EXPLORERS

*From Ancient Times
to the Space Age*

Simon & Schuster Macmillan
1633 Broadway
New York, NY 10019

Library of Congress Catalog Card Number: 98-8809

PRINTED IN THE UNITED STATES OF AMERICA

Printing Number

1 2 3 4 5 6 7 8 9 10

Library of Congress Cataloging-in-Publication Data

Explorers and discoverers: from ancient times to the space age/consulting editors,
    John Logan Allen, E. Julius Dasch, Barry Gough.
        p. cm.
    Includes bibliographical references and index.
    ISBN 0-02-864893-5 (set).—ISBN 0-02-864890-0 (v. 1).—ISBN 0-02-864891-9 (v. 2).—
ISBN 0-02-864892-7 (v. 3)
    1. Explorers—Biography—Dictionaries.   I. Allen, John Logan. 1941–
II. Dasch, E. Julius.   III. Gough, Barry M.
G200.E877   1998
910´.92´2—dc21   98-8809
[B]   CIP

EXPLORERS

From Ancient Times to the Space Age

Volume 2

Consulting Editors

John Logan Allen
Professor of Geography
University of Connecticut

E. Julius Dasch
Manager/Scientist
NASA National Space Grant Program

Barry M. Gough
Professor of History
Wilfrid Laurier University

Macmillan Library Reference USA

Simon & Schuster Macmillan
New York

Simon & Schuster and Prentice Hall International
London   Mexico City   New Delhi   Singapore   Sydney   Toronto

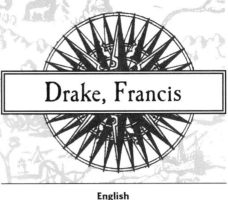

Drake, Francis

English
b between 1540 and 1542?; Tavistock, England
d January 28, 1596; at sea in the Caribbean
Sailed around world; explored California coast

circumnavigation journey around the world

privateer privately owned ship hired by a government to attack enemy ships

Spanish Main area of the Spanish Empire including the Caribbean coasts of Central America and South America

Sir Francis Drake became a famous and successful pirate and explorer in the service of Queen Elizabeth I of England.

Sir Francis Drake may be best known as an English pirate who caused great damage to Spanish shipping in the 1500s. He was also an important explorer. In 1577 the queen of England, Elizabeth I, asked Drake to sail to the Pacific Ocean. That voyage became the second **circumnavigation** in history—about 60 years after the first, which was led by Ferdinand MAGELLAN and Juan Sebastián de ELCANO. On his way around the world, Drake explored the west coast of North America and claimed the area for England. Several years later, he commanded English naval forces in a major victory against an invading Spanish fleet. His accomplishments as a pirate, explorer, and military leader helped Britain become the world's greatest sea power for the next 300 years.

A Troubled Childhood

Drake was the oldest of 12 boys in a poor Protestant farming family. When he was about seven years old, a violent Catholic uprising forced many Protestant families, including Drake's, to flee their homes. He developed a hatred of Catholics that fueled his career against Spain, Europe's most powerful Catholic nation.

Drake first went to sea when he was barely in his teens. He learned to pilot a small vessel that sailed along the coasts of France and the Netherlands. But he longed for greater adventure, so he approached a wealthy relative named John Hawkins, who was England's most successful sea merchant. Although Hawkins hired him as a record keeper, Drake became a captain by the age of 22.

A Pirate's Treasure

In 1570 Drake was licensed as a **privateer** by Queen Elizabeth. He prowled the waters of the **Spanish Main,** attacking Spanish ships and coastal settlements. He looted the town of Nombre de Dios in Panama, where the Spanish stored gold, and then crossed the narrowest part of Panama by land. From the top of a tree, he saw the Pacific Ocean, and he vowed to "sail an English ship in these seas."

Drake captured enough gold and silver to make himself a wealthy man by the time he returned to England in 1573. He purchased three ships and offered his services to the queen. But Elizabeth had just achieved a fragile peace with Spain, so she did not want Drake to continue his attacks on the Spanish. Drake therefore proposed a voyage to the southern Pacific Ocean through the Strait of Magellan, which no one had navigated since Magellan himself. When England's relations with Spain worsened, Elizabeth agreed to Drake's expedition. She instructed him to set up trading posts in the Pacific Ocean, but he also planned to attack Spanish settlements in South America.

The Strait of Magellan

Drake gathered a crew of 166 men, and on December 13, 1577, his five ships set out from Plymouth, England. Drake told his men that they were on a trade mission to Alexandria, Egypt. But when the ships headed into the Atlantic Ocean instead of the Mediterranean Sea, it was obvious that Egypt was not their true destination. Drake told his crew little about the trip, but he promised them great

This astrolabe—a navigational instrument used to determine latitude—was made in 1569 for Francis Drake. It has additional plates including a calendar and information about the moon and tides.

mutiny rebellion by a ship's crew against the officers

riches. He soon supported his promise by capturing a Portuguese ship. By the time Drake reached the coast of Brazil in early April 1578, however, the crew was uneasy. Thomas Doughty, one of only three men on board who knew Drake's plan, fueled the crew's fears by loudly criticizing Drake. Believing that Doughty was encouraging a **mutiny,** Drake had him put on trial and beheaded at San Julián, where Magellan had also put down a mutiny 58 years earlier.

Sailing southward, Drake reached the Strait of Magellan on August 21 and sank two of his supply ships. He thought that a smaller fleet would be able to stay together more easily in the strait. He also renamed his flagship the *Golden Hind* in honor of a supporter whose coat of arms included a type of deer called a hind. In the strait the ships fought fierce winds and rains, but they reached the Pacific Ocean in only 16 days—about half as long as Magellan had taken. One ship, however, was lost in a storm. Soon after completing the passage, Drake's ship was blown about 100 miles south of Tierra del Fuego, the island that lies south of the Strait of Magellan. This accident allowed Drake to prove that Tierra del Fuego was an island and not part of a continent. In November the ship *Elizabeth* returned to England, leaving the *Golden Hind* on its own.

California and the Pacific Ocean

On the west coast of South America, Drake raided Spanish outposts, capturing two merchant ships and about 40 tons of gold and silver bars. He then sailed north, perhaps as far as Vancouver Island in Canada, before turning south again. On June 17, 1579, he entered what is now Drake's Bay, north of the present-day site of San Francisco, to make repairs to the *Golden Hind.* He claimed the surrounding region for England and named it New Albion. The local Miwok tribe, seeing the English building structures on the beach, threatened them with arrows. But Drake convinced the Miwok that he had come in peace, and when he left on July 23, he wrote that the Miwok "took a sorrowful farewell of us."

Drake and his men saw no land for the next 66 days, until they reached a group of islands that were probably the Caroline Islands. The people there were so aggressive in attempting to steal goods from the English that Drake had to fire shots into the water to frighten them away. Twenty islanders were eventually killed in the violence. Drake proceeded to Mindanao, an island in the Philippines, then sailed south in search of the Spice Islands (now called the Moluccas). A local fisherman guided Drake to the island of Ternate (in present-day Indonesia), where the English received a warm reception from the local ruler. At the island of Celebes (now called Sulawesi), Drake spent a month repairing the *Golden Hind.*

After leaving Celebes, Drake considered traveling to China, but he decided to head home rather than risk a longer journey. After stops in Timor and Java (both in present-day Indonesia), he sailed west in March 1580. By the time he rounded Africa's Cape of Good Hope he had only 57 crew members and three barrels of fresh water

Spanish sailors came to fear the flag of England, which flew from the masts of Sir Francis Drake's ships.

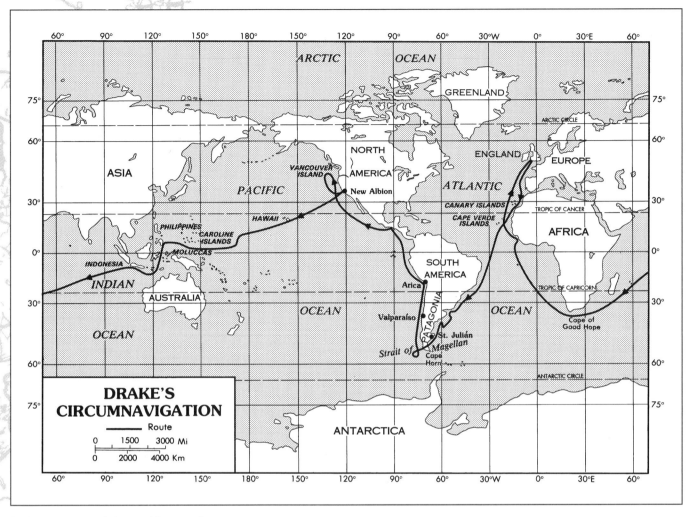

Drake's voyage around the world was only the second in history.

remaining. The *Golden Hind* reached England on September 26, 1580, after a voyage of 2 years and 10 months. Elizabeth, still wary of starting trouble with Spain, did not at first praise Drake's accomplishments. Later, however, she gave a banquet for Drake aboard the *Golden Hind* and made plans to preserve the ship as a historical monument.

Serving Queen and Country

In 1581 Drake became mayor of Plymouth, but four years later, he was at sea again, attacking the port of Vigo, Spain. In 1587 he set fire to dozens of Spanish ships in Portugal's Bay of Cádiz. This victory probably delayed by a year Spain's plan to invade England. When the fleet known as the Spanish Armada attacked in 1588, Drake was a vice admiral in the English navy and played a major role in defeating the Spanish.

In 1595 Drake sailed once again with his former employer, John Hawkins. They intended to capture Spanish settlements in the Caribbean. During this mission, Drake fell ill with **dysentery** and died on January 28, 1596, off the coast of Panama. At the time of his death, he was a very famous man, beloved in England and feared in the rest of the world.

dysentery disease that causes severe diarrhea

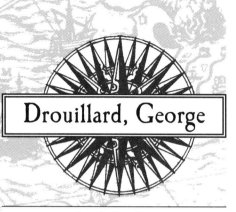

Drouillard, George

French-Canadian
b 1775?; ?
d 1809; Three Forks, Montana
Explored Rocky Mountains

SUGGESTED READING Robert Fleming Heizer, *Francis Drake and the California Indians* (University of California Press, 1947); J. H. Parry, *The Age of Reconnaissance* (World Publishing Company, 1963); James A. Williamson, *The Age of Drake* (Barnes and Noble, 1960); Derek Wilson, *The World Encompassed: Drake's Great Voyage 1577–1580* (Harper and Row, 1977).

George Drouillard, a fur trapper, took part in the expedition led by Meriwether LEWIS and William CLARK from 1804 to 1806. He was one of only two civilians who accompanied Lewis and Clark for the entire journey up the Missouri River, west to the Pacific Ocean, and back to St. Louis. In the years that followed, Drouillard explored the basins of the Tongue, Bighorn, and Yellowstone Rivers in the region that is now Montana and Wyoming.

Exploring the Rocky Mountains

Drouillard was the son of a French-Canadian father and a Shawnee Indian mother. Lewis and Clark hired him for his knowledge of western Indian tribes and their sign language, which was called hand talk. As a hunter and interpreter, he proved to be a valuable member of the expedition. In 1807, looking for more adventure, Drouillard joined the Missouri Fur Company, which was operated by Manuel Lisa. In April of that year, he headed up the Missouri River with Lisa and 40 other trappers. In May one of the men deserted, and Lisa sent Drouillard to bring him back—dead or alive. Drouillard caught the man and wounded him fatally. When the trappers returned to St. Louis the next year, both Lisa and Drouillard were tried for murder, but they were found not guilty.

During the spring of 1808, Drouillard made two journeys from Lisa's fort, located where the Yellowstone and Bighorn Rivers meet. While hunting beaver, he also hoped to find out how far north Spanish settlers had come from Mexico. During his travels, Drouillard made rough maps of the basins of the Tongue, Bighorn, and Yellowstone Rivers. He later presented these maps to Clark.

The Mistake on the Map

Drouillard's maps included two pieces of incorrect information that he had picked up from the Indians. One was that all the major western rivers had a common source. The other was that a person on horseback could reach the Spanish empire by riding south from the Yellowstone River for only 12 days—much less time than the trip would actually take. As a result, his maps showed that the Spanish settlements were much closer to American territory than they really were.

Clark used Drouillard's information in his own map of the Louisiana Territory, the western part of the United States at the time. Since Clark was the governor of the territory, his flawed map was accepted by the United States government. This mistaken view of the West led the government to increase its competition with Spain for the Rocky Mountain region. But Drouillard never had the chance to continue his explorations and correct his mistake. In 1809, while hunting near Three Forks, Montana, he was killed by Blackfoot Indians.

SUGGESTED READING M. O. Skarsten, *George Drouillard, Hunter and Interpreter for Lewis and Clark and Fur Trader, 1807–1810* (A. H. Clark Company, 1964).

Drygalski, Erich Dagobert von

German
b February 9, 1865; Königsberg, East Prussia
(now Kaliningrad, Lithuania)
d January 10, 1949; Munich, Germany
Explored Greenland and Antarctica

sledge heavy sled, often mounted on runners, that is pulled over snow or ice

dirigible large aircraft filled with a lighter-than-air gas that keeps it aloft; similar to a blimp but with a rigid frame

Dr. Erich Dagobert von Drygalski led expeditions to Greenland in 1891 and to Antarctica in 1902. Although the discoveries he made were minor, the scientific work he carried out was significant. Many scientists who worked with him in Antarctica made important contributions to the studies of oceans, weather, and magnetism.

In January 1902, Drygalski sailed for Antarctica on the *Gauss,* a ship that was specially built for polar travel. Shortly after land was sighted, the ship became locked in ice. Teams on **sledges** were sent out over the ice and discovered an extinct volcano, which they named Gaussberg. They named the surrounding mountains the Gaussberg Range. In February 1903, the explorers freed their ship by laying ash from the volcano on the surface of the ice. The ash collected the sun's heat, melting a path through the ice to open waters. However, Germany's King William II was disappointed that more dramatic discoveries had not been made. Germany stopped exploring Antarctica, and the *Gauss* was eventually sold to Canada.

Drygalski's work made him a respected scientist, and he won positions as a professor at German universities. He specialized in the study of the movements of polar ice. In 1910 his work took him to Spitsbergen, an island north of Norway, with a German noble named Count Zeppelin. The count investigated the possibility of flying **dirigibles** over the Arctic Ocean, a feat accomplished by Umberto NOBILE in 1926. Drygalski also spent about 25 years preparing the data he had gathered during his voyage to Antarctica. He published his findings in 20 volumes.

SUGGESTED READING Erich von Drygalski, *The Southern Ice-Continent: The German South Polar Expedition Aboard the* Gauss, *1901–1903,* translated by M. M. Raraty (Erskine Press, 1989); Wilhelm Filchner and others, *To the Sixth Continent: The Second German South Polar Expedition,* translated and edited by William Barr (Erskine Press, 1994).

Du Chaillu, Paul Belloni

French-American
b July 31, 1835; Paris, France
d April 30, 1903; St. Petersburg, Russia
Explored central Africa

Paul Belloni Du Chaillu traveled widely in the forests of western and central Africa and traced the courses of the Gabon and Ogowe Rivers. He located a tribe of small-statured Africans known as Pygmies and was also the first modern European to see a live gorilla. His discovery of the gorilla earned him worldwide fame, but he had to return to Africa to convince skeptics that gorillas really did exist.

Curiosity and Surprise

Du Chaillu grew up in Gabon, which lies near the equator on the west coast of Africa. His father traded rubber and dyes. While working for a few years at a trading post, Du Chaillu became fascinated by the mysterious African interior. He decided to go to the United States to seek funding for an expedition. He arrived in 1852, and

Paul Belloni Du Chaillu was the first European in modern times to see a live gorilla, but critics argued that he did not show proper scientific proof.

specimen sample of a plant, animal, or mineral, usually collected for scientific study or display

in the next three years he became an American citizen, studied natural history, and won financial support from the Philadelphia Academy of Natural Sciences.

During his four-year African expedition, Du Chaillu collected a variety of plants and shot thousands of animals, which he took back to America as **specimens.** In the interior highlands, he discovered and shot a large male gorilla. He later described the animal as "some hellish dream creature—a being of that hideous order, half-man, half-beast." Missionaries had previously found gorilla skulls in the area, but Du Chaillu was the first European in modern times to see the animal alive.

Accused of Lying

Du Chaillu became famous on his return to America in 1859. Two years later, he published a colorful account of his journey, titled *Exploration and Adventures in Equatorial Africa.* But some people challenged his claim to have seen a gorilla. Many critics complained that Du Chaillu had not obtained proper scientific proof, and some simply called him a liar. In 1863 he returned to Africa, where he took photographs of gorillas and captured a live specimen. Unfortunately, the animal died while being transported to Britain. On his second trip to Africa, Du Chaillu also encountered the Pygmies, a tribe later studied by scientists such as Delia Denning AKELEY.

Du Chaillu published a more scientific—and less controversial—book about his second journey. He then turned to writing children's books about Africa, for which he was well known and beloved as "Uncle Paul." He also published two books about Scandinavia after visiting there several times. Du Chaillu spent his last two years in Russia and died in St. Petersburg in 1903.

SUGGESTED READING Paul Belloni Du Chaillu, *The Country of the Dwarfs* (Negro Universities Press, 1969) and *The Land of the Long Night* (Tower Books, 1971).

Dulhut, Daniel Greysolon

French
b 1639?; St.-Germain-Laval, France
d February 25, 1710; Montréal, Canada
Explored land west of Lake Superior

Daniel Greysolon Dulhut spent about eight years exploring the land west of Lake Superior in North America. He established friendships with the area's Indian tribes, making it easier for later French explorers to enter the American West. He also took part in the French search for a mythical inland body of water known as the Western Sea.

War and Peace by the Great Lakes

Dulhut was born in France and moved to Québec, Canada, in 1674. There he sought the friendship of local Indians in order to learn more about the lands to the west. In September 1678, he left the city of Montréal with seven Frenchmen and three Indian slaves to explore the upper Great Lakes region. Ten months later, Dulhut reached the large Sioux Indian village on the shores of Lake Mille Lacs, southwest of Lake Superior. He found that the Sioux, the Chippewa, and other tribes were at war, and he persuaded them to sign peace treaties.

Meanwhile, Dulhut sent three of his men west with a Sioux war party. They returned with the news that Indians had told them about a nearby sea with water that was not good for drinking. Dulhut believed that the story referred to salt water in the legendary Western Sea, which was supposed to lead to the Pacific Ocean. The Indians probably meant the body of water that is now called Lake Winnipeg.

Dulhut headed west to find the source of these rumors. But when he reached the Mississippi River, he learned that Father Louis HENNEPIN had been taken prisoner by a band of Sioux. Dulhut called off the search for the Western Sea and hurried to the priest's rescue. Hennepin was freed and safely escorted back to Lake Michigan, but Dulhut was disappointed that relations with the Sioux had not been friendlier. He decided not to travel farther west.

Diplomacy and Retirement

Dulhut was recalled to France in 1681 to face accusations that he had organized a group of traders without a license. After being cleared of the charges against him, he returned to the Great Lakes region in 1683. The governor of **New France** instructed him to keep order among the Indians and to persuade the tribes north of Lake Superior to trade with the French instead of the British. Dulhut later supported military efforts against the Iroquois Indians. He spent his last 15 years in quiet retirement in Montréal. The present-day city of Duluth, Minnesota, is named for him.

SUGGESTED READING David J. Abodaher, *Daniel Duluth, Explorer of the Northlands* (P. J. Kennedy, 1966); Lawrence J. Sommer, editor, *Daniel Greysolon, Sieur Duluth: A Tercentenary Tribute* (St. Louis County Historical Society, 1979).

New France French colony that included the St. Lawrence River valley, the Great Lakes region, and until 1713, Acadia (now called Nova Scotia)

Duluth, Daniel Greysolon. See *Dulhut, Daniel Greysolon.*

Dumont d'Urville, Jules-Sébastien-César

French
b May 23, 1790; Condé-sur-Noireau, France
d May 8, 1842; near Meudon, France
Explored Pacific islands and Antarctica

Jules-Sébastien-César Dumont d'Urville was a French naval officer who pursued a wide range of interests. He was mainly concerned with studying the islands, waters, and peoples of the western Pacific Ocean. His search for the South Magnetic Pole led to the discovery of the Adélie Coast of Antarctica. His landing there allowed France to make a formal claim to Antarctic territory.

A Man of Many Talents

After the early death of his father, Dumont d'Urville was raised by his mother and his uncle. He went to sea in 1807 after failing the entrance examination for a technical college. He later transferred to a naval base at Toulon, where he studied insects and learned five languages. It is not clear how well he mastered any of these subjects, and later in his career, he was criticized for flaws in his scientific methods. Even so, he did acquire the basic skills he would need on his voyages of discovery.

specimen sample of a plant, animal, or mineral, usually collected for scientific study or display

scurvy disease caused by a lack of vitamin C and once a major cause of death among sailors; symptoms include internal bleeding, loosened teeth, and extreme fatigue

When his compass began spinning wildly, Jules-Sébastien-César Dumont d'Urville knew that he was close to the South Magnetic Pole.

In 1817, while on duty with the French navy in the Mediterranean Sea, he noticed a statue that had recently been dug up on the Greek island of Melos. He recognized the statue as the Venus de Milo, a great work of classical art. His report led France to obtain and preserve the statue. He was promoted and made a member of France's Legion of Honor. On an expedition to the Pacific Ocean five years later, he collected plants and used his findings to publish his first scientific paper.

Studying the Pacific Islands

Dumont d'Urville was promoted again in 1825 and was given command of a ship. He was directed to study the waters around the widely scattered islands of the western Pacific Ocean. He was also asked to study the island peoples and to gather plant and animal **specimens.** In addition, he was to learn the fate of the French expedition, led by Jean François de Galaup de LA PÉROUSE, that had vanished 40 years earlier. Dumont d'Urville renamed his ship the *Astrolabe* after one of La Pérouse's ships, and set sail on April 25, 1826. During his three-year voyage, he discovered several small islands and what is now known as Astrolabe Reef, near the island of Fiji. His explorations led to a better understanding of the islands of the region, which appeared to form three main groups: Polynesia, Micronesia, and Melanesia. He also found out that La Pérouse's ships had been wrecked in the Santa Cruz Islands.

Although these discoveries were important, their cost was high—about one-third of Dumont d'Urville's crew died of **scurvy.** When the expedition returned to France, some of Dumont d'Urville's observations were questioned by scientists. As a result, he did not receive the promotion he desired until August 1829, and even then he was not given a new mission. Since the navy was not keeping him busy, he wrote an account of his voyage. The book reestablished his good reputation. He also helped found the Paris Geographical Society, and after eight years, the navy called him back to duty.

The South Magnetic Pole

The French king, Louis-Philippe, suggested that an effort be made to break through the ice of the Weddell Sea, off the coast of Antarctica. While reading about the region, Dumont d'Urville also became interested in locating the South Magnetic Pole. The magnetic poles—not the geographic poles—are the places to which a compass points north or south.

The ships *Astrolabe* and *Zélée* left France on September 7, 1837, and encountered the Antarctic ice in January 1838. The French were unable to make much progress into the Weddell Sea, but they did survey the tip of the Antarctic Peninsula, which lies to the south of South America. The expedition then spent a year in the southern Pacific Ocean. Disease struck the crew once again, and the sick were left aboard the *Zélée* to recover at Hobart, Tasmania. The *Astrolabe* then headed for the magnetic pole. The party sighted the ice cliffs of Adélie Coast on January 19, 1840, and made a landing on a small island nearby. They knew that they were close to the pole because the compass was spinning wildly. But massive sheets of ice blocked the way farther south, and the expedition had to turn back.

Upon his return to France, Dumont d'Urville was promoted to rear admiral. Before he could publish the results of his mission, however, he and his wife and child were killed in a train accident outside Paris. Eighty-two years later, France made a formal claim to Antarctic territory based on Dumont d'Urville's landing. The French research station on Adélie Coast is named in his honor.

SUGGESTED READING Jules-Sébastien-César Dumont d'Urville, *Two Voyages to the South Seas*, translated by Helen Rosenman (University of Hawaii Press, 1992).

---

d'Urville, Jules-Sébastien-César Dumont. See *Dumont d'Urville, Jules-Sébastien-César*.

Duveyrier, Henri

French
b February 28, 1840; Paris, France
d April 25, 1892; Sèvres, France
Explored Sahara

Henri Duveyrier explored extensively in northern Africa's vast desert, the Sahara. He became the world's leading expert on the language and customs of the Tuareg people who lived in the region. The information he gathered about the Sahara's geography, history, and culture helped France to expand its colonial empire in Africa.

At age 17, Duveyrier traveled to Algeria, where he studied Arabic and prepared for his first expedition with the help of the great German explorer Heinrich BARTH. Duveyrier's journey through the northern Sahara earned him the Paris Geographical Society's gold medal when he was only 19. He continued to explore the area south of the Atlas Mountains, between Morocco and Tunisia, for two more years, making detailed notes about its geography. He also lived among the Tuareg, studying their culture and economy.

Three years of travel in the desert seriously damaged Duveyrier's health, and he returned to France in 1861 to recover. He later published an account of his travels that created public interest in Saharan exploration. Duveyrier felt that France could benefit from colonizing the Sahara, and he promoted efforts to extend French control there. He made several more trips to the region and also explored the salt lakes of Algeria and Tunisia. His books about these places served as references for later travelers in North Africa. Although he was hailed as one of the leading explorers of the Sahara, Duveyrier took his own life at the age of 52.

SUGGESTED READING Douglas Porch, *The Conquest of the Sahara* (Alfred A. Knopf, 1984); James Welland, *The Great Sahara* (E. P. Dutton, 1965).

Eannes, Gil

Portuguese
b ?; Portugal
d 1435?; ?
Explored western coast of Africa

Gil Eannes commanded one of the most important voyages in the history of Portuguese exploration, sailing south of Africa's Cape Bojador (in what is now Western Sahara). The prince of Portugal, known as Prince Henry the Navigator, had already sent several explorers on the same mission. But all of them had failed to pass the dangerous ridges of rocks and sand in the waters near the cape. By sailing past Cape Bojador, Eannes put to rest the sailors' fears and rumors about what lay beyond it.

Eannes had been raised as an attendant in the prince's household. In 1433 he was given command of a ship and was told to sail past the cape and as far as possible down the west coast of Africa. However, his crew pressured him into turning back when they reached the Canary Islands. Prince Henry was angry that Eannes had not completed his mission and told him not to return to the royal court until he was successful. Eannes set out the following year and managed to navigate the rough seas off the cape. He found the waters beyond the cape to be surprisingly calm, nothing like the "Sea of Darkness" that had long been thought to lie there. To prove that he had accomplished his task, Eannes brought Prince Henry the only plant life he could find in the area, an herb called roses of Santa Maria.

Prince Henry was delighted with Eannes's success and sent him out again the following year to sail farther down the coastline. In command of one or two **caravels,** Eannes and Alfonso Goncalves Baldaya sailed about 200 miles south of the cape before finding evidence of human settlement. Records show that Baldaya returned to Portugal, but what happened to Eannes from then on remains uncertain.

caravel small ship with three masts and both square and triangular sails

SUGGESTED READING Edgar Prestage, *The Chronicles of Fernão Lopes and Gomes Eannes de Zurara* (Voss and Michael, 1928).

Eiriksson, Leif. See *Erikson, Leif.*

Elcano, Juan Sebastián de

Spanish
b 1476?; Guetaria, Spain
d August 4, 1526; at sea in the Pacific Ocean
Served as pilot for Magellan

circumnavigation journey around the world

For a map of Elcano's route, see the profile of Ferdinand MAGELLAN in this volume.

scurvy disease caused by a lack of vitamin C and once a major cause of death among sailors; symptoms include internal bleeding, loosened teeth, and extreme fatigue

Juan Sebastián de Elcano was one of only a handful of sailors who survived the **circumnavigation** begun by Ferdinand MAGELLAN. Elcano returned to Spain in 1522, bringing with him not only spices and silks but also the strange notion that travelers who sailed west around the world lost a day by the time they returned home.

Twist of Fate

Elcano was not one of Magellan's strongest supporters on the expedition. Early in the voyage, off the coast of South America, he sided with the officers who wanted to abandon the mission and return to Spain. Magellan prevailed, and the ships sailed across the Pacific Ocean. Magellan and his highest-ranking officers, Duarte BARBOSA and Juan Serrano, died in the Philippines. After their deaths, command of the expedition passed from one person to another. At the island of Borneo, Elcano was made commander of the *Victoria,* which was by then barely seaworthy.

Elcano reached the Spice Islands (now called the Moluccas) in November 1521 with the help of a captured Filipino sailor. There the crew stocked the ship with cloves, gold, silks, sandalwood, cinnamon, and wax before heading for home. To avoid ports controlled by Spain's enemy, Portugal, Elcano was forced to sail 10,000 miles without touching land. After several months, he passed the

Juan Sebastián de Elcano was one of the few sailors to complete the voyage around the world begun by Magellan.

Cape of Good Hope, the southern tip of Africa. During the voyage, a storm destroyed the ship's masts, much of the food on board rotted, and the crew fell ill with **scurvy.**

A Narrow Escape

The few remaining Spaniards reached the Cape Verde Islands, controlled by Portugal, on what they believed to be July 9, 1522. When they found that it was actually July 10, they realized that because the earth rotates toward the east, people who travel around it to the west lose a day. While on the island, Elcano told the Portuguese that he had come from the Americas. They believed him until one of his men offered to pay for a purchase with spices. The Portuguese then knew that the ship must have come from eastern Asia, where Portugal was trying to control the spice trade. They prepared to attack the *Victoria,* but the Spanish sailed out of the harbor and escaped.

The *Victoria* was the only one of Magellan's ships to return to Spain. Elcano and his 17 surviving crewmen had completed the first circumnavigation. He was rewarded with a lifelong pension and made a nobleman. Elcano died four years later on a military expedition to the Moluccas.

SUGGESTED READING Mairin Mitchell, *Elcano: The First Circumnavigator* (Herder, 1958).

Ellsworth, Lincoln

American
b May 12, 1880; Chicago, Illinois
d May 26, 1951; New York, New York
First to fly over both polar regions

Lincoln Ellsworth, the son of a wealthy businessman, spent the first 45 years of his life drifting aimlessly. After his father's death, Ellsworth used his inheritance to finance several expeditions to the Arctic Ocean and Antarctica. He became the first explorer to fly across both polar regions. During his explorations, he claimed nearly 400,000 square miles of uncharted Antarctic territory for the United States.

Willing to Try

For most of his life, it appeared that Ellsworth would never achieve anything of importance. He flunked out of Yale University and dropped out of Columbia University. He then tried but failed to take a role in his father's coal-mining business. Ellsworth kept busy by working at a series of difficult outdoor jobs, but his father considered him a great disappointment. In 1925 Ellsworth met Roald AMUNDSEN, the famous explorer who had been the first to reach the South Pole in 1911. Ellsworth suggested that they ask his father for money for an expedition to the North Pole. They succeeded in getting money to purchase two seaplanes, which they intended to land on the ice at the pole. The resulting Arctic flight captured the world's imagination and launched Ellsworth's career as an explorer.

Lincoln Ellsworth was the first person to fly airplanes over both the Arctic Ocean and Antarctica.

dirigible large aircraft filled with a lighter-than-air gas that keeps it aloft; similar to a blimp but with a rigid frame

Air, Water, and Ice

Ellsworth and Amundsen set up a base at Kings Bay on Spitsbergen, a Norwegian island in the Arctic Ocean. With four crew members, they took off in both planes on May 21, 1925. But after only seven hours in the air, an engine on one of the planes malfunctioned. Both planes were forced to make a dangerous landing on small channels of open water between sheets of floating ice. It took 24 days of hard work to clear a waterway long enough for the remaining plane to take off. When the plane finally returned to Spitsbergen, carrying both crews, Ellsworth was a new Arctic hero. He and his crews had flown to within 156 miles of the North Pole.

The next year, Ellsworth, Amundsen, and Umberto NOBILE crossed the Arctic Ocean in the **dirigible** *Norge.* In 1931 Ellsworth took part in Sir George Hubert WILKINS's unsuccessful attempt to reach the North Pole in the submarine *Nautilus.* Ellsworth financed both of these expeditions with the fortune that had been left to him when his father died.

He then turned his attention to Antarctica, but he failed in his first two attempts to fly across the southern continent. In 1935 he succeeded in flying 2,300 miles across Antarctica with pilot Herbert Hollick-Kenyon. With this feat, Ellsworth became the first explorer to fly across both polar regions.

SUGGESTED READING Lincoln Ellsworth, *Beyond Horizons* (Doubleday, Doran and Company, 1938); Theodore K. Mason, *Two Against the Ice, Amundsen and Ellsworth* (Dodd, Mead, 1982).

Emin Pasha. See *Schnitzer, Eduard.*

Entrecasteaux, Antoine Raymond Joseph de Bruni d'

French
b 1739; Chateau d'Entrecasteaux, France
d July 21, 1793; at sea near Java, Indonesia
Charted coasts of southern Australia and Tasmania

species type of plant or animal

frigate small, agile warship with three masts and square sails

arsenal place where weapons are made or stored

Antoine Raymond Joseph de Bruni d'Entrecasteaux was an officer in the French navy who sailed in search of Jean François de Galaup de LA PÉROUSE. Although unsuccessful in locating La Pérouse, Entrecasteaux proved to be a capable leader on a difficult voyage. He charted large sections of Australia and Tasmania, and his scientists identified many previously unknown **species** of plants and animals.

Growing Up in the Navy

Entrecasteaux was born on his family's estate in southeastern France. At the age of 15, he joined the French marine guard, a naval force, and soon made a name for himself in a battle off the coast of Spain. Working his way up through the ranks, Entrecasteaux earned a promotion to lieutenant in 1770. Several years later, he successfully guided a **frigate** from the French port of Marseilles to the eastern Mediterranean Sea, escaping attacks by two powerful pirate ships. This feat earned him further recognition for his skills.

The following year, he was named assistant director of French ports and **arsenals,** and he later became director. After a nephew of

Despite tension on board his ship, Antoine d'Entrecasteaux charted significant sections of coastline in the southern Pacific Ocean.

scurvy disease caused by a lack of vitamin C and once a major cause of death among sailors; symptoms include internal bleeding, loosened teeth, and extreme fatigue

dysentery disease that causes severe diarrhea

his committed murder, Entrecasteaux asked to leave the navy, but instead he was chosen to be the commander of the French India Naval Station in 1785. In this post, he sailed to China and other ports in the western Pacific. From 1787 to 1789, he served as governor of Île de France (present-day Mauritius) and Bourbon (now Réunion) in the Indian Ocean.

The Search for La Pérouse

In 1791 the French National Assembly ordered Entrecasteaux to search for La Pérouse. The missing explorer had not been heard from after leaving Botany Bay in New Holland (present-day Australia) three years earlier. Entrecasteaux was also instructed to make detailed surveys of New Holland and Van Diemen's Land (now called Tasmania). He was promoted to rear admiral and given two ships, the *Recherche* and the *Espérance.* Neither ship was of high quality. Meanwhile, France was undergoing a political revolution, in which power was taken from the king and nobles by townspeople and farmers. On board Entrecasteaux's ships, tensions were high between the officers, most of whom were of noble birth, and the sailors, who were commoners. The ships left France on September 29, 1791, but the journey down the African coast took longer than expected, supplies of drinking water ran low, and maggots infested the food.

The small fleet reached Cape Town, South Africa, in January 1792. There Entrecasteaux heard rumors that inhabitants of the Admiralty Islands, in the western Pacific Ocean, had been seen wearing French uniforms. He decided to investigate and sailed east, reaching Tasmania in the spring. He spent over a month charting the coastline and naming Recherche Bay, Bruny Island, D'Entrecasteaux Island, D'Entrecasteaux Channel, and the Huon River. On shore, his scientists identified three species of eucalyptus tree and a species of kangaroo that were previously unknown to Europeans.

The expedition reached the Admiralty Islands in July but found no evidence of islanders in French uniforms. **Scurvy** soon broke out among the crew, forcing the expedition to spend a month recovering in the Moluccas. The French sailed again in October and discovered a group of islands on the west coast of New Holland that Entrecasteaux named the Recherche Archipelago. In the middle of December, they reached Nuyts Land on the southwest coast of New Holland. After exploring it carefully, the expedition returned to Tasmania one month later.

The End of a Difficult Voyage

From Tasmania, Entrecasteaux sailed to New Zealand, New Caledonia, the Santa Cruz Islands, and the Solomon Islands, but he found no information about La Pérouse. By then the crew was exhausted, and Entrecasteaux was suffering from scurvy and **dysentery.** He called off the search and headed for Java (in what is now Indonesia) on July 9. Less than two weeks later, Entrecasteaux died and was buried at sea. Sixty-six more sailors died of scurvy and dysentery before the ships reached the Dutch port of Surabaja on Java. The Frenchmen did not know that the Netherlands had gone to war on behalf of the French king. The Dutch imprisoned the common sailors. The officers were not jailed, but they were afraid to return to France. The official account of the expedition was not published until 1808.

SUGGESTED READING Frank Horner, *Looking for La Pérouse: d'Entrecasteaux in Australia and the South Pacific, 1792–1793* (Miegunyah Press, 1995); J. J. Houtou de La Billardière, *Voyage in Search of La Pérouse, 1791–1794* (Da Capo Press, 1971); Brian Plomley and Josiane Piard-Bernier, *The General: The Visits of the Expedition Led by Bruny d'Entrecasteaux to Tasmanian Waters in 1792 and 1793* (Queen Victoria Museum, 1993).

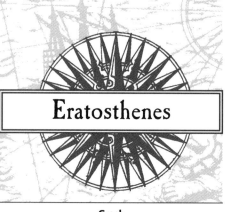

Eratosthenes

Greek
b 276 B.C.; Cyrene, Libya
d 192 B.C.; Alexandria, Egypt
*Calculated circumference of the earth;
developed system of grid lines for maps*

cartographer mapmaker

Eratosthenes was an ancient Greek mathematician whose ideas made important contributions to the work of explorers and **cartographers.** He used mathematics and astronomy to describe the physical world. Eratosthenes invented a method for measuring the circumference of the earth. He also developed a system of parallel grid lines for maps and suggested that it might be possible to sail all the way around the world.

How Big Is the Earth?

Before the time of Eratosthenes, people had often wondered how large the earth was, but no one had figured out a way to measure it. Eratosthenes discovered the solution as he was looking down a well at Syene (now Aswan), a town in Egypt about 500 miles southeast of the city of Alexandria. He noticed that at noon on the longest day of the year, the water in the well reflected the sun. This fact meant that at that time and place, the sun's rays hit the earth at a 90° angle. He also learned that at the same time in Alexandria, the sun's rays hit the earth at an angle of about 83°.

This difference in the angle of the sun's rays led Eratosthenes to two conclusions. First, since the difference in the angles is so small, the sun's rays are almost parallel when they reach distant points on the earth. Therefore, the sun must be very far away from the earth. Second, the 83° angle and the distance from Syene to Alexandria could be used to calculate the circumference of the planet. Eratosthenes expressed the circumference in stadia (plural of *stadium,* an ancient Greek unit of measurement). Since historians disagree on the unit's exact length, his figure may have been off by as much as about 4,000 miles or as little as about 125 miles. (The actual circumference is about 24,860 miles.) In spite of this difference, Eratosthenes' result and his method of measurement were remarkably accurate, as astronomers would prove thousands of years later.

Mapping the World

Eratosthenes also developed the use of grid lines to determine the location of places on a map. He divided the world using two main lines. The east-west line ran through the Greek island of Rhodes and the middle of the Mediterranean Sea. The north-south line ran through Alexandria. He then added lines that ran through other well-known locations. His map divided the earth into 60 rectangular areas of varying shapes and sizes. Eratosthenes knew that his system would be improved by later explorers and cartographers,

latitude distance north or south of the equator

longitude distance east or west of an imaginary line on the earth's surface; in 1884 most nations agreed to draw the line through Greenwich, England

circumnavigation journey around the world

but his basic method is still used today for the grid lines of **latitude** and **longitude.**

Eratosthenes made yet another contribution to exploration. He was curious about what lay beyond the two oceans, the Atlantic Ocean and the Indian Ocean, that were known to ancient Greeks. He measured the rise and fall of the tides in both oceans and discovered that the tidal patterns were similar. He reasoned that these oceans must be connected as part of one huge body of water. If that theory was true, he argued, a ship should be able to sail west into the Atlantic Ocean, circle the earth, and return from the east by way of the Indian Ocean. Eratosthenes was right, but his theory would not be proven correct until 1522, when Ferdinand MAGELLAN led the first **circumnavigation.**

SUGGESTED READING P. M. Fraser, *Eratosthenes of Cyrene* (Oxford University Press, 1971).

Ericson, Leif. See *Erikson, Leif.*

Erik the Red

Norse
b 950?; Jaeren, near Stavanger, Norway
d 1001?; near modern Julianehåb, Greenland
Established first European settlement on Greenland

Erik the Red left Iceland with a group of his family, followers, and slaves and established the first European community in Greenland in 982. At the time, other Norse were terrorizing much of Europe as they expanded their territory from their homelands in Scandinavia. Erik the Red's career as founder of the small, peaceful community contrasted with his own violent history. His decision to settle Greenland was also an important event in the history of exploration. It provided the opportunity for his son, Leif ERIKSON, to become the first European known to have set foot on the shores of North America.

From Violent Neighbor to Peaceful Settler

Erik's life provides an example of the kinds of pressures that led many Norse to leave Scandinavia between 760 and 1080. As a boy, he was forced to leave Norway with his father, Thorvald, when a neighborhood argument ended in murder. Erik and his father sailed west to Iceland, but they found little good land that was not already settled. With nowhere else to go, they set up a farm on the rocky coast of northwestern Iceland. Afer his father died, Erik found better pastureland to the south, but he began fighting with his neighbors. He had to leave the area after killing two of them, and he eventually settled on the islands of Breidha Fjord. Here he became involved in another fight, killing at least two more neighbors. The Icelanders finally had enough of Erik and ordered him to leave the country for three years.

A New Opportunity in Greenland

Although he was the first to establish a European settlement in Greenland, Erik was not the first person to discover the island. The **Inuit** had lived in Greenland for many years but had left long before Erik's arrival, probably because the climate there had become

Inuit people of the Canadian Arctic, sometimes known as the Eskimo

fjord narrow inlet where the sea meets the shore between steep cliffs

saga medieval Norse legend or historical account

too warm. Its existence had been reported by Norse sailors such as Gunnbjorn Ulf-Krakuson, who had sighted it around 900. On clear days, Greenland is actually visible from the mountaintops near where Erik had made his home in Iceland.

Forced to leave Iceland in 982, Erik decided to explore the land sighted by Gunnbjorn. After a sea voyage of some 450 miles, he found the barren southeastern shore of Greenland. He sailed on, rounding the island's southernmost point and discovering the grassy shores of its southwestern **fjords.** Calling the area a "green land," he explored it for the next three years.

Erik returned to Iceland with a boatload of sealskins and walrus tusks as proof of the land's riches. He persuaded a group of Icelanders to settle Greenland. A party of 25 ships set out, but only 14 reached their destination. A colony of about 400 people was established and eventually grew into two communities. The Eastern Settlement was located near the modern town of Julianehåb and the Western Settlement was near the site of present-day Godthaab.

The Norse Community in Greenland

Erik was remembered and glorified for his role as Greenland's founder in two **sagas,** *The Saga of the Greenlanders* and *Erik the Red's Saga.* The sagas describe Erik's activities as leader of the settlers. Little is known about his role in creating laws for the new community. But it is likely that the former outlaw played a key role in setting up the government, which was similar to that of Iceland.

Extensive trade made Greenland a part of Europe. For example, records show that the French duke of Burgundy paid a ransom in 1396 with "twelve Greenland falcons." In addition, the settlement was converted to Christianity soon after its establishment. Sixteen churches, a cathedral, and two monasteries were eventually founded in Greenland.

Both the Eastern Settlement and the smaller Western Settlement remained thriving, independent communities for almost 300 years. However, in 1261 the inhabitants granted authority over their settlements to the king of Norway. The loss of control over trade, combined with a change in climate that brought cooler temperatures, led to the colony's steady decline. By the time the region was visited by the English explorers Martin FROBISHER and John DAVIS in the 1500s, the Inuit had returned, and the descendants of Erik the Red were gone.

SUGGESTED READING Paul H. Chapman, *The Norse Discovery of America* (One Candle Press, 1981); Kirsten A. Seaver, *The Frozen Echo: Greenland and the Exploration of North America, ca. A.D. 1000–1500* (Stanford University Press, 1996); Rebecca Stefoff, *The Viking Explorers* (Chelsea House, 1993).

Erikson, Leif

Norse
b 980?; ?
d 1020?; Greenland?
Explored coast of North America

Leif Erikson is generally recognized as the first European to have landed in North America. Having set out from the Greenland colony established by his father, ERIK THE RED, Erikson explored three sites along the coast of North America. Historians still disagree about exactly where those landing sites were, especially the place he named Vinland—probably because of the wild grapevines he found there.

Many Norse explorers, including Leif Erikson, sailed in Norse ships such as the one shown above.

saga medieval Norse legend or historical account

temperate moderate, well balanced

Erikson's Early Life and Travels

Erikson's travels were first known through spoken stories before they were written down. The first written record of them appeared in two Icelandic **sagas.** *The Saga of the Greenlanders,* written around 1200, is considered more reliable because it was written about 50 to 75 years before the other one, *The Saga of Eric the Red.* The older saga describes Erikson as a "big, strapping fellow, handsome to look at, thoughtful and **temperate** in all things." He was raised in Greenland, where his father had settled after being forced to leave Iceland, and became a skillful sailor. In 999 or 1000, Erikson sailed from Greenland to Norway, but unlike other sailors, he did not stop at Iceland on the way. He sailed directly for Norway, becoming the first person known to have made a nonstop crossing of the Atlantic Ocean.

Back in Greenland, Erikson had often heard about the travels of Bjarni HERJOLFSSON, a merchant from Iceland. Herjolfsson had accidentally sailed west of Greenland in 985 or 986 and had reported seeing new lands in three separate places. Two of the areas he had sighted were wooded, exciting news for the Norse colonists, whose lands did not have large trees. They had to use earth and driftwood for shelter and fuel, so they welcomed the possibility of finding timber nearby.

Sailing to America

In the summer of 1001, Erikson bought Herjolfsson's boat and gathered a crew of 35 men, including a German named Tyrker. Erikson attempted to retrace Herjolfsson's path in reverse, making his first stop at the last place Herjolfsson had seen. It turned out to be a region of flat ledges and icy mountains that Erikson named Helluland, meaning Country of Flat Stones. Most scholars agree that Helluland is present-day Baffin Island, which lies directly west of Greenland. Since this land had no timber, Erikson continued down the coast to a flat, wooded land with broad white beaches. He named the area Markland, which means Land of Forests. This shore was most likely the coast of Labrador in Canada. Despite the timber, Erikson was not satisfied, and he sailed on.

The Discovery of Vinland

Erikson and his crew next came to an island where their ship ran aground at low tide. The crew ran up the beach, waited until the tide came back in, and then towed the ship onto the shore. They decided to spend the winter at a place on the island where a stream flowed out of a lake. Taking advantage of the relatively warm weather, the crew built several large houses. The grass did not wither from cold, so cattle could graze outdoors all winter. Salmon were plentiful in the waters.

After the houses were built, Erikson allowed the men to do some exploring. He divided them into two groups, with only one group going out each day. Erikson was a careful leader, so he told the men

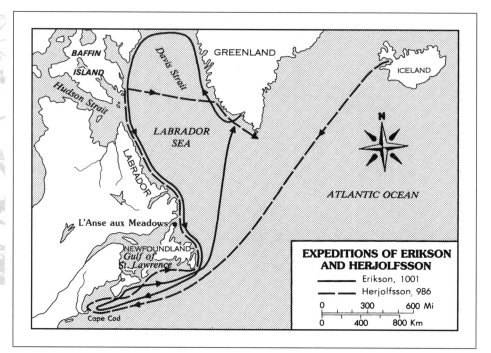

Leif Erikson investigated—and landed on—the coasts that Bjarni Herjolfsson had accidentally discovered.

to stay together at all times and to return by evening. One day Tyrker did not return with his group. Erikson led a search party to look for him. When the searchers found Tyrker, the German was so excited that all he could do was babble in his native language, which the Norse could not understand. After he calmed down, he told them in Norse that he had found grapes growing in the wild. This was important information because now the explorers would bring home two kinds of valuable goods—grapes and timber. Erikson named the country Vinland, which may have meant either Wineland or Meadowland.

Return to Greenland

When spring came, the Norse loaded their ship with timber, filled a small boat with grapes, and headed back to Greenland. According to the saga, Erikson found and rescued 15 sailors along the way who had been shipwrecked. This incident earned him the nickname "Leif the Lucky." Erikson never returned to Vinland because during the next winter, his father died, and Leif was left in charge of the Greenland colony. But he must have planned to return at some time, because he refused to sell the houses he had built there.

Other Greenlanders attempted to explore Vinland. One voyage was led by Erikson's brother, Thorvald, who thought that Leif had not been daring enough when investigating the new land. The saga reports that Thorvald was killed in an encounter with the people of Vinland, whom Erikson and his crew had never seen. Another expedition, led by Thorfinn KARLSEFNI, attempted to establish a colony in Vinland but was also driven away by the local people.

The Mystery of Vinland

One of the mysteries of Erikson's voyage is the location of Vinland. The few bits of evidence that do exist are confusing. The geographical

The raven was used as a symbol and banner by some Norse leaders of Leif Erikson's time, and it may have flown over North America.

landmarks mentioned in the saga suggest either the northern tip of Newfoundland or the southern coast of Cape Cod (in present-day Massachusetts). Wild wheat described in the saga has been identified by some scholars as Lyme grass, which grows along shores from Iceland to Cape Cod. The saga also says that the winter days were longer in Vinland than in Iceland, implying that Vinland was farther south.

The grapes that probably gave Vinland its name have been one of the greatest sources of confusion about its location. Cape Cod is about as far north as wild grapes grow today, so many scholars believe that Vinland could have been anywhere between Cape Cod and Florida. But it seems unlikely that Erikson could have sailed south from Labrador to Cape Cod without seeing any other land, such as Newfoundland, along the way. That island does not have wild grapes today, but the climate there was warmer in Erikson's day, so grapes may have grown there at that time. Some who argue for Newfoundland as the site of Vinland wonder whether the "wild grapes" might actually have been berries from which wine could be made.

There is also physical evidence of early Norse settlements in North America. Foundations of two great houses were uncovered in 1960 by the Norwegian archaeologist Helge Ingstad in a spot called L'Anse aux Meadows in Newfoundland. These houses are similar to Norse dwellings found in Greenland. However, there is no proof that the houses found by Ingstad represent Erikson's Vinland settlement.

Even if the mystery of Vinland is never solved, it is clear that Leif Erikson was an ideal explorer. He was bold in his search for new lands, yet he was careful not to risk the lives of his crew. He returned with all of his men as well as the 15 rescued sailors. He has earned a unique place in history as the first European to have set foot in North America, almost 500 years before Christopher COLUMBUS.

SUGGESTED READING Hjalmar R. Holand, *Westward from Vinland: Norse Discoveries and Explorations in America, 982–1362; Leif Erikson to the Kensington Stone* (Dover Publications, 1969); Kirsten A. Seaver, *The Frozen Echo: Greenland and the Exploration of North America, ca. A.D. 1000–1500* (Stanford University Press, 1996); Erik Wahlgren, *The Vikings and America* (Thames and Hudson, 1986).

Escalante, Silvestre Vélez de

Spanish
b 1751?; Santander Mountains, Spain
d ?; ?
Explored American Southwest

New Spain region of Spanish colonial empire that included the areas now occupied by Mexico, Florida, Texas, New Mexico, Arizona, California, and various Caribbean islands

pueblo Indian village or dwelling in the American Southwest, often built of sun-dried bricks

From 1776 to 1777, Father Silvestre Vélez de Escalante journeyed about 1,500 miles through what is now called the American Southwest. While exploring previously uncharted territory from Colorado to Utah, he discovered the only point at which the Colorado River could be crossed at that time. The site was named the Crossing of the Fathers in honor of Escalante and another priest who traveled with him.

Holy Purpose

Escalante was born in a small mountain village in Spain. When and why he came to **New Spain** is unknown. At the age of about 17, he joined a religious order in Mexico City and became a Franciscan priest. In 1775 he moved to the mission at the **pueblo** of the Zuñi Indians in what is now New Mexico. The reasons for his expedition are not clear, but he did want to find a route from Santa Fe to Monterey, California. He also hoped to convert Indians to Christianity. Although Escalante was not one of the leaders of the expedition, he inspired his companions and kept a record of the trip.

The party left Santa Fe on July 29, 1776, crossed the Rio Grande, and headed into Colorado. The men followed a series of canyons and **plateaus** until they reached the place where the Gunnison and Uncompahgre Rivers meet. Then they traveled northwest into un-explored lands. They crossed the White River and the Green River (which Escalante named the San Buenaventura River) and entered what is now Utah. There they heard tales of a bearded tribe living on the shores of an impassable river that flowed west. When the Spanish entered the Great Salt Lake basin near Utah Lake, they realized that this was the "river" they had heard about.

From the Desert to Discovery

The group then headed south, avoiding the area's salt desert, and went even farther south when snow began to fall. While passing through what is now the Escalante Desert, they found only dried seeds and cactus to eat and almost died of thirst. When they entered northern Arizona, they discovered the only place at which the Colorado River could be crossed. If they had continued south instead of heading east, they would also have discovered the Grand Canyon. Traveling southeast through the land of the Zuñi tribe, they returned to Santa Fe on January 2, 1777. Nothing is known of Escalante's life after this time. The Spanish authorities in New Spain did not send any further expeditions to investigate the Utah region. That task fell to the American fur trappers of the 1800s, such as James BRIDGER.

SUGGESTED READING Walter Briggs, *Without Noise of Arms: The 1776 Domínguez-Escalante Search for a Route from Santa Fe to Monterey* (Northland Press, 1976); Ted J. Warner, editor, *The Domínguez-Escalante Journal: Their Expedition Through Colorado, Utah, Arizona, and New Mexico in 1776*, translated by Angelico Chavez (University of Utah Press, 1995).

plateau high, flat area of land

Everest, George

English
b July 4, 1790; Gwernvale, Wales
d December 1, 1866; London, England
Surveyed India

surveyor one who makes precise measurements of a location's geography

From 1816 to 1843, the British **surveyor** Sir George Everest worked to create a precise geographical map of India. While surveying the vast Indian subcontinent, he developed a system of measurement that made it possible to calculate the heights and positions of the many soaring peaks in the Himalaya mountain range. His success is indicated by the fact that the world's highest peak, Mount Everest, is named after him.

Everest first saw the Indian subcontinent in 1806 as a 16-year-old cadet in the British army. In his mid-20s, he was employed for two years surveying the Indonesian island of Java. In 1816 he was chosen by the British East India Company to help survey India. Two years later he became assistant to William Lambton, the superintendent of the British effort to map the subcontinent. When Lambton died in 1823, Everest was named superintendent. Seven years later, he was given an additional title, surveyor general of India, and he served in that post until his retirement in 1843.

The British survey of India was a complex, organized, and highly ambitious undertaking. It employed many people—both British and Indian—and lasted for several decades. One of the greatest challenges facing Everest and his surveyors was how to measure the jagged, snow-covered Himalayan peaks. It would be too difficult and too time-consuming to climb each icy mountain. Everest developed an innovative way to use mathematical calculations to determine the height and position of each peak.

The people of Tibet called one of the peaks Chomolungma, which means "Goddess Mother of the World." The surveyors found that it was 29,028 feet high—the tallest mountain in the world—and they named it Mount Everest. Several attempts to climb it resulted in failure and even death. In 1953 Edmund HILLARY of New Zealand and Tenzing Norgay of Nepal became the first people to reach the summit of Mount Everest.

SUGGESTED READING Matthew H. Edney, *Mapping an Empire: The Geographical Construction of British India, 1765-1843* (University of Chicago Press, 1997).

The world's highest peak was named for George Everest in honor of his efforts to map the Indian subcontinent.

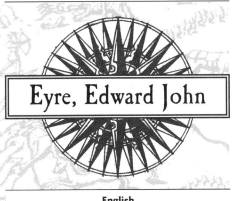

Eyre, Edward John

English
b August 5, 1815; Hornsea, England
d November 30, 1901; Tavistock, England
Explored southern Australian deserts

In 1841 Edward John Eyre crossed more than 1,000 miles of desert in an effort to move livestock across southern Australia. He also made several journeys into the interior of Australia and proved the possibility of land communication between Western and South Australia.

The Muddy Lakes of South Australia

When Eyre was young, his father encouraged him to leave England because of his poor health. In 1834 Eyre went to Australia, where he managed sheep stations near Canberra, New South Wales. He made several successful journeys driving livestock from the ranches to new settlements. He then moved to Adelaide, South Australia, in 1838. From there he led two expeditions to find new grazing lands and a route to Western Australia. The first journey, in May 1839, took him north across the Flinders Ranges and then west across what is now the Eyre Peninsula to Streaky Bay.

On his second trip, Eyre planned to explore central Australia and travel to Port Essington on the north coast. In June 1840, Eyre and seven companions left Adelaide. After a month, they reached Lake Torrens and what is now Lake Eyre. The water had evaporated, exposing the lakes' muddy, salt-covered bottoms. The men attempted to cross the lakes but had to turn back after six miles because of the deep mud. Eyre concluded that the lakes were an impassable barrier. His discouragement is shown in the names he gave to two nearby mountains: Mount Desolation and Mount Hopeless.

Crossing the Continent

In late February 1841, Eyre led an expedition to move livestock across the southern coast of Australia. Accompanied by an assistant named John Baxter and three Australian Aborigines, he left Fowler's Bay and headed west across the Nullarbor Plain. Instead of new grazing land, the men found only barren sands and overwhelming heat. Eyre called the trip one of "never-ceasing torment."

Edward John Eyre not only explored Australia but also served as governor of the islands of Antigua and Jamaica.

About a week after departing, the party reached the last watering hole in the area, but they continued on the journey. Eyre and Baxter survived because the Aborigines showed them how to find water in wells in the sand, in holes in rocks, and in the roots of plants. Near the site of the town that now bears his name, Eyre spent almost three weeks digging six feet into the sand to get water.

In these conditions, tensions ran high. On April 28, two of the Aborigines murdered Baxter and took most of the food. Eyre was left alone with a young Aborigine boy named Wylie. Rain began to fall a week later and continued throughout the rest of the journey. In June the pair reached a bay near Esperance, where a French fisherman gave them food and water. About one month later, Eyre finally reached his destination at King George Sound.

Despite his efforts, Eyre's sponsors considered the trip a failure because he could not successfully move livestock across the Nullarbor Plain. But Britain's Royal Geographical Society recognized Eyre's courage and endurance with a medal. He later became an official of the government of South Australia and was responsible for the welfare of the Aborigines in the Murray River region.

From 1846 to 1865, Eyre served the British government in several posts, including that of governor of Jamaica. He ordered about 400 executions in reaction to an uprising on the island in 1865. This controversial decision led to his resignation. But the British government could make no case against him, and in 1874 he retired to Walreddon Manor, where he lived the rest of his life.

SUGGESTED READING Geoffrey Dutton, *In Search of Edward John Eyre* (Macmillan, 1982); Edward Stokes, *The Desert Coast: Edward Eyre's Expedition, 1840–41* (Five Mile Press, 1993).

Fadlan, Ahmad Ibn. See *Ibn Fadlan, Ahmad.*

Fa-Hsien. See *Faxian.*

Faxian

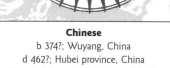

Chinese
b 374?; Wuyang, China
d 462?; Hubei province, China
Traveled in central Asia and India

Faxian was a Chinese pilgrim whose religious devotion led him to make a great journey. He traveled for 15 years across the Asian continent in search of knowledge about his religion, Buddhism. Faxian produced the earliest known account of an overland journey from China to India, a book that is prized today for its wealth of information about the Asian peoples and lands he visited.

The Ancient Scrolls of Buddhism
Faxian was born in the Shanxi province of northern China, around the year 374. His parents had already had three other sons who had died as infants. His father promised that this fourth son would devote himself to Buddhism. When Faxian fell ill, his father sent him to live with Buddhist monks in the nearby city of Ch'ang-an (present-day Xi'an). The boy recovered and decided to stay and study with the monks. Known for his courage, intelligence, and honesty, he became a monk at the age of 20.

Faxian wanted to spend his life studying the many writings about Buddhism. But he feared that his copies of these texts might contain errors or be incomplete. The religion had originated in India about 800 years earlier and had spread through much of Southeast Asia, central Asia, and China. Buddhist writings were transported, copied, and translated many times over the centuries. Faxian knew that people who copy and translate texts often make mistakes. It was even possible that entire scrolls had been lost or stolen while being carried across Asia.

Faxian felt that he could not truly understand Buddhism by reading these faulty Chinese versions of the ancient texts. He decided that he had to travel to India to find the sacred writings in their original language, Sanskrit. He hoped to bring the Sanskrit texts back to China in order to create new and more accurate translations.

Demons of the Desert

The journey Faxian planned was highly unusual—and very dangerous—but he believed that his mission was more important than any risks he might face. In 399 he set out from Ch'ang-an together with three or four other monks. More people joined the group along the way. But over the course of the long journey, some turned back, some settled down in the cities they passed, and some died.

The monks first traveled west, following a route used by trade **caravans.** From Xining, China's westernmost city, they crossed the western part of the Gobi Desert to reach the town of Dunhuang. Dunhuang was built on the edge of a harsh desert called the Takla Makan. The city's military governor gave the travelers supplies and advice to prepare them for the journey across the Takla Makan.

Faxian later said: "In this desert there are a great many evil demons. . . . There are no birds or beasts to be seen; but so far as the eye can reach, the route is marked out by the bleached bones of men who have perished in the attempt to cross the desert." For 17 days, Faxian and his companions struggled through the barren sands. They survived the crossing and arrived at the Buddhist kingdom of Hotan on the desert's southern edge.

The Paths to Knowledge

After a short stay in Hotan, the travelers resumed their journey, heading west through the towns of Yarkant (present-day Shache) and Kashgar (present-day Kashi). They then turned south and entered the Pamir Mountains. Faxian described the dizzying and dangerous experience of walking along icy mountain trails high above the Indus River. "On looking over the edge," he said, "[your] sight becomes confused, and then, on advancing, the foot loses its hold and you are lost." When at last they came down from the mountains, Faxian and a few remaining companions followed the Kabul River into what is now Pakistan. Before them lay the vast Indian subcontinent. After six years of travel, Faxian was ready to begin his search for Buddhist writings.

Fortunately, he was not disappointed. He spent three years studying in the capital city of Magadha, a state in eastern India. After visiting sacred sites along the Ganges River, he passed another two years in

caravan large group of people traveling together, often with pack animals, across a desert or other dangerous region

the port city of Tamralipti (now called Tamluk) before sailing to the island of Ceylon (present-day Sri Lanka). There he obtained some Buddhist texts that Chinese followers of the religion had never seen before.

Lost in Stormy Seas

Around 413 Faxian gathered his collection of books and scrolls and boarded a ship for a return voyage to China. A violent storm arose, and the ship was blown off course. When the ship sprang a leak and was in danger of sinking, the merchants on board threw their cargo into the sea in order to lighten the ship's weight. Faxian could only pray that they would not force him to abandon his sacred texts. Finally the storm ended, leaving the ship lost and at the mercy of pirates. Faxian recalled: "The merchants were full of terror, not knowing where they were going. The sea was deep and bottomless, and there was no place where they could drop anchor and stop." After 90 days, the ship's pilots were able to find their way to the island of Java (now part of Indonesia). Faxian spent five months there before boarding another ship bound for the port of Guangzhou (also known as Canton) in southern China.

Once again fierce winds and rains drove his vessel off course. His shipmates, who were followers of the Hindu religion, feared that the presence of a Buddhist on board was bringing them bad luck. They threatened to find an island and abandon him on its shores. But a man who had befriended Faxian warned the Hindus that if they treated the monk badly, the emperor of China would be furious with them. They agreed not to harm Faxian, but their luck did not improve—the ship continued to drift for 70 days without sighting land. At last the crew turned the ship to the northwest, and the weary travelers managed to reach the coast of northern China. Faxian completed his journey by land, arriving in the capital city, Nanjing, in 414.

At a Buddhist monastery in Nanjing, Faxian began the long task of translating the scrolls he had brought. He was helped by a monk from India. Faxian also found time to give an account, which may have been written down by another monk, of the travels that had taken him through 30 countries in 15 years. Faxian retired to a monastery east of Nanjing and lived there until his death.

SUGGESTED READING M. A. Giles, translator, *The Travels of Fa-Hsien (399–414 A.D.)*, or *Record of the Buddhistic Kingdoms* (reprint, Susil Gupta, 1923); James Legge, translator, *A Record of Buddhistic Kingdoms, Being an Account by the Chinese Monk Fâ-Hsien of His Travels in India and Ceylon (A.D. 399–414) in Search of the Buddhist Books of Discipline* (reprint, Paragon, 1965).

Federmann, Nikolaus

German
b 1505?; Ulm, Germany
d 1542; Madrid, Spain
Explored Venezuela and Colombia

El Dorado mythical ruler, city, or area of South America believed to possess much gold

Nikolaus Federmann was a German adventurer who explored the interior of what is now Venezuela and Colombia. His most famous expedition was the search for **El Dorado,** the legendary city of gold said to exist in the Andes Mountains. After almost three years of traveling, he arrived in Colombia only to discover that the Spanish had already claimed the land.

Early Expeditions in South America

Little is known about Federmann's life before 1530, when he was appointed second-in-command of the German colony in Coro,

Venezuela. The Welsers, a powerful family of German bankers, had been given the right to govern this region by King Charles I of Spain. Hoping to profit from the riches that were available in South America, the Welsers ordered Federmann to explore the interior. In 1531 he traveled south to the **llanos** near the Portuguesa River. After exploring the foothills of the Cordillera Mérida, a group of mountain ranges east of Lake Maracaibo, Federmann returned to Coro in 1532.

llanos vast grassy plains of South America

In Pursuit of Treasure

The next year, he joined an expedition under the command of Georg von Speier to look for El Dorado in what is now Colombia. Disobeying orders, Federmann left the main group with about 500 men. He traveled southeast, ascending the Meta River and crossing the floodplains of the Orinoco River. When the men reached the Guaviare River in Colombia, they climbed the Andes Mountains while being attacked by the Chibcha Indians. The Chibcha were fighting a losing battle to protect their empire.

plateau high, flat area of land

Federmann finally reached the **plateau** of Bogotá in 1539. The journey had taken nearly three years, and only one-third of his force had survived. But when he arrived, he found that a Spanish army led by Gonzalo JIMÉNEZ DE QUESADA was already there. Quesada wanted to avoid a war over the region, so he gave Federmann gold and food for his men. Then Quesada, Federmann, and Sebastián de BENALCÁZAR, another Spaniard who claimed the area, agreed to present their cases to the **Council of the Indies** in Spain. The council eventually ruled in favor of Spain, though neither Quesada or Benalcázar was named governor. Federmann received nothing for his efforts. Later the Welser family took away his lands in Venezuela and began legal action against him for his disobedience. Federmann died in Madrid, Spain, in 1542.

Council of the Indies governing body of Spain's colonial empire from 1524 to 1834

SUGGESTED READING Robert Silverberg, *The Golden Dream: Seekers of El Dorado* (Ohio University Press, 1996).

Fernandez de Quirós, Pedro. See *Quirós, Pedro Fernandez de.*

Fitzroy, Robert

English
b July 5, 1805; Suffolk, England
d April 30, 1865; Norwald, England
Explored South America and the
Pacific Ocean with Charles Darwin

Robert Fitzroy spent nearly 10 years charting the coasts of South America. From 1831 to 1836, Charles DARWIN was a passenger aboard Fitzroy's ship, the *Beagle.* While Darwin studied plants, animals, and natural history, Captain Fitzroy made important contributions to the science of **meteorology.**

Travels in Argentina

Fitzroy was born into a wealthy noble family. He attended the Royal Naval College as a young man and was made a lieutenant at the age of 19. In 1828 he was given command of the *Beagle* when the ship's captain committed suicide. Fitzroy was ordered to continue a survey of Patagonia and Tierra del Fuego in Argentina. This task called upon his skills not only as a sailor but also as a

meteorology the scientific study of weather and weather forecasting

hydrographer scientist who studies bodies of water to make navigation easier

hydrographer and meteorologist. When he returned to England in 1830, he brought back a small group of Fuegians. At Fitzroy's expense, they were taught Christianity and the English culture. He then took them back to South America, hoping that they would spread Christianity, but his efforts did not succeed.

An Unlikely Friendship

From 1831 to 1836, Fitzroy charted the coasts of South America with Darwin aboard the *Beagle.* Fitzroy found that his Christian beliefs differed from many of Darwin's scientific ideas, but the two men became close friends. Darwin named a species of dolphin after Fitzroy who named Mount Darwin in Tierra del Fuego after the naturalist. In 1837 Fitzroy received the gold medal of the Royal Geographic Society for his work, and two years later, he published *Voyage of the* Adventure *and the* Beagle.

After two years as a member of the British Parliament, Fitzroy was appointed governor and commander in chief of New Zealand in 1843. He arrived just after an uprising by the Maori people of the region. His sympathy for the Maori angered the British colonists, and he was forced to leave his post after two years. He retired from the navy in 1850 and was placed in charge of the meteorological department of the Board of Trade in 1854. Seven years later, he published a book on meteorology that led to the storm warning system in use today. Depressed by opposition to his work, he took his own life in 1865.

SUGGESTED READING Loren Eisely, *Darwin's Century* (Doubleday, 1958); Robert Lee Marks, *Three Men of the Beagle* (Knopf, 1991); Alan Moorehead, *Darwin and the Beagle* (Harper and Row, 1969).

Flinders, Matthew

English
b March 16, 1774; Donnington, England
d July 19, 1814; London, England
First to sail around Australia

hydrographer scientist who studies bodies of water to make navigation easier

circumnavigate to travel around

specimen sample of a plant or animal, usually collected for scientific study or display

Matthew Flinders is regarded as one of the world's most successful navigators and **hydrographers.** In 1803 he became the first person to **circumnavigate** Australia, then known as *Terra Australis.* While surveying and charting the continent, Flinders also made several advances in the field of navigation. The naturalists on his expedition collected hundreds of new plant and animal **specimens.**

A Taste for Adventure

Since his father and grandfather were both surgeons, Flinders was also expected to study medicine. But reading Daniel Defoe's book *Robinson Crusoe* inspired him to seek adventure, so he joined the Royal Navy at the age of 15. Early in his military career, he served under Captain William BLIGH in the South Pacific and West Indies. In 1794 he took part in the Battle of Brest, off the northwestern coast of France. The next year, he sailed to the British colony of New South Wales, Australia, aboard the *Reliance.*

Upon arriving in Sydney, Flinders explored the region's bays with the colony's governor, John Hunter. Flinders was later ordered to survey the Furneaux Islands, which lie north of Van Diemen's Land (present-day Tasmania). After being promoted to lieutenant, Flinders was sent to join George Bass, the ship's surgeon, to search for a water passage between Van Diemen's Land and the southern coast of Australia. The pair discovered the channel, which was

Matthew Flinders sailed around Australia and explored the Great Barrier Reef.

sloop small ship with one mast and triangular sails

species type of plant or animal

marsupial animal whose babies are carried in a pouch on the front of the mother's body

brig small, fast sailing ship with two masts and square sails

named Bass Strait, and circumnavigated Van Diemen's Land, proving that it was an island. In 1800, Flinders returned to England to raise money for an exploration of the coasts of Australia. He received support from Sir Joseph BANKS, who had explored Australia's Botany Bay 30 years earlier.

Discovery and Disaster

The following year, Flinders was given command of the **sloop** *Investigator* with a crew of 88 men, including the naturalist Robert Brown. The expedition left Spithead, England, in July. Sailing south around Africa, the ship reached Cape Leeuwin on the southwest coast of Australia in early December. The crew spent almost a month at nearby King George Sound, where Brown gathered specimens of 500 previously unknown flowers as well as specimens of kangaroos, snakes, lizards, and fish.

In January 1802, Flinders sailed east along Australia's southern coast. In the Recherche Archipelago, Brown identified many plants, along with seabirds, blue penguins, and a **species** of small kangaroo. The *Investigator* then reached a group of islands that Flinders named after the ship. On February 21, a small group of sailors went to the mainland near what is now Spencer Gulf to look for fresh water. Neither the boat nor the landing party was ever seen again. The place where they disappeared is now known as Cape Catastrophe.

Sailing up Spencer Gulf, Flinders saw a range of red mountains and named one of them Mount Brown, after the ship's naturalist. The mountain region was named the Flinders Ranges. Continuing east, Flinders explored the Gulf of St. Vincent and Kangaroo Island, where the crew hunted kangaroos for food.

The Great Barrier Reef

In April, Flinders met a French explorer, Nicolas BAUDIN, at a site near the Gulf of St. Vincent that became known as Encounter Bay. Although France and England were at war, the two men had a friendly breakfast together before going their separate ways.

Later that month, Flinders explored the Bass Strait as well as the northeast coast of what is now called King's Island. The ship's scientists went ashore and found more plant species on the island than anywhere else on their travels. They also encountered **marsupials,** such as wallabies and wombats, and many flocks of a waterbird called the short-tailed shearwater. In May, Flinders landed in Port Jackson, on Australia's east coast, and had dinner with Philip Gidley King, the governor of the prison colony of New South Wales. The governor gave Flinders a small **brig** with a crew of prisoners and two Australian Aborigines who could act as interpreters for the remainder of the voyage.

Sailing north in July, Flinders investigated Hervey Bay and a group of seventy small islands near Keppel Bay. He soon reached the world's largest coral reef, the Great Barrier Reef. After careful examination, he determined that the reef was made up of the outer shells and skeletons of tiny sea creatures called polyps. During this time, he also became one of the first navigators to understand the way in which the iron parts of a ship affect its magnetic compass. Unfortunately, the brig given to Flinders was damaged by hitting the reef and

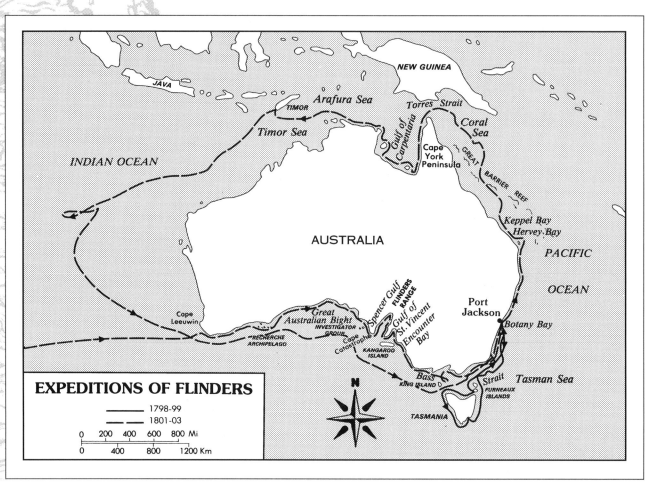

EXPEDITIONS OF FLINDERS

——— 1798-99
– – – 1801-03

```
0    200  400   600   800 Mi
0       400      800     1200 Km
```

Matthew Flinders studied the coast of Australia so thoroughly that it was said that he had left nothing for other explorers to do.

schooner fast, easy-to-maneuver sailing ship with two or more masts and triangular sails

had to return to Port Jackson. Flinders continued north in the *Investigator* for about 500 miles before finding a safe route to open waters.

Completing the Circumnavigation

Flinders sailed the rest of the way up Australia's east coast and then headed west through the Torres Strait, between Australia and New Guinea. From November 1802 to March 1803, he explored the coast and islands along what is now the Gulf of Carpentaria. At the end of March, the ship rounded the western and southern coasts of Australia, making Flinders and his crew the first to circumnavigate the continent.

Two months later, Flinders returned to Port Jackson before departing for England as a passenger aboard the *Porpoise*. But the ship was wrecked on a reef, and Flinders spent the next two weeks rowing 700 miles back to Port Jackson for help. Governor King gave him a **schooner** in which to return to England, but it was barely seaworthy. With a sick crew and very little food, Flinders decided to land at Île de France (now Mauritius) to ask for aid. He did not know that the war between England and France had intensified. The French accused Flinders of being a spy and took him prisoner on December 17, 1803. He spent nearly seven years in jail before he was released. Despite the fact that many of his records had been taken by the French, Flinders wrote an account of his voyage that was published on the day he died.

SUGGESTED READING Matthew Flinders, *Narrative of His Voyage in the Schooner Francis, 1798,* edited by Geoffrey Rawson (Golden Cockerel Press, 1946); Geoffrey C. Ingleton, *Matthew Flinders: Navigator and Chartmaker* (Genesis Publications in association with Hedley Australia, 1986).

Forster, Johann Georg Adam

German
b November 27, 1754; Nassenhuben, Prussia, (near present-day Gdańsk, Poland)
d January 12, 1794; Paris, France
Assisted as naturalist on James Cook's second voyage

Johann Georg Forster and his father, Johann Reinhold Forster, served as naturalists on James Cook's second voyage around the world.

From 1772 to 1775, Johann Georg Adam Forster was one of the naturalists aboard one of Captain James Cook's ships, the *Resolution.* His journal provides a general account of Cook's second major expedition. Forster also contributed to Europe's growing knowledge of the natural history of the southern Pacific Ocean.

A Teenage Explorer

Forster was born in Prussia, a former German state that is now a part of Poland. His father, Johann Reinhold Forster, was a pastor and schoolteacher with an interest in the natural sciences. When he was 11 years old, the younger Forster—known as Georg—joined his father on an exploration of Russia. At 17 he sailed with his father on Cook's ship *Resolution.* Cook, an officer in the British navy, was searching for *Terra Australis Incognita,* the legendary southern continent that was supposed to exist somewhere in the southern Pacific Ocean. During the three-year voyage, Forster proved to be an easygoing and likable shipmate. He was a bright young man and had a talent for drawing.

Controversial Writings

During the voyage, Forster kept a journal. Among other topics, he wrote about the ship's visit to the island of Tahiti. He described the shock he felt regarding his shipmates' sexual relationships with the Tahitian women. At the same time, Forster could see why the simple island life enchanted the sailors.

Although Forster was well liked on board, his father quarreled with Cook and the rest of the crew throughout the voyage. After the ship returned to England in 1775, Cook told the elder Forster not to publish an account of the expedition. Cook planned to earn money from his own writings. But Georg Forster published *A Voyage Round the World* six weeks before Cook's book was completed. In his book, Forster did not accurately describe the way Cook had behaved as the ship's commander. Some historians believe that his father persuaded Georg to write a falsely negative report.

Life as a Professor and Politician

Georg Forster returned to Germany two years after his book was published. He was a professor of natural history at two German universities and also studied medicine. He became a librarian for a German prince in Mayence (now called Mainz) in 1788. Forster's work in natural history strongly influenced Baron Alexander von Humboldt, a German naturalist, traveler, and statesman. From 1790 to 1791, Forster accompanied Humboldt on a trip to Belgium, Holland, England, and France.

When Forster returned to Germany, he became involved in politics. France had taken control of Mayence in 1792. The people of the city sent Forster to Paris to ask the French government if the city could become a part of France. But Forster's requests were ignored. In the meantime, the Germans regained Mayence, and they accused Forster of betraying his country. He spent his final days in Paris, where he died in 1794.

SUGGESTED READING Michael E. Hoare, *Three Men in a Boat: The Forsters and New Zealand Science* (Hawthorn Press, 1975).

Forster, Johann Reinhold

German
b October 22, 1729; Dirschau, Prussia
(now Tczew, Poland)
d December 9, 1798; Halle, Germany
Served as naturalist on James Cook's second voyage

circumnavigation journey around the world

anthropology the scientific study of human societies

From 1772 to 1775, Johann Reinhold Forster held the post of naturalist during Captain James COOK's second **circumnavigation.** While traveling in the southern Pacific Ocean, Forster completed extensive studies of the plant and animal life of the region. His findings greatly expanded upon the work done by Sir Joseph BANKS and Daniel Carl Solander on Cook's first voyage. He also made major contributions in the field of **anthropology.**

From the Schoolroom to the Open Sea

Forster was born in Prussia in 1729 and spent his early adulthood as a pastor and schoolteacher. He had few experiences with the sea or with sailors, other than a scientific expedition to Russia aboard the *Volga* in 1765. He moved to London in 1766, and by 1772 he had published two widely read books on natural history. He also translated an account of Louis-Antoine de BOUGAINVILLE's circumnavigation.

During that same year, Cook was planning a Pacific expedition to search for the legendary southern continent, *Terra Australis Incognita.* He had hired Sir Joseph Banks to serve as the ship's naturalist. But Banks decided not to go on the trip after an argument over the amount of space he and his assistant would have aboard the ship, the *Resolution.* Forster was offered a large sum of money to replace Banks. He accepted the post and brought along his son, Johann Georg Adam FORSTER, as an assistant.

Misery and Success

Forster was not used to life at sea, and he suffered from seasickness. He was a mean-spirited man and argued with almost everyone on board, but he still managed to do his job with care and precision. Wherever the *Resolution* sailed, he added to the plant and animal life studies begun on Cook's previous journey. Forster was the first European to describe the Australian sea lion. In Tahiti he added a swallow, a parrot, and many plants to the list of **species** known to Europeans. When the ship reached Antarctic waters, Forster did not let his **rheumatism** stop him from working. He identified four species of penguins and two other seabirds. He also studied the Pacific islanders and classified cultural groups among them.

species type of plant or animal

rheumatism physical condition that causes pain in the joints or muscles, making movement uncomfortable

Despite Forster's contributions to the expedition, he and Cook did not get along. When the *Resolution* returned to England in 1775, Cook refused to allow Forster to publish anything about the expedition—but Forster eventually did write several books about the trip.

In 1780 Forster became a professor of natural history. He was also named director of botanical gardens for the king of Prussia, Frederick II. Seven years later, Forster published a volume on voyages and discoveries. He died at the age of 69.

SUGGESTED READING Johann Reinhold Forster, *Observations Made During a Voyage Round the World,* edited by Nicholas Thomas and others (University of Hawaii Press, 1996); Michael E. Hoare, *The Tactless Philosopher: Johann Reinhold Forster (1729–98)* (Hawthorn Press, 1975).

Foucauld, Charles-Eugène de

French
b September 15, 1858; Strasbourg, France
d December 1, 1916; Tamanrasset, Algeria
Explored Morocco

rabbi Jewish teacher or religious leader

cartographer mapmaker

Charles-Eugène de Foucauld was a Christian missionary to the French colonies of North Africa.

While serving in the French army, Charles-Eugène de Foucauld developed a deep interest in the barren beauty of North Africa. After leaving the army, he disguised himself in order to explore Morocco, a region that was closed to Europeans. Foucauld later became a monk and worked among the Tuareg people of Algeria.

A Man of Many Faces

Foucauld was born into a well-known French family, but he was a lazy student and did poorly in school. At the age of 20, he enrolled in a military academy, and two years later, he went to Algeria as a soldier in the French army. Foucauld saw little military action, but he became fascinated by the desert region of the Sahara. He resigned from the army and moved to Algiers.

Foucauld wanted to explore Morocco, but European Christians were not welcome in the region. He disguised himself as a Russian **rabbi** in order to enter the country. Foucauld wanted to gather information about the geography of the land so that **cartographers** could draw maps based on his report. In 1888 he published *Reconnaissance of Morocco,* the result of almost a year of exploration. The Paris Geographical Society awarded him its gold medal for his achievement.

A Change of Heart

By 1890 Foucauld had decided to become a monk, believing that religion would help the French secure control of North Africa. He wrote: "If we do not manage to make Frenchmen out of the natives, they will drive us from their land. The only way, however, of turning them into Frenchmen, is by making them Christians first." He entered a monastery, took his vows in 1901, and lived as a hermit in Beni Abbès, Algeria, for two years. Foucauld then agreed to travel with a friend to the Hoggar Mountains in southern Algeria. After stopping in Adrar to learn the language of the region's Tuareg people, he continued across the desert to the Hoggar Mountains. He decided to settle in Tamanrasset, a small village in the middle of Tuareg territory. The Tuareg ruler liked Foucauld so much that he moved the tribe's capital to Tamanrasset. By making peace with the Tuareg, Foucauld achieved one of the main goals of the French military.

During the last 11 years of his life, Foucauld produced extensive geographical studies of the Sahara region. He proposed locations for roads, railroads, and irrigation systems. Foucauld also compiled a complete dictionary of the Tuareg language. In 1916 Foucauld was murdered by a group of Muslims, who may have suspected him of being a military spy for the French.

Foxe, Luke

English
b October 20, 1586; Hull, England
d July 1635; Whitby, England
***Explored Hudson Bay and
discovered Foxe Channel***

courtier attendant at a royal court

Northwest Passage water route connecting the Atlantic Ocean and Pacific Ocean through the Arctic islands of northern Canada

SUGGESTED READING S. C. Lorit, *Charles de Foucauld, the Silent Witness* (New City Press, 1991); Margaret Trouncer, *Charles de Foucauld* (G. G. Harrap, 1972).

Luke Foxe completed the work begun by Thomas BUTTON, William BAFFIN, and Robert BYLOT in mapping the area of Hudson Bay in what is now Canada. After sailing along the entire western coast of Hudson Bay, he discovered what became known as the Foxe Channel, between Southampton Island and Baffin Island.

Preparing for Departure

Foxe was an excellent navigator who had been trained by his father, a seaman stationed at Hull. After many voyages to the Mediterranean and Baltic Seas, Foxe became interested in exploring the Arctic Ocean. He learned much about the region from books, and he also gathered information from other sailors. When ships returned to England from the Arctic Ocean, Foxe interviewed the captains, officers, and others who had sailed on the expeditions. He later wrote a book in which he included this valuable historical and geographical information.

Bound for the Arctic Ocean

Foxe befriended Henry Briggs, a famous Oxford mathematician and astronomer, who told an important **courtier** about Foxe's navigational skills. Foxe was then chosen to lead an expedition to Hudson Bay. A group of London merchants supplied him with an old gunboat called the *Charles* and a crew of 23 men. The party left England on May 5, 1631, and landed at Frobisher Bay on Baffin Island, Canada, in June. They navigated the Hudson Strait and then sailed south as far as what is now James Bay. On the way, the *Charles* met a rival expedition sent out by merchants from Bristol, England. Foxe had dinner with the ship's captain, Thomas James.

James stayed in the southern part of the bay and suffered through a difficult winter. Foxe traveled directly north in search of the **Northwest Passage,** though Baffin had reported that there was no such route out of Hudson Bay. Foxe discovered what is now known as Foxe Channel, between Southampton Island and Baffin Island. He then followed the coast of Baffin Island northward. But he soon realized that there was no way to pass through the ice, and he returned to England.

Foxe had finally made it to Arctic waters. He wrote an interesting and vivid book, in which he called himself "North-west Foxe." But since he had not found a way through the ice, his mission was considered a failure, and he died neither rich nor famous.

SUGGESTED READING Luke Foxe, *North-West Fox or Fox from the North-West Passage* (reprint, Johnson Reprint, 1965).

Francis Xavier. See *Xavier, Francis.*

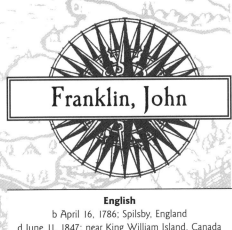

Franklin, John

English
b April 16, 1786; Spilsby, England
d June 11, 1847; near King William Island, Canada
Explored Arctic Ocean off northern coast of Canada

Northwest Passage water route connecting the Atlantic Ocean and Pacific Ocean through the Arctic islands of northern Canada

Admiralty governing body of Britain's Royal Navy until 1964

For more than 10 years, the disappearance of Sir John Franklin was a mystery that obsessed the British public.

During his lifetime, Rear Admiral Sir John Franklin was regarded as a hero for his expeditions to the Arctic Ocean. But his determination to complete his missions, no matter what the danger, caused him to make some deadly mistakes. On the first expedition that he commanded, half of his party died of starvation. Twenty-six years later, Franklin and all 129 of his crew members died when their ships became trapped in Arctic ice. Though this voyage ended in tragedy, Franklin's work eventually led to the discovery of the **Northwest Passage.**

A Sailor at Heart

Franklin grew up only a few miles from England's eastern coast. He had a gentle nature, so his father thought that the boy should become a minister. But as soon as Franklin saw the waves of the North Sea, he wanted to become a sailor. At the age of 14, he joined the Royal Navy as a volunteer aboard the *Polyphemus.* He soon saw combat in the Battle of Copenhagen, in 1801. Over the next several years, he fought in other naval battles and worked his way up to the rank of lieutenant.

After Britain's war with France ended, the **Admiralty** decided to use its naval forces to explore the Arctic Ocean. Many geographers of the time believed that the polar ice was a ring beyond which lay an open polar sea. The navy decided to send an expedition from Spitsbergen, a Norwegian island in the Arctic Ocean, eastward to the Bering Strait, which separates Siberia from Alaska. Franklin was appointed second-in-command to Captain David Buchan. They sailed on April 25, 1818, but their two ships, the *Dorothea* and the *Trent,* did not get far before they were stopped by ice. A strong gale forced both ships to seek shelter with the ice as a windbreak. The crews struggled to sail the ships through stormy waters, but Franklin calmly steered the *Trent* to safety. Later both vessels became trapped in the ice north of Spitsbergen for three weeks. Buchan admitted that the expedition had failed, and he ordered the crews to return to England.

Success and Failure

By the time he was 33 years old, Franklin had proved that he was a talented sailor who could perform well under pressure. The Admiralty decided to send him to the northern coast of North America to continue the search for the Northwest Passage. Neither Franklin nor his superiors knew much about this region. Franklin was given the challenge of charting the Arctic coast of North America by foot and canoe. He was to travel east from the Coppermine River to a point where William PARRY, another English explorer, might have been able to meet him. Only one European, Samuel HEARNE, had ever before made it to the mouth of the Coppermine River. Although Hearne was an experienced overland explorer, he had searched for three years before finding a group of Indians who led him to the river. All of Franklin's experience had been at sea, not on land, so he had little hope of success.

Despite his fears, Franklin charted 550 miles of the northern coast of Canada, east of the Coppermine River. He accomplished this feat in about three years, about the same amount of time it had taken Hearne to do much less. The expedition was not a complete

This illustration of John Franklin's expedition shows one method of cutting through ice in the Arctic Ocean.

voyageur expert French woodsman, boatman, and guide

frigate small, agile warship with three masts and square sails

success, however, partly because of events beyond Franklin's control and partly because of his stubbornness. The companies that were supposed to supply food and water for the crews never made the deliveries. But Franklin insisted that the officers in his party would not carry heavy loads or hunt for food. Everyone in his party nearly starved, and nine men died. One of the Canadian **voyageurs** ate a dead Englishman and was executed for this crime. Despite the fatal turn of events, the British people were captivated by the story. They admired Franklin's persistence and honored him upon his return to Britain.

The Struggles of a Hero

Franklin was not discouraged by the tragedy of his first trip to the Arctic Ocean. But when he left for his next voyage, in February 1825, he was well prepared. He made sure that he had enough supplies, and he brought along light boats that he had designed for river and coastal travel. John Richardson and George BACK, who had served on Franklin's first expedition, even volunteered for this journey. When the party reached the mouth of the Mackenzie River, Franklin and Back turned west to explore the coast of Canada in the direction of the Bering Strait. Richardson led a second party east toward the Coppermine River. Franklin traveled halfway up the coast before bad weather forced him to turn back. But he had charted the southern edges of the Northwest Passage. When he returned to England, he was made a knight for his achievement.

Franklin then turned his attention away from Arctic exploration. He commanded the **frigate** *Rainbow* in 1830 on a tour of the Mediterranean Sea. In 1837 he was appointed lieutenant governor of Van Diemen's Land (now called Tasmania), off the coast of Australia. Although he did his best to govern this prison colony, he was not well liked by other politicians there, and he was dismissed from the job in 1843.

When he returned to England, he was able to persuade the Admiralty to let him lead the next expedition to seek the Northwest Passage. He set out with the *Erebus* and the *Terror* in 1845. Franklin first tried to sail north through the Wellington Channel, located west of Devon Island, to what he still thought was an open Arctic Sea. Unable to break through the ice in the channel, he then headed south through Peel Sound and the waterway now called Franklin Strait. Franklin did not know about the existence of the ice-free Simpson Strait, south of King William Island. He sailed west of the island instead. But his two ships were too large to navigate the ice-clogged waters. In September 1846, the ships became stuck in the ice and never escaped. The only surviving record reports that Franklin died a year before his men abandoned the trapped ship. They walked south, but all died before reaching a settlement. Some of them made it as far as Simpson Strait, the last part of the Northwest Passage that had not yet been discovered.

The Long Search for Franklin

By 1848 the British had not heard from Franklin's expedition, and the public became obsessed with the missing hero and his crew. More than 50 separate rescue expeditions were sent to the Arctic Ocean. In 1859 Franklin's wife, Lady Jane Franklin, financed an expedition led by Francis McClintock. He discovered the graves marking the site of the shipwreck on King William Island. The work done by these many rescue missions resulted in the complete charting of the Northwest Passage.

SUGGESTED READING Owen Beattie and John Geiger, *Frozen in Time: Unlocking the Secrets of the Franklin Expedition* (Reprint, Plume, 1990); Sir John Franklin, *Narrative of a Journey to the Shores of the Polar Sea in the Years 1819-22*, edited by Leslie H. Neatby (Reprint, M. G. Hurtig, 1971); Paul Nanton, *Arctic Breakthrough: Franklin's Expeditions, 1819-1847* (Clarke Irwin, 1970).

Fraser, Simon

Canadian
b 1776; Bennington, New York (now part of Vermont)
d April 19, 1862; St. Andrew's, Canada West
(now Ontario)
Explored Fraser River

Simon Fraser's journals suggest that he felt he was competing against Alexander Mackenzie, who had explored the Fraser River 15 years earlier.

Simon Fraser was an adventurous Canadian fur trader. After spending several years establishing trading posts on the western side of the Rocky Mountains, he was sent to find a river route from the Pacific Ocean to the Canadian interior. In 1808 Fraser undertook a dangerous journey down the raging river that now bears his name. He followed the Fraser River all the way to its mouth on the Pacific Ocean at the site of present-day Vancouver, British Columbia.

Early Years

Fraser's father fought on the side of the British in the American Revolution, but he was captured and died a prisoner. After the war, Fraser's mother took the family to Canada. Fraser began working for the North West Company at the age of 16. By 1802 he had been made a partner in the company.

Following Mackenzie

In 1805 Fraser was sent to set up trading posts west of the Rocky Mountains. The North West Company hoped to find new sources of furs and an easy water route to the Pacific Ocean. This new route would allow the company to ship supplies and goods inland from the Pacific coast instead of making the long and expensive journey overland from Montréal. Twelve years earlier, another North West Company trader named Alexander Mackenzie had crossed the Rocky Mountains from the east. Mackenzie had tried to follow the Fraser River to the coast, thinking that he was on the Columbia River. But along the way, Indians told him that the river would become too difficult to navigate, so he turned back and took an overland route. Now the company wanted Fraser to try following the river. There was no hurry, however, so Fraser spent three years in the area he named New Caledonia (now central British Columbia). He developed the company's business and planned his expedition.

His priorities changed when he heard surprising news. The president of the United States, Thomas Jefferson, had sent Meriwether Lewis and William Clark up the Missouri River to the Pacific Ocean. The expedition had succeeded in 1805. Although the border between the United States and Canada had not yet been established, the United States was claiming much of the territory around the

portage transport of boats and supplies overland between waterways

latitude distance north or south of the equator

Columbia River. Suddenly the Canadians were in a great hurry to compete for the land. Fraser was told to travel down the Columbia River (which was actually the Fraser River) as quickly as possible.

On May 28, 1808, Fraser set out from Fort George (present-day Prince George) with a party of 24 men. He met Indians who warned him that the river ahead was full of rapids and falls between steep, rocky cliffs. The cliffs made **portaging** around the rapids very dangerous. Mackenzie had listened to these warnings and turned back. But Fraser and his party pressed ahead, determined to carry out their orders. They found the river to be as difficult as they had been told. Although the canoes swirled through the rapids and almost tipped over many times, the men decided that they would rather risk the rapids than haul the canoes up the rocky cliffs.

Adventures on the Wrong River

Fraser did not completely ignore the warnings of the Indians. He sent some men to observe the river ahead and decided that the Indians were right—the river could not be navigated. By determining that the river could not be used to transport goods, he had achieved the main goal of his journey. But Fraser had also been ordered to reach the coast. The men began to walk along the cliffs, following narrow, slippery paths. These trails had been worn into the cliffs by generations of Indians who were familiar with the rocky route. Fraser's men were following it for the first time.

They passed the mouth of another river, and Fraser named it the Thompson River after his fellow trader and explorer, David THOMPSON. Past the Thompson River, the Fraser River became calmer. But farther downstream, the party found difficult rapids in a huge canyon. They were forced to make portages along the steep riverbanks. The explorers came to a spot where the river divided into several channels. They followed one of these waterways, now called the Strait of Georgia, to a bay of the sea. Fraser was disappointed not to find open water, for he did not realize that Vancouver Island was blocking his view of the nearby Pacific Ocean. He took a **latitude** reading and discovered that he was far north of the place where the Columbia River emptied into the sea. Fraser realized that he had followed the wrong river.

A Speedy Return

Confronted by hostile Indians and running low on supplies, Fraser's party decided to turn around and head for home. During the first part of the return journey, Indians followed Fraser and his men, shooting arrows and dropping stones from the cliffs above the river. In a moment of panic, some of the men threatened to leave the group and try to return overland. Fraser convinced them that it would be better to stay together, and the party returned safely on August 6. The journey to the sea had taken 36 days. Though the return trip required the men to paddle upstream, it took them only 37 days.

But Fraser was disappointed because he had failed to follow the Columbia River to the Pacific Ocean. Since he had been on the wrong river the entire time, he could not claim the land along the Columbia for Great Britain. However, the Fraser River is a major waterway in western Canada, and he had succeeded in following it under very challenging conditions.

SUGGESTED READING Simon Fraser, *Simon Fraser: Letters and Journals, 1806–1808*, edited by W. Kaye Lamb (Macmillan of Canada, 1960); Bruce Hutchinson, *The Fraser* (Rinehart, 1950).

Frémont, John Charles

American
b January 21, 1813; Savannah, Georgia
d July 13, 1890; New York, New York
Surveyed and mapped American West

topographer person who describes and maps the physical features of geographic regions

John Charles Frémont attracted settlers to the frontier with the exaggerated descriptions of Western exploration that he wrote with his wife.

John Charles Frémont did more than any other explorer to make the American West attractive to settlers. Between 1842 and 1845, he led three expeditions to chart the region on behalf of the United States government. His highly publicized journeys contributed to Americans' knowledge of the West and their interest in settling there.

The Soldier and the Senator's Daughter

Born in Georgia, Frémont grew up to be talented, handsome, and independent. After attending Charleston College for a short time, he taught mathematics in the navy. In 1835 he joined the Topographical Corps of the United States Army. This unit was responsible for surveying and mapping lesser-known areas of the United States. Three years later, Frémont was promoted to second lieutenant. He became the assistant to Joseph Nicollet, a respected **topographer** who was mapping the area between the upper Mississippi and Missouri Rivers.

Frémont then went to Washington, D.C., with Nicollet to report the results of their studies. There the young soldier met and fell in love with Jessie Benton, the beautiful, smart, and strong-willed daughter of Senator Thomas Hart Benton of Missouri. The senator thought that Frémont was too poor to marry his daughter, but John and Jessie were secretly married in 1841. Benton then decided to use Frémont's surveying experience to promote Manifest Destiny, the belief that the United States had the right and the duty to extend its territory to the Pacific Ocean.

At the time, Mexico controlled the region that is now the southwestern United States. The Oregon Territory in the northwest was owned by both the United States and Great Britain. Benton and others in the U.S. government wanted to take control of the West from Mexico and Britain. They devised a plan to build permanent American settlements in Oregon and California. Frémont was sent to survey and map the unknown parts of the West so that Americans could make their homes there more easily. He was also told to write enthusiastic reports that would make people dream of heading west.

Peak of Adventure

Frémont's first major expedition was a survey of the route from the Mississippi River to the South Pass, which is a 20-mile-wide opening in the Rocky Mountains. This route was the beginning of the Oregon Trail, a path that many settlers would later follow west. In May 1842, Frémont arrived in St. Louis to gather his party. On the way,

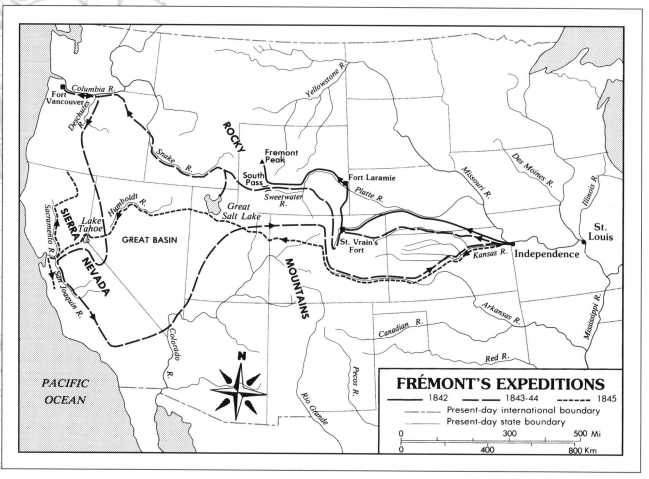

FRÉMONT'S EXPEDITIONS

— 1842   – – 1843–44   - - - - - 1845
— · — Present-day international boundary
—— Present-day state boundary

| 0 | | 300 | | 500 Mi |
| 0 | 400 | | 800 Km | |

Nicknamed "the Pathfinder," Frémont mapped the route that eventually brought thousands of settlers to the West.

he hired the famous mountain man Christopher CARSON as a guide. Frémont and his men traveled along the Platte River to St. Vrain's Fort (in what is now Colorado) and then turned north to Fort Laramie (in what is now Wyoming). Frémont ignored rumors of hostile Indians and pushed west through the South Pass.

After turning north again, Frémont saw what he believed to be the highest peak in the Rocky Mountains, and he decided to climb it. One eyewitness said that Frémont barely made it to the top, but Frémont's version of the story made the climb seem much more heroic. When he returned to Washington, D.C., his wife Jessie helped him write an exaggerated report of his western adventures. It fueled Americans' growing attraction to the frontier.

In the spring of 1843, Frémont headed west again with orders to follow the Oregon Trail all the way to the Pacific coast. His mission was to map a road for settlers as well as to locate campsites, wood, water, and Indian tribes to be found on the way. The government also wanted him to suggest sites where forts could be built along the route. With a party of 40 men, including Carson, Frémont tried to blaze a new trail by following the Kansas River rather than the Platte River. He then turned north and rejoined the main trail at the Sweetwater River. In September the party sighted the Great Salt Lake in what is now Utah. Frémont's report described this desert

From 1841 to 1842, Frémont carried an American flag with 26 stars and an eagle. The other side showed a butterfly and the words "Rocky Mountains 1841."

region as well suited to settlement, enticing the religious leader Brigham Young to bring his followers there. Young later criticized Frémont for misrepresenting the dry land.

Beyond the Call of Duty

From Utah, Frémont headed northwest to Oregon. When he reached Fort Vancouver, he had officially completed his mission, but he went south again to explore the land between Oregon and California. He wanted to search for the Buenaventura, a legendary river that was supposed to lead to the Pacific Ocean. The explorer Benjamin BONNEVILLE had already stated that the Buenaventura River did not exist. Frémont hoped that proving this fact would motivate the United States to take control of the Oregon Country, where the Columbia River provided the needed water route to the Pacific Ocean.

In November 1843, Frémont led his men along the Deschutes River. They continued south until they reached what seemed like a good place to cross the mountains of the Sierra Nevada. Despite the onset of winter, Frémont and his party trudged into the mountains. Clearing trails through snowdrifts that were almost over their heads, they suffered cold, hunger, and fatigue for 30 days. Their Indian guides deserted them, and one man went mad from fear and cold. But Frémont finally led his men out of the mountains. The party rested at Captain John Sutter's ranch on the American River and then followed the San Joaquin Valley south. The men then crossed the Sierra Nevada into the desert of the Great Basin. Frémont was the first to identify and map this region between the Sierra Nevada and the Rockies. While moving east over the trail blazed by Jedediah SMITH and others 10 years earlier, Frémont's group met Joseph Reddeford WALKER, a mountain man. Walker led the expedition back east through some of the most barren land in North America. Back home, Frémont wrote another account of his travels, which also was received with wild enthusiasm by the American public.

Acts of Rebellion

In March 1845, Frémont was put in charge of an expedition to survey the Arkansas and Red Rivers in order to help mark the western border of the United States. A month after Frémont received his assignment, the Republic of Texas became part of the United States. Since Texas had declared independence from Mexico only nine years earlier, the United States government knew that Mexico might declare war. Ignoring his orders, Frémont left someone else in charge of the river expedition. Instead, he blazed a new route through the central Rockies and across the Great Basin to California, where he planted an American flag. But Frémont's presence in Mexican territory—with a band of armed Americans—alarmed the Mexicans. He and his men were ordered to leave, and they retreated to the Oregon Territory.

Not long after this incident, a secret message from Washington, D.C., sent Frémont hurrying back to California. When a group of American settlers in California proclaimed independence from

Mexico, Frémont came to their aid in what became known as the Bear Flag Revolt. The United States and Mexico officially went to war in May 1846. Frémont and his men joined the army forces in California, and Frémont was appointed major of a battalion. When the Mexicans surrendered in August, Frémont was named military governor of California. However, an army general had also received orders to establish a government in California, and he viewed Frémont as a threat to his authority. He ordered Frémont to disband his unit. When Frémont refused, the general had him arrested and put on trial for disobeying orders. Although he was found guilty, President James K. Polk offered to let Frémont stay in the army. But Frémont was angry over the way he had been treated, and he resigned.

In 1848 Frémont made his last major expedition to the West. Senator Benton and others were interested in building a railroad that would cross the North American continent. Frémont's task was to blaze a trail along a straight line from St. Louis to San Francisco. Frémont insisted on carrying out his mission in the middle of winter to prove that the route would be practical in any weather. Despite warnings against such a course of action, Frémont headed into the San Juan Mountains (in modern-day Colorado) in mid-December. The snow was more than 10 feet deep, and the temperature fell far below freezing. Ten members of the party died, and Frémont was forced to retreat to Taos, New Mexico. However, in his usual style, Frémont described the mission as a total success that proved the route was practical even in winter.

The End of Glory

In spite of his successes as a young man, Frémont seemed to fail at everything he tried in later life. He became wealthy when gold was discovered on land he owned in California, but he managed his money poorly and lost his fortune. He ran for president of the United States in 1856 but was defeated by James Buchanan. During the Civil War, he served as a general in the Union army, but President Abraham Lincoln removed him from command. John Charles Frémont died in poverty in 1890, but despite his failures, he had played a major role in leading America westward.

SUGGESTED READING Ferol Egan, *Frémont: Explorer for a Restless Nation* (Doubleday, 1977); Donald Jackson and Mary Lee Spence, editors, *The Expeditions of John Charles Frémont* (University of Illinois Press, 1970); Allan Nevins, *Frémont, Pathmarker of the West* (University of Nebraska Press, 1992); Fredrika Shumway Smith, *Frémont: Soldier, Explorer, Statesman* (Rand McNally, 1966).

Frobisher, Martin

English
b 1540?; Altofts, England
d November 22, 1594; Plymouth, England
Discovered Frobisher Bay and Baffin Island

The English sailor Sir Martin Frobisher was one of Queen Elizabeth I's boldest and most adventurous **sea dogs.** He was feared by both the French and the Spanish for his **privateering.** Frobisher's fame as an explorer resulted from his three expeditions to what is now northeastern Canada. He made the first well-documented attempt to explore the northern waters west of Greenland in search of a **Northwest Passage** to eastern Asia. He thought that he had found such a passage, but it was only a bay of an island in the

sea dog old or experienced sailor or pirate

privateer privately owned ship hired by a government to attack enemy ships

Northwest Passage water route connecting the Atlantic Ocean and Pacific Ocean through the Arctic islands of northern Canada

archipelago large group of islands or a body of water with many islands

Martin Frobisher never explored what he believed to be the entrance to the Northwest Passage because he thought he had discovered gold in the region.

huge, ice-clogged **archipelago** of northern Canada. Although he was far from the riches of China, he had discovered what became known as Frobisher Bay and Baffin Island.

Survival on the Sea

Frobisher was born into a wealthy Yorkshire family in about 1540. At the age of 13, he made his first sea voyage, a highly profitable but dangerous trip to Guinea in West Africa. The trip was funded by London businessmen and commanded by a Portuguese captain. Fewer than 40 of the 120 crewmen survived the heat and diseases of western Africa. But the deadly conditions did not stop Frobisher from returning to the continent the following year. On that trip, he was captured by African tribesmen and was then taken hostage by Portuguese, who eventually released him.

As he gained more experience as a sailor, he also became a skilled pirate. Occasionally, England arrested Frobisher for his attacks on the Spanish and French, especially when he interrupted trade. But he was never held in jail for long. In that period of unstable relations with Spain and France, piracy could be useful to the English government. In 1571 Queen Elizabeth rewarded Frobisher with command of a ship to serve in her effort to control Ireland. Frobisher still found time to continue his career as a pirate until 1573, when Elizabeth made piracy illegal.

Testing a New Idea

Frobisher turned his attention away from privateering and developed a deep interest in the idea of reaching eastern Asia through a Northwest Passage. He may have been influenced by Sir Humphrey GILBERT's book, *Discourse of a Discoverie for a New Passage to Cataia.* This famous geographical work argued that there might be a passage above North America similar to the passage around South America at Cape Horn.

Attempts to find such a water route had already been made by England's John Cabot at the end of the 1400s and by France's Jacques Cartier in the 1530s. They had explored Newfoundland and the St. Lawrence River, but Gilbert's book suggested searching farther north. Geographers of Frobisher's time were beginning to realize the true size of North America. They knew that a northern passage would be much longer than the one around South America, and that it would probably enter Arctic waters. Although the ice presented a problem, geographers believed that it could be overcome. They thought that near the North Pole, the summer climate would be mild because the sun stayed over the horizon 24 hours a day. If a polar ocean existed, they reasoned, it would be too warm and perhaps too deep to freeze. For these reasons, explorers hoped that the northern ice was only an obstacle on the way to open waters that would take them to Asia. Frobisher decided to test these theories in the Arctic seas of North America.

Dodging Danger

In June 1576, Frobisher left the Shetland Islands, off the coast of Scotland, on his first expedition in search of the Northwest Passage.

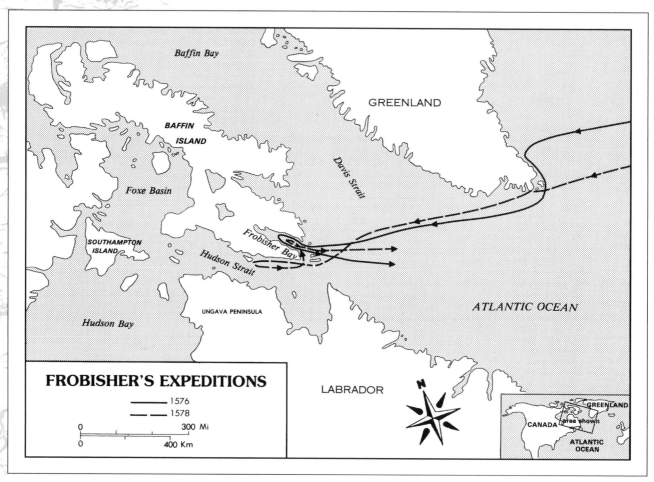

FROBISHER'S EXPEDITIONS

——————— 1576
— — — — 1578

0 .... 300 Mi
0 .... 400 Km

The frozen seas between England and Greenland called for skillful navigation. Frobisher quickly made his way back and forth on three expeditions.

pinnace small boat that can sail in shallow waters

mizzenmast mast that is third from the front of a ship

Inuit people of the Canadian Arctic, sometimes known as the Eskimo

He was equipped with three ships: the *Gabriel,* the *Michael,* and a **pinnace.** The first part of the voyage, from England to Iceland, was difficult because the sailors could not see land for several days. West of Iceland, land was almost always in view, but steering through the icebergs and fog was a problem. Storms also presented a challenge, wrecking the pinnace and separating the two larger ships. Heavy ice forced the *Michael* to return to England. Frobisher pressed ahead aboard the *Gabriel* with only 18 crew members. When he reached the coast of Greenland, he mistakenly thought it was "Frisland," an imaginary place on a flawed map published by Nicolo Zeno in 1558. This error later caused confusion when Frobisher reported his findings to others.

Unable to land, Frobisher turned south to escape the fog and icebergs, but he encountered another storm. The high waves caused the *Gabriel* to turn on its side and fill with water. Frobisher saved the ship—and its crew—by cutting off the **mizzenmast.** This desperate act restored the ship to its upright position.

The *Gabriel* turned west again and on August 11 reached a bay of what is now called Baffin Island. Frobisher thought that the bay was actually the beginning of the Northwest Passage he was looking for. Soon he and his crew made contact with the **Inuit,** who traded goods with the Englishmen and eventually offered to guide the ship westward through the bay. Then the *Gabriel*'s small boat

For more information about the map of Nicolo Zeno, see the profile of Antonio ZENO in Volume 3.

disappeared with five crew members. It is not clear from the voyage's records what happened. The sailors may have deserted, or they may have been tricked into coming ashore by hostile Inuit. Frobisher believed that the Inuit had kidnapped the men, so he captured an Inuit and tried to arrange a trade of hostages. But the missing men did not return, so Frobisher was left with a crew of 13 men and only one vessel. He felt that he could not continue exploring, so he returned to England with the captured Inuit as a trophy.

The Illusion of Wealth

Frobisher also brought back a heavy rock that interested Michael Lok, his sponsor. Lok thought that it contained gold, but only two scientists who examined the rock agreed. The queen's official examiners did not find any traces of the precious metal. But Lok still managed to convince investors, including the queen herself, to form a company for the purpose of mining gold. Frobisher was made high admiral of the new Cathay Company. He made his next two expeditions to Frobisher Bay, in 1577 and 1578, for business purposes rather than for exploration.

In 1578 Frobisher wandered into the previously undiscovered Hudson Strait after becoming lost in fog. But since he was on a mining mission, he did not explore this channel, which he called Mistaken Strait. He also landed on Greenland, the first European known to do so since Norse settlers had thrived there in the 1200s.

The Cathay Company went bankrupt when it was finally proven that the rocks contained no gold. Frobisher returned to privateering against the Dutch and the Spanish under the protection of the English crown. War with Spain soon followed. In 1588 Frobisher helped defeat an invading fleet, the Spanish Armada, and was made a knight for his leadership aboard the *Triumph*. Six years later, Frobisher fought the Spanish again at Brest, France. He was badly wounded and died of his injuries soon after returning to England.

SUGGESTED READING W. A. Kenyon, *Tokens of Possession: the Northern Voyages of Martin Frobisher* (Royal Ontario Museum, 1975); Brendan Lehane, *The Northwest Passage* (Time-Life Books, 1981); Frank Rasky, *The Polar Voyages* (McGraw-Hill Ryerson, 1976); Vilhjalmur Stefansson, *The Three Voyages of Martin Frobisher,* 2 volumes (Argonaut, 1938).

Fuchs, Vivian Ernest

English
b February 11, 1908; Isle of Wight, England
living
Explored Antarctica

geologist scientist who studies the earth's natural history

glacier large, slowly moving mass of ice

The **geologist** Sir Vivian Fuchs spent his early career studying equatorial Africa. But after World War II, he devoted himself to exploring and surveying Antarctica. In 1957 Fuchs succeeded in carrying out Sir Ernest SHACKLETON's abandoned plan to cross Antarctica by land.

Fuchs joined the British effort to explore Antarctica in 1947, when he began work in the Falkland Islands, off the coast of Argentina. In 1955 he began two years of preparation for his expedition to cross Antarctica. Following Shackleton's basic route—but with far more advanced technology—Fuchs's party planned to travel in snow tractors to the South Pole from a base in the

In 1957 Sir Vivian Fuchs crossed Antarctica on land. He was knighted on his return to England.

Weddell Sea. His partner, the explorer Sir Edmund HILLARY of New Zealand, was instructed to lay supply stations between the Ross Sea and the American research station at the pole.

Fuchs and his party departed from the Filchner Ice Shelf on November 24, 1957. His tractors had a difficult time plowing through the deep snow on the polar plains. Fuchs and Hillary met at the South Pole on January 20, 1958. Fearing that the tractors would not be able to handle the terrain, Hillary advised Fuchs to postpone the final part of his trip from the pole to the Ross Sea. But Fuchs was determined to carry out his plan, and he continued the journey. The rest of the 2,158-mile trip was successful, and Fuchs reached Scott Base on the Ross Sea on March 2. During this leg of the journey, Fuchs performed experiments to measure the depth of the ice.

Until his retirement in 1973, Fuchs was the director of the British Antarctic Survey. This effort involved over 1,200 people who conducted comprehensive studies of the polar region's plant and animal life, natural history, minerals, **glaciers,** and weather.

SUGGESTED READING Sir Vivian Fuchs, *Of Ice and Men: The Story of the British Antarctic Survey, 1943-73* (Anthony Nelson, 1982) and *A Time to Speak: An Autobiography* (Anthony Nelson, 1990).

Gaboto, Giovanni. See *Cabot, John.*

Gaboto, Sebastiano. See *Cabot, Sebastian.*

Gagarin, Yuri Alekseyevich

Russian
b March 9, 1934; near Gzhatsk (now Gagarin), Soviet Union
d March 27, 1968; near Moscow, Soviet Union
First person in space

Soviet Union nation that existed from 1922 to 1991, made up of Russia and 14 other republics in eastern Europe and northern Asia

cosmonaut Russian term for a person who travels into space; literally, "traveler to the universe"

Yuri Gagarin was a carpenter's son who became a hero of space exploration in 1961. He was the first person to leave the earth, circle the planet, and return safely to describe what he had seen and felt in space. His feat won a political victory for his country, the **Soviet Union,** and it also marked a triumph of science, engineering, and human daring.

A Race to Space

Gagarin was born in a large farming community near the city of Gzhatsk. When he was seven years old, Germany invaded the Soviet Union, and he and his mother were forced to hide while his father served in the army. After the war, Gagarin returned to school and later found work in a steel factory. He then attended college to pursue his interest in science and technology. While in college, he became fascinated with the airplanes and pilots at a nearby airport. He studied in a pilot training school for two years, during which he met his future wife, a medical student named Valentina Ivanovna. He joined the Soviet air force and became a highly skilled pilot. In 1959 he volunteered to be trained as a **cosmonaut** and was accepted.

Space exploration was a thrilling new kind of adventure in the 1950s. It was also the focus of intense competition between the

satellite object launched into space to circle a planet or moon

orbit stable, circular route; one trip around; to revolve around

rocket vehicle propelled by exploding fuel

capsule small early spacecraft designed to carry a person around the earth

Soviet Union and the United States. Each country tried to demonstrate its superiority by being the first to send **satellites** and people into space. This contest became known as "the space race." The Soviets won an early victory with *Sputnik 1,* the first satellite to **orbit** the earth. Soviet hopes of launching the first human space traveler rested on Yuri Gagarin—28 years old, five feet two inches tall, with a round face and a broad smile.

A Hero for Earth

On the morning of April 12, 1961, the young explorer stood before his **rocket** and spoke to a group of technicians and reporters. "Am I happy, starting on my space flight?" he asked out loud. "Of course I am. Indeed, in all times . . . people considered it the greatest happiness to take part in new discoveries."

The rocket blasted into space, carrying Gagarin in his **capsule,** which was called the *Swallow.* In a flight that lasted 108 minutes, Gagarin circled the planet once. Far from the earth and its gravity, Gagarin enjoyed his sensation of weightlessness. He also marveled to see the beauty and spherical shape of the earth from nearly 200 miles above its surface.

The *Swallow* descended into the earth's atmosphere on schedule and landed in a potato field near Saratov, the city where Gagarin had studied aviation. "I returned from outer space to exactly the same spot where I first learned to fly an aircraft," he later said. "How much time had passed since then? Not more than six years."

Gagarin was hailed as a hero around the world, even by Americans, and he paid public visits to several nations. In his speeches, he always gave full credit for his achievement to the scientists and workers who had designed and built his spacecraft. Everyone was impressed by his humor, modesty, and thoughtfulness. He was wildly popular with the Russian people, who renamed many streets—and even his hometown—in his honor. Gagarin remained involved with the Soviet space program, becoming commander of the cosmonaut team in 1963. Five years later, he and another pilot died when their two-seated jet plane crashed outside Moscow.

SUGGESTED READING Philip Clark, *The Soviet Manned Space Program* (Crown, 1988); Yuri Gagarin, *Road to the Stars: Notes by Soviet Cosmonaut No. I,* translated by G. Hanna and D. Myshne (Foreign Languages Publishing House, 1962); George P. Kennedy, *First Men in Space* (Chelsea House, 1991); Evgeny Riabchikov, *Russians in Space* (Doubleday, 1971).

Russian cosmonaut Yuri Gagarin, the first person to orbit the earth and return from space, became an international hero.

Galaup, Jean François. See *La Pérouse, Jean de Galaup de.*

Gama, Vasco da

Portuguese
b 1460?; Sines, Portugal
d December 24, 1524; Cochin, India
Sailed around Africa to India

In the 1400s and 1500s, Portugal produced many expert sailors and brave explorers. One of the greatest of them was Vasco da Gama. Setting out from Lisbon, Portugal, in the summer of 1497, Gama made a voyage to find a sea route to the valuable spices of the East. Ten years earlier, his countryman Bartolomeu Dias had turned back after sailing around Africa's Cape of Good Hope. Gama followed Dias's path but then continued up the eastern coast of Africa and

More than half of the sailors who accompanied Vasco da Gama on his voyage to India did not survive.

caravel small ship with three masts and both square and triangular sails

on to India. Gama's successful expedition helped transform the tiny nation of Portugal into an international power.

Sailing into the Unknown

Vasco da Gama was born in about 1460 in Sines, a seaside town south of Lisbon. Little is known about his early life. The first mention of him in official records appears in 1492, when he was instructed to capture French ships in Portugal as a response to the seizure of Portuguese property in France. Although Gama appears to have carried out his orders well, he is not mentioned again until his voyage to India.

In the late 1400s, the Islamic nations of the Middle East and North Africa controlled all of the known land and sea routes to Asia, a continent famous for its spices. For Christian Europeans, it was almost impossible to use these routes. The only way to avoid the Islamic lands and reach India was to sail around Africa into the Indian Ocean. In 1487 Dias had rounded the southern tip of Africa. But his crew, frightened by the violent storms and hostile Africans they had encountered, had refused to sail any farther. No one in Europe knew how far India was from the Cape of Good Hope, but the Portuguese were determined to find out.

Gama was given four vessels, including two medium-sized, three-masted sailing ships—the *São Rafael,* which was commanded by Gama's brother Paulo, and the *São Gabriel.* The other vessels were a **caravel** called the *Berrio* and an unnamed supply ship. The expedition also included three interpreters who spoke Arabic, the language of the Islamic world, and Bantu, an African language. The king supplied a priest for each vessel as well as several convicted criminals, who were to be given the dirtiest, most dangerous jobs.

No Land in Sight

Although the four ships were manned by experienced sailors, the Portuguese public was not confident that the expedition would succeed. Nevertheless, on July 8, 1497, Gama and 170 crew members departed from Lisbon. The fleet traveled south to the Canary Islands and then stopped at the Cape Verde Islands, off the coast of northwest Africa. The crews rested there for a week and repaired some damage that the ships had suffered from stormy weather; then they set out again.

On the advice of Dias, Gama avoided sailing close to the west coast of Africa, with its dangerous offshore winds and currents. Instead he sailed into the uncharted waters of the southern Atlantic Ocean. As his ships pushed south, they were actually closer to Brazil than to Africa.

But the voyage across the vast, unfamiliar emptiness of the southern Atlantic Ocean seemed unending. Long stretches of calm were broken by sudden, violent storms. Supplies of food and water ran low, and men began to fall ill as the ships turned eastward. After 96 days without sighting land, the crews spotted the hills above St. Helena Bay (in what is now South Africa) on November 7.

Gama anchored his fleet there, and the Portuguese traded for fresh food with the tribes of the area, who seemed to be friendly.

Then one day a sailor, who had been invited to dinner at a local village, was seen running across the shore, chased by an angry tribesman. The sailor escaped, but fighting broke out, and four Portuguese were wounded—including Gama, who was struck in the leg by an arrow. The incident was not the last problem Gama's crew had with people they met on their journey.

Setting a New Standard

On November 16, Gama sailed south again. Battling unfavorable winds, the ships rounded the Cape of Good Hope four days later. The crews put ashore in what is now called Mossel Bay, where they rested for 13 days. There Gama destroyed his supply ship, transferring rations to the other vessels. The three remaining ships then headed northeast.

By late December they had passed what is now the Great Fish River—the point at which Dias and his men had turned back. Continuing along the coast, Gama stopped on December 25 at a place he named Natal, in honor of Jesus Christ's birth. Today the spot is the site of the South African port of Durban, in a province that still carries the name that Gama gave to the region.

Proceeding north, the fleet reached the Quelimane River (in what is now Mozambique) on January 25, 1498. After more than six months at sea, many of the sailors were sick with **scurvy,** so Gama and his crews stayed in the area to rest for about a month. During this time, Paulo da Gama won a reputation for kindness, generously sharing his personal medical supplies with the crews. It was unusual for a captain to show such concern for common sailors. Unfortunately for many of the men, the medicine was useless. Historians do not know exactly how many men died there, but approximately two-thirds of those who had sailed with the fleet did not survive the voyage.

For the men who lived, the most frightening part of the expedition was over. Now they were about to sail northward along the East African coast toward territory that was known to Europeans. Pêro da COVILHÃ, another Portuguese explorer, had journeyed overland to India a decade earlier. He had sent back reports that Arab vessels crossed the Indian Ocean and traded at various African and Indian ports. Covilhã also believed that Prester John, a legendary Christian king, lived somewhere in Africa. Gama planned to sail north along the coast and investigate these reports.

First Encounter with Muslims

On March 5, the Portuguese sighted Mozambique, a major port city. While most of the coastal lands they had passed were ruled by local tribes, this region was under Arab influence. At the time, the Arabs controlled the Indian Ocean. They had become wealthy by trading slaves and goods throughout the region.

The people of Mozambique had had little experience with Christian Europeans, so when Gama met the Arabs, he pretended that he and his men were Muslims—followers of the Islamic religion that dominated the Arabic world. At first the Portuguese were well received by the local **sultan.** They gathered information about inland

scurvy disease caused by a lack of vitamin C and once a major cause of death among sailors; symptoms include internal bleeding, loosened teeth, and extreme fatigue

sultan ruler of a Muslim nation

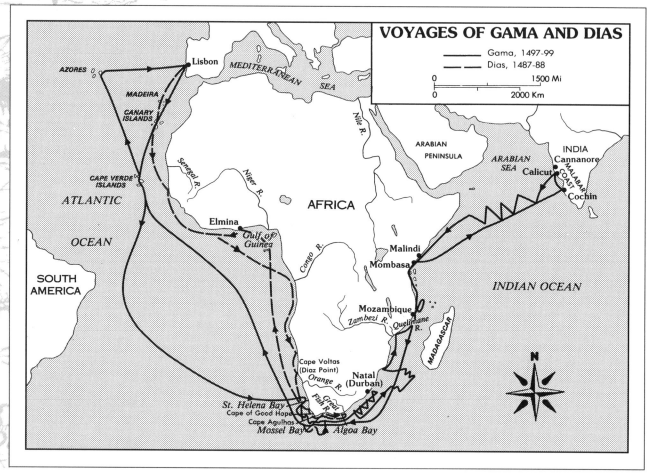

VOYAGES OF GAMA AND DIAS

——— Gama, 1497-99
– – – Dias, 1487-88

The route pioneered by Gama through the southern Atlantic Ocean was so efficient that it is still widely used by vessels sailing from Europe to Africa.

Africa, the continent's eastern coast, and the Arabian Sea. The Portuguese also asked many questions about Prester John, but this made their hosts suspicious. However, the sultan agreed to provide guides to help them cross the Indian Ocean.

Then Gama happened to met two Christians from India who had been taken captive and brought to Mozambique. The Indians noted the religious nature of the sculptures on the front of the *São Gabriel* and the *São Rafael* and realized that the Portuguese were fellow Christians. The sudden friendship between the Portuguese and the Indian slaves confirmed the Muslims' suspicions that Gama had lied about his religion. Fighting broke out, and Gama was ordered to leave.

More Trouble and Violence

As Gama's fleet prepared to depart, one of the Muslim guides deserted. The other guide was held aboard ship while Gama led a party toward shore in two small boats, intending to capture the runaway. Suddenly the Portuguese saw six boats, loaded with heavily armed men, heading toward them and preparing to attack. Gama and his crewmen hurriedly returned to their vessels and sailed for the open sea. But over the next few days, weak winds and currents forced them back toward shore. Low on supplies, they landed and became involved in a battle as they tried to stock their ships. In the fighting, several Muslims were killed, and the guide who had escaped was recaptured. Finally the winds improved, and the ships headed up the coast.

Unfortunately for Gama, his Muslim guides were totally unreliable. When he realized that they were lying to him about his fleet's location, he had them beaten. While at sea, Gama's party met another Arab, who was sailing in a **dhow.** The Portuguese took him prisoner and tortured him for information about the route to India.

On April 7, the fleet anchored at Mombasa (in present-day Kenya), the wealthiest port on Africa's east coast. The local **sheikh** welcomed Gama with fresh supplies. But Gama was suspicious of the sheikh's generosity, and he feared an attack. Instead of sending his officers to offer the sheikh valuable gifts, Gama sent two of the Portuguese criminals with a string of coral beads. Despite Gama's concerns, the two men were well treated by the sheikh.

The next day, two of the Portuguese ships collided in the harbor. During the confusion that followed, the Muslim guides jumped overboard and swam to shore. Enraged, Gama seized four Arabs who were on board and ordered that they be tortured with fire drops, a boiling oil that was poured on their bare skin. In severe pain, the hostages confessed that the sheikh planned to attack the Portuguese that night. Later, when Muslim soldiers swam toward the ships, Gama's crew was prepared and held off the attack. On the morning of April 13, the Portuguese fleet escaped.

Crossing the Indian Ocean

Gama's luck finally began to improve. Sailing north, he dropped anchor off Malindi, a port about 50 miles north of Mombasa. The local ruler, a rival of the sheikh of Mombasa, thought that the Portuguese might become useful allies. He promised to provide a guide to lead them across the Indian Ocean.

In the Malindi harbor at the same time were four merchant vessels from India. The Indians, who were followers of the Hindu religion, thought that the Portuguese were Hindus as well, and Gama's men thought that the Indians were Christians. To celebrate such a coincidence, the Indians and the Portuguese feasted for a week. But Gama grew impatient with the sheikh because the promised guide had not been delivered. He seized hostages, and the sheikh gave in to his demands, providing an Arab named Ahmad ibn Majid, who knew the sea route to India's west coast, known as the Malabar Coast. On April 24, Gama's fleet left Africa and headed east. In less than a month, the ships reached the Indian city of Calicut.

A Cold Welcome

The Malabar Coast was divided into many small states, both Muslim and Hindu. Calicut, then the most important trading center of southern India, was controlled by the Hindus. The ruler of Calicut, called the zamorin, was at first friendly to Gama, who then offered the zamorin the gifts sent by Portugal's King Manuel. Unfortunately, perhaps because Manuel had not thought that Gama would ever reach India, his gifts were cheap. The zamorin's **courtiers** were insulted by the cloth, hats, coral beads, and jars of honey that the Portuguese presented.

dhow Arab vessel with triangular sails, widely used in the Mediterranean Sea and Indian Ocean

sheikh Arab chief

courtier attendant at a royal court

Vasco da Gama most likely sailed with this flag, which is based on the coat of arms of Portugal.

Even worse, Gama was soon exposed as a liar. He had exaggerated in describing the size of his fleet, but Arab merchants quickly told the zamorin the truth. The Arabs also reported the violent behavior of the Portuguese in African ports. To the officials and merchants of Calicut, Gama and his men seemed no better than pirates.

The presence of the Christian Portuguese also posed a threat to the Muslim merchants who controlled the profitable spice trade in India. Some Muslims even offered the Hindus bribes to destroy Gama's ships. Despite the tense situation, Gama managed to avoid disaster. He even obtained a small supply of spices to take back to Portugal. At the end of August, having promised that he would one day return to India, Gama set sail for home.

The Price of Fame

The return voyage was fatal for many members of Gama's crew. For three months, the ships battled the winds of the Arabian Sea. Scurvy killed 30 more men. By the time Gama reached Malindi on January 7, he did not have enough sailors to operate his three ships. He ordered that the *São Rafael* be burned and its crew transferred to the remaining vessels. On March 10, the *Berrio* and the *São Gabriel* rounded the Cape of Good Hope.

A month later, the two ships were separated in a fierce storm in the Atlantic Ocean. The *São Gabriel,* commanded by Gama, landed at the Cape Verde Islands. His brother Paulo was close to death, perhaps from scurvy, so Gama sailed on to the Azores, where he hoped that his brother would recover. But Paulo died on the island of Terceira. Meanwhile, on July 10, 1499, the *Berrio* arrived in Lisbon. On September 9, Gama proudly entered Portugal's capital. He received many rewards, including money, private lands, and a noble title.

New Voyages to India

The Portuguese wanted to build quickly on Gama's success. In March 1500, King Manuel appointed Pedro Álvares CABRAL leader of a fleet of 13 heavily armed ships. The voyage to India was a disaster—7 ships were lost, including one commanded by Bartolomeu Dias. At Calicut, Cabral managed to acquire a large supply of spices and other exotic goods from the zamorin. But the Portuguese offended both the Muslims and the Hindus of the city.

Cabral set up a warehouse on shore, and one day the Indians attacked it without warning, killing 50 Europeans. In response Cabral seized 10 Muslim ships, took their cargoes, killed their crews, and then sailed back to Portugal. Cabral's expedition was considered a great success, but some of King Manuel's advisors believed that the Indians had to be taught to respect the Portuguese. Gama was chosen as the man to teach that lesson.

In February 1502, Gama—now known as "the Admiral of India"—left Lisbon with a fleet that eventually numbered 20 ships. It was the largest, most heavily armed fleet Portugal had yet sent to the East. Gama had orders to punish the Africans and Indians who had been hostile to the Portuguese, to destroy Arab shipping, and to win control of the spice trade.

emir Muslim ruler in parts of Asia and Africa

Acts of Cruelty

When they reached the east coast of Africa that summer, the Portuguese reinforced their growing reputation for cruelty. On the island of Kilwa Kisiwani, Gama confronted the **emir,** Ibrahim, who had been unfriendly to Cabral and had refused to accept Christianity. Gama threatened to burn Ibrahim's city if he did not pay a large ransom and pledge his loyalty to Portugal. The emir gave in to Gama's demands.

Slowed by bad weather, Gama sailed toward the Malabar Coast of India. The fleet anchored off Cannanore, where it waited to prey on Muslim ships. The worst act of terror committed by the Portuguese was against the *Meri,* a merchant vessel. It carried about 300 Muslim men, women, and children who were returning to India from the holy city of Mecca, in what is now Saudi Arabia. Facing the powerful Portuguese ships, the sailors of the *Meri* knew that it would be useless to resist. They obeyed Gama's command to hand over the ship's cargo. Then Gama ordered the Muslims to go below deck and instructed his men to set the *Meri* on fire. Everyone on board died in the flames except 20 young boys, who agreed to convert to Christianity.

Gama sailed on to Calicut, where he demanded that the zamorin force every Muslim to leave the city. To show that he was serious, Gama captured 38 local fishermen, hanged them, cut up their bodies, and threw them into the sea. The following day, his fleet attacked the city. Leaving six ships to blockade the Calicut harbor, Gama sailed to Cochin, where he signed a trade agreement with the local ruler. Meanwhile, a diplomat arrived from Calicut, saying that the zamorin wanted peace.

Gama returned, anchored off Calicut, and found that the offer of peace was a trap. His ship was attacked, but the crew managed to hold off the Indians until more Portuguese ships arrived to help. Gama then returned to Cochin, where he loaded his ships with precious cargo before sailing back to Calicut. On February 5, 1503, he fought an Indian fleet. Although he could not win a clear victory, the communities of the Malabar Coast were more fearful than ever of Portuguese power. With his ships fully stocked, Gama sailed for home. He arrived in Lisbon on October 11.

A Last Voyage

Gama was again treated as a hero. He hoped to settle down to a life of luxury and ease, but circumstances did not turn out as he had planned. He returned to Sines, his birthplace, but he quarreled with the town's religious officials and was eventually ordered to leave. Gama also argued with King Manuel, and despite his past achievements, he lost support at Manuel's court.

In 1521 Manuel died, and his eldest son, John III, took the throne. Three years later, John ordered Gama to return to India to strengthen Portugal's trading position there. On April 9, 1524, Gama left Lisbon one last time, with a fleet of 14 ships. He arrived on the Malabar Coast in September, and he successfully reformed Portugal's trade colony there, but his administration did not last long. He fell ill, and he died on December 24, 1524.

Although he was ruthless and cruel, Vasco da Gama's bravery made him one of history's most renowned explorers. His voyage marked the beginning of the rise of Portugal's empire. Gama's courage, seamanship, and leadership were later celebrated in *The Lusiads,* a famous Portuguese poem that became one of his country's greatest literary classics.

SUGGESTED READING Henry H. Hart, *Sea Road to the Indies* (William Hodge, 1952); Rebecca Stefoff, *Vasco da Gama and the Portuguese Explorers* (Chelsea House, 1993); Sanjay Subrahmanyam, *The Career and Legend of Vasco da Gama* (Cambridge University Press, 1997).

Garcés, Francisco Tomas Hermenegildo

Spanish
b 1741?; Aragon, Spain
d 1781; mouth of Gila River, Arizona
Explored southwestern United States

mission settlement founded by priests in a land where they hoped to convert people to Christianity

New Spain region of Spanish colonial empire that included the areas now occupied by Mexico, Florida, Texas, New Mexico, Arizona, California, and various Caribbean islands

presidio Spanish settlement in the Americas that was defended by soldiers

While founding **missions** in southwestern Arizona, Father Francisco Garcés established the first overland route from Tubac, Arizona, to Monterey, California. The valuable knowledge he gained of the deserts, mountains, and rivers in the region helped settlers and traders reach Spanish outposts on the Pacific coast of North America. Garcés learned a great deal about the lands he explored from the Indians he met during his travels.

Desert Crossings

Francisco Garcés is thought to have been born around 1741 in Aragon, Spain. In 1768 he was sent to Pimería Alta (the region that is now northwestern Mexico and southern Arizona) to serve as a priest. Three years later, after rebuilding a damaged mission at San Xavier del Bac (near the site of present-day Tucson, Arizona), he began his explorations to find a land route from **New Spain** to northern California. The Spanish thought that it might be quicker to transport supplies to their western settlements by land than to carry them up the Pacific coast by ship.

On his first trip, Garcés headed north from San Xavier to the Gila River and then turned west to the Colorado River. After temporarily being lost near the mouth of the Colorado River, Garcés pushed northwest and crossed the Yuma Desert. Then he traveled through the Mojave Desert and Death Valley in California and reached the southern edge of the mountains of the Sierra Nevada. Despite haze in the air, he sighted two openings in the mountains. He thought that the openings were passes that would lead him to the Spanish outposts. However, Garcés was afraid that he might not find water if he continued, so he returned to the San Xavier mission.

Discovery and Duty

Several years later, Captain Juan Bautista de ANZA, the commanding officer of the **presidio** at Tubac, agreed to search for a route to Monterey, California, with Garcés. After receiving permission from Spanish officials, their expedition left Tubac on January 8, 1774. Garcés led them through the territory he had already explored, and a Yuma Indian served as guide for the rest of the trip. On this journey, Anza and Garcés established a land route from southern Arizona to the coast of northern California.

In October 1775, the pair traveled to the Colorado River, where Garcés established a mission among the Yuma at the site of present-day Yuma, Arizona. He was then persuaded by Spanish officials to open a route from New Mexico to the southern California missions.

Traveling up the Colorado River to the present site of Needles, California, Garcés crossed the Mojave Desert and arrived at the San Gabriel mission (near what is now Los Angeles). After further travels in California, Garcés returned to the mission at San Xavier in the summer of 1776.

Three years later, he helped found two more missions among the Yuma. But by 1781, the Indians had become unhappy with the Spaniards. The Yuma revolted, killing Garcés and others near the mouth of the Gila River.

SUGGESTED READING Francisco Garcés, *A Record of Travels in Arizona and New Mexico, 1775-1776*, edited by John Galvin (John Howell Books, 1967).

Garnier, Francis

French
b July 25, 1839; St.-Étienne, France
d December 21, 1873; near Hanoi, Vietnam
Explored Southeast Asia and China

specimen sample of a plant, animal, or mineral, usually collected for scientific study or display

Determined to help build a French empire in Southeast Asia, Francis Garnier explored a land of dense rain forests, steep mountains, and deadly fevers.

Driven by the desire to see the French flag flying over Southeast Asia, Francis Garnier followed the Mekong River through the dense rain forests of Vietnam, Cambodia, and Laos in the 1860s. After the death of the expedition's leader, Garnier took command. He mapped thousands of miles of territory along the courses of several rivers in the interior. His efforts helped to expand the French empire in Southeast Asia, which lasted until the mid-1900s. Garnier ranks among history's greatest river explorers, such as John Hanning SPEKE and Alexander MACKENZIE.

The French in Vietnam

Garnier grew up in southeastern France. As a young man, he joined the navy, and in 1861 he served as an officer in a French force that conquered Cochin, the southern part of Vietnam. With this victory, France was ready to build a colonial empire in Southeast Asia that would rival Dutch Indonesia and British India. But at the time, Europeans were familiar only with the southern coastal areas of France's new colony. The rain forests and mountains farther inland—and the rivers that flowed from there—were a mystery.

Garnier was eager to expand France's knowledge and control of Southeast Asia. He was especially interested in the Mekong River. If the river flowed from China, as he suspected, it might prove to be a profitable route for trade. He knew that a busy exchange of goods, money, and merchants would carry French influence inland. He also knew that France would need accurate maps in order to control the region.

Only a year or two earlier, a French butterfly collector named Henri Mouhot had collected **specimens** along stretches of the Mekong River. Reaching Laos alone, Mouhot had died a painful death from a tropical fever, but this grim fate did not discourage Garnier. The aspiring explorer began lobbying his superiors for permission to lead an expedition up the Mekong River.

The Unknown River

Garnier's persistence was rewarded when the French authorities in Cochin created the Commission for the Exploration of the Mekong River. Garnier was named second-in-command to another officer, Ernest Doudart de Lagrée. The expedition consisted of about six Frenchmen and a larger number of Vietnamese servants and assistants.

The party left Saigon in 1866 and headed north through Cambodia, which had recently come under French control. Almost at once, it was obvious that the explorers had brought far too much clumsy equipment and that progress would be slow and difficult. It also became clear that the Mekong River was not the open waterway into the heart of Asia that Garnier had dreamed of finding. The river's course was blocked by numerous rapids and waterfalls, some of which were extremely dangerous. Garnier navigated the worst stretch of rapids, in northeastern Cambodia, with a single companion.

Pushing upriver despite disappointments and delays, the expedition reached Luang Prabang in Laos, where its members saw Mouhot's grave. Lagrée decided to continue into China, but the travelers needed passports to enter that country. Unfortunately, the papers were waiting back in Phnom Penh, Cambodia's capital city. Garnier left the main party and returned to Phnom Penh on foot to pick up the passports. He then hurried back to Laos, making a short detour along the way to see the immense ruins that Mouhot had spotted at a place called Angkor. Abandoned for several hundred years, these jungle-covered ruins were the remains of the capital of Cambodia's ancient Khmer civilization. Garnier rushed north from Angkor, and after a two-month journey of more than 1,000 miles, he caught up with his companions and handed them their passports.

Once the group had entered the Yunnan province of southwestern China, Garnier made another side trip. He explored the Red River (also known as the Hong or the Yuan) and found that it could be navigated from the highlands of southwestern China to Tonkin, the northern part of Vietnam. Then he and three of the other Frenchmen made a last effort to find the source of the Mekong. They failed, but not before reaching a remote region of western Yunnan that no European had visited since Marco POLO had passed through 600 years before.

Despite these achievements, exhaustion and fever were taking their toll on the expedition. Lagrée died in March 1868. Garnier took command and led the weary travelers east on the Chang Jiang (also known as the Yangtze River), crossing China to the port of Shanghai, where they boarded a ship for Cochin.

Exploration and Empire

Garnier returned to France to report his findings. He received much praise for having explored and mapped more than 3,000 miles of the Mekong, Red, and Chang Rivers. Britain's Royal Geographical Society gave him a medal despite the rivalry between Britain and France. Yet some people, especially in France, accused him of being immodest and not showing proper respect for his deceased commander, Lagrée.

Garnier still believed that he should help establish France's claim to Southeast Asia. He returned to Asia, and in 1873 he traveled alone into western Yunnan and Tibet. He scouted the routes over which Chinese traders carried tea and silk through thousands of miles of rugged territory.

Later that same year, Garnier became involved in the politics of building an empire. A French trader named Jean Dupuis had organized a private army of bandits and was trading illegally on the Red River. When the Vietnamese rulers of Tonkin tried to stop him, Dupuis took control of part of Hanoi, Tonkin's capital, and asked the French governor of Cochin for support. The emperor of Tonkin asked the governor to control and discipline Dupuis.

In response to the emperor's request, the governor sent Garnier to Hanoi, in command of two gunships and 100 men, to remove Dupuis from the city. But Garnier could not resist the chance to bring Tonkin under French control, and he joined forces with Dupuis. Within a few weeks, Garnier had conquered part of Tonkin, but he was killed in a skirmish with an army loyal to the emperor.

SUGGESTED READING J. M. Gullick, *Adventures and Encounters: Europeans in South-East Asia* (Oxford University Press, 1995); Milton Osborne, *River Road to China: The Mekong River Expedition, 1866–1873* (Liveright, 1975).

Gilbert, Humphrey

English
b 1539?; Devon, England
d September 10, 1583; Atlantic Ocean
Led early sea expedition to Newfoundland

Northwest Passage water route connecting the Atlantic Ocean and Pacific Ocean through the Arctic islands of northern Canada

In the summer of 1583, Sir Humphrey Gilbert led an expedition across the Atlantic Ocean, hoping to establish a permanent English settlement on the Penobscot River (in what is now Maine). He was one of the first Englishmen to recognize the importance of colonizing North America for both short-term and long-term gain. Gilbert's mission failed, but his work motivated others to pursue colonial expansion in the region.

A Man with Vision

Sir Humphrey Gilbert was a man of both action and ideas. As a soldier, he was knighted for his part in the defeat of an Irish rebellion in 1569. As a thinker, he argued for the existence of a **Northwest Passage** to Asia. In 1576 Gilbert published a paper in which he suggested that starting English colonies in North America would provide trade opportunities and jobs for his unemployed countrymen.

Gilbert presented his ideas to Queen Elizabeth I, one of his strongest supporters. On June 11, 1578, the queen granted him the right to "discover, searche, finde out, and viewe such remote heathen and barbarous landes, countries, and territories not actually possessed of any Christian prince or people." He was also given permission to settle any lands between Labrador and Florida and to attack any vessel in any harbor of these lands.

Gilbert spent the summer of 1578 preparing for his voyage and trying to keep his plans secret. He knew that the Spanish would try to block any English attempt to settle in the Americas. He concealed his destination so well that historians are still not sure where he intended to go. What is known is that an expedition of 10 well-armed ships sailed out of Plymouth, England, in November 1578. But all of the vessels had to turn back before reaching North America. Gilbert's first voyage, financed mostly with his family's money, was a complete failure.

The Rewards of Perseverance

Gilbert was determined to sail to North America, but first he had to raise money for the voyage. His efforts to sell his rights to the lands

The day before his death, while his ship sailed through rough seas, Humphrey Gilbert was seen out on deck, calmly reading a book.

he intended to settle were not successful. He had to finance the second trip with the remainder of his own money and additional funds from his friends.

Gilbert planned to build a settlement near a city called Norumbega on the Penobscot River. Norumbega was a myth, but Gilbert thought that it really existed. On June 11, 1583, he left England with five ships and 260 men, taking the northern route across the Atlantic Ocean.

At the end of July, the expedition arrived on the coast of Newfoundland. About one week later, Gilbert anchored his fleet at the port of St. John's and formally took possession of Newfoundland for England. No one in Gilbert's time seems to have known that John CABOT had already claimed the island for England's King Henry VII in 1497. When Gilbert's ships arrived in the harbor, it was filled with fishing boats from Spain, Portugal, France, and England. But there was no fighting among the sailors from the rival nations, and no one disputed Gilbert's authority.

For two weeks, Gilbert and his men feasted with the fishermen. But as Gilbert prepared to sail south, the captains of two of his ships said that they were ill and could not travel farther. The three remaining vessels departed from Newfoundland on August 20.

Death at Sea

One of the three ships was soon wrecked on a sandbar off Sable Island, near Nova Scotia. The men on the other ships were concerned about setting up a colony with winter coming, and they convinced Gilbert to return to England. On the trip home, Gilbert sailed aboard the smaller of the two vessels, even though it was overloaded with guns—the extra weight made crossing the Atlantic Ocean more dangerous.

The ships encountered stormy weather north of an island group called the Azores, and on September 9, Gilbert's ship nearly sank. Later that night, the men on the other English vessel could not see any lights from Gilbert's ship. Their commander and his crewmen had apparently drowned. Nevertheless, his hope to found a permanent English settlement in North America was not forgotten. Two years later, his half brother, Sir Walter RALEIGH, sent the first English colonists to what is now North Carolina.

SUGGESTED READING Donald B. Chidsey, *The Life of Sir Humphrey Gilbert, England's First Empire Builder* (Greenwood Press, 1970); Humphrey Gilbert, *The Voyages and Colonising Enterprises of Sir Humphrey Gilbert*, 2 volumes, edited by David Beers Quinn (Hakluyt Society, 1940).

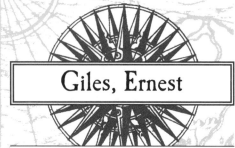

Giles, Ernest

Australian
b July 20, 1835; Bristol, England
d November 13, 1897; Coolgardie, Australia
Crossed Australia

Ernest Giles was an adventurer who was fascinated by the idea of exploration. He made several journeys into the interior of Australia and was the first person to cross the continent from east to west and back again. On those trips, he traveled through two of the harshest deserts in the world.

Desperate Times and Desperate Measures

Born in England in 1835, Giles was educated in London. In 1850 he moved to Adelaide, South Australia, where his parents were living. After spending several years working in gold fields and doing clerical jobs in Melbourne, he was hired to find new grazing lands for livestock. From 1861 to 1865, he surveyed the territories northwest of the Darling River.

In 1872 Giles and five companions attempted to cross the Australian continent. Departing from the town of Charlotte Waters on the east coast, they traveled along the route of an overland telegraph line, intending to reach the Murchison River, 1,000 miles to the west. Although Giles did not achieve his goal, he did discover Mount Olga, the Finke River, and a plant believed to be 2,000 years old.

The following year, Giles set out with Alfred Gibson, who had no experience in the wilderness. Together they explored the area west of the Petermann Ranges, but Gibson became lost in the long stretches of sand and died. Giles later named the desert after his companion. After carrying a 45-pound keg of water on his back for 60 miles, Giles finally emerged from the barren region nearly starved. When he spotted a dying baby kangaroo, as he later described, he "pounced upon it and ate it, living, raw, dying—fur, skin, bones, skull and all."

Not to Be Outdone

Giles continued his efforts to cross Australia even though he knew that other explorers had already accomplished this feat. In December 1873, John W. Lewis journeyed to the west coast of the continent. The following year, John Forrest became the first person to cross Australia from west to east. Nevertheless, on May 6, 1875, Giles departed from Port Augusta on the southern coast with Henry Tietkins as his second-in-command. The expedition also included an Afghani camel driver named Saleh, an Australian Aborigine named Tommy, and 22 camels. After traveling through the southern part of the Great Victoria Desert, the group reached the west coast of Australia in mid-November, having crossed 2,500 miles of barren land in five months. During that journey, they were forced to endure a stretch of approximately 330 miles without any water.

After a brief rest, Giles left Perth on January 13, 1876, and headed east. The same team accompanied him, except for Tietkins, who was replaced by Alec Ross. Their route took them north of their first crossing and through the Gibson Desert. Along the way, they were attacked by hordes of flies and stinging ants, and Giles temporarily lost his sight. The party finally reached the telegraph station at Peake in late August. Giles later said, "Exploration of 1,000 miles of Australia is equal to 10,000 miles in any other part of the earth's surface, always excepting Arctic and Antarctic travel."

Giles won recognition and praise around the world for his journey across Australia and back. However, his adopted homeland largely ignored his achievement because he had failed to find new grazing lands, which were among the country's most pressing needs. In 1897, while working again as a clerk in Western Australia's gold fields, Giles died of pneumonia.

At one point on their 1875 expedition across Australian deserts, Giles and his team went 330 miles without water.

SUGGESTED READING Geoffrey P.H. Dutton, *Australia's Last Explorer: Ernest Giles* (Barnes and Noble, 1970); Ray Ericksen, *Ernest Giles: Explorer and Traveller, 1835-1897* (Heinemann Australia, 1978).

Glenn, John Herschel, Jr.

American
b July 18, 1921; Cambridge, Ohio
living
First American to orbit the earth

---

orbit stable, circular route; one trip around; to revolve around

supersonic faster than the speed of sound, which is about 740 miles per hour

astronaut American term for a person who travels into space; literally, "traveler to the stars"

John H. Glenn, Jr., one of America's first seven astronauts, boosted the nation's confidence with his space flight around the earth.

John Herschel Glenn, Jr., was the first American to **orbit** the earth. He became a symbol of American success and of the bold spirit of exploration. Not long after his space flight, he said: "People are afraid of the future, of the unknown. If a man faces up to it and takes the dare of the future, he can have some control over his destiny. That's an exciting idea to me, better than waiting with everybody else to see what's going to happen."

A Pilot in War and Peace

Raised in a small Ohio town, Glenn excelled in school and sports and gained a reputation as a hardworking and religious young man. He was attending Muskingum College in Ohio when the United States entered World War II in 1941. After taking a flying class run by the navy, he enlisted in the Marine Corps to be a fighter pilot. Glenn flew dozens of missions in both World War II and the Korean War, earning many medals and promotions. In peacetime he became a test pilot for new and experimental military jets. In 1957 he made the first **supersonic** flight across North America, flying from Los Angeles to New York in less than 3½ hours.

In 1959 Glenn was among seven military pilots chosen to be the first U.S. **astronauts.** As part of the Mercury space program, they underwent intensive physical, psychological, and technical training in a short time. Some of this urgency came from the United States's desire to match the space program of its rival, the **Soviet Union.** In April 1961, Americans were shocked to learn that the Soviet **cosmonaut** Yuri GAGARIN had orbited the earth.

America into Space

The U.S. government raced forward with the Mercury program. To Glenn's disappointment, Alan SHEPARD and Virgil Grissom were the first astronauts to go into space, in May and July 1961—although they did not actually orbit the earth. In August the cosmonaut Gherman Titov orbited an amazing 17 times. Finally it was Glenn's turn to make history.

During several frustrating delays, Glenn lay strapped inside his tiny space **capsule,** the *Friendship 7,* high atop a massive Atlas **rocket.** On February 20, 1962, the entire nation watched the successful launch on television. Over the next five hours, Glenn sped around the world three times. He was touched when the people of Perth, Australia, turned on every light in the city to greet him as he passed high above in the night sky. But the flight was not entirely free of worry, especially when the capsule's automatic steering system

Soviet Union nation that existed from 1922 to 1991, made up of Russia and 14 other republics in eastern Europe and northern Asia

cosmonaut Russian term for a person who travels into space; literally, "traveler to the universe"

capsule small early spacecraft designed to carry a person around the earth

rocket vehicle propelled by exploding fuel

NASA National Aeronautics and Space Administration, the U.S. space agency

Goes, Bento de

Portuguese
b 1562; Villa Franca do Campo, Azores
d April 11, 1607; Jiuquan, China
Explored India and China

mercenary soldier who is hired to fight, often for a foreign country

Jesuit member of the Society of Jesus, a Roman Catholic order founded by Ignatius of Loyola in 1534

khan title of an Asian ruler

malfunctioned. An experienced test pilot, Glenn was able to fly his spacecraft by manual control. At last the *Friendship 7* splashed into the Atlantic Ocean north of Puerto Rico and was picked up by a U.S. Navy vessel.

Glenn returned home to a whirlwind of parades and honors. But in 1964 he developed ear problems from a fall in the bathtub and had to leave active military duty. After a career in business, he was elected to the U.S. Senate in 1974 and ran unsuccessfully for president in 1984. In 1998, **NASA** decided to send the 77-year-old Glenn back into space for a scientific study of the effects of space travel on older people.

SUGGESTED READING Michael Collins, *Liftoff: The Story of America's Adventure in Space* (Grove Press, 1988); Gordon L. Cooper, John H. Glenn, and others, *We Seven: By the Astronauts Themselves* (Simon and Schuster, 1962); Gregory P. Kennedy, *First Men in Space* (Chelsea House, 1991).

Bento de Goes was a soldier, a missionary, and a diplomat before starting his career as an explorer. In 1602 he made a five-year journey along Marco POLO's route into China. Goes hoped to establish the identity of Christians who were reported to be living in Asia and to determine whether the country known as Cathay was actually China.

Solving Mysteries

Goes began his travels early in life. While still a very young man, he went to India as a **mercenary.** He then became interested in the Society of Jesus, a Roman Catholic religious group whose members are called **Jesuits.** Goes began studying to become a Jesuit but then changed his mind. Instead he traveled to an area near the Strait of Hormuz, in the eastern Persian Gulf. But several years later, he decided to accompany a group of Jesuits on a missionary journey. He went to Lahore (in what is now Pakistan) with Jerome Xavier, great-nephew of Francis XAVIER, in an attempt to convert the Moguls, the dynasty of Turkish-Mongolian descendants who ruled India at the time.

In Lahore, Goes earned the confidence of Akbar the Great, the Mogul **khan.** Akbar asked him to end a dispute between the Moguls and the Portuguese settlers in central India. Goes traveled to Goa, and his diplomatic efforts impressed Father Pimenta, the head of the Jesuit mission there. While with the Moguls, the Jesuits were intrigued by stories of people practicing Christianity in western Tibet. The missionaries wondered if these people had been led to central Asia by the legendary Christian king Prester John. Father Pimenta, who served as director of all Jesuit work in Asia, chose Goes to lead an expedition to central Asia to locate the lost Christians. He also wanted Goes to identify the country Marco Polo had referred to as Cathay.

On the Road to China

In 1602 Goes left for Cathay. He disguised himself as an Indian and called himself Banda Abdullah. Accompanied by two Greeks and an Armenian, he headed to Lahore and then to Kabul (now in Afghanistan), where the Greeks abandoned the expedition.

Determined to complete his task, Goes continued east through what is now Afghanistan, across the Takla Makan Desert to the western frontier of China. Along the way, he met a group of merchants from Cathay. The traders said that they knew Matteo RICCI, a Jesuit who had been a missionary to China, and they had papers to prove it. Goes now had the evidence he needed to show that Cathay and China were the same land. He also learned of a large uncharted area lying north of the known regions of India and China. But Goes did not have the opportunity to explore these territories, nor did he have the chance to search for the lost Christians. He died of exhaustion in the Chinese frontier town of Suchow (present-day Jiuquan) in 1607.

SUGGESTED READING Fernão Guerreiro, *Jahangir and the Jesuits* (R. M. McBride and Company, 1930); Wilfred P. Schoenberg, *Garlic for Pegasus*, (Newman Press, 1995).

Gray, Robert

American
b May 10, 1755; Tiverton, Rhode Island
d Summer 1806; at sea off east coast of United States
Explored northwest coast of North America;
sailed around world twice

circumnavigate to travel around

Though other explorers had failed before him, Captain Robert Gray succeeded in sailing up the mouth of the Columbia River.

Between 1787 and 1793, Robert Gray made two trading voyages around the world from Boston, Massachusetts, to the Pacific Northwest and then back by way of China. His first voyage made him the first American to **circumnavigate** the globe. On his second voyage, he found and named the Columbia River. This discovery later helped the United States claim a large portion of the Oregon Territory.

Around the Globe

As a young man, Gray served in the Continental Navy during the American Revolution. After the war, he joined a Massachusetts trading company. In 1787 a group of six Boston merchants agreed to sponsor a trading voyage by sea to the northwest coast of North America. Gray was named captain of the *Lady Washington,* and John Kendrick commanded the *Columbia.* The goal of their trip was to trade with Indians for sea otter skins and then to take the furs to China to exchange them for tea, which in turn could be sold at a profit back in Boston.

The *Columbia* and the *Lady Washington* left Boston in the autumn of 1787, but the vessels became separated in heavy storms while rounding South America's Cape Horn. The ships eventually reunited, and in September 1788, they reached Nootka, an island off what is now Vancouver Island. At that time, Nootka was a center of sea otter trading. During the spring of the following year, Gray worked hard at trading with the Indians, and he grew annoyed with Kendrick's laziness. Kendrick eventually transferred command of the *Columbia* to Gray.

On July 30, 1789, Gray headed for China, where he traded the sea otter skins for tea. But since he did not have experience in this business, he did not make the best possible profit. Nevertheless, Gray returned to Boston in triumph on August 10, 1790, having traveled almost 42,000 miles. He was the first American to sail around the world. Although his trip did not bring large financial rewards, it showed Boston merchants the potential for future riches.

Northwest Explorations

After just a month ashore, Gray sailed again on the *Columbia* to resume the sea otter trade. In June 1791, he arrived at Vancouver

bar ridge, usually of sand or rock, on the bottom of a river or other body of water

Island. Gray was carrying a letter of instructions signed by both President George Washington and Secretary of State Thomas Jefferson. The letter warned Gray not to enter any port held by the Spanish and forbade him to trade in Spanish territory. Gray followed his orders and avoided Nootka, the scene of conflict between the Spanish and the British. Instead he traded at various points up and down the coast. He traveled as far north as the large group of islands off the southern tip of what is now Alaska and as far south as what is now Oregon.

When winter came, Gray dropped anchor not far from Nootka and built another ship, the *Adventure.* The following spring, the *Adventure* sailed north to trade, and Gray took the *Columbia* south. Facing intense competition from other traders, Gray was looking for a bay or river mouth where Indians who were inexperienced in trading would take lower payments for their furs.

Gray knew that several years earlier, Bruno de HEZETA of Spain had noticed a major river in the region. But Hezeta had been unable to get past the strong currents and the **bar** that surrounded the river mouth. Hezeta's discovery appeared on Spanish maps, and for 17 years, explorers had sought the river without success. Near the end of April, Gray felt strong currents, indicating that he had reached a river mouth. But the bar caused the river to churn violently, and Gray abandoned his attempt to sail up the river. He sailed north and dropped anchor to think about his next step.

Navigating the Mighty River

After a friendly encounter with the British captain George VANCOUVER, Gray sailed north and entered a harbor that now bears his name, on the coast of what became the state of Washington. He then headed south again, hoping to navigate the mighty river he had seen.

On the morning of May 11, 1792, Gray carefully guided the *Columbia* across the dangerous bar and into the river, which he named after his ship. He continued up the river for about 25 miles. Along the way, the crew exchanged goods with local Indians, but the trading was disappointing, and Gray left after about 10 days.

He sailed again to China and then back to Boston, but he never returned to the Columbia River. After this second circumnavigation, Gray did not sail beyond the Atlantic coast of North America. He is reported to have been buried at sea after dying in 1806 of yellow fever, a tropical virus spread by mosquitoes.

Gray's explorations of the Columbia River had a lasting impact on U.S. history. Before his expedition, Britain, Spain, and Russia had been competing for the land in the Pacific Northwest. Gray's discovery gave the United States a strong claim to the territory. That claim was strengthened by Meriwether LEWIS and William CLARK when they explored the Columbia River in 1805. The disputed land later became the states of Oregon, Washington, and Idaho.

SUGGESTED READING Francis E. Cross and Charles M. Parkin, Jr., *Sea Venture: Captain Gray's Voyages of Discovery, 1787–1793* (Valkyrie Publishing House, 1981); J. Richard Nokes, *Columbia's River: The Voyages of Robert Gray, 1787–1793* (Washington State Historical Society, 1991).

Greysolon, Daniel Dulhut. See *Dulhut, Daniel Greysolon.*

Groseilliers, Médard Chouart des

French
b 1621 or 1625?; Charly-Saint-Cyr, France
d 1696; Trois-Rivières, Canada
Opened up Hudson Bay to fur trade

New France French colony that included the St. Lawrence River valley, the Great Lakes region, and until 1713, Acadia (now called Nova Scotia)

Jesuit member of the Society of Jesus, a Roman Catholic order founded by Ignatius of Loyola in 1534

mission settlement founded by priests in a land where they hoped to convert people to Christianity

A fur trader by profession, Médard Chouart des Groseilliers was also a smart businessman. He traveled around Lake Superior in search of beaver pelts and discovered that the best furs came from an area between the lake and Hudson Bay. Working with his brother-in-law, Pierre Esprit RADISSON, Groseilliers developed the idea that started England's Hudson's Bay Company.

A Family Business

Groseilliers arrived in **New France** in his late teens. By 1646 he was serving as an assistant to the **Jesuits** at a **mission** to the Huron Indians near Georgian Bay. After learning the Huron language, he gave up missionary life and became a fur trader. Groseilliers eventually settled on an estate near Trois-Rivières, Québec. He called his property Groseilliers, meaning Gooseberry Bushes after his family's farm in France.

In 1653 Groseilliers married the widowed half sister of Pierre Radisson. His new brother-in-law had arrived in New France a few years earlier, spent time living with the Iroquois Indians, and then worked as an interpreter. The two men joined forces in business and formed an extremely effective partnership. Radisson was the fast-talking salesman, while Groseilliers was the organizer.

A Fortune in Fur

Between 1659 and 1660, the partners made a fur-trading expedition north of Lake Superior. They may have traveled as far as the upper Mississippi River. On the journey, they often shared campfires with the Cree, Sioux, and Huron tribes. The Indians told them about ponds between Lake Superior and Hudson Bay that were rich in beaver. Groseilliers and Radisson knew that carrying furs to Québec by an overland route was slow and difficult. They quickly realized that it would be much easier to ship their beaver pelts to market by sea from Hudson Bay.

Groseilliers and Radisson returned to Québec loaded with furs. The partners expected to be praised for finding a new source of beaver pelts. Instead the French government arrested them, took away their goods, and demanded that the men pay a heavy fine for trading without a license. This treatment made Groseilliers and Radisson so furious that in 1666 they took their business and their ideas to England.

The men eventually met King Charles II, who sent them on a fur-trading voyage to Hudson Bay. The expedition left England in June 1668 with Radisson on one ship and Groseilliers on another. A violent storm forced Radisson's ship to turn back, and he spent the next two years in London while Groseilliers completed the voyage.

The success of Groseilliers's trip led to the formation of the Hudson's Bay Company, which still exists today. Groseilliers and

Radisson worked for the company until 1674, when they began to feel undervalued by the English and switched their loyalties back to France. However, the French still did not appreciate their countrymen's trading efforts. They raised taxes on the fur trade, causing Groseilliers to retire in disgust. He died at Trois-Rivières in 1696.

Radisson wrote the account of his expeditions with Groseilliers and received most of the publicity. But historians agree that Groseilliers's achievements were equal to, if not greater than, the accomplishments of his partner.

SUGGESTED READING Morden H. Long, *Knights Errant of the Wilderness; Tales of the Explorers of the Great North-west* (Macmillan Company of Canada, 1920); Grace Lee Nute, *Caesars of the Wilderness: Médard Chouart, Sieur des Groseilliers and Pierre Esprit Radisson, 1618-1710* (reprint, Minnesota Historical Society, 1978).

Hadley, John

English
b April 16, 1682; Hertfordshire, England
d February 14, 1744; East Barnet, England
Invented the quadrant

quadrant navigational instrument used since the Middle Ages to determine distance north or south of the equator

latitude distance north or south of the equator

longitude distance east or west of an imaginary line on the earth's surface; in 1884 most nations agreed to draw the line through Greenwich, England

sextant optical instrument used by navigators since the 1750s to determine distance north or south of the equator

John Hadley advanced the ability of explorers to find and report the locations of their discoveries.

John Hadley was a mathematician who used his skills to help others explore both the heavens and the earth. In 1721 he constructed the first telescope powerful enough to observe the stars and planets effectively. More important for explorers, he later invented a navigation device called the double-reflecting **quadrant.**

Invisible Lines

By the year A.D. 150, the Greeks ERATOSTHENES, HIPPARCHUS, and PTOLEMY had developed and refined a system for locating any place on the earth, using lines called **latitude** and **longitude.** Lines of latitude run parallel to the equator, while lines of longitude run from the North Pole to the South Pole and cross the latitude lines. But these lines—called parallels and meridians—appear on maps, not on the earth's land and sea surfaces. Explorers needed a way to determine their position in relation to the lines on their maps.

Stars As a Guide

In 1730 Hadley invented his quadrant and made latitude measurement simple. Working independently, Thomas Godfrey of Philadelphia invented a quadrant the same year. Hadley's device enabled sailors to measure the height above the horizon of the sun and stars. To use a quadrant, a navigator sighted a known star along one of the instrument's sides. The angle between the star and the horizon was measured by a string that hung from the upper corner of the quadrant and crossed a curved arc that was marked in degrees. Consulting a star chart, the navigator then used the angle of the star's elevation to calculate degrees of latitude. Hadley's quadrant included a level, which told the sailors when they were holding the device perfectly straight. This feature enabled them to make accurate readings even if they could not see the horizon.

Hadley's quadrant was a huge leap forward in navigational technology. But the constant motion of a ship at sea often made it difficult to take reliable measurements. The **sextant,** a later, improved version of the quadrant, was easier to use and measured latitude even more precisely. Determining a ship's exact longitude, however,

chronometer clock designed to keep precise time in the rough conditions of sea travel

cartographer mapmaker

Northwest Passage water route connecting the Atlantic Ocean and Pacific Ocean through the Arctic islands of northern Canada

This title page was printed in 1598 for the first volume of Richard Hakluyt's history of English navigation.

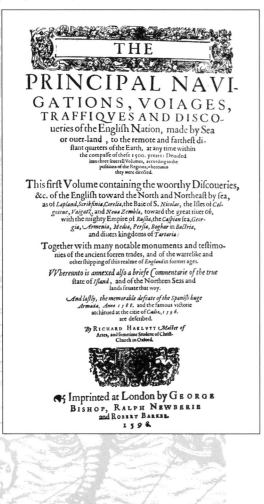

was not possible until John HARRISON invented the first accurate marine **chronometer** in 1762.

SUGGESTED READING *Biographical Account of John Hadley* (Fisher, Son and Company, 1835).

Although Richard Hakluyt never left Europe, almost everything known about exploration during the reign of Queen Elizabeth I is due to his dedicated work. His writings had tremendous political influence, motivating England to explore overseas and eventually to establish an empire. In addition, Hakluyt's appealing writing style made his three-volume work, *The Principal Navigations, Voyages, and Discoveries of the English Nation,* a classic of English literature.

Geographic Scholar

Hakluyt was born in or near London in 1552. His wealthy family had ties to the English nobility as well as to the growing business class. His father, also named Richard, was a London merchant. Little is known about his mother, Margery. Both parents died while Hakluyt was still young, and he was raised by a cousin—or as some sources say, an uncle—who was a lawyer with an interest in geography.

Hakluyt graduated from Oxford University in 1574, earned a master's degree three years later, and then became a minister. Although he worked as a minister for the rest of his life, Hakluyt devoted himself primarily to geography. He eventually became the first teacher to lecture on the subject at Oxford.

In the 1500s, many geographers blended fact and fantasy in their accounts of the newly discovered lands across the seas in order to entertain their readers. Hakluyt, however, was a serious scientist and scholar and did his best to record only the truth. His job was not easy. Spain, England's main rival at the time, often refused to share information about its new colonies. But like a skilled detective, Hakluyt tracked down firsthand information brought home by voyagers returning from the Americas.

As a young man, he exchanged letters with the leading international authorities on geography. These experts included Gerardus Mercator, the great Flemish **cartographer,** and Abraham Ortelius, a Dutchman who assembled the first modern atlas. In London, Hakluyt regularly talked to well-known seamen. He was a good friend of Sir Francis DRAKE, who returned in 1580 from a voyage around the world. Hakluyt also associated with Sir Martin FROBISHER and Sir Humphrey GILBERT, seagoing adventurers who were seeking a **Northwest Passage.** In addition, Hakluyt kept close contact with the captains of England's Muscovy Company, which had begun trading with Russia.

Promoting Exploration

Among Hakluyt's earliest writings were two small volumes on the discoveries in North America. By this time, the English knew that there was no easy sea route to Asia by way of the

Canadian Arctic, but Hakluyt still believed that England would benefit by exploring North America. He also understood that the secret to overseas wealth was not to mine gold, as the Spanish had done, but to establish a network of colonies for trade.

In 1582 Hakluyt published *Divers Voyages Touching the Discovery of America.* This book encouraged England to expand its activities in the Americas. Two years later, at the request of Sir Walter RALEIGH, he privately published *Discourse on Western Planting,* urging Queen Elizabeth I to support overseas colonies.

Eager for More Knowledge

In 1583 Hakluyt was named chaplain to the English ambassador in Paris, Sir Edward Stafford. In this position, he learned even more about explorations by other nations, particularly about French expeditions. Like England, France had explored much of northern North America in the quest for the Northwest Passage. But when war broke out between England and Spain, Hakluyt returned home in 1588. That same year, Sir Francis Drake defeated the fleet known as the Spanish Armada off the English coast. His victory ended the threat of invasion and severely damaged Spain's naval power.

Over the next 10 years, Hakluyt gained influence at Queen Elizabeth's court. As a minister in Westminster, he had access to the queen and her ministers. He continued to collect and edit materials on English voyages and the accounts of foreign travelers.

Hakluyt died on November 23, 1616. He was buried in London's Westminster Abbey, the resting place of many great English writers. More than 200 years later, the Royal Geographic Society honored him by founding the Hakluyt Society, which publishes works on exploration and travel.

SUGGESTED READING Irwin R. Blacker, editor, *Hakluyt's Voyages* (Viking Press, 1965); George Bruner Parks, *Richard Hakluyt and the English Voyages,* second edition (Frederick Ungar, 1961); Delbert A. Young, *According to Hakluyt: Tales of Adventure and Exploration* (Clarke, Irwin, 1973).

Hall, Charles Francis

American
b 1821; Rochester, New Hampshire
d November 8, 1871; northwestern Greenland
***Explored Canadian Arctic;
attempted to reach North Pole***

Inuit people of the Canadian Arctic, sometimes known as the Eskimo

Charles Francis Hall was a newspaper publisher in Cincinnati, Ohio, when he left his family and became a full-time Arctic explorer. He was inspired by the Arctic adventures of Elisha Kent KANE and was convinced that he could find survivors of Sir John FRANKLIN's lost expedition. Often working alone, he made many discoveries during his 17 years in the polar region. However, Hall is best known for his detailed knowledge of **Inuit** life.

Uncovering the Past

In May 1860, Hall set out on the *Henry George,* a whaling ship headed for the Arctic region. He planned to leave the whaler at Cumberland Sound and travel to King William Island, the site of the Franklin disaster. Hall had plenty of determination and self-confidence—but none of the skills of an Arctic explorer. He brought along a tiny boat and just a few supplies. Luckily for Hall, he met two Inuit, Tookolito and Ebierbing, who became his guides and lifelong friends. While on Baffin Island, he heard Inuit tales of another white man. Hall realized that the stories were about Martin FROBISHER, who had explored

Charles Francis Hall's enthusiasm for Arctic exploration was undiminished by his lack of training or experience.

sledge heavy sled, often mounted on runners, that is pulled over snow or ice

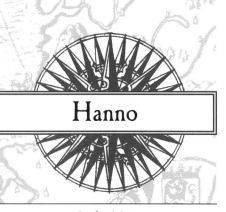

Hanno

Carthaginian
b 500 B.C.?; ?
d ?; ?
Explored Africa

the island in the 1500s. Hall did not reach King William Island as planned, but his first trip to the Arctic was not a failure. He spent a year uncovering artifacts from the Frobisher expedition and exploring what is now called Frobisher Bay.

Hall also learned about Inuit culture. He lived as they did, eating their traditional foods such as seal's blood soup. He began to admire the Inuit lifestyle. However, he could not accept their practice of leaving the old and sick to die alone. Hall once broke into an igloo and comforted an elderly woman for 12 hours, until she passed away.

The Search for Franklin

After returning from the Arctic in 1862, Hall began to prepare for another trip north. He had been impressed by the accuracy of the Inuit's stories and was convinced that they would know what had happened to Franklin. He journeyed for five years, finally reaching King William Island in 1869. There he discovered items from Franklin's fateful voyage and heard tales of how the explorers had starved to death. Hall never found any survivors from the Franklin expedition.

Hall made one last trip to the polar region in August 1871. This time he was on a government-funded expedition to reach the North Pole. With 32 crew members, including his Inuit friends, Hall sailed the *Polaris* up Smith Sound, between Greenland and Ellesmere Island. He then traveled by **sledge** across part of Greenland and discovered an area, later named Hall Land, full of plants and wildlife. After returning to the ship, he fell ill, and he died two weeks later. He may have been murdered by poisoning, but this theory has not been proven.

After Hall's death, the crew decided to return home. On the way, some members of the expedition, including Tookolito and Ebierbing, became stranded on a large sheet of floating ice. The hunting, cooking, and building skills of the Inuit kept the stranded party alive. When the public learned of their amazing 1,300 mile drift to Labrador, however, little attention was paid to the heroic role played by the Inuit.

SUGGESTED READING Charles Francis Hall, *Life With the Esquimaux*, edited by George Swinton (reprint, M.G. Hurtig, 1970); Chauncey Loomis, *Weird and Tragic Shores: The Story of Charles Francis Hall, Explorer* (Alfred A. Knopf, 1971); David Mountfield, *A History of Polar Exploration* (Dial Press, 1974).

In the 500s B.C., Hanno led a large expedition from the ancient Mediterranean civilization of Carthage and established a settlement in western Africa. Some historians believe that as many as 60 ships, carrying 30,000 men and women, traveled to what is now Morocco. Hanno's voyage was recorded in a document known as the Periplus of Hannon. Despite doubts regarding the accuracy of the Periplus, this document provides reliable evidence that Hanno and his people visited much of Africa's western coastline. There they founded several communities and engaged in trade.

Seeking New Territory

Carthage was located on the Mediterranean coast of Africa (in what is now Tunisia). By Hanno's time, the Carthaginians had already established several settlements in Morocco. However, conflicts with the Greeks in nearby Sicily made the Carthaginians eager to expand their territories and trade routes along the west coast of Africa.

Hanno and his party left their homeland and sailed west across the Mediterranean Sea, through the Strait of Gibraltar, and down the coast of Africa. They established the city of Thymiaterion, later named Kenitra, and built a temple at what later became known as Cape Meddouza. They also founded five other communities farther south. These included the Carian Fortress (believed to be the modern city of Essaouira) and a trading post named Cerne. The location of Cerne is uncertain, but it may have been on Hern Island at the mouth of the Río de Oro in Western Sahara.

Hanno may have explored south of Cerne, but the account of his travels does not make this clear. A river described in the Periplus may have been the modern Senegal River. Hanno's party also reported seeing streams of fire, which they described as a "Chariot of the Gods." This may have been an active volcano, probably either Mount Kakoulima (in modern Guinea) or Mount Cameroon (in Cameroon).

The Carthaginians had some commercial success in their new colonies. Reports from that time show that they traded gold with the tribes of the area near Cerne. However, none of the colonies had any lasting economic importance. After the Romans defeated Carthage in a series of wars in the 200s B.C. and took over that portion of Africa, the Romans never traded in the region.

Doubts and Questions

Historians have several doubts about the report of Hanno's voyage. It contains many errors of geography, such as its claim that the Lixus (now Larache) River was south of Cape Meddouza. Most of the settlements listed in the Periplus were never mentioned in other records, nor have archaeologists been able to locate them. Historians suspect that the size of Hanno's party was greatly exaggerated, and some doubt that his voyage took place at all. However, many scholars believe that the Carthaginians, who were extremely protective of their trade routes, gave misleading information to confuse their enemies.

SUGGESTED READING B. H. Warmington, *Carthage* (Frederick Praeger, 1966).

Hargraves, Edward Hammond

English
b October 7, 1816; Gosport, England
d October 29, 1891; Sydney, Australia
Discovered gold in Australia

Edward Hammond Hargraves discovered gold along Summerhill Creek in New South Wales, Australia. Whether he was the first person to find gold in that country is still disputed. However, his discovery started the gold rush that tripled Australia's population to 1.5 million people by the 1860s.

Learning the Tools of the Trade

Hargraves was born in England in 1816. At the age of 16, he traveled to Australia as a member of the merchant marine. After spending a short time on land, he served on a ship that sailed the Torres

Edward Hammond Hargraves discovered gold in Australia, producing a rush of immigration and settlement.

tributary stream or river that flows into a larger stream or river

Strait between Australia and New Guinea to hunt tortoises for their shells. He grew to be a big, husky man with a taste for adventure. In 1848 he left Australia to join the California gold rush. Although he found no gold during his two years there, he learned how to use a pan and cradle to sift river bottoms for gold nuggets. He believed that he would be able to use this skill when he returned to Australia.

Following the Scent of Gold

The terrain of the California gold country reminded Hargraves of land he knew near the Blue Mountains, located northwest of Sydney. He returned to Australia in 1850, convinced that he would find gold there. But when he told his countrymen about his theory, as he later wrote, they treated his "views and opinions as those of a madman."

Nevertheless, Hargraves set out in search of gold. On February 12, 1851, he rode along Summerhill Creek, a **tributary** of the Macquarie River, with John Lister as his guide. Hargraves's belief that he was "surrounded by gold" proved correct. Four out of every five pans he sifted produced the valuable nuggets.

Hargraves returned to Sydney and offered to sell the location of his goldfield. In May the newspapers reported his find, and the gold rush began. By the end of the month, 1,000 prospectors were working the creek, with more coming each day. So many people came to the region that the rest of the country experienced a shortage of labor, and wages rose in those areas. Hargraves's discovery was followed by even richer finds in Victoria.

In 1855 Hargraves published *Australia and Its Gold Fields.* He was later named commissioner of Crown Land and granted a large sum by the government of New South Wales. He died in 1891, having lured many new settlers to Australia with the magical promise of gold.

SUGGESTED READING Frank Clune, *Golden Goliath* (The Hawthorn Press, 1946); Lynette Ramsay Silver, *A Fool's Gold?: William Tipple Smith's Challenge to the Hargraves Myth* (Jacaranda Press, 1986).

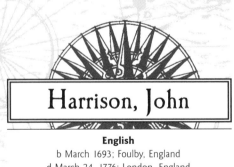

Harrison, John

English
b March 1693; Foulby, England
d March 24, 1776; London, England
Invented first accurate marine chronometer

chronometer clock designed to keep precise time in the rough conditions of sea travel

John Harrison, the son of a carpenter, designed the first accurate marine **chronometer.** His instrument allowed navigators to calculate their **longitude** to within 10 miles. Since longitude was always more difficult to determine at sea than **latitude,** Harrison's invention of the chronometer overcame a major obstacle to world exploration.

In the Middle of the Ocean

By the 1700s, mariners had long had an effective way to determine latitude. They calculated the angles of the sun and stars above the horizon. Then they compared this measurement to the known positions of these heavenly bodies. In 1730 John HADLEY improved on

John Harrison's chronometer solved a problem that had plagued navigators for centuries. A late version of his timepiece is shown at lower left.

longitude distance east or west of an imaginary line on the earth's surface; in 1884 most nations agreed to draw the line through Greenwich, England

latitude distance north or south of the equator

quadrant navigational instrument used since the Middle Ages to determine distance north or south of the equator

Hartog, Dirck

Dutch
b 1500s; ?
d 1600s; ?
Sighted Western Australia

westerlies winds that blow from west to east midway between the equator and each of the poles

trade winds winds that blow from east to west in the tropics

this method with the invention of the double-reflecting **quadrant,** an instrument that provided an almost exact measurement of latitude.

However, sailors did not yet have a useful tool for finding longitude. To measure longitude, navigators needed to know what time it was at a certain place when it was noon aboard their ship. British navigators used as their fixed reference a north-south line, known as the prime meridian, that ran through the Royal Observatory in Greenwich, England. The difference in time between Greenwich and the ship's location would tell the sailors how far east or west they were of the prime meridian.

The clocks of Harrison's day were not accurate enough to measure longitude. All clocks were run by either weights or pendulums. At sea, changes in temperature and the rocking motion of a ship made these clocks function poorly. This problem caused many navigational errors and even some disasters at sea.

In 1714 the British government offered a substantial reward to "such person who shall discover longitude at sea." To win the prize, a person was required to determine a ship's longitude to within 34 miles after a journey of six weeks. John Harrison began work in 1728 and completed his first chronometer seven years later. But it was not accurate enough to win the prize, so he returned to his workshop, where he designed three more devices. Finally, in 1762, he finished his famous No. 4 Timekeeper, which won the prize. On a nine-week voyage to Jamaica that year, the No. 4 Timekeeper lost only one and one-fourth minutes of longitude. However, Sir Isaac Newton, the politically influential physicist and mathematician, preferred to find an astronomical solution rather than a mechanical one. Because of Newton's opposition, Harrison did not receive all of his prize money until 1774.

Even so, Harrison's invention was regarded as a major advance in navigation at sea. Captain James Cook used the No. 4 Timekeeper on his second voyage to the Pacific Ocean in 1772. He called it "our never-failing guide" and "trusty friend."

SUGGESTED READING Dava Sobel, *Longitude: The True Story of a Lone Genius Who Solved the Greatest Scientific Problem of His Time* (Walker and Company, 1997).

Dirck Hartog, a navigator for the Dutch East India Company, was the first European to set foot on the west coast of Australia. He discovered the coast entirely by accident.

In the early 1600s, sailors for the Dutch East India Company could reach Asia by a route that had been established by the Portuguese. From Africa's Cape of Good Hope, they would turn northeast to Madagascar and then sail past the Seychelles to the Maldives, off the coast of India. They would then head east to their Indonesian trading outpost at Batavia (now Jakarta) on the island of Java. In 1611 the Dutch captain Hendrick Brouwer discovered a faster route. He sailed directly east from the southern tip of Africa for about 4,000 miles and then headed north to Java. This alternative route enabled ships to take advantage of the **westerlies** and the southeastern **trade winds,** and it soon became the standard route for the Dutch.

While headed for Java on a trading voyage, Dirck Hartog accidentally discovered the west coast of Australia.

longitude distance east or west of an imaginary line on the earth's surface; in 1884 most nations agreed to draw the line through Greenwich, England

In January 1616, Hartog commanded the ship *Eendracht* heading for Bantam, a trading post on Java. Upon reaching the Cape of Good Hope in August, he headed east. Hartog could only estimate when to turn north, since sailors of that time had no accurate way to measure **longitude.** As a result, he sailed too far east, landing at what he described as "some islands" on October 25. He came ashore on an island that stretched across the mouth of what is now Shark Bay. Across the bay, he could see the west coast of Australia. Hartog and three crew members spent three days on the island. Before they left, Hartog scratched their names and the date of their visit on a tin plate, which he nailed to a post. The plate was eventually found in 1697 by the Dutch voyager Willem de Vlamingh; it is now in the Museum of Amsterdam.

Hartog reached Java in December 1616, probably by sailing north along the Australian coast. Although no record of his voyage survived, word of Hartog's discovery soon reached the Dutch East India Company. Their records began to refer to a place they called "Eendrachtsland," named for Hartog's ship. A company map drawn in 1627 shows this region extending 300 miles southward from what is now the North West Cape to just below Shark Bay. Following Hartog's discovery, all Dutch ships sailing to the islands of Southeast Asia were required to use Brouwer's route. Several of these ships reached the shores of Western Australia. The map that was begun after Hartog's discovery was finally completed in 1629, when François Pelsaert made a continuous voyage along Australia's western coast.

SUGGESTED READING R. Copley, *Hartog and Tasman* (Longmans, 1965).

Hawqal, Ibn. See *Ibn Hawqal*.

He, Zheng. See *Zheng He*.

Hearne, Samuel

English
b 1745; London, England
d November 1792; London, England
Reached Arctic Ocean overland from Hudson Bay

Northwest Passage water route connecting the Atlantic Ocean and Pacific Ocean through the Arctic islands of northern Canada

quadrant navigational instrument used since the Middle Ages to determine distance north or south of the equator

Samuel Hearne lived among the Chipewyan while exploring the far northern reaches of Canada.

Samuel Hearne made one of the most remarkable journeys ever undertaken in North America. He was the first European to reach the Arctic Ocean by an overland route. Hearne completed the expedition with the help and guidance of Matonabbee, a Chipewyan Indian.

Hearne's Early Attempts

Samuel Hearne entered Britain's Royal Navy at age 12 and served for six years. In 1766 he joined the Hudson's Bay Company, a group of adventurers and profit seekers authorized by the king to develop the fur trade in the area surrounding Hudson Bay. The company was supposed to explore as well as trade, and it was now under pressure for having neglected exploration. Responding to this pressure, as well as to rumors of rich copper mines in the Canadian northwest, the company's directors decided to act.

In 1769 the directors chose Hearne to lead an overland expedition to discover the copper mines and search for the **Northwest Passage.** Hearne set out from Fort Prince of Wales (now Churchill, Manitoba) on November 6, 1769. He was accompanied by two servants and two Cree Indians. A group of Chipewyan, an Indian tribe that roamed the northern parts of North America, happened to depart at the same time. Three weeks later, the Chipewyan stole Hearne's food supply and fled. Although the expedition was 200 miles away from the fort, Hearne managed to bring his men back safely.

When spring came, Hearne made a second attempt. He spent nine months in the barren lands northwest of the fort, a harsh region that extends across the top of North America. The terrain is so difficult to walk on that explorer R. A. J. Phillips compared it to wading through "porridge sown with razor blades." Hearne went as far west as Dubawnt Lake before breaking his **quadrant.** The next day, a group of Chipewyan stole his gun and some other possessions.

Lost and lacking supplies for the coming winter, Hearne trudged southward for three days, struggling to keep from starving or freezing to death. It was then that he met Matonabbee, a Chipewyan whom Hearne soon came to respect and admire. Matonabbee led Hearne back to the fort and offered to serve as his guide on later expeditions.

Traveling with the Chipewyan

After two weeks at the fort, Hearne left to join Matonabbee's family. He traveled west and then north with them, following the caribou, a type of large deer, across Canada. He adopted the Chipewyan way of life and feasted with them on caribou stomachs and raw ox. However, he refused to join them when they dined on lice from

Inuit people of the Canadian Arctic, sometimes known as the Eskimo

their own heads. The group stayed in the forest as long as possible before heading out across the barren lands. Matonabbee, Hearne, and a small group of Chipewyan eventually left the main group of women and children and went on toward the Coppermine River.

On the way to the river, Hearne's party was joined by a mysterious band of Indians. It became clear in time that these Indians were planning a massacre of their traditional enemies, the **Inuit.** On July 17, they brutally attacked a group of Inuit at a spot Hearne later named Bloody Falls. Helpless to prevent the slaughter, Hearne and his party could only stand by and watch. At one point, an Inuit woman wrapped herself around Hearne's legs while her attackers plunged spears into her.

After this incident, Hearne's group proceeded to the copper mine. But four hours of searching produced only one good chunk of copper. Hearne's supervisors had been deceived by the Indians, who were known for telling Europeans what they wanted to hear. The journey to the Arctic Ocean ended in disappointment as well. When they reached Coronation Gulf at the mouth of the Coppermine River, they found the Arctic Ocean covered in ice. Hearne realized that if the ocean was still frozen in July, this waterway was not the Northwest Passage he was seeking. The party then returned south, picking up the women and children. Crossing Point Lake and MacKay Lake, they went into the forest. They reached Great Slave Lake on December 24, 1771, and were back at Fort Prince of Wales by June 30, 1772.

Hearne's Later Life

Hearne remained with the Hudson's Bay Company for many more years, and he served a term as governor of Fort Prince of Wales beginning in 1775. During the American Revolution, the fort was captured by French troops led by Jean François de Galaup de LA PÉROUSE. Hearne was captured and taken to France as a prisoner. Although the French seized Hearne's records of the expedition, La Pérouse later arranged for Hearne's release on the condition that he publish these journals. Hearne went back to Canada in 1783, but poor health forced him to return to London after four years. He died in London in 1792, and his journals were published three years later.

According to Hearne, most of his accomplishments involved disproving the mistaken ideas of others. He showed that the plan to establish copper mines in northwestern North America was based on myth rather than reality. He also proved that there was no Northwest Passage through Hudson Bay. However, his most lasting achievement was his book describing life among the Chipewyan. It is still considered a classic work in the literature of exploration.

SUGGESTED READING Samuel Hearne, *A Journey to the Northern Ocean*, edited by Richard Glover (Macmillan of Canada, 1958); Gordon Speck, *Samuel Hearne and the Northwest Passage* (Caxton Printers, 1963).

Heçeta, Bruno de. See *Hezeta, Bruno de.*

Hedin, Sven Anders

Swedish
b February 19, 1865; Stockholm, Sweden
d November 26, 1952; Stockholm, Sweden
Explored Middle East, central Asia, and China

The Swedish explorer Sven Hedin won the respect of kings, governments, and mountain tribesmen.

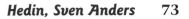

During more than 40 years of travel, Sven Anders Hedin mapped vast regions of central Asia that were previously unknown. He explored Turkistan (a region including much of central Asia), the rugged mountains of the Himalaya, and the wild and barren deserts of northwestern China and Mongolia. He found the source of India's holy rivers, the Indus and the Brahmaputra. Hedin charted large stretches of the Takla Makan and Gobi Deserts, uncovering ancient cities buried beneath the sands. He located Lop Nur, the fabled Wandering Lake in northwestern China. Hedin even mapped the dangerous mountains between India and Tibet, now known as the Hedin Trans-Himalayan Range.

Hedin's Early Travels

Hedin was born to an important family with ties to Swedish royalty. Hedin's father was the official city architect of Stockholm, and two of his uncles held high posts in government. His uncle Svente Hedin was a famous actor and a friend of King Carl XI. Hedin was a good student and well liked by his classmates. He enjoyed exercise, sketching, and mapmaking, and he took interest in geography and exploration. At the age of 20, Hedin accepted a job tutoring the son of a Swedish engineer who was living in the city of Baku on the Caspian Sea (now in Azerbaijan). There Hedin learned to speak Persian and Tartar. After working as a tutor for one year, he traveled extensively in Persia (now Iran).

Hedin then returned to Europe, where he attended Uppsala University in Sweden. He continued his studies in Germany, where he became friends with Ferdinand von RICHTHOFEN, the greatest expert on Asian geography at that time. Hedin also published a book about his travels in the Middle East, the first of the 30 volumes he was to write.

Hedin returned to Persia in 1890 at the request of the Swedish government. He was appointed to serve as an interpreter for Swedish diplomats who visited the court of the ruler of Persia in Tehran. During this mission, Hedin impressed Sweden's King Oscar II. When the job ended, Hedin received funding from the Swedish government to explore central Asia. He traveled to Tashkent (now the capital of modern-day Uzbekistan) and to Samarkand, an important city on the Silk Road—the route that merchants had traveled across Asia and the Middle East in ancient times. Hedin made a difficult crossing of the Pamir Mountains to Kashi, the westernmost city in China. This journey introduced him to the region's harsh terrain and prepared him for later expeditions.

Exploring the Takla Makan Desert

After completing advanced studies in Germany, Hedin received another grant from the Swedish government for further exploration. In late January 1894, Hedin left western Turkistan with three servants, crossed the Pamirs, and returned to Kashi. The mountain ice was dangerous, and the party was almost lost in snowstorms. Hedin's courage,

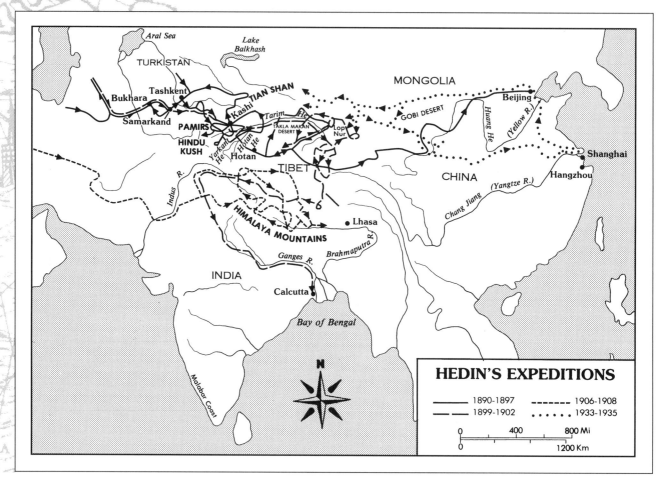

Sven Hedin traveled throughout Asia, undaunted by blazing deserts, civil wars, and tales of evil spirits.

humor, and generosity won him the respect of the Kirghiz tribesmen who were his guides. Once across the mountains, the group rested by the shore of Lake Karakul. There Hedin amazed and delighted his guides by building and sailing a small sailboat, the first the Kirghiz had ever seen.

Hedin wanted to explore the Takla Makan Desert, which stretches from northwestern China into Mongolia's Gobi Desert. Europeans knew little more about this area than they had when Marco POLO traveled along its edges in the late 1200s. The Takla Makan is crossed by three rivers: the Yarkant He, the Hotan He, and the Tarim He. The people who lived on the western border of the desert along the Yarkant He told legends of sandstorms that had buried ancient cities. They considered the desert an evil place where spirits bewitched unwary travelers and led them to their deaths.

On April 10, 1895, Hedin left the Yarkant He and traveled east into the Takla Makan. He was accompanied by three servants—Islam Bai, Kassim, and Mohammed Shah—a guide named Yolchi, and several camels and other animals. The local people had tearfully begged the adventurers not to go. Within three weeks, the party ran out of water. The men slaughtered a sheep and tried to drink its blood. However, the heat of the desert quickly caused the blood to thicken and become undrinkable. The camels began to die of thirst, and the group wandered apart.

Hedin and Kassim stayed together, crawling over great sand dunes toward some trees they saw on the horizon. They knew that any sign of plants meant that they were near the Hotan He. When they reached the trees, Kassim collapsed, but Hedin struggled on toward the river and stumbled into the water. After satisfying his thirst, Hedin revived Kassim, and the pair rested by the Hotan He. Soon they were joined by Islam Bai, who had saved himself by following one of the camels to the water. Mohammed Shah and Yolchi were never heard from again. By the fall of 1895, the survivors had made their way back to Kashi.

Further Explorations in China

Hedin was determined to explore the Tarim He basin. After gathering new instruments to replace those he had lost in the desert, he headed east again with Islam Bai in December 1895. Near the city of Hotan, they uncovered the remains of a 2,000-year-old town. Following the Tarim He, Hedin and Islam Bai reached the shallow body of water known as Lop Nur. Hedin determined that Lop Nur was the "Wandering Lake" referred to in ancient Chinese records. His calculations suggested that the changing geography of the region caused the lake to shift back and forth across the desert. Later scientific investigation proved that he was right.

The party returned to Hotan in April after covering 1,200 miles. Next Hedin decided to journey over land to Beijing. Along the way, he charted parts of northern Tibet and western China that were so remote that even the tribes of the region had no names for them. Traveling by camel through the southern Gobi Desert, Hedin reached Beijing and won the praise of Europe. Islam Bai's role in the expedition was not forgotten: Sweden's King Oscar awarded him a gold medal.

In 1899 Hedin returned to western China for additional surveys of the Tarim He basin. There he uncovered Lou-lan, an ancient city that had thrived 1,800 years earlier. In 1901 Hedin disguised himself as a Mongolian monk in order to enter the sacred Tibetan city of Lhasa. However, aides to Tibet's spiritual leader, the Dalai Lama, discovered Hedin's scheme. They arrested him and ordered him to leave the country. The disappointed Hedin made his way to India and eventually back to Sweden.

Hedin's Final Journey and Later Life

In 1906 Hedin undertook one last trip to India to explore the Himalaya, much of which had never been mapped. The sources of India's great rivers, the Indus and the Brahmaputra, were believed to be in these mountains. For two years, Hedin hiked back and forth across the rugged mountains that now bear his name—the Hedin Transhimalayas. He mapped the region and discovered the rivers' sources. This journey was one of his greatest triumphs. On returning to Stockholm, Hedin wrote books about his travels and his political observations. These writings included works about Germany's armies during World War I.

Hedin joined another expedition to central Asia in 1926. Germany's Lufthansa Airlines sponsored this trip in order to establish an air route to China. Although the project was unsuccessful, the Chinese government asked Hedin to remain there and make a detailed map of the Silk Road. Despite his age—he was almost 70 years old—and despite the civil war then raging in China, Hedin agreed. He completed the project in 1935. Later, during World War II, he served as an unofficial Swedish ambassador to Berlin, Germany. Although some of his ancestry was Jewish, Hedin supported the Nazis because he sympathized with their war against the **Soviet Union.** Hedin used his influence to save the lives of some Jewish friends and Norwegian resistance fighters, but his reputation was hurt by his relationship with the Nazis. He died in Stockholm at age 87.

Soviet Union nation that existed from 1922 to 1991, made up of Russia and 14 other republics in eastern Europe and northern Asia

SUGGESTED READING John Lennox Cook, *Six Great Travellers* (Hamish Hamilton, 1960); Sven Hedin, *My Life as an Explorer,* translated by Alfhild Huebsch (Kodansha International, 1996); George Kish, *To the Heart of Asia: The Life of Sven Hedin* (University of Michigan Press, 1984).

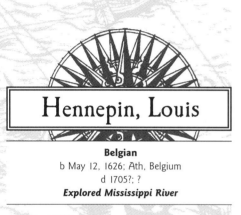

Hennepin, Louis

Belgian
b May 12, 1626; Ath, Belgium
d 1705?; ?
Explored Mississippi River

Father Louis Hennepin was the first European to describe Niagara Falls in detail and to see the upper Mississippi River. He claimed to have reached the mouth of the Mississippi before René Robert Cavelier de LA SALLE. However, most historians reject that claim.

Hennepin was one of five priests chosen by France's King Louis XIV to serve as missionaries to **New France.** This assignment gave Hennepin a way to express both his religious enthusiasm and his love of adventure. In 1676 he joined a **mission** in Ontario, Canada; two years later, he was ordered to accompany La Salle on his explorations. La Salle instructed Hennepin and a small group to build a ship and a fort on the Niagara River. On December 8, 1678, Hennepin reached Niagara Falls, which he described as "the most beautiful and altogether the most terrifying waterfall in the universe."

This painting depicts Father Louis Hennepin at the Falls of St. Anthony. Settlers later built Minneapolis, Minnesota, around the falls.

New France French colony that included the St. Lawrence River valley, the Great Lakes region, and until 1713, Acadia (now called Nova Scotia)

mission settlement founded by priests in a land where they hoped to convert people to Christianity

Hennepin traveled with La Salle from August 1679 to February 1680. After the expedition built Fort Crèvecoeur on the Illinois River, La Salle ordered Hennepin and two other men to proceed to the Mississippi River. Hennepin later claimed that from February 29 to March 25, his party had canoed to the mouth of the Mississippi. However, such a journey would have been impossible, since by April 10, they had returned to the fort. The group would have had to travel more than 3,000 miles in a little more than a month.

On April 11, a group of Sioux Indians captured Hennepin and his men. But when Hennepin's group offered the peace pipe and gifts to the Sioux, the Indians decided to spare the explorers' lives. The Sioux and their captives traveled up the Mississippi and then marched for five days to a Sioux village in the Thousand Lakes area of what is now Minnesota. While he was held prisoner, Hennepin studied the customs and language of the Sioux.

In August, Hennepin accompanied a Sioux hunting party to the Wisconsin River. There the priest met the French explorer Daniel Greysolon DULHUT, who persuaded the Indians to release Hennepin. The explorers spent the winter where Lake Michigan empties into Lake Huron. In April 1681, they set out for Québec, and later that year, Hennepin returned to France. Hennepin eventually wrote a famous and exaggerated account of his travels. The details of Hennepin's last years are unknown.

SUGGESTED READING Father Louis Hennepin, *A New Discovery of a Vast Country in America* (Coles Publishing Company, 1974).

Henson, Matthew Alexander

American
b August 8, 1866; Charles County, Maryland
d March 9, 1955; New York, New York
Explored Arctic Ocean with Robert Edwin Peary

surveyor one who makes precise measurements of a location's geography

Inuit people of the Canadian Arctic, sometimes known as Eskimo

Matthew Alexander Henson served as personal assistant to the Arctic explorer Robert Edwin PEARY for 23 years. Henson is credited with being the most valuable member of Peary's polar expeditions. He accompanied Peary on a historic journey to the North Pole. However, because he was an African-American, Henson did not receive the recognition he deserved for his accomplishments until later in his life.

Overcoming Many Obstacles

Matthew Henson was born to a poor family in 1866, when being African-American meant being treated as a second-class citizen. In his early 20s, while working in a clothing store, Henson met Robert Edwin Peary, a **surveyor** for the U.S. Navy. Peary, who was white, was looking for an assistant to accompany him to Nicaragua. The two men immediately made a deal. Henson later said of their meeting: "I recognized in him the qualities that made me willing to engage in his service." Henson later credited his relationship with Peary with giving him an opportunity to escape from poverty and gain an education.

Henson seems to have accepted white society's attitude toward his race. He claimed to be satisfied in his role as "the faithful and constant companion" of a white man. When he reached the North Pole with Peary and four **Inuit,** Henson expressed pride that "it was I, a lowly member of my race, who had been chosen by fate to represent it, at this, almost the last of the world's great work."

The African-American educator Booker T. Washington thought that Henson did not give himself enough credit for his contributions to Peary's success. Washington, who wrote the introduction to Henson's book about the North Pole expedition, felt that Henson was an inspirational role model for African-Americans. Henson described himself as a "splendid follower." But Washington believed that given the opportunity, Henson would have been a great leader as well.

Reactions to Henson's Role

After Peary and Henson returned from the pole, racist doubters asked Peary why he had taken a black man to the polar region—instead of someone whom they would have considered a more reliable witness. Peary answered by praising Henson's excellent navigational skills. However, he also believed that Henson was not qualified to lead a supply party because of his race. Peary said that only whites could do this job.

In fact, Peary did not always take advantage of Henson's abilities as a navigator. In 1909 many people doubted that Peary had actually reached the North Pole. He claimed to have taken accurate **latitude** readings at the pole, but he had not allowed Henson to check them. As a result, Peary never had firm proof that he had reached the pole.

Nevertheless, Henson's true value to Peary's journey was recognized by Donald MacMILLAN, another member of the party. MacMillan, who was white, returned to base with a supply team before the final journey to the pole. He later became an explorer in his own right. He wrote that Peary

> never would have reached the Pole without Henson. Matt was of more real value than the combined services of all of us. With years of experience, an expert dog driver, a master mechanic, physically strong, most popular with the Eskimos, talking the language like a native, clean, full of grit, he went to the Pole because Peary couldn't get along without him.

Henson's Life After the Pole

Despite the important role he played in Peary's polar expedition, Henson never had the opportunity to become the leader that Booker T. Washington had imagined. His achievements were soon forgotten, and again he was treated as a second-class citizen. He worked as a parking lot attendant and customs clerk in New York City, earning very little money.

His accomplishments as an explorer were ignored until the late 1930s, when he was honored by the Explorers' Club of New York. Later in his life, he received many honors, including personal congratulations from President Dwight D. Eisenhower. The president invited Henson to the White House to celebrate the 45th anniversary of the day Peary's team was said to have reached the North Pole. Henson died the following year, at the age of 88.

SUGGESTED READING Pauline K. Angell, *To the Top of the World: The Story of Peary and Henson* (Rand McNally, 1965); Matthew A. Henson, *A Black Explorer at the North Pole* (reprint, Arno Press, 1969); Bradley Robinson, *Dark Companion* (Medill McBride, 1948); Laurie Rozakis, *Matthew Henson and Robert Peary: The Race for the North Pole* (Blackbirch Press, 1994).

latitude distance north or south of the equator

Matthew Henson's life was marred by poverty and prejudice, but he holds a place of honor in the history of Arctic exploration.

Herbert, Walter William

English
b October 24, 1934; York, England
living
Crossed Arctic Ocean by dog sledge

sledge heavy sled, often mounted on runners, that is pulled over snow or ice

Wally Herbert wanted to lead an Arctic expedition by dog sledge, although the polar region had already been explored with modern vehicles.

dirigible large aircraft filled with a lighter-than-air gas that keeps it aloft; similar to a blimp but with a rigid frame

orbit stable, circular route; one trip around; to revolve around

In 1968 Walter William Herbert became the first person to cross the Arctic Ocean by dog **sledge.** Despite this achievement, Herbert received little recognition for his feat. By that time, both the North Pole and South Pole had been reached, and most of the polar region had been mapped. There was no real scientific purpose for the expedition. Nevertheless, his story is inspiring because of his courage and determination.

A Fascination with the Arctic

Although Herbert did not have a formal education, he had the experience necessary to manage an Arctic expedition. Herbert had gained navigational skills while serving in the British army and improved these skills by working as a surveyor in Antarctica under Sir Vivian Fuchs from 1955 to 1958. During his travels with the New Zealand Antarctic Expedition between 1960 and 1962, Herbert became an expert dog driver. His work with Fuchs caused him to become obsessed with leading an Arctic expedition of his own.

In the early 1900s, when Robert Peary was exploring the Arctic region, newspaper editors would have paid for such an expedition for the sake of the publicity it would bring. At that time, the polar ice was a source of great mystery, and people were eager to learn about it. But by Herbert's day, the public was interested in a new frontier: outer space. Herbert recognized that he had been born 60 or 70 years too late to make a fortune by exploring the Arctic Ocean, but his love of adventure inspired him to go after his dream.

Seeking Support

Although Herbert believed that his journey would be "the culmination of four centuries of human endeavor," he had a difficult time raising enough money for the trip. No one seemed to think that there was much reason to travel across the Arctic Ocean by sledge. It had already been crossed by airplanes and **dirigibles.** Submarines were studying the Arctic Ocean floor, and floating observatories were tracking the weather in the region. Herbert compared his plan to Fuchs's crossing of Antarctica, but Fuchs's journey had been a serious scientific undertaking. Herbert's proposed expedition was seen as personal recreation.

In a small room in his parents' house, Herbert conducted a three-year campaign to obtain the financing he needed. He wrote hundreds of letters to wealthy and influential people, requested support from the Royal Geographical Society without success, and borrowed money to live on. Only when Fuchs put together a committee of supporters did Herbert's project become a practical possibility. Herbert's greatest advantages were his stubborn persistence and his persuasive words. In addition to Fuchs's generous support, Herbert was able to get private sponsors to back his old-fashioned adventure.

Across the Arctic

After five years of planning, Herbert and four companions set out from Point Barrow, Alaska, on February 25, 1968, the same year that Apollo 8 **orbited** the moon. They reached the North Pole on April 5, 1969, and Svalbard on May 29. Two months later, American

astronaut American term for a person who travels into space; literally, "traveler to the stars".

astronaut Neil ARMSTRONG stepped onto the surface of the moon. Herbert and his party made the 3,600-mile journey in 16 months. He later wrote an account of the trip, *Across the Top of the World,* which contains beautiful descriptions of the extraordinary polar landscape. The book gives an honest account of the difficulties he endured to achieve his dream, but it also includes a good deal of self-promotion.

After the expedition, Herbert continued to work in the Arctic region. In 1977 he **circumnavigated** Greenland, using a dog sledge and animal skin boats, another remarkable achievement that would have been widely recognized in an earlier age. In the 1980s, he wrote a well-received book on Peary and his competitor, Dr. Frederick COOK. One reviewer called the volume a "graceful, meticulous, superbly informed and gentlemanly effort." In the book, Herbert declared that Peary's major flaw was that he had held onto the mistaken idea "that fame is the proof of greatness." He argues convincingly in the work that both Peary and Cook faked their claims that they had reached the North Pole. Herbert wrote about the controversy surrounding these explorers with compassion and fairness, probably because he had suffered through some of the same trials himself.

circumnavigate to travel around

SUGGESTED READING Wally Herbert, *Across the Top of the World* (Longmans, Green, 1969).

Herjolfsson, Bjarni

Norse
b 900s; ?
d ?; ?
Sighted eastern coast of North America

Bjarni Herjolfsson was a wealthy Norse shipowner who is credited with having been the first European to sight the eastern coast of North America. His discovery was accidental, the result of his ship being blown off course on the way to Greenland.

Searching for Greenland

Herjolfsson made his living trading between Norway and Iceland. Although he loved the sea, he faithfully spent every other winter on his father's farm in Iceland. In 986 he arrived in Iceland, only to discover that his father had moved to the colony established in Greenland by ERIK THE RED. Herjolfsson persuaded his crew to sail west with him to Greenland even though none of them had ever been there before.

As soon as they left Iceland, their ship was blown off course by stormy weather that lasted several days. When the weather cleared, Herjolfsson and his crew were within sight of an unknown land covered by low, wooded hills. Herjolfsson knew that this was not Greenland, which he had been told was icy and mountainous. He ordered his crew to sail north, and they soon sighted land again. This place was wooded and flat, indicating that they had not yet reached their destination. Three days later, the Norsemen came to a mountainous land covered with **glaciers.** From descriptions he had been given, Herjolfsson concluded that this also was not the site he was seeking. After sailing with a southerly wind for four days, Herjolfsson and his crew finally reached Greenland. Amazingly, they sailed right into the **fjord** where Herjolfsson's father had established his home.

glacier large, slowly moving mass of ice

fjord narrow inlet where the sea meets the shore between steep cliffs

Reports of New Lands

Since little evidence of Herjolfsson's voyage exists, scholars are not sure exactly what parts of the North American coast he saw. The most commonly accepted theory is that the first sighting was part of Newfoundland, the second was the coast of Labrador, and the third was Baffin Island. But some historians place the first viewing as far south as Cape Cod. Whatever the locations of his sightings, most experts agree that Herjolfsson was the first European to see the eastern coast of North America. In fact, it was Herjolfsson's reports of unknown lands that led Leif ERIKSON to mount an expedition to North America some 15 years later.

SUGGESTED READING Rebecca Stefoff, *The Viking Explorers* (Chelsea House Publishers, 1993); C. Keith Wilbur, *Early Explorers of North America* (Chelsea House Publishers, 1996).

For a map of Herjolfsson's route, see the profile of Leif ERIKSON in this volume.

Hernández, Juan Josef Pérez. See *Pérez Hernández, Juan Josef.*

Herodotus of Halicarnassus

Greek
b 484 B.C.?; Bodrum, Turkey
d 420 B.C.?; near Corigliano Calabro, Italy
Traveled throughout Asia Minor, Mediterranean Sea, and North Africa

Herodotus of Halicarnassus was a pioneering historian and geographer.

galley ship with oars and sails, used in ancient and medieval times

Herodotus of Halicarnassus was one of the most widely traveled individuals of the ancient world. His journeys ranged from Babylon in Persia (present-day Iran) to the deserts of Libya in North Africa, and from the northwest shores of the Black Sea to southernmost Egypt. His writings, called the *Histories,* are one of the great works of Western civilization and a primary source of information about life in ancient times. These volumes are filled with detailed observations about the cultural traditions, religions, myths, and politics of the peoples Herodotus encountered during a lifetime of traveling. Some scholars have called Herodotus "the Father of History."

A Fearless Traveler

The exact details of Herodotus's life are uncertain. Most of what is known about him comes from the *Histories.* He was born in Halicarnassus, a Greek colony on what is now the west coast of Turkey. He was well educated, and historians believe that he came from a wealthy family. As a young man, he was forced to leave his homeland by Lygdamis, a cruel dictator who had defeated the colony's government. While he was in exile, Herodotus traveled throughout the Ionian Islands in the Aegean Sea, between Greece and Turkey. He then returned to Halicarnassus to help overthrow Lygdamis. Democracy was restored, but instead of settling down, Herodotus chose to continue his journeys.

Herodotus's decision was bold, since travel in his time was extremely dangerous. Sea voyages were so hazardous that **galleys** rarely left the shore. Wandering the roads may have been even riskier because bandits frequently robbed and killed travelers. However, such dangers did not discourage Herodotus. Historians estimate that in his travels, he covered 1,700 miles from east to west and 1,600 miles from north to south.

Fascinated by the World

The sequence of Herodotus's travels and their original purpose are unclear. At first he may have intended to expand the work of the geographer Hecataeus of Miletus, who had written about the countries bordering the Mediterranean Sea. The first book of the *Histories* deals largely with the war between the Greeks and the Persians, which ended in 478 B.C. However, some historians believe that Herodotus did not originally plan to write about the war, since he did not report some of the most important events of the conflict. The Persian king Darius I conquered the kingdom of Scythia in the region that is now Bulgaria and Romania. However, when Herodotus traveled to the Black Sea region, he made no effort to investigate Darius's invasion route. In his later journeys, though, Herodotus examined and described battlefields in detail.

Whatever his original purpose in writing, Herodotus was fascinated by the physical world. He tried to guess the size of Africa, which he incorrectly believed to be part of the continent of Asia. The entire second volume of the *Histories* is a careful account of his trip to Egypt. He was particularly interested in the Nile River, and he studied the various theories of his day about its source. Although he traveled 700 miles down the river to the site of modern Aswan, he never determined its origin. The source of the Nile remained a mystery for over 2,200 years. It was finally discovered by the English explorers Richard Francis BURTON and John Hanning SPEKE in 1862.

Mixing Fact with Fiction

Herodotus's work reflects not only keen observation but also the ignorance and superstition of his times. As a result, his writings have received criticism as well as praise. He is sometimes called "the Father of Lies" because of the many false stories contained in the *Histories.* Herodotus reported that in Egypt a mare once gave birth to a rabbit. He also told a story of headless creatures, living in western Africa, that had eyes in their breasts. Herodotus doubted such tales himself, but he felt that it was his duty to report them and let his readers decide whether or not the stories were true.

Nevertheless, Herodotus was a great storyteller and traveler. He was one of the first scholars to employ firsthand investigation and research as part of his work, an important milestone in written history. Despite his work's flaws, Herodotus's *Histories* are still read and enjoyed today.

SUGGESTED READING Herodotus, *The Histories,* translated by Aubrey de Selincourt (Penguin, 1954); James S. Romm, *Herodotus* (Yale University Press, 1998); Aubrey de Selincourt, *The World of Herodotus* (Little, Brown, 1962).

Heyerdahl, Thor

Norwegian
b October 6, 1914; Larvik, Norway
living
*Crossed Atlantic and Pacific Oceans on rafts
modeled after ancient vessels*

anthropologist scientist who studies human societies

Thor Heyerdahl is an **anthropologist,** author, and adventurer who dedicated his life to showing that people of ancient cultures could have crossed the oceans long before the Europeans did. To prove his theory, he made three voyages in simple craft that he believed were similar to the boats used by the earliest ocean explorers.

Dreams of Paradise

Heyerdahl is the son of a successful Norwegian businessman. He was raised as an only child, and according to a friend, he spent more time daydreaming than playing with others. He sometimes wrote

Thor Heyerdahl (far right) constructed simple vessels and took them to sea to prove the possibility that ancient sailors had crossed the oceans.

specimen sample of a plant, animal, or mineral, usually collected for scientific study or display

zoology the scientific study of animals

schooner fast, easy-to-maneuver sailing ship with two or more masts and triangular sails

stories about children who ran off to tropical islands—as he himself would do in later life. As a boy, he showed a strong interest in natural history, and he collected **specimens** that included starfish, shells, insects, and snakes. When he went to the hospital to have his appendix removed, he asked the doctors to preserve the organ in a jar of alcohol so that he could add it to his collection. He even constructed a freshwater aquarium and built a small museum for his collection in the courtyard of his house. In 1933 he went to Oslo to study **zoology** and geography at the university.

While in Oslo, Heyerdahl read everything he could about the southern Pacific islands of Polynesia. He persuaded his girlfriend to travel with him to the islands so that they could live simply and naturally. They married on Christmas Eve of 1936 and soon sailed aboard an ocean liner bound for Tahiti. When the couple arrived at their destination, they were adopted by Chief Teriieroo, who helped them learn the ways of the islanders. They then took a **schooner** to the island of Fatu Hiva, where they lived for the next year.

Heyerdahl and his wife quickly found out that Fatu Hiva was not the paradise they had hoped to find. The couple longed for sausages and other Norwegian food. They were bothered by poisonous insects, disease-carrying mosquitoes, and open sores on their feet that the islanders called *fefe.* To make matters worse, bugs began to eat the couple's house, which the islanders had built from green bamboo. The islanders had known that bugs preferred the fresh wood to hardened, mature wood and that their choice of construction would guarantee them repair work. When the schooner arrived to pick up the couple, they were glad to leave. Upon his return to Norway, Heyerdahl wrote: "There is no paradise to be found on earth today."

Kon-Tiki

During his stay in Fatu Hiva, Heyerdahl became interested in the giant stone carvings he saw on the island and the pale, bearded god the Indians called Tiki. The islanders claimed that Tiki had led their people to the islands from the east. Heyerdahl realized that the only eastern place they could have come from was South America. Later, Heyerdahl saw pictures of carvings from British Columbia in Canada that resembled Tiki. From this evidence, Heyerdahl believed that the southern Pacific islands had been populated by two migrations—one from the Malay Peninsula and the other from Peru. He also suggested that the migrations from South America might have been led by Europeans nearly 1,000 years before the time of Christopher COLUMBUS.

To test his theory, Heyerdahl built of logs and bamboo a 45-foot-long raft that he named *Kon-Tiki,* after the Polynesian god. On April 28, 1947, Heyerdahl and five crewmen aboard the raft were towed out of the harbor at Callao, Peru, and set adrift in the Pacific Ocean. Wind and currents carried the raft north along the coast of South America. Then, just south of the equator, the raft turned west into the open ocean. After floating 4,300 miles in 101 days, *Kon-Tiki* and its crew reached the Tuamotu Islands.

Heyerdahl published an account of the voyage in 1948, and his documentary film about the trip won an Academy Award in 1951. Two years later, he published *American Indians in the Pacific,* a controversial book that challenged the accepted theory that the people who had settled the Pacific came only from the west. In 1953 Heyerdahl found remains of the Inca culture in the Galápagos Islands. He later traveled to Easter Island to study its huge stone sculptures.

The Ra *Expedition and Other Travels*

Heyerdahl's second great voyage was inspired by his fascination with the existence of pyramids in both the Middle East and South America. He believed that the South American pyramids were evidence that the ancient Egyptians could have crossed the Atlantic Ocean. In 1969 he set out to prove his theory. Heyerdahl built a papyrus-reed raft, *Ra II,* and traveled on it across the Atlantic from Morocco to Barbados. He claimed that if he could make this voyage, the Egyptians could have done the same.

On a later adventure in the Middle East, he further proved the possibility of sea voyages by ancient peoples. Heyerdahl built a boat out of reeds grown in the Tigris-Euphrates Valley of Asia Minor (the peninsula now occupied by Turkey). He and a crew of 11 sailed the craft through the Persian Gulf and around the Arabian Sea to Pakistan's Indus Valley, a total of 4,200 miles. The vessel was designed to resemble pictures found on ancient Sumerian seals.

Even though some anthropologists reject Heyerdahl's theories, he has won many significant international awards for his voyages. Heyerdahl retired in 1979, stating that he had proved that ancient cultures could have traveled across the oceans. He added that "the burden of proof now rests with those who claim the oceans were necessarily a factor in isolating civilizations."

SUGGESTED READING Thor Heyerdahl, *Early Man and the Ocean* (Doubleday, 1979), *Fatuttiva: Back to Nature on a Pacific Island* (New American Library, 1976), *Kon-Tiki: Across the Ocean by Raft* (Garden City Books, 1950), and *The Ra Expeditions* (New American Library, 1972); Arnold Jacoby, *Señor Kon-Tiki* (Rand McNally, 1967).

Hezeta, Bruno de

Spanish
b 1750?; Bilbao, Spain
d ?; ?
Discovered mouth of Columbia River

New Spain region of Spanish colonial empire that included the areas now occupied by Mexico, Florida, Texas, New Mexico, Arizona, California, and various Caribbean islands

latitude distance north or south of the equator

scurvy disease caused by a lack of vitamin C and once a major cause of death among sailors; symptoms include internal bleeding, loosened teeth, and extreme fatigue

In 1775 Bruno de Hezeta, a Spanish naval officer, led an expedition along the western coast of North America as far north as what is now Nootka Sound, off Vancouver Island. On his return voyage, he became the first European to find the mouth of what was later to be called the Columbia River. However, he did not enter it because of strong currents and an ailing crew. Seventeen years after Hezeta's discovery, the American merchant captain Robert GRAY managed to sail into the river.

Claiming Territory

Hezeta arrived in San Blas, **New Spain,** the headquarters for Spanish naval operations in California, in 1774. At the time, it was rumored that Russia was expanding eastward from what are now the Aleutian Islands. The Spanish believed that they could stop Russian advances in the area by establishing a presence along the northwest coast of North America. In 1775 Hezeta was put in charge of three ships and instructed to sail to a **latitude** of 65° north. He was to avoid foreign settlements, go ashore to claim land wherever it was safe to do so, and establish friendly relations with the Indians. Juan Francisco de la BODEGA Y QUADRA was appointed commander of one of the expedition's three ships.

On March 16, 1775, the party left San Blas. By mid-July, Hezeta had reached the coast of what is now the state of Washington, where he went ashore to take possession of the land. At this point, most of his crew was sick with **scurvy,** and he decided to turn to the south, even though he had only reached a latitude of 49° north. Bodega y Quadra proceeded north, eventually reaching 65° north latitude.

Sighting the Columbia River

On the evening of August 17, while sailing down the North American coast, Hezeta sighted a large bay between two cliffs. Hezeta attempted to enter the bay, but the current was too strong, and he had to give up. He decided not to land nearby; his men were so weak that he feared that they would not be able to raise the ship's heavy anchor once it had been dropped. Hezeta believed that the bay was the "mouth of some great river or of some passage to another sea." It was actually the mouth of the river now called the Columbia. He named it Bay of the Assumption of Our Lady after a feast day celebrated on August 15. Hezeta charted the river mouth based on what he could see from outside the bay. The waterway later appeared on maps as "Entrada de Hezeta," meaning Hezeta's Entryway.

Bruno de Hezeta was a cautious commander who chose to turn back rather than risk unknown waters with a sick crew. Though most of the glory from his expedition would go to Bodega y Quadra, Hezeta had made the most significant discovery of the voyage.

SUGGESTED READING Bruno de Hezeta, *For Honor and Country: The Diary of Bruno de Hezeta* (Western Imprints, 1985).

Hillary, Edmund Percival

New Zealander
b July 20, 1919; Auckland, New Zealand
living
Explored Antarctica and Himalaya

Sir Edmund Percival Hillary is best known as being part of the first team to reach the summit of Mount Everest, which was considered the world's highest peak at the time. He also led an important expedition to Antarctica in 1957. The following year, Hillary became the first person since English explorer Robert Falcon SCOTT to reach the South Pole by an overland route.

The Mountaineer

Hillary was born on New Zealand's North Island and raised on a small farm in the village of Tuakau, south of the city of Auckland. He was a good student and recalled that he filled his time "with reading and dreaming. Books of adventure became my greatest support—Edgar Rice Burroughs, Rider Haggard, John Buchan. . . . In my imagination . . . I was always the hero." Hillary's first chance to fulfill his dreams of adventure came at the age of 20, when he climbed Mount Oliver on New Zealand's South Island. He continued his mountaineering, and in 1950 he traveled in the Austrian and Swiss Alps.

In May 1951, Hillary made his first of many trips to the Himalaya. At the end of the summer, he was invited to join the British expedition to climb to the top of Mount Everest. However, icefalls and avalanches prevented the team from reaching their goal. Hillary returned to the mountain in 1953 as part of a British team led by Colonel John Hunt. On May 29, Hillary and a Nepalese Sherpa tribesman named Tenzing Norgay became the first people ever to reach the summit of Mount Everest. Britain's Queen Elizabeth II knighted Hillary for his achievement.

Exploring Antarctica

In 1955 Hillary was invited to lead an expedition to Antarctica. His mission was to support the voyage of Dr. Vivian FUCHS, who wanted to cross the continent from the Weddell Sea to the Ross Sea. Fuchs planned to make scientific observations along the way. Hillary was to establish a base on the Ross Sea and set up supply depots along the route to the pole.

Later that year, Hillary accompanied Fuchs on a trip to the Weddell Sea. After spending over a month there with their ship trapped in ice, they reached the Filchner Ice Shelf and set up Shackleton Base. Hillary returned to New Zealand in March 1956 and spent the next eight months lecturing and raising money for the expedition to

Sir Edmund Hillary was part of the first team to reach the summit of Mount Everest.

surveyor one who makes precise measurements of a location's geography

geologist scientist who studies the earth's natural history

meteorology the scientific study of weather and weather forecasting

glacier large, slowly moving mass of ice

plateau high, flat area of land

cross the polar continent. On December 21, he and his party departed for Antarctica aboard the ship *Endeavor.* His team included three **surveyors,** two **geologists,** an expert in biology and **meteorology,** three New Zealand Air Force pilots, and five other experienced scientists.

The expedition first established Scott Base at McMurdo Sound in the Ross Sea. Using planes to fly in materials, they set up the first supply depot at the foot of Skelton **Glacier** by the end of January 1957. The group then journeyed by dog team to establish a second depot on the polar **plateau,** about 290 miles from Scott Base.

Hillary's party planned to use tractors to set up depots closer to the South Pole. However, while testing a tractor in March, Hillary almost fell into a deep, snow-covered crack in the ice. When his team finally left camp, they covered only 12 miles on the first day. The explorers realized that they would have to prepare themselves better to deal with the conditions in the polar region. After returning to base camp, they spent most of the winter adapting their tractors and other equipment so that the machines would function in deep snow and temperatures as low as –60° Fahrenheit.

Reaching the South Pole

When the weather warmed, Hillary again tried to establish supply depots closer to the pole. He eventually set up five depots. The last one, called Depot 700, was 500 miles from the pole. At this point, Hillary decided to try to reach the pole himself. His team headed south from Depot 700 on December 20, 1957. They traveled for two extremely difficult weeks through soft snow, abandoning all but the most essential supplies.

On January 4, 1958, Hillary reached the South Pole with only 20 extra gallons of fuel. Hillary's team also identified many of the dangerous areas and established a route from McMurdo Sound to the pole. Fuchs joined them at the pole on January 20. During their two-month return trip to Scott Base, Fuchs performed a series of measurements to determine the depth of the ice layer. The explorers left Antarctica in March 20. For his accomplishments, Hillary won *Argosy* magazine's Explorer of the Year Award in 1959.

Hillary's Later Adventures

After his historic journey to the South Pole, Hillary organized a Himalayan expedition to look for the legendary creature called the yeti—also known as the abominable snowman. He returned to Antarctica in 1967 to climb Mount Herschel on the western shore of the Ross Sea. He then traveled for 16 days over unstable sea ice and around deep cracks to obtain rock samples from the north shore of Robertson Bay. Hillary undertook this dangerous journey to assist Dr. Larry Harrington, who was studying the theory that the continents slowly drift over the earth's surface.

Hillary later wrote several books about his experiences. At the end of his 1975 autobiography, he remarked: "I can see a mighty river to challenge; a hospital to build; a peaceful mountain valley with an unknown pass to cross; an untouched Himalayan summit and a shattered Southern glacier—yes, there is plenty left to do."

Hind, Henry Youle

Canadian
b June 1, 1823; Nottingham, England
d August 9, 1908; Windsor, Nova Scotia
Explored Canadian plains and Labrador

geologist scientist who studies the earth's natural history

geology the scientific study of the earth's natural history

SUGGESTED READING Pat Booth, *Edmund Hillary: The Life of a Legend* (Moa Beckett, 1993); Sir Vivian Fuchs and Sir Edmund Hillary, *The Crossing of Antarctica* (Little, Brown, 1958); Sir Edmund Hillary, *High in the Thin Cold Air* (Doubleday, 1962) and *Nothing Venture, Nothing Win* (G. P. Putnam, 1975).

Henry Youle Hind was a **geologist** on the Red River Exploring Expedition of 1857, which surveyed the territory between Lake Superior and the Selkirk Settlement (present-day Winnipeg). The following year, he was put in charge of this expedition, examining much of what is now southern Manitoba and Saskatchewan. From his travels, Hind concluded that the fertile Canadian plains could support thousands of people. His work eventually led to the settlement of what would become the Canadian provinces.

Surveying the Canadian West

In 1857 Britain's Hudson's Bay Company controlled the vast expanse of territory west of Hudson Bay. This land was unknown to anyone except the company's fur traders, who refused to share their valuable information about the region with outsiders. However, the company's trading license was due to be renewed in 1859, and Canada and Britain were interested in opening the territory to settlement. The parliaments of both countries decided to organize explorations to learn more about the area. The stated purpose of the Canadian expedition was "to ascertain the practicability of establishing an emigrant route between Lake Superior and the Selkirk Settlement, and to acquire some knowledge of the natural capabilities and resources of the Valley of the Red River and the Saskatchewan."

The man chosen to head the Canadian Red River Exploring Expedition of 1857 was George Gladman, a former official of the Hudson's Bay Company. However, the most inspiring leader in the party was its geologist, Henry Hind, a professor of chemistry and **geology** at Trinity College in Toronto. In 1858 Gladman was removed from his post. Hind was put in charge of a party whose mission was to explore the Assiniboine and Saskatchewan Rivers, which formed the southern and northern borders of the area to be studied.

Swarms of Insects

Although Hind and his men did not suffer as much as some earlier explorers, they experienced their share of hardships. They occasionally missed a meal, and their food was often unappetizing. The explorers also encountered dangerous rapids on their canoe trips along the rivers and faced the danger of attacks by hostile Indians. However, their greatest annoyances were mosquitoes and grasshoppers. In one passage in his report, Hind described spotting some large and delicious-looking wild raspberries that were surrounded by a swarm of mosquitoes. He wrote:

> *I offered the Cree guide a piece of tobacco for a tin cup full of the raspberries, he tried to win it, but after a short struggle with these terrible insects he rushed from the hillside and buried his face in the smoke of the fire we had lit in the hope of expelling them from the neighborhood of our camp.*

Hind also reported that the grasshoppers would

attack any substances presented to them, even such indigestible articles as leather, travelling bags, woollen garments, saddle girths, and harness. In a few minutes they ate the varnish from the leather case of a telescope I left on the ground in 1858, and so disfigured a valise that the owner . . . could not recognize it after it had lain ten minutes on the grass.

Despite these troubles, Hind seems to have enjoyed his mission.

Opening the Door to Western Settlement

From his own observations and his discussions with settlers who were already farming the land, Hind concluded that the southern Canadian prairies could support thousands of settlers. He even laid out a combined land and water route that could bring settlers from Liverpool, England, to Fort Garry on the Red River in just 22 days. His only significant error was in underestimating the number of people the land could support. Hind mistakenly believed in the myth of a Great American Desert at the center of the continent. This idea had first been proposed by Zebulon PIKE in 1810 and made popular by Stephen Harriman LONG in 1823. Hind therefore suggested that the area of the Saskatchewan River valley farther north had greater potential for farming than the prairies.

After the expedition, Hind was unable to raise funds for further exploration of the South Saskatchewan River and the Rocky Mountains, so he turned his attention to the east. In 1861 Hind explored the rivers of Labrador with his brother. He then made a geological survey of New Brunswick in 1864. From 1869 to 1871, he surveyed gold fields in Nova Scotia. Later, while exploring northern Labrador, he discovered new cod-fishing areas. Hind retired from exploration in 1890 to become president of a religious school in Nova Scotia.

SUGGESTED READING W. L. Morton, *Henry Youle Hind, 1823-1908* (University of Toronto Press, 1980).

Hipparchus

Greek
b 165 B.C.?; Nicaea (now in Turkey)
d 127 B.C.?; Rhodes, Greece?
Refined Eratosthenes' grid system for maps

Hipparchus is widely considered to be the greatest of all ancient astronomers. He improved ERATOSTHENES' system of grid lines for maps, and he discovered why the measured positions of the stars appear to change slightly over time. He also compiled a catalog of over 850 stars and developed an early form of trigonometry, the branch of mathematics that deals with the characteristics of triangles. In addition, Hipparchus computed the length of a year to within six and one-half minutes.

Mapping the Earth

Hipparchus was greatly influenced by the ancient Greek belief that the universe is a logical, orderly place. His determination to seek order and balance was reflected in his descriptions of the natural world. For example, he believed that each mass on the surface of the earth must be balanced by a similar mass in the opposite hemisphere. According to this theory, undiscovered landmasses would exist in the Southern Hemisphere, balancing the known lands of the Northern Hemisphere.

Hipparchus's contributions to mapmaking have influenced geography and exploration from the time of ancient Greece to the present.

longitude distance east or west of an imaginary line on the earth's surface; in 1884 most nations agreed to draw the line through Greenwich, England

latitude distance north or south of the equator

Hipparchus's most important contribution to world exploration was his improvement on the global grid system first devised by Eratosthenes, an ancient Greek geographer. Eratosthenes had developed a system of parallel grid lines for maps by dividing the sphere of the earth into 60 rectangles. But he drew each of these lines through an important place in the ancient world, so the rectangles on the map were not all the same size.

Hipparchus used his knowledge of mathematics and astronomy to divide the sphere of the earth into 360 equal parts. He argued that the lines should be set in relation to astronomical events, which appear the same from all places on the earth. For example, he proposed that the **longitude** of a place on the earth could be calculated from the exact times when a solar eclipse began and ended, as viewed from that place.

Earlier geographers had already used parallel lines of **latitude** to divide the earth into zones. According to these geographers, the length of the longest day of each year was the same for all locations within a zone. Hipparchus refined this system as well, estimating a place's latitude from the ratio of the lengths of the longest day and the shortest day at that location.

Using Hipparchus's system, any place on earth could be located by giving its longitude and latitude, a method still used by modern geographers. Some historians believe that PTOLEMY, not Hipparchus, invented the terms *latitude* and *longitude*. However, Hipparchus created the evenly spaced grid system that those terms describe.

Movement in the Heavens

Hipparchus is also well known for discovering an occurrence that he called "the procession of the equinoxes." For many years, astronomers had noticed that the measured positions of the stars seemed to shift over time, but they could not explain why. Hipparchus reasoned that it was not the stars that moved, but the ground from which they were observed—the earth. He compared his observations with those of earlier Babylonian astronomers. Hipparchus correctly concluded that the earth wobbles slightly as it rotates on its axis.

SUGGESTED READING Hipparchus, *The Geographical Fragments of Hipparchus* (University of London, Athlone Press, 1960).

Ho, Cheng. See *Zheng He*.

Hornemann, Friedrich Konrad

German
b September 1772; Hildesheim, Prussia (now Germany)
d February 1801?; Nigeria?
Explored North Africa

Friedrich Konrad Hornemann, one of the earliest explorers of North Africa, was the first European to travel across the Sahara from Egypt to Hausaland (in what is now northern Nigeria). He explored southern Libya, where he visited the community of Murzuch in the Fezzan region. The information he collected there would later help the British to establish trade in that part of Africa.

Exploring Northern Africa

Hornemann came from a long line of German clergy and studied for the ministry. However, he was never able to let go of his childhood dream of exploring Africa. On the night before his final examinations in 1795, he left the **seminary** to apply for a position as an explorer. He was accepted by the newly formed African Association of London on the condition that he learn the Arabic language. In 1797 he was sent to Cairo, Egypt, and instructed to join a trading **caravan** that would take him southwest to Hausaland. Hornemann's departure from Cairo was postponed by a **plague** that caused the city to be quarantined—no one could enter or leave Cairo until the plague ended. But by September 1798, he left with a caravan bound for the Fezzan region of southwestern Libya.

To avoid arousing suspicion and hostility among his traveling companions, Hornemann disguised himself as an Arab. He accompanied the caravan to the oasis towns of Siwa and Aujila. Then he continued southwest to Temissa in Fezzan, arriving in Murzuch in November. During the six months that he spent in that lively trading community, he studied its culture and economy thoroughly. After leaving Murzuch, Hornemann decided to travel north to the city of Tripoli (now in Libya) to send his journals to London. He was planning a trip south to the Niger River and feared that the journals might be lost if he failed to return.

Mysterious Fate

Unfortunately, Hornemann's concerns were proven true. He left Tripoli in December 1799 and was never heard from again. The African Association later learned that he had returned to Murzuch and may have even reached Timbuktu and Lake Chad. Some historians believe that he died in Nigeria in February 1801, possibly of **dysentery.** However, one source told British officials in Tripoli that the explorer had been seen in Nigeria in 1803. To this day, no one really knows what became of Hornemann.

SUGGESTED READING *Missions to the Niger; The Journal of Friedrich Hornemann's Travels from Cairo to Murzuk in the Years 1797-98; The Letters of Major Alexander Gordon Laing, 1824-26,* volume I (University Press, 1964).

Hongzu, Xu. *See Xu Hongzu.*

Houghton, Daniel

Irish
b 1740?; ?
d 1791; West Africa
Explored course of Niger River

In 1790 Daniel Houghton, a retired officer of the British army, sailed from England to the west coast of Africa, determined to discover the course of the Niger River. He experienced a series of misfortunes while traveling to Timbuktu, in what is now Mali, and he died on the way, under mysterious circumstances. The Scottish explorer Mungo PARK traveled through the same area years later. Park concluded that Houghton had traveled farther inland than any European at that time.

Houghton spent part of his youth and a portion of his army career in Morocco. He also served in a fort off the coast of Senegal. After retiring from the army with the rank of major, Houghton turned to exploring. He made plans to chart the still-undiscovered course of the Niger River and presented them to the African Association, a British organization founded by the naturalist Sir Joseph BANKS to promote exploration in the interior of Africa. Houghton wanted to travel east from the Atlantic coast of Africa as far as Timbuktu and Houssa and then return across the Sahara. The association supported his plan, and Houghton set off from England on October 16, 1790.

After he arrived on the west coast of Africa, Houghton followed the Gambia River for several hundred miles. He then prepared for a long overland journey by hiring a guide and buying a horse and five donkeys. However, the expedition quickly became dangerous. A group of river merchants feared that Houghton was a potential competitor, and they plotted to kill him. Houghton, who had learned some of the local language during his youth, overheard their conversation and managed to escape with his life. Later a fire destroyed a hut next to the one in which he was sleeping. During the commotion, Houghton's interpreter fled with a horse and three donkeys. News of these and other dramatic incidents reached Britain in a series of written reports that Houghton sent periodically to the African Association.

Despite these problems, Houghton continued toward Timbuktu, bribing some local merchants to guide him. The merchants took the gun and the tobacco he offered them and then led him in the opposite direction. When Houghton finally realized that he had been deceived, the merchants robbed him and fled. Houghton died there, either from wounds or from starvation.

Neither Houghton nor the journals from his long trip were ever discovered. However, prior to his death, he managed to determine the course of the upper Niger River. He accurately reported that it runs eastward, a fact previously unknown to European geographers and later confirmed by Park.

SUGGESTED READING Brian Gardner, *The Quest for Timbuctoo* (Harcourt, Brace, and World, 1969).

Hsia-K'o, Hsü. See *Xu Hongzu.*

Hsüan-chuang. See *Xuan Zang.*

Hsüan-tsang. See *Xuan Zang.*

Hsü Hsia-K'o. See *Xu Hongzu.*

Hsü Hung-tsu. See *Xu Hongzu.*

Hudson, Henry

English
b ?; ?
d 1611; Hudson Bay, Canada
Explored Arctic Ocean, eastern coast of North America, Hudson River, and Hudson Bay

Northeast Passage water route connecting the Atlantic Ocean and Pacific Ocean along the Arctic coastline of Europe and Asia

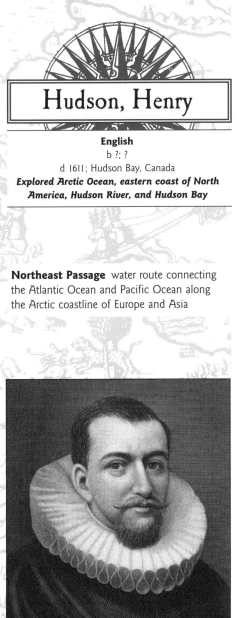

Hudson's final crossing of the Atlantic Ocean took 10 weeks—an unusually long time—and was perhaps a sign that problems with his crew began early in the voyage.

mutiny rebellion by a ship's crew against the officers

Northwest Passage water route connecting the Atlantic Ocean and Pacific Ocean through the Arctic islands of northern Canada

The English navigator Henry Hudson made four voyages of discovery in an attempt to find a northern route from Europe to Asia. His last two trips led him to North America, where he was the first European to sail up the Hudson River in what is now New York. He was also the first to enter Canada's Hudson Bay.

Search for the Northeast Passage

Nothing is known of Hudson's life until his final four years, when he emerged as one of the world's great explorers. By 1607 he had established a reputation as a skilled navigator. That year he was hired by England's Muscovy Company to sail across the North Pole to China in search of a **Northeast Passage.** No one knew for sure what the pole was like in summer, but respected geographers thought that it might be warm enough to keep the polar sea free of ice. If Hudson could not get through the ice, he was instructed to sail east to China on the "warm sea."

In April 1607, Hudson left England aboard the ship *Hopewell.* With him were his young son, John, and 10 crewmen. They sailed north along the east coast of Greenland until they were stopped by ice just south of the pole, proving that the Arctic Ocean remained frozen in summer. Their voyage had taken them farther north than any Europeans had previously sailed. The vessel then turned east and proceeded to Spitsbergen, a Norwegian island in the Arctic Ocean. Confused by inaccurate charts, bad weather, and icebergs, Hudson turned back and reached England in mid-September. Though Hudson had not found a Northeast Passage to Asia, the voyage provided English ships with access to the profitable whaling industry off Spitsbergen.

The English Muscovy Company again sent Hudson out to search for a trade route to Asia the following year. This time he was instructed to sail along the north coast of Russia. He reached the island of Novaya Zemlya and then spent 10 days trying unsuccessfully to find a passage through the island. When his crew threatened **mutiny,** Hudson headed for home. The crewmen forced him to sign a document saying that he had freely chosen to return, although actually, he had wanted to continue. By giving in to his crew, Hudson started a dangerous practice that would become a more serious problem on his later voyages.

A Change of Course

After two failures, the Muscovy Company was not interested in sponsoring another expedition by Hudson. But in 1609 the Dutch East India Company hired him to try once again to find a Northeast Passage. In a ship called the *Half Moon,* Hudson and a crew of English and Dutch sailors headed northeast into the icy waters of the Barents Sea. The Dutch sailors, who were used to sailing in tropical waters, were shocked by the cold weather, thick fog, and violent storms they encountered. By May there was talk of mutiny. Once again Hudson gave in to the crew's demands and turned back.

Hudson may have welcomed the change in plans. He was eager to test the theory of his friend Captain John SMITH of the Jamestown colony in Virginia. Smith believed that a **Northwest Passage** to Asia

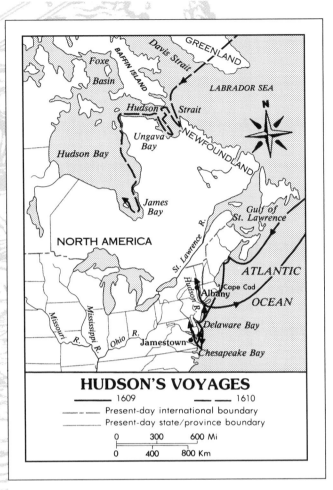

HUDSON'S VOYAGES
———— 1609   ———— 1610
——·——— Present-day international boundary
————— Present-day state/province boundary

0		300		600 Mi
0	400		800 Km	

On his last voyage, Hudson was instructed to see if "any passage might be found to the other ocean called the South Sea."

mate assistant to the commander of a ship

might lie somewhere north of the Virginia colony. After the near mutiny, Hudson convinced the crew to sail west across the Atlantic Ocean instead of heading home. By mid-July they had reached the coast of Maine.

Hudson sailed south to what is now Chesapeake Bay and then turned north to look for a passage to the Pacific Ocean. He explored the mouth of Delaware Bay, but he decided that it was too full of sandbars to be the passage he was seeking. Sailing up the coast of what later became New Jersey, he reached the mouth of a huge open bay on September 2, 1609. It was the lower bay of today's New York harbor. The Italian navigator Giovanni da VERRAZANO had sailed into this bay in 1524, but no one had followed up on his discovery. From the strength of the current, Hudson realized that he was at the mouth of some great river or strait. He hoped that this was the Northwest Passage. For several days, the crew fished and explored the surrounding shores. They were impressed by the large number of fish and by the beauty of the land. They also met the local Indians, who came aboard dressed in clothes made of fur and feathers to trade with the Europeans.

Hudson sailed on and eventually anchored off the coast of a tree-covered island that the Indians called Manna-hatta (present-day Manhattan). He then headed north up the river that now bears his name. After dropping anchor near what is now Albany, he sent a smaller boat farther upriver to check the water's depth. He soon learned that the river became too shallow for his ship to pass. Hudson realized that this was not the Northwest Passage. Although he was disappointed, the voyage was not a failure. Within a year, the Dutch colonized Manhattan and claimed the Hudson River valley.

Setting Out One Last Time

Hudson arrived in England in early November and sent a report to the Dutch East India Company in Amsterdam. He hoped to travel there later, but the English authorities were impressed with the news of his voyage and would not let him go. Instead a group of wealthy English merchants sponsored another Hudson expedition to America to locate a passage to Asia. Hudson was again joined by his son and by Robert Juet, his **mate** on previous voyages. Also on board his ship, the *Discovery,* was a sailor named Abacuk Prickett, who recorded the details of the trip in his journal. Prickett wrote that Juet made fun of Hudson's hope to reach Java by February.

On June 25, Hudson entered the strait, now named after him, that lies between Baffin Island and the Canadian province of Québec. It was too early in the year to pass through the strait, which was still full of ice and fog. As the *Discovery* sailed back and forth between what is now Ungava Bay and Baffin Island, the dreary landscape frightened the crew. Like Hudson's previous

In what is now New York, Hudson and his crew traded with the Indians for tobacco, corn, beans, and oysters.

scurvy disease caused by a lack of vitamin C and once a major cause of death among sailors; symptoms include internal bleeding, loosened teeth, and extreme fatigue

crews, they refused to go any farther, but this time Hudson persuaded them to proceed.

Following the Wrong Path

Hudson pushed on against the current and the ice flowing from the west. He took this flow of water to mean that the Pacific Ocean was nearby. Confident that he was on the right path, he turned south into Hudson Bay. But his hopes were crushed when he encountered the marshy waters of the south shore of James Bay, the southern extension of Hudson Bay. Unable to accept the fact that he would not find the Northwest Passage by traveling farther, Hudson sailed aimlessly for weeks. Convinced that Hudson had lost his mind, the crew confronted their commander. Hudson reacted angrily and accused Juet of mutiny. He replaced Juet with Robert BYLOT.

Hudson planned to spend the winter in James Bay. He dropped anchor on the south shore, where the ship became locked in ice until spring. The winter was long and hard, and the crew had barely enough food to survive. To add to the misery, most of the men had **scurvy.** When spring came, the men were so close to starvation that they ate frogs and lichen, a type of fungus, to stay alive. By June the *Discovery* was able to sail, but supplies would last only two more weeks. Nevertheless, Hudson told his crew that he planned to

shallop open boat used in shallow waters and equipped with oars, sails, or both

continue the search for the Northwest Passage. On June 22 or 23, a full mutiny broke out, led by Juet and another crew member. The men put Hudson, his son, and six others into a **shallop** towed by the *Discovery,* saying they wanted to search the ship for food they believed Hundson was hoarding. Then the rebels cut the shallop loose. Hudson and the others probably died from starvation and exposure to the cold. The exact details of what happened to them are not known.

Hudson's tragic death does not overshadow his many accomplishments. He was a skilled and courageous navigator, although his lack of leadership skills led to his ultimate failure. In just four years, he added immensely to the world's knowledge of areas as widespread as the Arctic Ocean and the Hudson River valley.

SUGGESTED READING Donald S. Johnson, *Charting the Sea of Darkness: The Four Voyages of Henry Hudson* (Kodansha International, 1995); Louis B. Wright and Elaine W. Fowler, editors, *West and by North: North America Seen Through the Eyes of Its Seafaring Discoverers* (Delacorte, 1971).

Huien-tsiang. See *Xuan Zang.*

Humboldt, Alexander von

German
b September 14, 1769; Berlin, Prussia (now Germany)
d May 6, 1859; Berlin, Prussia (now Germany)
Explored South America and Mexico

geology the scientific study of the earth's natural history

meteorology the scientific study of weather and weather forecasting

zoology the scientific study of animals

botany the scientific study of plants

A man of many interests and skills, Baron Friedrich Wilhelm Karl Alexander von Humboldt was both a great naturalist and a great explorer. Between 1800 and 1804, he journeyed more than 6,000 miles throughout Peru, Ecuador, Venezuela, and Colombia. He also traveled widely in Mexico, Cuba, and the United States. He explored remote rain forests and the great river system of Venezuela, climbing some of the highest volcanic mountains in the world. Humboldt also discovered the cold Pacific Ocean current that bears his name. Unlike earlier explorers of South America, Humboldt sought knowledge, not gold or silver. Wherever he traveled, he kept detailed notebooks filled with statistics and measurements, maps, sketches, and observations. The information he gathered enriched the sciences of **geology, meteorology, zoology, botany,** and geography. Famous all over the world, he was considered one of the great thinkers of his time.

Early Interest in Nature

Alexander von Humboldt was born at his family's estate just north of Berlin. His father, an army officer, died when Humboldt was nine years old. He and his older brother Wilhelm were raised by his mother. A curious, energetic child, Humboldt called his home "the Castle of Boredom" and spent much of his time exploring nearby forests and collecting rocks and flowers. He also enjoyed reading, particularly books by explorers such as Charles-Marie de LA CONDAMINE, James BRUCE, and Captain James COOK.

Humboldt studied at various universities, but the greatest influence on his future career came from the naturalist and explorer

Alexander von Humboldt's exploration of South America was only one episode in a long life of innovation and fame.

specimen sample of a plant, animal, or mineral, usually collected for scientific study or display

llanos vast grassy plains of South America

tributary stream or river that flows into a larger stream or river

cacao seeds that are used to make chocolate

Johann Georg Adam FORSTER. On a trip to England in 1790, Forster taught the eager Humboldt about art and nature. Humboldt later studied at a mining school in Saxony. He joined the school's staff in 1792 and was quickly promoted to chief inspector. By the age of 27, Humboldt was one of the most successful men in Prussia. He worked long hours and had an extensive knowledge of the world. He was also popular, known for his sense of humor, friendliness, and charm.

First Explorations

When his mother died in 1796, Humboldt inherited a fortune, enabling him to quit his job and pursue his two great loves—natural history and exploration. The next year, he planned expeditions to Italy and Egypt, but war in those lands forced him to cancel both trips. In 1799 Humboldt and his friend, botanist Aimé Bonpland, set out to explore the interior of South America.

The two men landed at Cumaná, Venezuela, and proceeded through the rain forest. They stopped at Caripe to study the Chayma Indians and collect plant **specimens** before going on to Caracas. Humboldt and Bonpland then journeyed to the land between the Orinoco and Amazon Rivers and began the first scientific exploration of these lands by Europeans. Traveling at night to avoid the extreme heat, they first crossed the great **llanos.** Humboldt described the region as a "vast and profound solitude" that "looked like an ocean covered with seaweed." After reaching a village called Villa de San Fernando, they went east on the Apure River until it met the Orinoco River. They followed the Orinoco upriver to the Great Cataracts (the present-day Atures and Miapures Rapids).

Hardships Rewarded

Although little was known of the Orinoco River beyond this point, Humboldt and Bonpland continued on their journey. They hoped to reach the upper Orinoco, find its source, and explore its **tributaries.** Along the way, the party battled the currents of the Orinoco, endured endless rain storms, and had "hands and faces swollen by mosquito bites." They traveled as far as San Carlos on the Río Negro, at the border of Brazil and Venezuela, living on bananas, water, and a little rice. By this time, Humboldt had collected 25 creatures, including tropical birds and 8 monkeys—all sharing the boat with the 13 people in the party.

On the return trip to the northern coast of Venezuela, the members of the expedition faced even worse conditions as they traveled along the Casiquiare Canal. The heat was overwhelming, and a thick layer of insects covered the canal. When the men ran out of supplies, they ate ants and dry **cacao** to survive. Despite these hardships, Humboldt accomplished one of his main goals. He

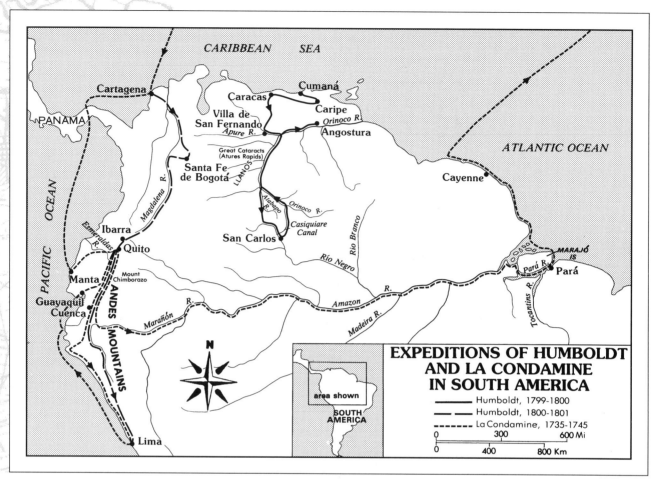

Alexander von Humboldt and Charles-Marie de La Condamine were two of the outstanding scientific explorers of South America.

latitude distance north or south of the equator

longitude distance east or west of an imaginary line on the earth's surface; in 1884 most nations agreed to draw the line through Greenwich, England

plateau high, flat area of land

proved that the Casiquiare Canal was a natural waterway connecting two large river systems, the Orinoco and the Amazon. It is the world's only natural canal of this kind. The expedition ended on June 13, 1800, at the mouth of the Orinoco in Angostura (present-day Ciudad Bolívar). Humboldt had measured the **latitude** and **longitude** of over 50 specific places and gathered data on climate and plant geography. He also collected about 12,000 plant specimens, many of them new to science.

On to the Andes

In late 1800, Humboldt set out on a two-year expedition to the Andes Mountains of Colombia, Ecuador, and Peru. On the trip that would earn him international fame, he first traveled through 500 miles of uninhabited forests along Colombia's Magdalena River. He then climbed 9,000 feet to the **plateau** of Bogotá and received a hero's welcome at the city of Santa Fe de Bogotá (present-day Bogotá). He next crossed a treacherous, snow-covered pass over the eastern end of the Andes on his way to Quito, Ecuador. Humboldt spent six months exploring major volcanoes of the area, collecting data that would change the field of geology.

His group then followed the route used by La Condamine from Quito to Peru. While traveling along the Amazon River, the party crossed the magnetic equator, the spot where the needle on a compass points neither north nor south. Humboldt's measurement of the earth's magnetic intensity at this point was used by geographers for the next 50 years.

The expedition ended in Lima, Peru, on October 22, 1802. There Humboldt tried to determine the reason for the dry weather pattern along western South America. In the process, he discovered a cold ocean current that flows north along the west coasts of Chile and Peru. It was named the Humboldt Current in his honor.

To Mexico and Beyond

Humboldt headed for the city of Acapulco in March 1803 and spent the next year traveling around Mexico. He made a detailed map of the country and researched its economy and politics. Before returning to Europe, he made a detour to the United States to meet President Thomas Jefferson, a man whom Humboldt greatly admired. Humboldt arrived in Philadelphia in May 1804 and was welcomed by the American scientific community. In Washington, D.C., he charmed everyone he met and used his new maps to help Jefferson determine the border between the United States and Mexico. On June 30, Humboldt left for France.

Humboldt spent many years in Paris, publishing the writings from his expeditions. He made one last expedition in 1829, traveling across Siberia on a mining survey for Czar Nicholas I of Russia. When he died in 1859, Humboldt had finished five volumes of a work he called *Cosmos,* which he had intended to be a complete record of the physical world.

Humboldt's explorations of South America offered new insights and observations about the continent. Today statues honor his memory around the world, and many cities and geographical features bear his name.

SUGGESTED READING Douglas Botting, *Humboldt and Cosmos* (Harper and Row, 1973); Lotte Kellner, *Alexander von Humboldt* (Oxford University Press, 1963); Helmut de Terra, *Humboldt: The Life and Times of Alexander von Humboldt, 1769–1859* (Octagon Books, 1979); Victor Wolfgang von Hagen, *South America Called Them: Explorations of the Great Naturalists* (Knopf, 1945).

Hume, Hamilton

Australian
b June 19, 1797; Parramatta, Australia
d April 19, 1873; Yass, Australia
*Discovered Murray River;
discovered Darling River with Charles Sturt*

bush land that has not been cleared or settled, usually covered with short trees and other plants

From 1814 to 1824, Hamilton Hume explored the region south and west of Sydney, Australia. His extensive experience in the Australian **bush** led to the discovery of the Murray River in 1824. Five years later, he joined Captain Charles STURT on an expedition across the Blue Mountains. During their journey, they found the Darling River near the site of present-day Burke.

Hamilton Hume was born in 1797 near Sydney, New South Wales. His father, Andrew Hume, worked as a supervisor of prisoners and had a bad reputation. Beginning at the age of 17, Hamilton spent 10 years exploring the area near his home, both on his own and as a government guide. He visited the Berrima and Bong Bong districts, the Sutton Forest, the Goulburn River, Lake Bathurst, Jervis Bay, the Yass Plains, and the Clyde River.

By 1824 Hume was very familiar with the unsettled regions of his homeland. That year he teamed up with William Hovell, a former

Hamilton Hume carried on a personal feud for 50 years with William Hovell, his partner in the exploration of Australia.

sailor, to explore the mountain ranges between Sydney and Port Phillip Bay. On October 22, Hume, Hovell, and six convicts left Lake George and crossed the Murrumbidgee River on a raft made from their wagon and a piece of canvas. They next reached what became known as the Murray River, though they called it the Hume River, after the explorer's father.

Instead of heading southwest along the river, Hume and Hovell traveled directly south. During their journey, they used fallen trees to cross the Ovens and Goulburn Rivers. They found good grazing land along the Goulburn, but beyond it the land was full of leeches and razor grass. After surviving a brushfire, the explorers crossed the Great Dividing Range. They reached the southern coast of Australia near Geelong on December 18. Hume and Hovell quarreled for most of the trip. Hovell would not accept the fact that Hume had more experience in and knowledge of the bush.

From December 1828 to March 1829, Hume traveled with Captain Charles Sturt. They set out on an expedition across the Blue Mountains to explore the Macquarie Marshes. They reached the Darling River only to find that its water was too salty to drink. The government later gave Hume 1,200 acres of land in honor of his discoveries. He retired to Yass, where he died in 1873.

SUGGESTED READING Rosemary Boyes, *Overland to Port Phillip Bay: Journey South West* (Interprint Services, 1974).

Hung-tsu, Hsü. See *Xu Hongzu.*

Hunt, Wilson Price

American
b 1782?; Hopewell, New Jersey
d April 1842; St. Louis, Missouri
***Blazed trail across Rocky Mountains
south of Lewis and Clark's route***

In 1811 Wilson Price Hunt led the second great crossing of the Rocky Mountains, following the expedition of Meriwether LEWIS and William CLARK several years earlier. Although Hunt made a disastrous decision along the way, his expedition discovered Union Pass in what is now western Wyoming. A major portion of the trail Hunt blazed later became part of the Oregon Trail, which Americans used to settle the Oregon Territory.

Into the Wilderness
Born in New Jersey, Hunt moved to St. Louis in 1804 and managed a general store. In 1810 he met John Jacob Astor, a wealthy businessman who wanted to enter the fur trade west of the Rocky Mountains. Astor hired two men to recruit trappers for an overland expedition to the Oregon Territory. One was Canadian Donald MCKENZIE, an experienced trapper. The other was Hunt, who had never before been into the wilderness.

The expedition left St. Louis in the fall of 1810. Traveling north up the Missouri River, Hunt and his party reached what is now St. Joseph, Missouri, where they camped for the winter. While in St. Joseph, Hunt received a letter from Astor giving him full command of the mission. The decision enraged McKenzie.

Nevertheless, in April 1811, the party continued up the Missouri to the region now named South Dakota. There they traded with the

Arikara Indians, eventually getting the horses they needed for an overland crossing. In mid-July they traveled through the plains into territory no European had ever seen before. The party was impressed—and frightened—by the huge herds of buffalo and the possibility of a stampede. In September the trappers reached the Wind River in what is now Wyoming. Hunt found a way to cross the Rocky Mountains at what is now called Union Pass. By September 26, the party had reached the Snake River, a **tributary** of the Columbia, and Hunt made the decision that turned the rest of the journey into a disaster.

tributary stream or river that flows into a larger stream or river

Struggle to Survive

Local Indians warned Hunt that the Snake was a dangerous river, but he ignored them. He released the expedition's horses, requiring the men to travel the river in canoes. For nine days, everything went well, but then the party reached the swirling waters they called Cauldron Linn (probably in what is now southern Idaho). There a canoe was destroyed, and a man drowned.

For 12 days, the expedition searched for a way to proceed to the Pacific Ocean. Scouts went ahead and reported that the river continued its violent course. Then the party found a faint trail made by animals. Leaving behind most of their supplies, the men set out on foot on November 9. They struggled through the bitter winter and across rugged terrain toward the Columbia River. Struggling to survive, they ate squirrels and beaver paws. A few men left the group to live among the Indians, and several others became lost. A small group led by McKenzie staggered into Fort Astoria at the mouth of the Columbia on January 18, 1812. Hunt arrived with the main party about a month later.

Despite Hunt's poor judgment at the Snake River, the journey was mostly successful. Hunt had discovered an important new route through the Rocky Mountains, opening up the Wind and Snake Rivers to trappers and the Oregon Territory to settlement.

SUGGESTED READING *The Overland Diary of Wilson Price Hunt*, edited by Hoyt C. Franchere (Oregon Book Society, 1973).

Iberville, Pierre Le Moyne d'

French-Canadian
b July 1661; Montréal, Canada
d July 1706; Havana, Cuba?
***Explored Mississippi River;
established French outposts on Gulf of Mexico***

New France French colony that included the St. Lawrence River valley, the Great Lakes region, and until 1713, Acadia (now called Nova Scotia)

Pierre Le Moyne d'Iberville was a soldier whose military goals led to exploration. He hoped to drive the English from North America—or at least to contain them along the Atlantic coast. With this mission, Iberville explored the Mississippi River northward from the Gulf of Mexico and also established three fortified posts on the gulf.

Campaigns Against the British

Born in **New France,** Iberville joined the French navy at the age of 14, but he did not start his military career in North America until 1686. That year he and two of his brothers took part in a campaign against the English at James Bay, the southern part of Hudson Bay. During the fighting, Iberville established his reputation for bravery. As the leader of a French attack on Fort Moose, he found himself alone inside the fort, separated from his troops. With a gun in one

From 1686 to 1697, Iberville traveled and fought in French Canada in an attempt to keep the area out of English hands.

hand and a sword in the other, Iberville held off the English soldiers until his men rescued him.

Iberville also served in various other campaigns against the English, including one at Corlaer (present-day Schenectady, New York). During the battle, the entire settlement was burned, and 60 English inhabitants were massacred. Iberville later took control of St. John's, the fortified English settlement in Newfoundland. He then destroyed 36 English villages and fisheries nearby. But none of Iberville's victories against the English achieved permanent results. As soon as he left, the English began rebuilding their settlements and reasserting their claims to the region.

In 1697 Iberville launched his last campaign in Hudson Bay. As usual he made daring and swift attacks against his enemy. In one battle, he used his naval skills to sink one English ship and easily capture another. While a third enemy ship fled, Iberville was forced to abandon his own sinking ship. After leading his men ashore, he attacked the strongest English fort, and within a week, he had forced the English to surrender. After this victory, Iberville left for France and never returned to Hudson Bay.

Travels to the South

Iberville's exploits in North America impressed the French king and his advisers. They decided to send him to establish a French presence in Louisiana. René Robert Cavelier de LA SALLE had tried, but failed, to accomplish this goal 10 years before. In October 1698, Iberville departed from France in order to find "the mouth [of the Mississippi], . . . select a good site which can be defended with few men, and . . . block entry to the river by other nations."

Iberville sailed first to St. Domingue (present-day Santo Domingo, Dominican Republic), then north to Florida. He headed up the west coast of Florida, passing the Spanish settlement at Pensacola. On March 2, 1699, the ship was driven by a storm into the mouth of the Mississippi River. Iberville was not sure whether he had found the right river, but he sailed up it anyway until he met the Bayagoula Indians. Their chief was wearing a blue cloak, which he had received 13 years earlier from Henri de Tonti, one of La Salle's companions on the Mississippi. Later Iberville's brother discovered a letter that Tonti had left for La Salle. Convinced that he had reached the Mississippi, Iberville returned to the river's mouth. Along the way, he explored Lake Maurepas and Lake Pontchartrain.

After building a fort at Biloxi, Iberville returned to France, but he was immediately ordered back to Louisiana to fortify the region. He again traveled up the Mississippi, visiting the Natchez Indians—a sun-worshiping people—and their relatives, the Taensas. On the way back down the river, Iberville built a wooden fort 40 miles from the mouth of the river. On a third expedition in 1701, he built a fort at Mobile Bay.

Iberville's Last Expedition

Ill health forced Iberville to return to France and remain there for a few years. In 1706 he was finally well enough to revisit America.

He sailed with a group of 12 ships that had been sent to harass the English in the West Indies. Iberville managed to capture the island of Nevis, but he died in Cuba soon after. After Iberville's death, his reputation was damaged when evidence was found indicating that he had planned to take part in illegal trade by selling a cargo of French iron in the Caribbean islands.

Despite the circumstances under which he died, Pierre Le Moyne d'Iberville has been called the first truly Canadian hero. Not only was he born there but he also displayed the tough character that seemed typical of so many natives of that newly explored land. Iberville was devoted to France and dedicated to his task of driving the English out of North America.

SUGGESTED READING Nellis Maynard Crouse, *Lemoyne d'Iberville: Soldier of New France* (Cornell University Press, 1954); Pierre Le Moyne d'Iberville, *Iberville's Gulf Journals* (University of Alabama Press, 1991).

Ibn Battuta

Arab
b February 24, 1304; Tangier, Morocco
d 1368 or 1369; Morocco
Traveled throughout Middle East, Asia, Europe, and Africa

For Ibn Battuta, what began as a journey to the holy sites of Islam turned into 26 years of extensive travel. A devout Muslim, Ibn Battuta eventually reached every major Islamic territory in the world except central Persia (now Iran), Armenia, and Georgia. Motivated by his intense curiosity about foreign lands, he covered some 75,000 miles. The *Rihlah,* Ibn Battuta's record of his experiences, is one of the world's most famous travel books. Ibn Battuta was the greatest Arab traveler of the Middle Ages.

A Career of Travel

Ibn Battuta's full name was Abu Abd Allah Muhammad ibn Abd Allah al-Lawati at-Tanji ibn Battuta. He was born in 1304 into a family that included many Muslim judges. Little is known of his early life, but given his family's social position, he was certainly well educated. Ibn Battuta left home at age 21 for a journey to Medina and Mecca, two Islamic holy cities in what is now Saudi Arabia. He wanted to make the once-in-a-lifetime journey to Mecca required of all devout Muslims and to study with great scholars of the Middle East. The trip to Mecca was supposed to prepare him for his career, but instead travel itself became his career. He developed a passion "to travel through the earth." Ibn Battuta pledged that he would never take the same road twice, suggesting that he traveled for the pure joy of visiting new lands and learning about their peoples.

On the way to Mecca, Ibn Battuta traveled east along the Mediterranean Sea to Cairo, where he boarded a boat for a trip down the Nile River. He then went to the port of Aidhab, on the Red Sea. From there he planned to sail across the Red Sea to Jidda (now in Saudi Arabia), but a local war made the trip impossible, and he returned to Cairo. In the *Rihlah,* Ibn Battuta implies that by this time, he had already decided to visit all of the world's countries—except the Christian lands. That decision would explain the indirect route he took from Cairo to Mecca and Medina. He traveled far out of his way to the north, taking time to explore Syria. He finally reached the Islamic holy cities and visited them briefly.

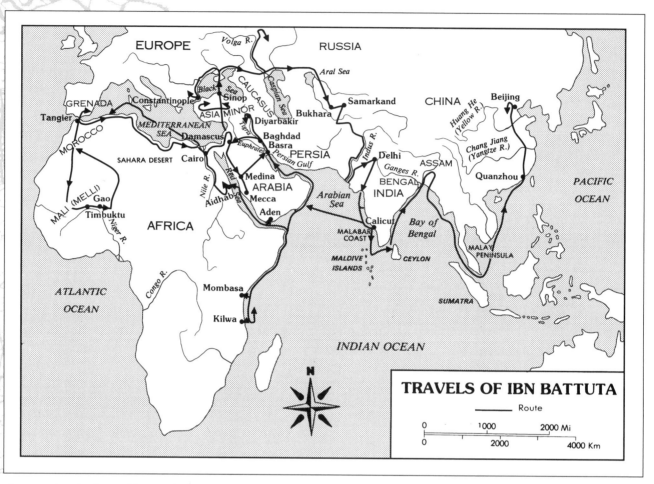

TRAVELS OF IBN BATTUTA

Ibn Battuta's vow when he began his travels was never to pass a second time over any road.

sultan ruler of a Muslim nation

On to East Africa

Ibn Battuta next set out across Arabia to Basra (now in Iraq). From Basra he followed the Euphrates River to Baghdad and then proceeded along the Tigris River to Diyarbakir (now in Turkey) before returning to Mecca. He spent the next several years studying—probably law and religion—before the urge to travel overwhelmed him again. In 1330 Ibn Battuta formed an expedition to explore East Africa. He sailed to the south end of the Red Sea, where he waited for the winds to turn in his favor. On the Indian Ocean, the expedition made stops along the east coast of Africa at Mombasa (now in Kenya) and Kilwa (now in Tanzania). Kilwa, Ibn Battuta reported, was "one of the most beautiful and well-built of cities. It is built entirely of timber."

Overland to India

After sailing back up the African and Arabian coasts to the Persian Gulf, Ibn Battuta made his third trip to Mecca. He then decided to sail to India. He had heard that the **sultan** there showed hospitality toward educated foreign travelers. To avoid taking a route he had traveled before, Ibn Battuta sailed north on the Red Sea and then crossed Asia Minor (the peninsula now occupied by Turkey) by land.

From the port of Sinop, Ibn Battuta sailed across the Black Sea and then journeyed to the Caucasus region. After a trip up the frozen Volga River, he made a detour to Constantinople (present-day Istanbul, Turkey). Ibn Battuta then made his way across the dry plains of Russia, around the north side of the Caspian and Aral Seas, and passed through the city of Bukhara before entering Afghanistan. He reached the northwestern border of India on September 12, 1333.

A Judge's Life

Upon arriving in Delhi, Ibn Battuta met the sultan Mohammed bin Tughlak. The sultan was as kind and generous as Ibn Battuta had heard. Tughlak gave him robes of honor, an annual salary, and an estate. Soon the sultan made him a judge over the city, a position he kept for nine years. Ibn Battuta's comfortable life, however, took a dangerous turn. He was arrested after he happened to meet a **sheikh** who was plotting against the sultan. Ibn Battuta reported: "Then the Sultan commanded that four slaves were to watch over me in the audience hall and not to move from my side. Such an order usually means that the person under guard does not escape with his life." Although the sultan could be as cruel as he was kind, he showed mercy and let Ibn Battuta resume his work as a judge.

Shortly after, the sultan appointed Ibn Battuta to lead a diplomatic mission to the emperor of China. The first attempt ended quickly. Soon after the expedition left Delhi in 1342, it was attacked by rebel Indians, and Ibn Battuta barely managed to escape. The second attempt was just as disastrous. After journeying by land and sea from Delhi to Calicut, all of the party's ships sank during a fierce storm in the Arabian Sea. Ibn Battuta was the only survivor. He happened to be in a **mosque,** praying for the success of the expedition, when the storm struck.

Other Indian Ocean Travels

Ibn Battuta chose not to return to Delhi. Instead he sailed south from Calicut to the Maldive Islands. After working there as judge for 18 months, he tried to return to India, but his ship was driven off course and he landed on Ceylon (now Sri Lanka). "The entire coast of the land of Ceylon is littered with the trunks of the cinnamon tree," Ibn Battuta observed, "which come floating down the rivers from the mountains." He saw other exotic items as well, including rubies "which were larger than hen's eggs" and a spoon made of precious stones.

Ibn Battuta then traveled from Ceylon to India's west coast, known as the Malabar Coast. After being shipwrecked and robbed, he returned to the Maldives by way of Calicut. He next decided to make one more attempt to get to China. He sailed for 43 days along the east coast of India until he reached Bengal and Assam, then turned southeast and landed on Sumatra (in what is now Indonesia). The ruler of that island gave him a **junk,** in which Ibn Battuta made a 71-day voyage across the South China Sea to Quanzhou (or as he called it, Zayton), in China.

sheikh Arab chief

mosque Muslim house of prayer and worship

junk Chinese ship with sails made of fiber mats

The Long Trip Home from China

Like Marco POLO, Ibn Battuta was fascinated by Quanzhou and the other cities he visited in China, including Beijing. But his description of these places is not vivid, perhaps because of his personal reactions to the culture of the country. He wrote: "I did not like the land of China, in spite of the many beautiful things it may have possessed. On the contrary, I was greatly troubled at the idolatry that prevailed there."

From Quanzhou, Ibn Battuta began his slow return to Egypt, passing through Sumatra, Calicut, Arabia, Persia, and Asia Minor. In Syria he witnessed the terrible **bubonic plague** epidemic that was called the Black Death of 1348. From Cairo he made a final journey to Mecca and then decided at long last to return to his home. By the time he arrived in Morocco in November 1349, he was 45 years old and had spent almost half his life traveling.

On the Road Again

After only a year, Ibn Battuta was once again eager to travel. He set out for a new destination—Granada—a region of Spain under Muslim control. In 1352 Ibn Battuta was sent by the sultan of Morocco to explore the interior of Africa, primarily to learn more about the empire of Mali. The ruler of Mali had stirred curiosity about his land when he had passed through Cairo with a large and wealthy **caravan** on his way to Mecca. Ibn Battuta traveled across broad stretches of the Sahara before spending a total of eight months in Timbuktu and Gao, two cities in Mali. He had not wanted to make the trip, and he found it an unpleasant experience.

Ibn Battuta finally returned to Morocco in 1353. At the request of the sultan, he described his extensive travels to the writer Ibn Juzayy. It was Ibn Juzayy who created the *Rihlah* by adding bits of poetry to Ibn Battuta's simple words. The famous traveler then spent his final years as a judge in Morocco.

SUGGESTED READING Daniel J. Boorstin, *The Discoverers* (Random House, 1983); Frank Debenham, *Discovery and Exploration* (Crescent Books, 1960); Ross E. Dunn, *The Adventures of Ibn Battuta, a Muslim Traveler of the 14th Century* (University of California Press, 1986); H. A. R. Gibb, editor, *The Travels of Ibn Battuta,* 3 volumes (Cambridge University Press, 1958–71).

bubonic plague deadly, highly contagious disease spread by fleas from infected rats; symptoms include rashes and high fever

caravan large group of people traveling together, often with pack animals, across a desert or other dangerous region

Ibn Fadlan, Ahmad

Mesopotamian
b ?; ?
d 900s; ?
Traveled from Middle East to Russia

Ahmad Ibn Fadlan was a diplomat who traveled from the city of Baghdad (in what is now Iraq) to southern Russia in the A.D. 900s. He provided one of the earliest accounts of the Rus, a people who were descended from the Norse of Scandinavia. The record of his journey is remarkable for the factual way in which he reported the Rus customs, which he found at various times strange, beautiful, and even horrifying.

A Messenger to Unknown Lands

Ibn Fadlan's life is a mystery. History contains no record of him aside from the book he wrote about his travels. Details in the book have led some scholars to suggest that Ibn Fadlan was not an Arab, although he was a Muslim. In 921 he left Baghdad as part of a

caliph Muslim political and religious ruler

caravan large group of people traveling together, often with pack animals, across a desert or other dangerous region

group of officials in the service of the city's **caliph.** They hoped to reach the east bank of the Volga River (now in Russia) to teach Islamic law to the Bulgars, a people who had recently converted to Islam.

The travelers took a route that first led them northeast along **caravan** routes through Persia (present-day Iran) to the central Asian cities of Samarkand, Bukhara, and Khiva. They then turned northwest and entered the region around the Caspian Sea. There the diplomats encountered several Turkish tribes, including the Oghuz, Pecheneg, and Bashkir peoples. They also met the Khazars, a Turkish tribe that had converted to Judaism and lived at the southern end of the Volga River.

To Teach and to Learn

A year's travel brought the caliph's officials to the Bulgar capital. Ibn Fadlan does not say how long he stayed there, but it was clearly long enough to study the Bulgars' government and way of life. Ibn Fadlan did not think that the Bulgars were as advanced or civilized as the Muslims of Baghdad, but he did report some of their customs. For example, the Bulgars admired obesity, and Bulgar women favored a certain kind of apple that they believed would make them fat. Bulgar women held higher status than was typical of women in the Islamic world. On formal occasions, the queen sat publicly with the king. Ibn Fadlan was disturbed that Bulgar men and women did not consider it immoral to bathe together in the river.

During his time with the Bulgars, Ibn Fadlan had many opportunities to observe the Rus. These Norse people had migrated to the Volga River region and established settlements among the Bulgars. Ibn Fadlan was fascinated by the Rus culture, which was closely related to that of Scandinavia. At the time, the Norse of Scandinavia were terrorizing much of western Europe with attacks on coastal villages. Many accounts of Norse culture that were written by Europeans characterized the Norse as violent, cruel barbarians. However, Ibn Fadlan approached the Rus with less bias, making his report especially important to historians. Although Ibn Fadlan clearly disapproved of some of the practices of the Rus, his eyewitness account vividly captures the details of their society.

He admired the Rus fine metalwork, noting that Rus women always carried knives and scissors in containers made of iron, copper, silver, or gold, depending on their wealth. He also described the customs of Rus merchants. Whenever a group of Rus traveled far to conduct trade, their first act on arrival at their destination was to pray for good business. After a successful business deal, they thanked their god by sacrificing an animal and giving some of the meat to the poor.

The Funeral of a Rus Chieftain

Ibn Fadlan was often careful to tell his readers that he had witnessed events in person, perhaps to dispel any doubts that the strange things he described were true. For example, one of the best-known passages in the book describes the traditional funeral given to a Rus chieftain. The Rus had temporarily buried their fallen leader while they prepared for his funeral ceremony. Ten days later, they opened the grave, removed the body, dressed it in fine silks and furs, and carried it to the riverbank. The dead man's boat had been hauled ashore, and the mourners placed his body under a roof that they had built on the deck. They arranged food, drink, and flowers next to the corpse and then sacrificed a dog, two horses, two cows, and two chickens in a series of elaborate rituals.

Next the Rus bound a slave woman who had served the dead chieftain. Another woman—who was known as the Angel of Death—gave the slave a great quantity of alcohol to drink and then stabbed her in the heart. The Rus placed the dead girl next to the chieftain's body and set the boat on fire with torches. The fire consumed the boat and the bodies. A Rus man standing nearby said to Ibn Fadlan, "You Arabs . . . take your dearest and most honored men and lay them in the earth, where they are eaten by insects and worms. We, on the contrary, burn them in fire in the twinkling of an eye, so that they immediately enter Paradise, without any delay."

Ibn Fadlan's Report

When Ibn Fadlan returned to Baghdad, he wrote an account of his journey. His original manuscript disappeared long ago, but modern scholars have pieced his story together from many copies and translations. Historians have also confirmed the accuracy of many of his reports by comparing them with those obtained from other sources. Although Ibn Fadlan included a few fables and myths in his account, he never insisted that an incident or custom was true unless he had seen it with his own eyes.

SUGGESTED READING Pier Giovanni Donini, *Arab Travelers and Geographers* (Immel Publishing, 1991); A. Torayah Sharaf, *A Short History of Geographical Discovery* (George G. Harrap and Company, 1967).

Ibn Hawqal

Arab
b 920?; Nasibin (present-day Nusaybin, Turkey)
d 990?; Iraq?
Traveled in Islamic lands in Europe, Africa, and Asia

Abu al-Qasim ibn-Ali al-Nasibi ibn Hawqal was one of the most important Islamic geographers and mapmakers of the A.D. 900s. He was part of a medieval Islamic civilization that stretched from Spain across North Africa and the Middle East. Over a 30-year period, he traveled from one end of this territory to the other. Ibn Hawqal then wrote an account of his travels that is filled with firsthand observations of the customs and economies of the lands he visited. Its text and maps gave Islamic scholars useful information about the widespread Islamic world and some of the lands beyond its borders, including western Europe and western Africa.

Islamic Spain

Historians know few details about the life of Ibn Hawqal. His home was a city called Nasibin (now Nusaybin, Turkey). He may have been a religious scholar and was probably a merchant as well. His book contains many details about trade, products, and prices in the lands he visited.

In 943 Ibn Hawqal left his home for what became a very long journey. Over four years, he traveled west through North Africa

dynasty succession of rulers from the same family or tribe

mosque Muslim house of prayer and worship

caravansary inn that provided food and lodging for traders, travelers, and their animals

caravan large group of people traveling together, often with pack animals, across a desert or other dangerous region

tributary stream or river that flows into a larger stream or river

desertification process by which fertile land becomes desert, often because of changes in agriculture or climate

to Morocco. From there he crossed the Strait of Gibraltar to Spain, which was then ruled by an Islamic **dynasty** called the Umayyads. Ibn Hawqal's description of Spain focused on two themes: the riches and resources of the country, and the poor horsemanship and cowardice of its soldiers. At times he seemed to suggest ways in which the Umayyads could be conquered. Some historians suspect that Ibn Hawqal may have been a spy working for the Fatimids, a rival Islamic dynasty from North Africa.

Córdoba was the capital of Islamic Spain. Ibn Hawqal admired the city's "huge markets, clean thoroughfares, [and] impressive **mosques,** not to mention its many public baths and **caravansaries.**" The people of the city showed their wealth, he said, by wearing fine garments of linen and silk, riding "nimble steeds," and eating well.

The Merchants of Morocco

From Spain, Ibn Hawqal returned to North Africa. By 951 he was in southern Morocco, which was home to many merchants from Iraq (at that time, the name for the region of Mesopotamia between Baghdad and the Persian Gulf). Ibn Hawqal's description emphasized the region's prosperity. The Iraqis, he wrote, reaped "considerable wealth, huge gains and remarkable profits" from trade with merchants in **caravans.** He also recorded information of practical interest to travelers, such as the number of days it took to travel from one city to the next "when traveling without baggage."

Leaving Morocco, Ibn Hawqal journeyed south to the region of western Africa that lies south of the Sahara desert region (today including Mali, Ghana, and other nations). He was careful to note points of economic interest, such as the area's trade in gold and salt. He also saw the Niger River, which he mistakenly believed to be a **tributary** of the Nile River.

Ibn Hawqal then headed north and east, recrossing the Sahara. He described repeated sandstorms in the Sudan region, south of Egypt, that forced people to abandon farmlands and caravan routes. These passages in his book interest modern geographers as early evidence of the **desertification** that troubles the region today.

Islamic Lands and Ancient Cities

Passing through Egypt, Ibn Hawqal continued to the northeast and visited the lands, now called Armenia and Azerbaijan, which lie south of Russia on the shores of the Caspian Sea. The people there had recently converted to Islam, although Ibn Hawqal complained about their lack of enthusiasm for their new religion. Turning south, he passed through Syria and eventually returned to his homeland. He visited the southern Iraqi city of Basra in 961, but the length of his stay is unknown.

When Ibn Hawqal resumed his travels, he went east into southern Persia (present-day Iran) and by 969 he had reached the city of Gorgan in northern Persia. To the north and east lay the cities of the ancient caravan routes of central Asia. Ibn Hawqal visited some of these cities, including Bukhara and Samarkand.

Ibn Hawqal, like other Arab geographers, was especially interested in the ways in which people made use of the natural world.

He carefully described the irrigation system that made the countryside around Samarkand lush and fertile. The residents had built canals to carry water to their city from natural sources. The water enabled the people to create welcoming green oases in a desert environment. "In all the world," he wrote, "there is no place more delightful and more health giving than the plains of Samarkand."

The Island of Sicily

Ibn Hawqal returned to Basra by way of southern Iran in 969. By then he had already written the first version of his travel book. It was closely based on an earlier book by another Arab geographer, al-Istakhri. Ibn Hawqal said that al-Istakhri had asked him to rewrite the book and correct its mistakes.

Ibn Hawqal's last recorded journey, in the early 970s, took him to the Mediterranean island of Sicily, which Muslims had ruled for about 150 years. Ibn Hawqal wrote a lengthy and detailed account of Sicily and of the capital city, Palermo. He listed the island's chief products and expressed his admiration for the excellence and low cost of locally made cloth. He also praised Palermo's "impressive and awe-inspiring stone walls."

Ibn Hawqal was struck, however, by the large number of mosques in Palermo. "I have never met with such a profusion of mosques anywhere," wrote this experienced traveler, "even in cities twice as big as Palermo." He soon learned that Palermo had many mosques because its residents, "out of excessive pride," all wanted to have mosques of their own. He wrote that brothers living as neighbors had been known to build two separate mosques so that each would have his own personal place to pray.

Ibn Hawqal added his account of Palermo to the final version of his book, which he wrote in 988. Titled *On the Shape of the Earth,* it became a chief source of knowledge for medieval Islamic scholars about the Islamic empire and its neighbors.

SUGGESTED READING S. M. Ziauddin Alavi, *Arab Geography in the Ninth and Tenth Centuries* (Aligarh Muslim University, 1965); Pier Giovanni Donini, *Arab Travelers and Geographers* (Immel Publishing, 1991).

I-Ching. See *Yi Jing*.

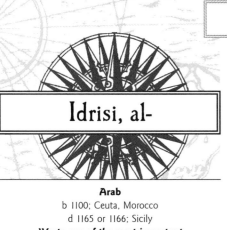

Idrisi, al-

Arab
b 1100; Ceuta, Morocco
d 1165 or 1166; Sicily
***Wrote one of the most important
medieval works of descriptive geography***

The Arab geographer al-Idrisi spent much of his adult life working for a Christian king—a rare relationship at a time when Christian and Islamic lands were often in conflict. As a young man, al-Idrisi traveled extensively across northern Africa, western Europe, and Asia Minor. Then, in about 1145, he was invited by Roger II, the king of Sicily, to become the official court geographer. His fellow Muslims would later criticize al-Idrisi for working for a Christian. But he accepted the position and stayed in Palermo, the Sicilian capital, for the rest of his life. His achievements there included several world maps and a book of geography.

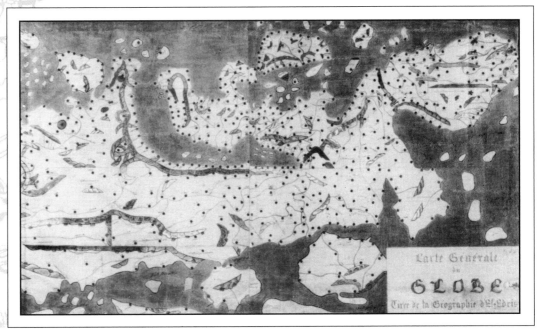

Al-Idrisi's immense silver map was destroyed by a mob only a few years after it was made, but copies of his second map still exist.

Famous Family Ties

Al-Idrisi's full name was Abu Abd Allah Muhammad ibn Muhammad ibn Abd Allah ibn Idris al-Hammudi al-Hasani al-Idrisi. His family traced its roots back to the eldest grandson of Muhammad, the prophet and founder of the Islamic religion. Their ancestors, the Hammudids, had once ruled parts of Spain and North Africa.

Using clues found in al-Idrisi's work and other evidence, historians have been able to piece together an outline of his early life. At various times, he lived in Córdoba, Spain; in Marrakesh, Morocco; and in Qustantinah, Algeria. His accurate, detailed knowledge of North Africa and Spain suggests that he spent a number of years traveling throughout these regions. Other journeys probably took him to Asia Minor (the peninsula now occupied by Turkey), Portugal, the Atlantic coast of France, and southern England.

By the age of 45, al-Idrisi had collected a substantial amount of firsthand geographical information. It was at that time that he accepted Roger's invitation to become his official court geographer and make a map of the world. It is puzzling why a Muslim who may have descended from Mohammed would work for a Christian king. One reason may have been that some of al-Idrisi's Hammudi relatives already occupied powerful positions in the Muslim community in Sicily. Some scholars believe that Roger convinced al-Idrisi that his family background put him at risk in lands ruled by rival Muslim families. Roger may have assured al-Idrisi that he would be safe in Sicily.

Combining the Old and New

Al-Idrisi used several different sources as he began to draw his map and to compile his book on geography. Believing in the value of eyewitness reports, he sent out a number of people to explore various countries. Some of these travelers were skilled artists, who were assigned to bring back sketches of the geographical features they saw.

Al-Idrisi sent one expedition to northern Europe in order to locate the tribes of Gog and Magog. Both the Christian Bible and the Islamic holy book, the Koran, warned that these savage cannibals would one day invade from the north. No one had ever discovered the precise location of Gog and Magog, so the threat of their invasion seemed even more frightening. Al-Idrisi's men went searching for the legendary wall that held back these violent tribes.

Al-Idrisi also relied on the work of earlier geographers and **cartographers.** One of his maps featured a grid system of horizontal and vertical lines that was similar to the system used on Chinese maps. Grid maps of China probably reached the Arabs in Sicily by way of the Arab colony at Guangzhou (also called Canton), China. Another key resource was the *Megiste* (or *Almagest*), an important work on geography and astronomy by the ancient Greek mathematician PTOLEMY. This book had been translated into Arabic by the A.D. 800s and was used by both Arab and European scholars.

Al-Idrisi relied heavily on Ptolemy for his drawings of the lands beyond the Mediterranean Sea and southeastern Europe. In fact, al-Idrisi's map is not much better than one that a cartographer in Ptolemy's day might have drawn. But al-Idrisi was able to name some of the islands in the Indian Ocean. He also knew from Arab sea captains that Africa did not extend as far to the east as Ptolemy had thought, but was surrounded by open sea.

Results of His Work

After al-Idrisi finished his research, he produced two maps of the world and one book on geography. One map, engraved on a silver plate, measured 12 feet by 5 feet and included a detailed key to its features. The other map used al-Idrisi's grid system, which divided the world into 70 sections using 10 vertical and 7 horizontal lines.

His maps were not as accurate as they might have been, since al-Idrisi had not mastered the physical and mathematical aspects of geography. For example, even though he was familiar with many places near the Baltic Sea, he did not properly outline some of the countries in the region. Al-Idrisi also did not take advantage of some of the important geographic advances of the era and did not question the accuracy of some of his earlier Greek and Arab sources.

Nevertheless, al-Idrisi earned a reputation as one of the greatest geographers of the Middle Ages as a result of his work. His book, completed in 1154, was often called *The Book of Roger* in honor of Roger II. Its Arabic title means "The Pleasure Excursion of One Who Is Eager to Traverse the Regions of the World." This volume contains an abundance of important geographic information, especially about the Mediterranean area and the lands of southeastern Europe.

Al-Idrisi had other talents besides geography and **cartography.** He put together a book that listed the common drugs of his time, naming each in 12 different languages. He also studied Arabic

cartographer mapmaker

cartography the science of mapmaking

literature and was a successful poet. Some of al-Idrisi's poetry survives to this day.

SUGGESTED READING *India and the Neighboring Territories in the Kitab Nuzhat al-Mushtaq Fi'Khtiraq al-'Afaq of al-Sharif al-Idrisi* (E. J. Brill, 1960).

Irala, Domingo Martínez de

Spanish
b 1487; Vergara, Spain
d 1557; Asunción, Paraguay
Explored South America

Domingo Martínez de Irala was the first governor of Paraguay and one of its earliest European colonists. Although there is some doubt as to whether he founded Asunción, Paraguay's capital, Irala is credited with developing the city into a powerful colonial center. His style of colonization was unusual for the era. He not only made friends with the Indians of the region but also tried to adapt to their lifestyle.

Shelter at Asunción

Irala first came to South America to search for silver. He was a member of the massive Spanish-German expedition led by Don Pedro de Mendoza. At the end of 1535, the explorers reached the mouth of the Río de la Plata and built a settlement there (at the present site of Buenos Aires, Argentina). However, they experienced severe famine and were attacked by the local Indians. Of the more than 2,500 Spaniards in the expedition, nearly 2,000 died—most of hunger.

Irala was among the survivors who escaped from Buenos Aires and headed north into the interior of the continent. After traveling almost 1,000 miles, they stopped at the point where the Paraguay and Pilcomayo Rivers join. In 1537 they built a fort that they named in honor of the Roman Catholic holy day of Assumption—Asunción in Spanish. Unlike the first settlement, Asunción was surrounded by fertile land, and the local Indians were friendly.

These Indians, the Guaraní, lived in small communities of six families, each surrounded by a protective wall. But they did not have to fear Irala and his men, who lived peacefully with the Guaraní. Irala even encouraged the Spaniards to marry Indian women. Although the Spanish soon dominated the region, Irala let the Guaraní culture thrive. He insisted that his men and later missionaries learn their language rather than force the Indians to speak Spanish. The settlers credited Irala's leadership with their success at Asunción and peaceful expansion in the region, and they elected him governor of Paraguay. In 1539 the king of Spain confirmed Irala's appointment.

Further Explorations

With Asunción as a base, Irala explored other areas of La Plata, a vast region that included the lands that are now Paraguay, Uruguay, Argentina, and portions of Bolivia and Chile. His men established new settlements in the area and made contact with Spanish settlers in Peru. Irala also helped Spain strengthen its claim to parts of Brazil. He built a series of forts along the boundary line between La Plata and the eastern part of Brazil, which was controlled by Portugal.

Jesuit member of the Society of Jesus, a Roman Catholic order founded by Ignatius of Loyola in 1534

Jansz, Willem

Dutch
b late 1500s; ?
d after 1629; ?
Explored northern coast of Australia

mate assistant to the commander of a ship

Asunción continued to grow in size and importance, and it remained the political center of the region's Spanish colonies for more than 60 years. An educational system was developed when **Jesuit** missionaries started the first school in Paraguay in 1544. Irala played a great role in Spain's early colonial success in central South America. In his 22 years there, he proved to be a resourceful and effective leader, praised for his cooperation with the Indians of the region.

SUGGESTED READING Edward J. Goodman, *The Explorers of South America* (Macmillan, 1972).

A sea captain from Amsterdam, Willem Jansz is credited with being the first European to investigate the Australian mainland. In the early 1600s, he explored the continent's northern coast.

Early Voyages
In 1598 Jansz made the first of many voyages to the islands of Southeast Asia as a **mate** aboard the *Hollandia*. While aboard this vessel, he met Jan Lodewycksz van Roossengin, who later accompanied Jansz on his exploration of the Australian coast. Eventually, Jansz was made skipper of the *Duyfken* (Dove) under Admiral Steven van der Hagen. When van der Hagen captured the island of Amboina in the Moluccas (also called the Spice Islands), he left Jansz there to explore the region.

Exploring Australia
Jansz left the north coast of Java (in present-day Indonesia) on November 18, 1605. He sailed first to the Aru Islands, west of New Guinea, and then to New Guinea itself, near what is now False Cape. From there Jansz sailed into Australia's Gulf of Carpentaria and reached the west side of what is now the Cape York Peninsula. Heading south across the mouth of Albatross Bay, he charted the coast as far south as Cape Keerweer and then returned to the bay.

Going ashore near the mouth of the Batavia River, Jansz encountered Aborigines, who attacked and killed some of his men. He then continued north to a point about 30 miles southwest of Cape York. Sailing west past Prince of Wales Island, Jansz turned north and reached the southern coast of New Guinea.

Amazingly, Jansz covered 200 miles of Australian coastline without finding the Torres Strait, the waterway that separates Australia from New Guinea. He mistakenly thought that the western part of the strait was part of a long bay, and he believed that the Cape York Peninsula and the southern coast of New Guinea were part of the same coastline. Jansz's record of the trip was lost. But when the region was mentioned in the books of the Dutch East India Company, which controlled most of the trade with the islands of Southeast Asia, the entry read: "No good to be done here." Apparently, Jansz was not impressed by what he saw.

In 1618, on a voyage heading east from Africa's Cape of Good Hope, Jansz found what he believed to be a large, inhabited island.

It was probably the peninsula now called the North West Cape, on the west side of Australia's Exmouth Gulf.

Jansz later served as a naval commander in the Dutch wars against the Portuguese and the English. He retired to the Netherlands with the rank of admiral after a long and distinguished career with the Dutch East India Company.

SUGGESTED READING T. D. Mutch, *The First Discovery of Australia: With an Account of the Voyage of the "Duyfken" and the Career of Captain Willem Jansz* (D. S. Ford, 1942).

Jiménez de Quesada, Gonzalo

Spanish
b 1510?; Córdoba, Spain
d February 16, 1579; Bogotá, Colombia
Explored Colombia and founded city of Bogotá

conquistador Spanish or Portuguese explorer and military leader in the Americas

On a plateau in Peru, Gonzalo Jiménez de Quesada persuaded two rival explorers to resolve their dispute without warfare.

A lawyer by profession, Gonzalo Jiménez de Quesada was unique among the Spanish **conquistadors.** Instead of violence, Jiménez de Quesada used diplomacy during his conquests. In 1536 he led an extraordinary expedition through the rain forest and rugged terrain of Colombia, discovering the empire of the Chibcha Indians. During the next three years, he took control of the Chibcha region and explored much of what is now Colombia.

Exploring Colombia's Rain Forest

Jiménez de Quesada was born in about 1510 in Córdoba, Spain. By his early twenties, he was a practicing lawyer, but he left Spain in 1535 to go to South America. He accepted a government position in Santa Marta, a settlement on the Caribbean coast of Colombia. In 1536 he was chosen to lead an expedition into the interior of Colombia. His mission was to observe the region's geography and to try to reach Peru by way of the Magdalena River.

Jiménez de Quesada left Santa Marta on April 5, 1536, with about 600 men. Traveling during the rainy season, the party headed south along the flooded Magdalena River. They endured attacks by crocodiles and other wild animals, swarms of insects, and intense heat. Five ships were supposed to meet them at a point on the Magdalena that had been chosen before they left. However, the ships never arrived—three had been wrecked, and two had returned to port. Nevertheless, Jiménez de Quesada persuaded the party to continue. Three supply ships eventually met the expedition, but not before the men had been forced to eat snakes, lizards, and bats to survive after their food ran out.

The men proceeded slowly, hacking their way through the underbrush and moving carefully through swamps filled with snakes. It took them eight months to travel 300 miles. Jiménez de Quesada then decided to leave the Magdalena and travel farther inland to the east. He had heard tales of an advanced Indian nation that mined gold and emeralds beyond the Andes Mountains. By March 1537,

plateau high, flat area of land

Jiménez de Quesada and the 166 men left in his party reached the **plateau** of Bogotá, the land of the Chibcha Indians. There the Spaniards found gold, emeralds, and other jewels. The Chibcha were friendly to the foreigners and gave them gifts of gold. Jiménez de Quesada named the land he conquered New Granada and founded the city of Santa Fe de Bogotá (present-day Bogotá).

Trouble Avoided

In 1539 two other explorers, Nikolaus FEDERMANN and Sebastián de BENALCÁZAR, reached Bogotá. Jiménez de Quesada managed to negotiate with them and thus avoid a war over New Granada. The three men agreed to submit their claims to the land to the **Council of the Indies** in Spain. Unfortunately for Jiménez de Quesada, Benalcázar was given control over the area.

Council of the Indies governing body of Spain's colonial empire from 1524 to 1834

In 1551 Jiménez de Quesada—now marshal of New Granada—returned to Bogotá where both the Indians and the Spaniards respected his leadership. In 1569 he made one last expedition, a search for **El Dorado,** the legendary city of gold. The mission was unsuccessful, and Jiménez de Quesada spent his last years writing an account of his conquest of New Granada.

El Dorado mythical ruler, city, or area of South America believed to possess much gold

SUGGESTED READING Germán Arciniegas, *The Knight of El Dorado; The Tale of Don Gonzalo Jiménez de Quesada and His Conquest of New Granada, Now Called Colombia* (Viking Press, 1942).

Jing, Yi. See *Yi Jing.*

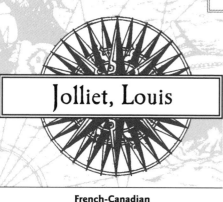

Jolliet, Louis

French-Canadian
b 1645; Beauport, Canada
d 1700; Gulf of St. Lawrence?
Explored upper Mississippi River

Louis Jolliet was a French-Canadian explorer who led a five-month, 2,500-mile expedition along the Mississippi River in 1673. On this voyage, he displayed skill, caution, and diplomacy toward the Indian tribes of the region. As a result of his journey, France controlled the Mississippi Valley for the next 90 years, until King Louis XV surrendered the region to the English.

Growing Up in Québec

In the early 1600s, Jolliet's parents, Jean and Marie, had moved from France to the province of Québec, where Louis was born in 1645. Jean, a wheelwright and wagonmaker, died when Louis was six years old. Marie remarried, and the family moved closer to central Québec. Louis and his two brothers, Adrien and Zacharie, attended a **Jesuit** school, where Louis excelled in mapmaking and music.

Jesuit member of the Society of Jesus, a Roman Catholic order founded by Ignatius of Loyola in 1534

When Jolliet was growing up, **New France** was a wilderness. French settlement had slowed down after the government had lost interest in the area and the French explorer Samuel de CHAMPLAIN had died. Settlers were also threatened by the fierce Iroquois Indians, who had tortured and killed a number of Roman Catholic missionaries. Even so, Jesuit missionaries and rugged fur trappers explored farther west each year. In 1638 Jean NICOLETT DE BELLEBORNE

New France French colony that included the St. Lawrence River valley, the Great Lakes region, and until 1713, Acadia (now called Nova Scotia)

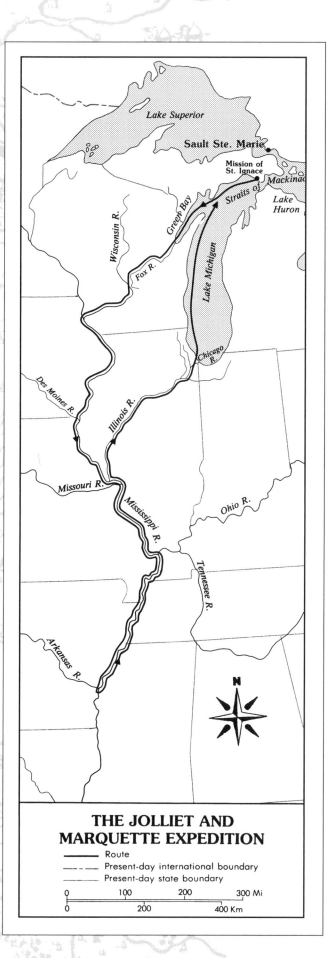

THE JOLLIET AND MARQUETTE EXPEDITION

—— Route
—·—·— Present-day international boundary
---- Present-day state boundary

0   100   200   300 Mi
0   200   400 Km

Jolliet's expedition down the Mississippi River turned back when the men discovered that they were heading into Spanish enemy territory.

(Marie Jolliet's brother-in-law) reached Lake Michigan. By 1670, Jesuit missionaries were preaching to Indians in what is now eastern Wisconsin.

In 1662 Jolliet joined the clergy. He remained at the **seminary** in Québec while his older brother, Adrien, started a fur trading business on the St. Lawrence River. During this time, Louis devoted himself to the study of music, and he became an accomplished performer on the harpsichord, flute, trumpet, and organ. By 1667 Louis had left the clergy and gone to France, where he probably studied **cartography.** His reason for leaving the seminary is not known.

France Explores the West

While Louis was overseas, a new governor, the Comte (Count) de Frontenac, arrived in New France. He was accompanied by a government official named Jean Talon. At the time, rumors about copper deposits near the Great Lakes were being spread by fur traders, missionaries, and Indians. These groups also described a "Big Water" still farther west that might lead to China. Talon commissioned several expeditions, one of which included Louis's brother Adrien, to investigate these reports.

By October 1668, Louis had returned from France, and he decided to join Adrien in the fur business. He borrowed money from a bishop for equipment, and in 1670 Louis and Adrien drew up a contract to trade with the Ottawa Indians. But by March of that year, Adrien had died. That summer Louis traveled to Sault Ste. Marie and set up a trading post. There he met Father Jacques MARQUETTE, a missionary who was an expert in Indian languages.

In the summer of 1672, Talon appointed Jolliet to explore westward in search of the great river reported by various Indian tribes. Like most French explorers, Jolliet was expected to pay for the trip himself. To help him recover his expenses, he was granted sole rights to trade with the Indians along the route. Jolliet carefully chose **voyageurs** to join him, including his younger brother, Zacharie. Louis also carried orders from the leader of the Jesuit **missions** on the Great Lakes. These orders added a final member to the company—Father Marquette.

seminary school for religious training

cartography the science of mapmaking

voyageur expert French woodsman, boatman, and guide

mission settlement founded by priests in a land where they hoped to convert people to Christianity

astrolabe navigational instrument used since ancient times to determine distance north or south of the equator

portage transport of boats and supplies overland between waterways

tributary stream or river that flows into a larger stream or river

Louis Jolliet was a skilled mapmaker, fur trapper, and musician. He made his mark by exploring the Mississippi River.

Monsters and Demons

Jolliet met Marquette in December of 1672 at the Mission of St. Ignace near the Straits of Mackinac, which join Lakes Michigan and Huron. They spent the winter making a map of their proposed route and interviewing Indians about the body of water known as the Messipi. In May 1673, Jolliet, Marquette, and five others set off in two birch-bark canoes. The canoes were loaded with supplies, including Jolliet's **astrolabe** and Marquette's portable altar. The party traveled around the northwest shore of Lake Michigan, covering about 30 miles a day. When they arrived at the mouth of the Fox River on Green Bay, the Menomini Indians warned the party to turn back. They claimed that the inhabitants of the Mississippi Valley were cruel savages. They also warned that the river itself held terrible monsters and demons. But Jolliet's party was determined to continue. They paddled up the dangerous Fox River. With the help of two Mascouten Indian guides, they then **portaged** to a **tributary** of the Wisconsin River. On June 17, 1673, Jolliet's party reached the Mississippi River.

The Frenchmen met no Indians on the river until they arrived at a friendly Illinois village, 200 miles below the mouth of the Wisconsin River. The legendary monsters turned out to be cliff paintings near what is now Grafton, Illinois. The demons were a myth, perhaps created to explain the rough waters where the Mississippi and Missouri Rivers meet. After more than 1,000 miles on the river, the men stopped when they encountered unfriendly Quapaw Indians near the Arkansas River. Fortunately, Marquette was able to make peace with the Quapaw, who told him that the Mississippi emptied into the Gulf of Mexico. Jolliet noticed that the Indians possessed Spanish trade goods, which proved that this claim was true. If the party continued, they would soon enter Spanish territory—enemy territory for the Frenchmen. The expedition turned back, arriving at Green Bay by late September 1673.

Up to this point, the trip had been a great success. Then disaster struck when Jolliet's canoe overturned on rapids just outside of Montreal. His two canoemen and a slave boy drowned. Jolliet lost his journal and map as well as all material evidence supporting the findings of his expedition. A diary supposed to have been written by Father Marquette did survive. This brief account is the main record of this first major exploration of the Mississippi.

Settling Down

Although he wished to settle along the Illinois River, Jolliet never returned west. Further exploration of the Mississippi River was left to René Robert Cavelier de LA SALLE. After he lost his papers, Jolliet was ignored by the French authorities. He also faced many legal problems over the profits from the trip. In 1675 he married and settled in Québec as a merchant. In 1679 Jolliet was granted valuable fishing rights in the Mignan Isles. That same year, he was asked to gather information about British forts on Hudson Bay. Jolliet managed this spy mission so well that he was awarded Anticosti Island at the mouth of the St. Lawrence River.

In his later years, Jolliet explored the coast of Labrador and produced a map and notes on the **Inuit** language. On a trip to France in 1695, he was named royal **hydrographer.** By 1697 he had returned to Québec to produce maps and open a school for pilots and mapmakers. In the winter of 1700, Jolliet set out for his landholdings in the north. He disappeared somewhere in the Gulf of St. Lawrence and was never seen again.

SUGGESTED READING Francis Borgia Steck, *The Jolliet-Marquette Expedition, 1673* (Arthur H. Clark, 1928).

Inuit people of the Canadian Arctic, sometimes known as the Eskimo

hydrographer scientist who studies bodies of water to make navigation easier

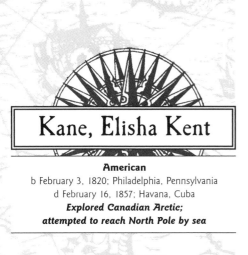

Kane, Elisha Kent

American
b February 3, 1820; Philadelphia, Pennsylvania
d February 16, 1857; Havana, Cuba
Explored Canadian Arctic;
attempted to reach North Pole by sea

Elisha Kane inspired other Arctic explorers with his colorful tales of the polar region.

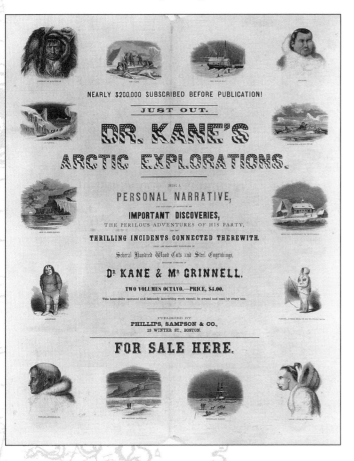

Elisha Kent Kane was a medical doctor whose desire for travel and adventure took him far from the laboratory and the clinic. From 1853 to 1855, he attempted unsuccessfully to reach the North Pole. Despite his failure, Kane's colorful tales of the expedition brought the Arctic region to life for many Americans.

The Adventurous Doctor

Kane had earned a reputation as a **physiologist** before he had even graduated from medical school. He became a navy surgeon and served on missions to Brazil, India, China, and West Africa. But this work did not satisfy his longing to travel to exotic places. He often took extended leave from his medical assignments in order to explore. While on a mission to the Asian island of Macao, he traveled to the Philippines, where he climbed down into the crater of a live volcano. His final adventure was an expedition to the northwest shores of Greenland.

The American merchant Henry Grinnell funded Kane's expedition to the polar region. It was the second American expedition sent by Grinnell to search for the lost party of Sir John FRANKLIN. Kane had been the ship's doctor on the first rescue mission in 1850, which had failed. Kane's real goal on this rescue expedition, however, was to reach the North Pole. He thought that the polar ice barrier must surround an open polar sea, and he planned to break through the ice.

On this trip, Kane traveled farther north than any person, other than the **Inuit,** had ever gone. He reached a record-high **latitude** in what is now Kane Basin. Then his ship, the *Advance,* was trapped in the ice. Kane and his men stayed with the ship for two winters, making a few short **sledge** trips. They were then forced to abandon the ship and head south on boats and on foot. The Inuit gave them a great deal of help. After a three-month struggle, the party finally reached Upernavik, Greenland, in August 1855. However, the Arctic

physiologist scientist who studies the parts and functions of living organisms

Inuit people of the Canadian Arctic, sometimes known as the Eskimo

latitude distance north or south of the equator

sledge heavy sled, often mounted on runners, that is pulled over snow or ice

Norse
b 980?; Skagafjord, Iceland
d ?; ?

Led first European attempt to found permanent settlement on North American mainland

saga medieval Norse legend or historical account

conditions damaged Kane's surprisingly weak health, and he died soon after his return.

Kane's Tall Tales

Kane's party made some important observations of the weather, magnetic conditions, and the tides in the polar region. Kane also brought back the exciting—but incorrect—news that there was an open polar sea just north of Kane Basin. He had seen some open water in Kennedy Channel and reported a major break in the ice.

Kane's contribution to Arctic exploration may have been small, but his published accounts of his Arctic adventure made him an American hero. He was the first explorer to make the cold north seem romantic, noble, and grand. He inspired a generation of Arctic explorers, including fellow American Charles Francis HALL.

SUGGESTED READING George Corner, *Doctor Kane of the Arctic Seas* (Temple University Press, 1972); William Elder, *Biography of Elisha Kent Kane* (Childs and Peterson, 1958); Jeannette Mirsky, *Elisha Kent Kane and the Seafaring Frontiers* (Little, Brown, 1954); Oscar M. Villarejo, *Dr. Kane's Voyages to the Polar Lands* (University of Pennsylvania Press, 1965).

Sometime around the year 1010, Thorfinn Karlsefni led an expedition to colonize the land called Vinland, in North America. His countryman Leif ERIKSON had discovered and named Vinland almost a decade earlier. Although the colonists failed to establish a permanent settlement, they lived on the North American mainland for three years. They are recognized as the first Europeans to found a community in North America.

Breaking Ground in North America

Karlsefni was a wealthy merchant from Iceland who sold his goods between Norway and Greenland. In about 1008, he spent the Christmas season with the children of ERIK THE RED. Early in the next year, Karlsefni married Gudrid, the widow of one of Erik's sons. Within the next few years, Karlsefni prepared to settle Vinland, which Leif Erikson had discovered around 1001. Karlsefni assembled an expedition of three ships, carrying about 160 men and women. The party included his pregnant wife Gudrid, Erik's daughter Freydis, and Freydis's husband.

Thorfinn retraced Erikson's journey. He sailed first past Helluland (probably Baffin Island) and then past the coast of Markland (probably Labrador). According to one Norse **saga,** Thorfinn next found Vinland and the houses that had been built by Erikson's party. The colonists settled on an island in a bay with strong currents. Some historians think that this area was present-day Belle Isle at the entrance to the Gulf of St. Lawrence. There Gudrid gave birth to Snorri, the first European child to be born in North America. The winter was more difficult than they had expected. The cattle they had brought suffered in the cold, and the fishing was poor.

A Change of Plans

The saga says that Karlsefni sailed south the next year in search of better land. He found this land at the mouth of a river that flowed into a small, land-locked bay. He also found the grapes and wild wheat for which Vinland was known. The Norse were visited by the local people, whom they called skraelings, meaning barbarians or weaklings. The first meetings were peaceful trading sessions. But when the skraelings returned the next summer, a battle took place. The saga says that the pregnant Freydis saved the day with a fierce war cry. Her wild behavior shocked the skraelings, and they retreated. The conflict convinced Karlsefni's party that the land was not safe for settlement. After one more winter, they set sail to return to Greenland. Karlsefni and his family eventually returned to Iceland.

SUGGESTED READING North Ludlow Beamish, translator, *Voyages of the Northmen to America* (B. Franklin, 1971).

Kelsey, Henry

English
b 1667?; East Greenwich, England?
d November 2, 1724; East Greenwich, England
Extended reach of Hudson's Bay Company to Saskatchewan River

In 1690 the Hudson's Bay Company sent Henry Kelsey to make contact with Indian tribes in the Canadian wilderness. At the time, the well-armed Cree Indians were preventing other tribes west of Hudson Bay from trading with the English. Kelsey's mission was to persuade these tribes, the Assiniboin and Gros Ventres, to ignore the threats of the Cree and to join the fur trade. He succeeded in his task mainly by adopting the ways of the Indians. Kelsey not only helped his company extend its fur trading territory but also helped prevent the Assiniboin and Gros Ventres from trading with the French to the south.

An Asset to the Company

Kelsey entered the service of the Hudson's Bay Company at the age of 17 and went to work with the great French fur traders Pierre Esprit RADISSON and Médard Chouart des GROSEILLIERS. His supervisors soon noticed that Kelsey liked to travel with Indians, and thus he was an important asset. Kelsey spoke Cree and possibly Assiniboin. He respected the Indians and their way of life, and they liked him as well. He also accepted the role that Indian women played in travel and even lived with these women, a practice that most Englishmen avoided.

On a Secret Mission

From 1688 to 1690, Kelsey traveled with an Indian to make contact with the **Inuit** north of the Churchill River. Afterward, he went to York Factory on the southwest shore of Hudson Bay. He was then sent out with the leader of a band of Assiniboin that had been trading at York. Unfortunately, Kelsey's journal is unclear about exactly where he traveled. He spent the next two years alone among the tribes along the Saskatchewan River. He journeyed as far southwest as the site of present-day Battleford, Saskatchewan, while trying to make peace between the Cree and the Gros Ventres.

Shortly after his return to York Factory in 1692, Kelsey traveled to London, where his efforts were praised by the British government. However, his daring peace mission was kept from the public because it was viewed as a trade secret. When his journal was

Inuit people of the Canadian Arctic, sometimes known as the Eskimo

discovered in 1926, many believed that it was nothing more than a romantic tale.

SUGGESTED READING Henry Kelsey, *The Kelsey Papers*, edited by Arthur G. Doughty and Chester Martin (King's Printer, 1929).

Khabarov, Yerofei Pavlovich

Russian
b 1600s?; Veliki Ustyug, Russia
d 1600s; near Kirensk, Russia
Explored and colonized Siberia

Yerofei Pavlovich Khabarov was one of the adventurous, ambitious, and often ruthless men who extended Russia's frontier to the Pacific Ocean in the 1500s and 1600s. These men brought northeastern Asia, known as Siberia, under the control of the Russian empire, making Russia the world's largest nation. Khabarov's contribution was the conquest and settlement of the Amur River region in southeastern Siberia. That river became the tense frontier between two great empires—Russia and China.

The Siberian Adventure

The Russian state was first established on the western side of the Ural Mountains. By the 1500s, however, Russians were beginning to look eastward, beyond the Urals. Rumors carried by a few venturesome fur traders spoke of a wide, wild land inhabited by warlords and savages.

Russia's advance into Siberia began in 1580, when Timofeyevich YERMAK led a band of more than 800 soldiers across the Urals. In the years that followed, other groups penetrated farther east into Siberia, fighting with the local tribes and building forts along the way. The Russian advance into Siberia was only partially supervised by the **czar.** Many of the explorers were renegades, outlaws, or troublemakers, drawn east by the idea of a freewheeling life beyond the frontier. They also hoped to make a fortune from Siberian gold, gems, and furs. One such man was Yerofei Pavlovich Khabarov.

czar title of Russian monarchs from the 1200s to 1917

Not much is known about Khabarov's birth or early life. He was originally from a village called Ustyug, about 450 miles northeast of the capital, Moscow. He made several trading journeys into remote regions of northern Russia. By 1636 he turned up near Yakutsk, a settlement on Siberia's Lena River. Yakutsk had been founded by **cossacks** a few years earlier to serve as a center of the area's fur trade and a base for further expansion. Khabarov appears to have been a good businessman. He operated a profitable salt mine and was also a grain merchant.

cossack horseman from southern Russia who served as a mounted soldier in the armies of Russian monarchs

A Pact for Conquest

In the mid-1640s, a group of cossacks ventured far into southeastern Siberia, returning to Yakutsk with a load of furs and also with accounts of a prosperous region called Daurien, along the Amur River. Eager to explore this region, Khabarov made a private and somewhat illegal arrangement with the czar's local representative, an official called the *voivode*. The *voivode* gave Khabarov weapons from the Russian government's supplies, with permission to organize an expedition to the Amur River on behalf of the czar.

dynasty succession of rulers from the same family or tribe

Khabarov and the *voivode* agreed to split any loot between themselves. The *voivode* did not notify the czar, who ruled from distant Moscow, until after Khabarov had set out in 1649.

On reaching the Amur region, Khabarov discovered that the Dauri—the people of Daurien—had fled before his approach. The previous group of cossacks had terrified the Dauri with violence, torture, and murder. However, Khabarov located supplies of grain hidden by the Dauri. Leaving a few men at a fort on the river, he returned to Yakutsk in 1650. He reported that with 6,000 men, the Russians could conquer Daurien and provide Yakutsk with plenty of grain.

At that point, neither Khabarov nor the other Russians in Siberia had a clear understanding of the political situation along the Amur River. Daurien lay on the river's north bank. On the south bank was Manchuria, a kingdom whose rulers, the Manchu, had just conquered China. The cossacks were trespassing on the edge of the homeland of China's powerful new **dynasty.**

A Violent Return

After spending a few months in Yakutsk, Khabarov returned to the Amur River with about 150 more men. In the spring of 1651, he and his men took boats down the river—fighting, burning, kidnapping, and looting as they went. They bombarded one Dauri settlement with cannons. In his report to the *voivode,* Khabarov wrote: "With God's help . . . counting big and little we killed six hundred and sixty one." By his count, the Russians had taken 243 women and 118 children prisoner and had captured 237 horses and 113 cattle. Khabarov's report describes how he and his men tortured prisoners to obtain information from them.

The Russians made camp for the winter of 1651 to 1652, unaware that a Chinese army was headed in their direction. When the two forces clashed, the cossacks won the battle. But they realized that a formidable power now stood against them. China would not allow another nation to colonize the Amur frontier. Khabarov prudently removed himself and his men up the Amur River to a safer distance from China.

Changing Fortunes

Word of Khabarov's achievements made its way to northern Siberia and western Russia. Khabarov was hailed as a hero—another Yermak who had conquered an important new region for Russia. Daurien's reputation for lawlessness and easy living attracted a stream of adventurers, convicts, and bandits to Khabarov's side. But in 1653, Khabarov received a less welcome visitor. A nobleman leading Russian troops had been sent by the czar to remove Khabarov from command and bring the Amur region under closer government control. This officer placed a man named Onufry Stepanov in charge of the area and took Khabarov back to Moscow.

In the Russian capital, Khabarov faced several criminal charges, including cruelty to his men. The czar's government seized Khabarov's property and nearly executed him. But he was able to restore himself to the good graces of government leaders. He described the potential riches in grain and furs that he had won for Russia. People came to agree that like Yermak, Khabarov may have been brutal, but he was also effective. The Russian government restored Khabarov's fortune, made him a noble, and placed him in charge of some villages near Kirensk, in southern Siberia. His career as an explorer, however, was over.

The Amur frontier remained a site of conflict between Russia and China, and Stepanov and many of his men died fighting the Chinese. Not until 1860 did Russia gain complete control of the north bank of the Amur River. In the 1850s, Russia honored Khabarov by founding a city called Khabarovka (present-day Khabarovsk) on the riverbank.

SUGGESTED READING Basil Dmytryshyn and others, editors, *Russia's Conquest of Siberia, 1558-1700*, (Western Imprints, 1985); F. A. Golder, *Russian Expansion on the Pacific, 1641-1850* (Peter Smith, 1960); Yuri Semyonov, *Siberia: Its Conquest and Development*, translated by J. R. Forster (International Publishers' Representatives, 1963).

K'ien, Chang. See *Zhang Qian*.

King, Clarence

American
b January 6, 1842; Newport, Rhode Island
d December 24, 1901; Phoenix, Arizona
Surveyed American West

geology the scientific study of the earth's natural history

latitude distance north or south of the equator

Between 1867 and 1873, Clarence King led a survey of the American West, carefully studying the mineral resources from the Sierra Nevada to the Rocky Mountains. King wrote a seven-volume report of the survey titled *Systematic Geology*. This work is considered a masterpiece in the field of **geology.**

After earning a degree in science at Yale University in 1863, King traveled to California, where he worked for the state's geological survey for three years. He then proposed a survey of the mineral resources in the area from Reno, Nevada, to Denver, Colorado. He wanted to aid in the construction of the final part of the transcontinental railroad.

Congress approved King's request. By July 1867, King and a group of fellow scientists were on the slopes of the mountains of the Sierra Nevada, ready to begin work. They spent close to six years making their way east along the line of **latitude** at 40° north. Although they were not the first explorers of this territory, they survived many of the same hardships as others had. Sometimes it was so hot that they huddled in the shadow of a flagpole for shade. At other times, they faced sudden mountain blizzards that destroyed their sense of direction. King had several close encounters with death. Once he was struck by lightning after setting up instruments on a mountain peak. On another occasion, he got stuck in a cave while trying to shoot a bear. He had to be pulled out of the cave by his ankles.

In 1879 Congress created the United States Geological Survey and asked King to serve as its first director. He agreed to take the

The Renaissance

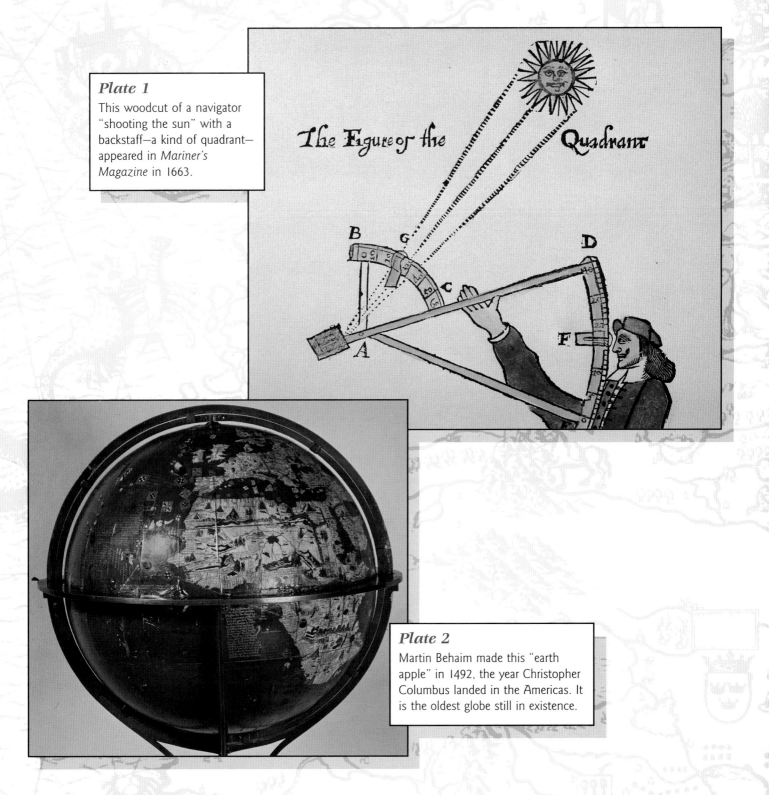

Plate 1

This woodcut of a navigator "shooting the sun" with a backstaff—a kind of quadrant—appeared in *Mariner's Magazine* in 1663.

Plate 2

Martin Behaim made this "earth apple" in 1492, the year Christopher Columbus landed in the Americas. It is the oldest globe still in existence.

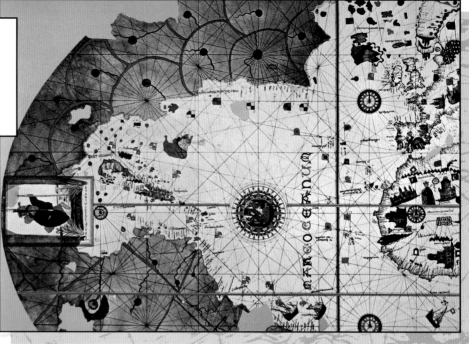

Plate 3
Juan de la Cosa's famous world map, created in 1500, was the first to show the newly discovered lands in the Americas, including Cuba, Hispaniola, and Jamaica.

Plate 4
This engraving of a two-masted caravel appeared in Theodore de Bry's *America*, a 13-part illustrated account of travels in the Americas, published between 1590 and 1634.

Plate 5
Sir Francis Drake combined exploration with piracy and warfare. In this engraving, his ship the *Golden Hind* (right) captures a Spanish treasure galleon (left).

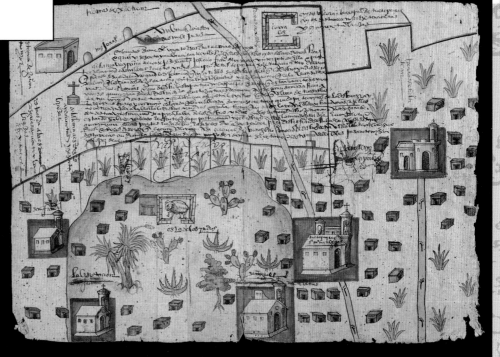

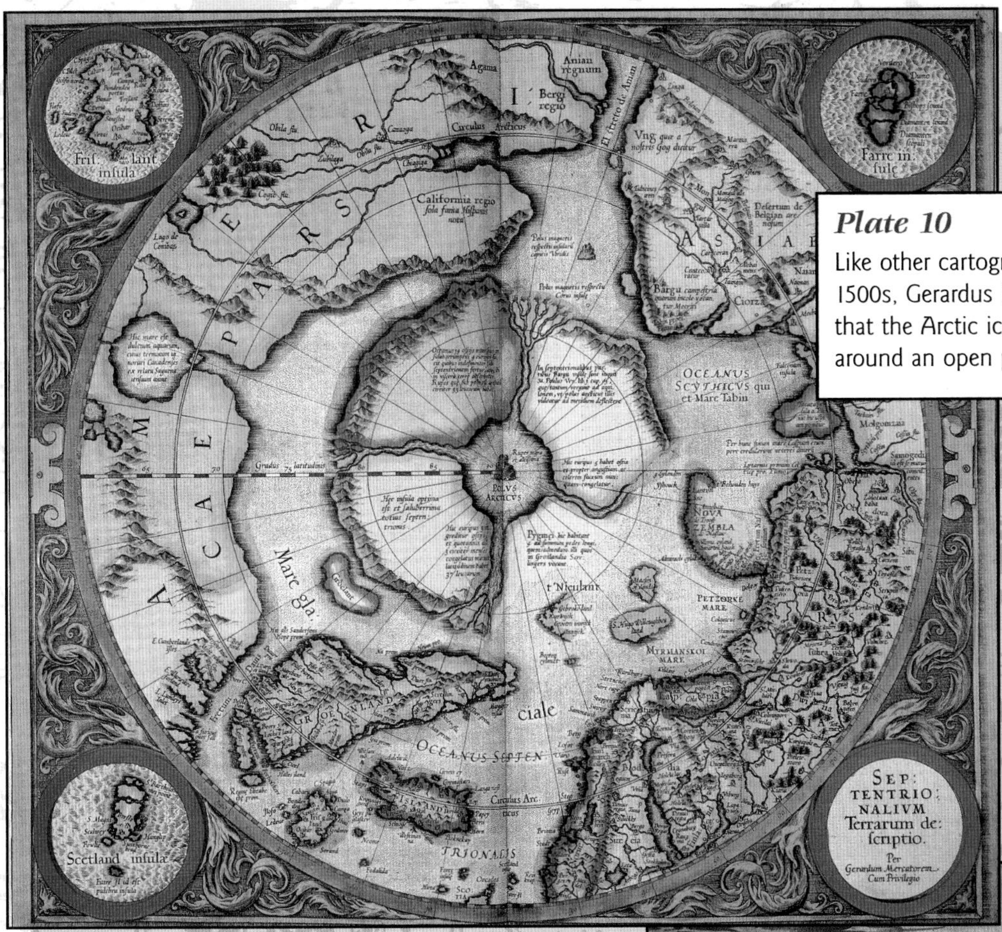

Plate 10
Like other cartographers of the late 1500s, Gerardus Mercator believed that the Arctic ice pack was a ring around an open polar sea.

Plate 11
James Cook dedicated his life to solving the geographic mysteries of the late 1700s. One of his crewmen painted this tribute to the *Resolution*, Cook's ship.

Plate 12

The Age of Exploration, which began in the 1400s, was also a time of conquest. This bronze statuette of a Portuguese soldier was made by an artisan from Benin in about 1600.

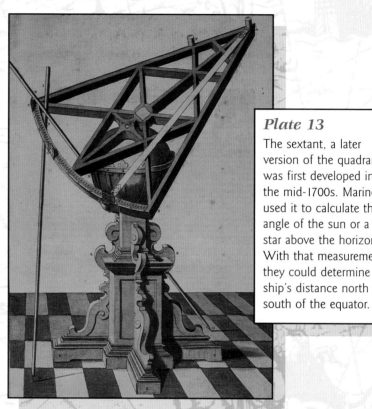

Plate 13

The sextant, a later version of the quadrant, was first developed in the mid-1700s. Mariners used it to calculate the angle of the sun or a star above the horizon. With that measurement, they could determine a ship's distance north or south of the equator.

Plate 14

In 1900 an artist in Abyssinia (now Ethiopia) depicted the battles his Muslim ancestors fought in the 1540s against the Portuguese.

Plate 15

John White, an artist, took part in England's attempt to establish a North American colony on Roanoke Island in the 1580s. In this watercolor, he showed the local Indians' methods of fishing.

Plate 16

Europeans came to know John White's paintings and drawings through engravings made by Theodore de Bry. This engraving features an Indian village in what became North Carolina.

Plate 17

This drawing from the 1500s presents an Aztec's view of the battle against the Spanish forces led by Hernán Cortés. The Spaniards were surrounded as they took refuge inside the walls of a palace.

Plate 18

European traders made their presence felt around the world. This Japanese screen painting from around 1600 shows a Portuguese merchant ship leaving India for Japan.

Clarence King *(far right)* and his team of scientists braved intense hunger, heat, and blizzards during their survey of the American West.

position only until a staff could be selected and the organization could begin its work. He resigned as director in 1881.

SUGGESTED READING Clarence King, *Mountaineering in the Sierra Nevada* (Yosemite Association, 1997); Henry Nash Smith, *Clarence King, John Wesley Powell, and the Establishment of the United States Geological Survey* (Mississippi Valley Historical Association, 1947).

Kingsley, Mary Henrietta

English
b November 13, 1862; London, England
d June 3, 1900; Simonstown, South Africa
Traveled through western equatorial Africa

specimen sample of a plant, animal, or mineral, usually collected for scientific study or display

Mary Henrietta Kingsley traveled extensively in central and western Africa for eight years. As she studied African culture and collected animal **specimens** for the British Museum, she developed a deep respect for the African people. She wrote books and gave lectures, expressing her wishes for a responsible British policy toward Africa. Kingsley demonstrated great cleverness and courage during the course of her African adventures.

A Dutiful Daughter

As a child, Kingsley led a difficult life. She once wrote: "The whole of my childhood and youth was spent at home, in the house and garden." From a young age, she accepted responsibility for many of the chores around the house without complaining. Her father was a physician who traveled a great deal. He was often hired by wealthy young noblemen to join expeditions to distant places, and he was only home for a few months at a time. At heart he was a dedicated naturalist, and he longed to study different cultures, but he mostly

While traveling in West Africa, Mary Kingsley lived among cannibals, fought off crocodiles, and climbed a volcano.

wandered the globe. He wrote long, funny letters about his travels, but his absence caused great hardship for his family. Meanwhile, Mary stayed at home and cared for her sick mother.

Mary, her mother, and her brother Charles had very little money, but they managed to save for Charles's education. Mary received no formal education except for a German language course. Her knowledge of German later became useful when she assisted her father with his research.

Although Mary resented her lack of schooling, she managed to educate herself in many areas. Her mother helped her learn to read, and Mary spent many hours in her father's library. She was interested in subjects that most Victorian girls ignored, such as travel, exploration, and piracy. Her favorite subjects were medicine and science.

When Mary was 24, the family moved to Cambridge, where Charles was attending the university. Mary made friends with some of the scientists at the university and started reading scientific books from the university library. She even helped her father conduct research on other cultures. Mary soon knew more about early African religions and law than her father did.

On Her Own

In 1888 Mary's mother became seriously ill, requiring the devoted daughter to serve as her mother's nurse night and day for the next four years. Then her father died unexpectedly from rheumatic fever, which he had caught on one of his overseas expeditions. Her mother died a few weeks later. Mary was now on her own, and at 30 years of age, she was ready to see the world. She undertook her first adventure, a holiday trip to the Canary Islands.

After returning to England, Kingsley decided to go to West Africa. She wanted to complete her father's research on African cultures. She may have hoped to finish the book that he had started to write on the subject. She asked officials of the British Museum to help her find a natural history project that required little money and no formal training. They suggested that she collect specimens of beetles and fish, since this work required only a few pieces of inexpensive equipment.

In August 1893, Kingsley set sail on the cargo ship *Lagos*. She was thrilled when she first saw Freetown (in Sierra Leone). She was finally visiting the world she had read about in books. Kingsley soon became friends with the sailors and traders of the region. They taught her about navigation and told her where she might find the specimens she was seeking. Kingsley later claimed that she had steered a 2,000-ton ship across the Niger River three separate times.

Kingsley kept no daily record of this first trip to Africa. But she did make reference to the journey in her writings. She sailed as far south as St. Paul de Loanda (now Angola) and explored the Congo (or Zaire) River. When she returned to England in January 1894, she had a solid reputation both as a traveler and a naturalist. The British Museum was so impressed by her fish and beetle collection that they agreed to equip her for further research.

Back to Africa

Near the end of 1894, Kingsley sailed again for the coast of West Africa. By now, she was treated like an "Old Coaster," the name given to those who had proved that they could withstand the dangers of Africa. These dangers included tropical diseases that wiped out entire European settlements. To avoid such diseases, Kingsley made it a rule never to drink unboiled water. She was not afraid of traveling alone, however, and she set out to explore the Ogowe River (in what is now Gabon). She planned to collect fish for the British Museum and continue her study of African culture.

In her travels, Kingsley met African people who had never seen a European. Many Africans considered Europeans to be a kind of devil. But Kingsley won their trust by pretending to be a trader. As she put it, "If you show yourself an intelligent trader who knows the price of things, they treat you with respect. . . ."

Having made friends with the local people, she traveled up the Ogowe River in a canoe rowed by crewmen from the area. They passed through a forest that was the home of a feared tribe called the Fans, who were believed to be cannibals. But Kingsley grew to love both the forest and the Fans. She described them as a "bright, energetic sort of African."

When Kingsley reached Kangwe, she spent several weeks at a Protestant settlement before boarding a steamer for the journey upriver to Njole. There she hired a canoe and crew for the extremely dangerous trip through the river above Njole. The water there swirled with rapids, whirlpools, and shallow, rocky patches. She returned four days later and described her survival as a joke that she had played on "King Death."

On July 22, 1895, Kingsley set out again from Njole for a journey to the Rembwe River. It may have been her most challenging adventure. In one week, she barely escaped death several times. She came face-to-face with a leopard and hit it over the head with a pot. She freed another leopard from a snare. Her canoe became trapped in a lagoon, where she had to beat off swarming crocodiles with her paddle. While visiting a village, she smelled something unpleasant and went to see what it was. She found a bag filled with the leftovers from a cannibal dinner. Despite these dangers, traveling alone had great benefits. She wrote: "Unless you live alone among the natives, you never get to know them; if you do this you gradually get a light into [their] true state. . . ." She observed and took notes on many aspects of African cultures, including religion, cannibalism, property laws, the role of women, and burial customs. She also found that her own religious beliefs were not very different from those of the Africans.

Kingsley next sailed to the island of Corisco, off the coast of Gabon, and collected shellfish. On her journey home, she stopped long enough to become the first European woman to climb the Mungo Mah Lobeh (also known as Mount Cameroon). This active volcano is one of the highest peaks in Africa. Her guides deserted her halfway through the climb, but she reached the summit by herself. However, she was frustrated by the mist that blocked her view from the top of the mountain.

A Serious Message

Kingsley reached England in November 1895 and began work on her book, *Travels in West Africa.* Her exciting adventures and interesting writing style made the book an immediate success. It contained a great deal of scientific and cultural information and presented her view of the African people. She disagreed with the popular view that Africans should be treated as children or as an inferior race. She believed that Africans were fellow human beings of great promise. Kingsley became a very popular lecturer and spoke to her audiences about her views on the British role in Africa. She warned that the British could do much damage to African cultures if they were not careful. This topic became the subject of her second book, *West African Studies.*

By 1900 Kingsley had decided to make a third trip to Africa. She no longer enjoyed life in England, and she missed the African people. The Boer War was underway in South Africa, and there was a great need for nurses, so she sailed to Cape Town to assist in this effort. She was assigned to a hospital in Simonstown, where many soldiers were dying of an intestinal fever. Within two months, Kingsley caught the fever herself and died. She was buried at sea with full military honors.

SUGGESTED READING Katherine Frank, *A Voyage Out: The Life of Mary Kingsley* (Houghton Mifflin, 1986); Mary Henrietta Kingsley, *Travels in West Africa* (Adventure Library, 1997); Caroline Oliver, *Western Women in Colonial Africa* (Greenwood Press, 1982); Marion Tinling, *Women into the Unknown* (Greenwood Press, 1989).

Kino, Eusebio Francisco

Italian
b August 10, 1645?; Segno, near Trent, Italy
d March 15, 1711; Magdalena, Mexico
Explored Baja California, northern Mexico, and southern Arizona

mission settlement founded by priests in a land where they hoped to convert people to Christianity

Jesuit member of the Society of Jesus, a Roman Catholic order founded by Ignatius of Loyola in 1534

New Spain region of Spanish colonial empire that included the areas now occupied by Mexico, Florida, Texas, New Mexico, Arizona, California, and various Caribbean islands

Father Eusebio Francisco Kino was a successful missionary and explorer who dedicated his life to the king of Spain and the Roman Catholic Church. He explored more than 50,000 square miles in northern Mexico and what is now the southwestern United States. Many of the Catholic **missions** that he founded have developed into modern towns. He also introduced to the Indians of the region the practice of raising farm animals. Kino was a master geographer and mapmaker. He produced the earliest maps that showed Baja California as a peninsula rather than as an island. His maps are also the first to include the Gila and Colorado Rivers and southern Arizona.

Kino's Promise

It is believed that Kino was born on August 10, 1645. He was raised in the Italian village of Segno and educated at the **Jesuit** College in nearby Trent. In 1663 he went to Hala, near Innsbruck, Germany (now in Austria), to continue his studies, but he fell ill with a deadly disease. Kino promised God that he would become a Jesuit missionary if he recovered. After he regained his health, Kino kept his promise and joined the Jesuit order in 1665. After studying at a number of European universities, he became a priest in 1677. Kino wanted to follow in the footsteps of his patron, Saint Francis XAVIER, by getting a missionary post in Asia. But posts were chosen by lottery, and he ended up in **New Spain.** However, he soon overcame

This statue of Eusebio Francisco Kino honors his role as a founder of Spanish settlements in the region that became the state of Arizona.

scurvy disease caused by a lack of vitamin C and once a major cause of death among sailors; symptoms include internal bleeding, loosened teeth, and extreme fatigue

whatever disappointment he felt. He was devoted to his Jesuit mission and eager to explore this new land.

On January 17, 1683, Kino left on his first expedition, commanded by Isidro de Atondo y Antillón. Their goal was to build Christian settlements in Baja California. When they reached La Paz Bay along the Gulf of California, Kino met Indians for the first time. He treated them with a peaceful and gentle manner. He gave them glass beads and handkerchiefs and made an effort to learn their language. A colony was founded at La Paz, but it was abandoned due to a lack of supplies.

"The Black Robe"

Atondo and Kino established another colony, called San Bruno, farther north on Baja California. From there they made several trips inland, to the west. They climbed a mountain they called La Giganta and explored a river they named Santo Tomás (now La Purísima). On New Year's Day 1685, they discovered a bay on the Pacific coast of Baja and named it Año Nuevo (now Laguna de San Gregoris). They were the first Europeans to cross California to the Pacific Ocean. But drought and a severe attack of **scurvy** forced them to leave the region. For the rest of his life, Kino hoped to return to California.

In 1687 Kino was sent to do missionary work in Pimería Alta, in the province of Sonora. Sonora included northwestern Mexico and what is now southwestern Arizona. Kino explored this vast area for the next 24 years. He peacefully extended the frontier of New Spain by founding a series of missions. Wherever he traveled, Kino was welcomed by the Indians, who called him "the Black Robe." He became known in the church as "the Apostle to the Pimas" for his work with the Upper Pima Indians in Pimería Alta.

Father Kino established the mission of Nuestra Señora de los Dolores in northwestern Sonora. This settlement became the headquarters for his work in Arizona. He later established missions throughout what became present-day Arizona and Sonora. He also made the first recorded journey to the lower Altar River, where he founded the mission village of Coborca. In 1697 he explored the San Pedro River valley and taught Christianity to the Indians in the region.

Further Explorations

In 1698 and 1699, Father Kino made several important journeys. First he traveled north along the Santa Cruz River to the Gila River near the site of modern Phoenix, establishing missions along both rivers. Next he traveled through southwest Arizona to Casa Grande in Sonora. Then he followed the Devil's Highway, perhaps the most difficult trail in the Southwest. It passed through rocky canyons and desertlike plains, where there was almost no water to be found. Kino was the first European to reach the end of the 200-mile-long trail. After reaching the Gila River near the modern town of Wellton, Arizona, he followed the river upstream. He then made the first recorded exploration between the Gila Bend Mountains and Sierra La Estrella in the Maricopa Mountains.

The Indian tribes in Arizona gave Kino blue shells that reminded him of shells he had found on the Pacific coast of Baja. He thought that they might have brought the shells by land from California. Looking for a land route to California, he traveled down the Gila River until he reached the Colorado River. Then he followed the Colorado to the Gulf of California. On his return trip, he rafted across the Colorado River into California. This journey proved that California could be reached by an overland route.

Father Kino made some 50 expeditions during his time in Pimería Alta, often traveling with only a few Indians or another priest. He died on March 15, 1711, after dedicating a new church at the mission of Magdalena in Sonora, Mexico. The records of his work were kept in Spanish libraries and were unknown to the rest of the world for many years. Today he is recognized as the founder of Arizona, and he is viewed as a great explorer. However, the only place that still bears his name is Bahía de Kino, a bay along the northwestern coast of Mexico.

SUGGESTED READING Herbert E. Bolton, *Rim of Christendom: A Biography of Eusebio Francisco Kino, Pacific Coast Pioneer* (Macmillan Company, 1936); Eusebio Francisco Kino, *Kino's Historical Memoir of Pimería Alta, 1683–1711,* translated by Herbert E. Bolton (University of California Press, 1948).

Kintup

Italian
b 1840s; Darjeeling?, India
d after 1914; India?
Explored Tibet

surveyor one who makes precise measurements of a location's geography

Kintup was one of several residents of India who helped the British explore remote regions of northern India and central Asia. These explorers, known as pundits, carried out many missions, often in highly dangerous circumstances. One of the most extraordinary ordeals was that of the pundit named Kintup, who suffered slavery and poverty while trying to learn the course of a river in Tibet.

Himalayan Mysteries

During the 1800s, the Indian subcontinent was ruled as a colony by the British, who had a great curiosity about the Himalaya Mountains on India's northern frontier. British geographers were eager to send **surveyors** to explore the region. But the mountains were home to several ancient kingdoms, including Tibet, Ladakh, and Nepal, whose rulers were determined to keep foreigners out of their lands. Europeans who tried to enter were turned back at the borders and sometimes even attacked or killed.

The British began training Indian men to act as geographical spies. These men could sneak into Tibet by disguising themselves as merchants or wandering monks. With careful training in the use of cleverly disguised surveying tools, these pundits compiled the information needed to map Tibet and the lands around it.

Some of the pundits, including Nain SINGH and Kishen SINGH, were well-educated men. Kintup, however, was a tailor from the city of Darjeeling in Sikkim, a kingdom in northeastern India. He

The British sent Kintup into the forbidden kingdom of Tibet on a daring and dangerous mission as a geographical spy.

lama Buddhist priest or monk of high rank in Tibet and Mongolia

pilgrimage journey to a sacred place

could neither read nor write, but he was a reliable person of "sturdy courage," according to one British official. From 1878 to 1879, Kintup served as assistant to a pundit named Nem Singh, who had surveyed several hundred miles of the Zangbo River (also called the Tsangpo) in Tibet. In 1880 the British assigned Kintup to continue that work.

The Zangbo River was a mystery. It flows through Tibet, but no one knew where it went. Many British geographers thought that the Zangbo was the same as the Brahmaputra River, which flows out of the Himalaya and empties into the sea at the eastern edge of India. Cliffs, rain forests, waterfalls, and hostile inhabitants made it difficult to travel up the Brahmaputra to find its source. Kintup's mission was to begin at the Zangbo and follow it downstream to see if it joined the Brahmaputra.

Entering a Forbidden Land

Because Kintup was unable to record the measurements he made, the British teamed him with a Mongolian **lama.** Kintup pretended to be the lama's servant as the pair traveled through Tibet. In this way, Kintup carried out his survey while the lama recorded their discoveries.

The plan backfired because the lama was far less reliable than Kintup. The two successfully entered Tibet, but the lama soon delayed them by beginning a long love affair with a village woman. He also treated Kintup badly, acting as though his partner were truly a servant. In the spring of 1881, after the travelers had explored part of the Zangbo River, the lama sold Kintup as a slave to a local official and then disappeared. Kintup labored for almost a year before he was able to escape.

To avoid being recaptured, Kintup begged the head lama of a local monastery for help. The lama took him in—again as a slave. About four months later, Kintup persuaded the lama to let him leave on a religious **pilgrimage.** Two and one-half years after entering Tibet, he was ready to begin his real mission.

Secret Success

Henry Harman, Kintup's British trainer, had worked out a backup plan in case Kintup was unable to complete the entire journey along the Zangbo River. Now, without money or freedom, Kintup decided to put that plan into action. He cut 500 logs, marked them in a certain way, hid them in the forest, and returned to his master. On his next leave of absence, he traveled to Lhasa, the capital of Tibet. There he found some fellow Sikkimese travelers who agreed to carry a message to Nem Singh in Darjeeling. The message told Singh and Harman to watch the lower Brahmaputra River for the marked logs, which Kintup would send down the Zangbo. If the logs appeared in the Brahmaputra, the watchers would know that the two rivers were one.

Kintup had to spend nine more months as a slave at the monastery before he was finally freed. He retrieved his logs and placed them in the Zangbo River, releasing 50 logs each day for 10 days. He then tried to follow the river to the sea, but he was turned back by a local tribe. He made a long, slow journey back to Lhasa and then crossed the Himalaya to return home. By the time he reached Darjeeling, he had been gone for more than four years.

Tragically, Kintup's devotion to duty was wasted. Harman had left India, Kintup's message had gone astray, and no one had been on the lookout for the logs in the Brahmaputra River. Had anyone been watching, however, they probably would have seen the logs, for the Zangbo does in fact become the Brahmaputra.

Kintup returned to his tailor's shop. Two years later, a British official finally interviewed him about his travels. The account appeared in a report in 1889, and Kintup made several other expeditions with the British. The British government awarded Kintup a small pension, but he received less attention than the better-educated pundits, whose reports were considered more reliable. He was last seen by the British in Darjeeling in 1914.

SUGGESTED READING John MacGregor, *Tibet: A Chronicle of Exploration* (Praeger Publishers, 1970); Derek Waller, *The Pundits: British Exploration of Tibet and Central Asia* (University Press of Kentucky, 1990).

Kotzebue, Otto von

Russian
b December 30, 1787; Reval (now Tallinn), Estonia
d February 15, 1846; Reval (now Tallinn), Estonia
Explored Pacific Ocean and northwest coast of America; sailed around the world twice

brig small, fast sailing ship with two masts and square sails

Northwest Passage water route connecting the Atlantic Ocean and Pacific Ocean through the Arctic islands of northern Canada

Otto von Kotzebue began a career of exploration when he went to sea at age 15. He later made several important discoveries for Russia in the Pacific Ocean and along the coasts of Alaska and California. Kotzebue wrote and published literary accounts of his two major ocean voyages.

Around the World

Kotzebue's father was the German poet and playwright August Friedrich Ferdinand von Kotzebue. Otto von Kotzebue was born in Reval (present-day Tallinn, Estonia). In 1803 Otto was a 15-year-old student at the St. Petersburg School for Cadets. His father asked that Otto and his younger brother, Martin, be allowed to join a major expedition. The commander, Adam Ivan von KRUSENSTERN, accepted the boys onto his crew. Otto served as a clerk on Krusenstern's three-year voyage around the world.

By 1815 Kotzebue was a lieutenant, and Krusenstern recommended him to command a **brig** on an expedition to find a **Northwest Passage** through the Bering Strait. With a crew of 32 men, Kotzebue rounded Cape Horn and sailed north up the South American coast. He then headed west to Easter Island. There he discovered Romanzof Island, named after the expedition's sponsor. He also discovered and named several other Pacific islands near what are now the Tuamotus and Kiribati.

Discovery and Disappointment

Kotzebue spent the summers of 1816 and 1817 looking for a safe place to anchor his ship and charting the northwest coast of Alaska.

kayak small canoe, usually made of sealskin stretched over a light frame of bone or wood

circumnavigate to travel around

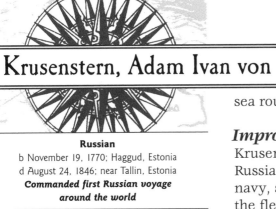

Krusenstern, Adam Ivan von

Russian
b November 19, 1770; Haggud, Estonia
d August 24, 1846; near Tallin, Estonia
Commanded first Russian voyage around the world

Adam Ivan von Krusenstern came up with a plan to link together Russia's distant trading posts.

He was aided by members of a Russian fur trading company and by Aleuts in **kayaks.** Kotzebue found a sound—a long, broad inlet—north of Bering Strait that he thought might lead to a Northwest Passage. It did not, but the sound still bears his name.

In July 1817, Kotzebue suffered an attack of angina, a painful respiratory disease, while preparing to enter the Bering Strait. The attack left him fainting and spitting up blood. He decided to return home, sailing west through the Pacific Ocean and around Africa's Cape of Good Hope. He arrived in St. Petersburg on August 3, 1818. From 1823 to 1826, Kotzebue commanded a second Pacific expedition, and again he **circumnavigated** the globe. He visited the Tuamotus, Tahiti, the Navigators Islands (now Samoa), the Marshall Islands, Kamchatka, and the northwest coast of America. Kotzebue retired in 1830 due to ill health and died in 1846.

SUGGESTED READING Otto von Kotzebue, *A Voyage of Discovery* (Longman, Hurst, Rees, Orme, and Brown, 1821).

Adam Ivan von Krusenstern helped put Russia on the same level as Great Britain and France in the field of naval exploration during the 1800s. He also established sea routes that improved Russian trade.

Improving Trade Relations

Krusenstern served in the Russian navy during the war between Russia and Sweden, from 1787 to 1790. He later joined the British navy, serving in Africa, Asia, and North America. In 1798 he left the fleet to spend a year in Guangzhou (also called Canton), China, before returning home. During his travels, he devised a plan to improve trade between Russia's ports on the Baltic Sea and its colonies in America and Siberia. Russia's emperor, Alexander I, approved the plan and put Krusenstern in charge of an expedition to the Pacific Ocean.

In August 1803, Krusenstern sailed from Kronstadt (now Kronshlot) on the Baltic Sea in two British-built ships, the *Nadezhda* and the *Neva.* He stopped in Denmark, England, and the Canary Islands before sailing to the coast of Brazil. The expedition's naturalist studied plant and animal life along the way. After rounding South America's Cape Horn in March 1804, the ships were separated in the southern Pacific Ocean. Krusenstern took the *Nadezhda* to the Marquesas Islands, where he traded with the islanders and witnessed their secret funeral rituals. After stopping at the Sandwich Islands (now Hawaii), he reached the Kamchatka Peninsula of Russia 35 days later.

Making the Connection

Krusenstern then sailed to Japan in hopes of repairing Russia's relations with that country. His party was met with hostility, but this response did not prevent him from charting the Japanese coast and exploring the northern island of Yeso (present-day Hokkaido). Krusenstern later reached Macao, off the coast of China, where his ships were reunited after 18 months apart. The Chinese tried to seize the ships, which barely escaped in February 1806. They sailed west around the world, reaching Russia just over three years after their departure.

Krusenstern had successfully charted an ocean route that linked Kamchatka, Russia's North American colonies, and China. He later published two books, an account of the voyage and *Atlas of the Pacific Ocean.* In 1815 he searched for the **Northwest Passage** but failed to find it. Krusenstern later achieved the rank of admiral and worked for several Russian naval committees and academies. He died on his Estonian estate in 1846.

SUGGESTED READING Ivan Fedorovich Kruzenshtern, *Atlas of the Voyage Round the World* (Da Capo Press, 1970).

Northwest Passage water route connecting the Atlantic Ocean and Pacific Ocean through the Arctic islands of northern Canada

La Condamine, Charles-Marie de

French
b January 27, 1701; Paris, France
d February 4, 1774; Paris, France
***Explored Amazon Basin;
measured earth's surface in Andes Mountains***

cartography the science of mapmaking

latitude distance north or south of the equator

Charles-Marie de La Condamine's explorations introduced Europe to many new substances, including rubber, platinum, and Indian medicines.

Charles-Marie de La Condamine was a French soldier, explorer, mathematician, and natural historian. His restless spirit and curious mind led him to Ecuador to help settle the debate over the shape of the earth. He would stay in South America for 10 years after that task was completed. During this time, he crossed the continent from the Pacific to the Atlantic Ocean, climbed the Andes Mountains, and led the first scientific exploration of the Amazon River.

From the Army to the Equator

Charles-Marie de La Condamine was born into a wealthy and noble French family. After attending college in Paris, he entered the military and won honors in a battle against Spain in 1719. But he was too restless and intellectually curious for the strict life of a soldier. He left the military and occupied himself with the study of mathematics, astronomy, **cartography,** and natural history. He soon joined the leading scientific circles in Paris. He made friends with the famous writer and philosopher Voltaire, who encouraged and supported La Condamine's ideas and explorations.

At the age of 29, La Condamine was elected to France's Royal Academy of Sciences. In 1731 he went on his first expedition to the African coast of the Red Sea and to Constantinople (present-day Istanbul, Turkey). Along the way, he made mathematical and astronomical observations. He presented a paper on his findings that earned him a firm reputation as a scientist.

La Condamine then got involved in the great scientific debate over the shape of the earth. The French astronomer Jacques Cassini believed that the earth's sphere stretched out at the poles. British scientist Sir Isaac Newton said that the earth was flattened at the poles and wider at the equator. Some measurements had been made in France, but more measurements would have to be taken at different points on the globe. Expeditions were sent to Lapland (in Norway) and to the equator for this purpose. Scientists would measure a degree of **latitude** in each place, compare the calculations, and decide which theory was correct.

La Condamine was selected to lead the Equatorial Expedition of 1735. Surprisingly, the king of Spain granted permission for the

French to enter South America. For 250 years, only the Spanish and the Portuguese had been allowed to explore South America openly. La Condamine's party was the first group of outsiders to be admitted.

Measuring the Earth

La Condamine's expedition arrived at Portobelo, Panama, on November 29, 1735. They traveled by land across the Isthmus of Panama and then by boat to Manta, on the west coast of Ecuador. Most of the men continued down the coast to Guayaquil. But La Condamine took the route through the jungle to Quito, the place chosen for the measurements of latitude. He traveled with Pedro Vicente Maldonado, the governor of the province of Esmeraldas. As they journeyed along the Esmeraldas River, they came across blood-sucking flies and mouse-size cockroaches. La Condamine was fascinated by the stretchy substance called *caoutchouc* that was drawn from trees. He had a bag made from it to protect his instruments. The substance is known today as natural latex, or rubber. Along the route, he also discovered a metal called *platina*. It was later classified as a precious metal and named platinum.

The two groups reunited at Quito in early 1737. The scientists faced great challenges as they tried to take the measurements of the chosen area. They had to climb steep volcanic mountains to complete their calculations. Also, the local people were highly suspicious of the French scientists. They thought that the surveying instruments were being used to find buried Inca treasure. The team took six years to complete their measurements, only to find out that the Lapland team had already proved that Newton's theory was correct. Though La Condamine's own measurements also supported Newton's theory, the years of work now seemed almost unnecessary. The expedition's members had suffered greatly during the course of the project. Two had gone insane, the team's medical doctor had been violently murdered, and two others had died—one of **malaria** and one in an accident.

malaria disease that is spread by mosquitoes in tropical areas

Down the Amazon River

La Condamine and Governor Maldonado then set out from Cuenca, Ecuador, and headed south to Borja, Peru. They reached Borja in June 1743 and traveled down the Marañón River by canoe until they reached the Amazon River. The gloom of the forest and the greatness of the river made this region very different from Quito. On the journey down the Amazon, La Condamine recorded its volume and depth and the speed of the current. He created a map so accurate that it could be used today to navigate the river. He also kept careful notes on the Indians he met along the river, describing their fishing methods and the ways in which they protected themselves from insect bites. However, he took a narrow and negative view of the Indians, and he failed to see much good in them.

La Condamine veered off onto the Río Negro for several miles and determined that it flowed from the northwest. His Amazon journey ended in Pará (present-day Belém) on the coast of Brazil

For a map, of La Condamine's route, see the profile of Alexander von HUMBOLDT in this volume.

in September 1743. There he discovered that Marajó, northwest of Pará, was a single island, not a series of islands as had been thought. La Condamine left Brazil in December and sailed to French Guiana. He stayed there for five months, conducting experiments.

Back in France

La Condamine returned to Paris in February 1745 after 10 years in South America. He brought back a wealth of scientific and geographical information, and his observations led to further explorations of the Amazon River. He spent the rest of his life writing of his experiences and campaigning for vaccination against smallpox. Since he had suffered from smallpox in his youth, he felt very strongly about this cause.

La Condamine married for the first time at age 55 and was elected to the respected French Academy in 1760. By the age of 62, he could no longer walk or move well and was almost deaf in one ear. He was forced to dictate his books and articles to his wife. La Condamine died in 1774, a highly respected member of the world's scientific community.

SUGGESTED READING Victor Wolfgang Von Hagen, *South America Called Them: Explorations of the Great Naturalists: Charles-Marie de la Condamine, Alexander Humboldt, Charles Darwin, Richard Spruce* (Scientific Book Club, 1949).

La Cosa, Juan de

Spanish
b 1460?; Puerto de Santa María, Spain
d February 28, 1510; near Cartagena, Colombia
Explored coast of South America

cartographer mapmaker

Spanish Main area of the Spanish Empire including the Caribbean coasts of Central and South America

Juan de La Cosa was a master **cartographer** who sailed with several Spanish expeditions, including the second voyage led by Christopher COLUMBUS. In 1500 La Cosa produced a world map, now famous, that incorporated the latest discoveries of the coast of South America and the islands of the Caribbean Sea. La Cosa also developed skills as a navigator and explorer. He led an expedition of his own to explore the area around the Gulf of Urabá in what is now Colombia.

A Map of Exploration

Nothing is known of La Cosa's life before 1493. In that year, he embarked on Columbus's second voyage as a sailor aboard the *Niña*. There has been some confusion among historians because there were two men named Juan de La Cosa who sailed with Columbus, both about the same age and both from the Basque region of Spain. One was the owner and pilot of the *Santa Maria,* the flagship of Columbus's first voyage, which took place in 1492. That La Cosa was disgraced when his ship ran aground off the coast of Hispaniola (the island now occupied by Haiti and the Dominican Republic). The more famous La Cosa, discussed here, was the cartographer and explorer of the **Spanish Main.** He credited Columbus with teaching him the skills of navigation, but no one knows how he learned to be a mapmaker.

In 1499 La Cosa sailed under the command of Alonso de OJEDA, piloting Ojeda's ships along the coastline of what is now Venezuela and British Guiana. He led the expedition into the Gulf of Venezuela and Lake Maracaibo; then he sailed around the Guajira Peninsula as far west as Cabo de la Vela (now in Colombia). The explorers returned to Spain with a large quantity of pearls and slaves, making La Cosa a wealthy man.

cartography the science of mapmaking

La Cosa then drew his map of the world, an important event in **cartography** and exploration. He was the first to show Cuba, correctly, as an island—although, when sailing with Columbus earlier, he had agreed to sign his captain's statement that Cuba was a peninsula of the mainland of Asia.

Good Advice and Bad Luck

In 1501 La Cosa sailed with Rodrigo de BASTIDAS, again exploring the coast of Colombia and what is now Panama. They were the first explorers to reach the mainland of Central America. This success assured La Cosa of the admiration and trust he had built at the royal court of Spain. He was so well regarded that Queen Isabella told another explorer, Cristóbal Guerra: "In navigation, I command you to follow what appears best to Juan de La Cosa, for I know that he is a man who knows well what he is talking about when he gives advice." Guerra would soon discover that the queen was right.

La Cosa left Spain again in late September 1504 and arrived at Margarita Island, off the coast of Venezuela. He gathered pearls along what is now known as the Pearl Coast (near present-day Cumaná, Venezuela). He also found brazilwood on the islands of the Curaçao **archipelago.**

archipelago large group of islands or a body of water with many islands

In the Bay of Cartagena, La Cosa encountered a shipwrecked band of Spanish explorers—the surviving members of a failed expedition led by Guerra. After helping them as best he could, La Cosa explored the Gulf of Urabá and ventured inland several times. On one such journey, he entered an abandoned hut in an Indian village and found a chest filled with gold masks and drums. Captured Indians told him that there was more gold on the other side of the gulf. La Cosa and his men then boarded small boats, navigated inland on the Atrato River, and raided villages for gold.

Returning to the Gulf of Urabá, La Cosa again had to rescue Guerra's men, whose boats had sprung leaks. But he soon had to abandon his own ships, which had been damaged by shipworms. The 200 survivors of both expeditions had to live on the beach of the gulf for almost a year. They were finally able to patch together a few boats and sail to Hispaniola. La Cosa returned to Spain in March 1506. Although his adventures had been profitable, he had lost all but 60 men to disease, starvation, and Indian attacks.

Poisoned Revenge

La Cosa next served as a commander of Spanish outposts in the Caribbean region until 1509. In November of that year, he left Hispaniola with Ojeda to establish a colony near the site of present-day Cartagena, Colombia. Against La Cosa's advice, Ojeda killed many Indians in the area. The Indians who survived soon took revenge with a vicious attack, killing the entire Spanish landing party except for Ojeda, who managed to escape. La Cosa died from wounds inflicted by the Indians' poisoned darts.

SUGGESTED READING John Frye, *Los Otros: Columbus and the Three Who Made His Enterprise of the Indies Succeed* (E. Mellen Press, 1992).

Laing, Alexander Gordon

Scottish
b December 27, 1793; Edinburgh, Scotland
d September 26, 1826; near Timbuktu, Mali
Explored Sahara; reached Timbuktu

headwaters source of a river

sheikh Arab chief

Alexander Gordon Laing was the first European to reach the fabled African city of Timbuktu.

Alexander Gordon Laing was the first European to reach the city of Timbuktu (in what is now Mali), after one of the longest journeys ever made across the Sahara desert region. Shortly before making that trek, he fell in love and married. Unfortunately, he did not live long enough to enjoy his marriage or the fame he might have won for his explorations. He was murdered outside Timbuktu just after beginning his return trip to Europe.

An Officer in Africa

Laing first went to Africa as a British army officer, stationed in the territory of Sierra Leone on the continent's west coast. He was assigned to find new trade routes to the interior, but his real interest was in exploring the Niger River. Although his request to lead an expedition inland was denied, he was given command of a patrol near the **headwaters** of the river. He became convinced that the Niger did not flow into the Nile River, and he was determined to prove his theory. Hostile Africans in the region blocked his efforts to follow the Niger, but he did discover the source of the Rokel River.

After serving in the Ashanti War from 1823 to 1824, Laing was assigned to give a personal report of the conflict to Lord Bathurst, the British secretary of state for war and colonies. The young officer used the opportunity to seek support for an exploration of the Niger River. Bathurst agreed, but he ordered Laing to begin at Tripoli (in what is now Libya), travel south to Timbuktu, and follow the Niger from there.

Journey to Timbuktu

When Laing arrived in Tripoli in May 1825, he fell in love almost immediately with Emma Warrington, the daughter of the chief British diplomat there. The young couple married on July 14, and Laing left for Timbuktu two days later. Accompanied by two officials from Tripoli, Laing was forced to travel through territory controlled by the hostile Tuareg tribe. In January 1826, his party was attacked by the Tuareg, and he was almost killed. Despite his injuries, he pressed on and arrived in Timbuktu on August 25, after a 1,500-mile journey across the Sahara.

Laing spent five weeks in Timbuktu, a city that had been glorified in Europe as an exotic and wealthy land. While he was there, Laing wrote letters stating that the city lived up to his expectations. However, Christians were not welcome in Timbuktu. Laing was treated well during his stay, but a friendly **sheikh** warned him that his life was in danger and begged him to leave. Laing did so on September 24, 1826; he was murdered by his own guide two days later on the outskirts of the city.

Apparently, Laing's presence was seen by the inhabitants of Timbuktu as a sign that more Christians would soon be intruding on them. Two years later, the French explorer René-Auguste CAILLIÉ arrived in the city, disguised as an Arab. He learned that Laing had been suspected of being a Christian spy and had been beaten to death by his guide for that reason.

SUGGESTED READING E. W. Bovill, *Missions to the Niger* (University Press, 1964).

Lander, Richard Lemon

English
b February 8, 1804; Truro, England
d February 6, 1834; Fernando Póo (present-day Bioko)
Traveled to mouth of Niger River

sultan ruler of a Muslim nation

Richard Lemon Lander was the first explorer to trace the course of the Niger River to its end, a task at which many had failed before him. He made his first voyage to the Niger as a servant to Sir Hugh CLAPPERTON. After Clapperton's death, Lander continued his former master's work, reaching the mouth of the Niger on his second journey. He returned to the river once more, but he was fatally wounded in a battle with Africans.

Sorrow and Slavery on the Niger

Lander, the son of an innkeeper, developed an interest in travel as a young man. He was employed as a servant to wealthy gentlemen and nobles and spent time in continental Europe, the Caribbean islands, and South Africa. In 1825 he joined Clapperton as a servant on the explorer's second expedition to the Niger River in 1825. The party traveled northeast from Badagri, a town on the coast of the Bight of Benin (near the present-day border of Benin and Nigeria). They then crossed the Niger near Bussa (now in Nigeria) and continued east. In July 1826, they reached Kano, where Lander stayed to recover from an illness.

Meanwhile, Clapperton traveled west to Sokoto to ask permission from a **sultan** named Bello to follow the Niger south to the Gulf of Guinea. Lander arrived in Sokoto to find that the request had been denied. Clapperton then fell seriously ill and died in Lander's care in April 1827. The loyal servant returned to England and had his employer's journals published.

Lander was determined to complete Clapperton's work, so he volunteered for a government-sponsored trip to the Niger. He left Britain in January 1830 with his younger brother John, again landing at Badagri and traveling to Bussa. By September the brothers had purchased a canoe and had begun their journey down the river.

On the Niger, they were attacked twice by African tribesmen. The first attackers retreated when they realized that the explorers meant no harm. But the second assault resulted in the brothers' capture by warriors of the Ibo tribe. All of the Landers' possessions and records were stolen or destroyed. Finally a slave trader purchased the brothers from the Ibo. John was held in the trader's home city while Richard finished the voyage down the river—as a slave on a chief's royal canoe. Both brothers were set free the following June.

A Fatal Return

After being honored in Europe for his achievement, Lander returned to Africa in 1832 to lead a private trading expedition up the Niger River. Problems plagued the journey from the start, including insufficient supplies and an unruly crew. Lander decided to turn back. About 100 miles from the mouth of the river, the party was attacked by Africans. Three crew members were killed, Lander was wounded, and all of his journals and papers were lost. After being pursued for several hours, Lander finally escaped. He retreated to the nearby island of Fernando Póo (now called Bioko), where he died a few days later from his injuries.

SUGGESTED READING Robin Hallett, editor, *The Niger Journal of Richard and John Lander* (Frederick Praeger, 1965); Mercedes Mackay, *The Indomitable Servant* (Collings, 1978).

La Pérouse, Jean François de Galaup de

French
b August 23, 1741; Albi, France
d 1788?; Santa Cruz Islands?
Explored Pacific Ocean

---

frigate small, agile warship with three masts and square sails

Northwest Passage water route connecting the Atlantic Ocean and Pacific Ocean through the Arctic islands of northern Canada

In 1785 the French navy chose Jean François de Galaup de La Pérouse, a military hero, to explore the Pacific Ocean.

Jean François de Galaup de La Pérouse led a French naval expedition to the Pacific Ocean in the 1780s. His goal was to fill any gaps in the extensive knowledge of the Pacific that had been gathered by the British explorer James COOK. La Pérouse sent word of his discoveries back to France with messengers, but he himself never returned. The fate of the commander and his crew remained a mystery for more than 40 years.

A Distinguished Military Career

La Pérouse joined the French navy in 1756 and fought the British off the coast of North America during the Seven Years' War. In 1759 he was wounded and taken prisoner. After his release, La Pérouse was promoted to the rank of ensign, and he served in North America and the Indian Ocean, eventually reaching the rank of commander.

During the American Revolution, the French navy fought against British ships off the Atlantic coast of North America. In 1779 La Pérouse captured a British **frigate** near Savannah, Georgia, and two years later, he seized two British ships at Cape Breton, Nova Scotia. In August 1782, he became a hero when he attacked and captured two British forts on the shores of Hudson Bay.

The Military Turns to Exploration

In 1785 the French navy chose La Pérouse to lead an ambitious expedition to the Pacific Ocean. Besides exploring the ocean's many island chains, he was expected to sail along the Pacific coasts of China and Russia and to establish a French outpost for whaling and fur trading in northern Pacific waters. His objectives also included a search for a western entrance to the **Northwest Passage.**

La Pérouse left France on August 1, 1785, with two ships, the *Boussole* and the *Astrolabe.* After several stops, he reached Cape Horn at the southern tip of South America on April 1, 1786. In February 1787, he visited the Spanish colony of Chile; in April he landed briefly at Easter Island in the Pacific Ocean.

Heading north, the expedition spent one day in May on the island of Maui in the Sandwich Islands (present-day Hawaii) before

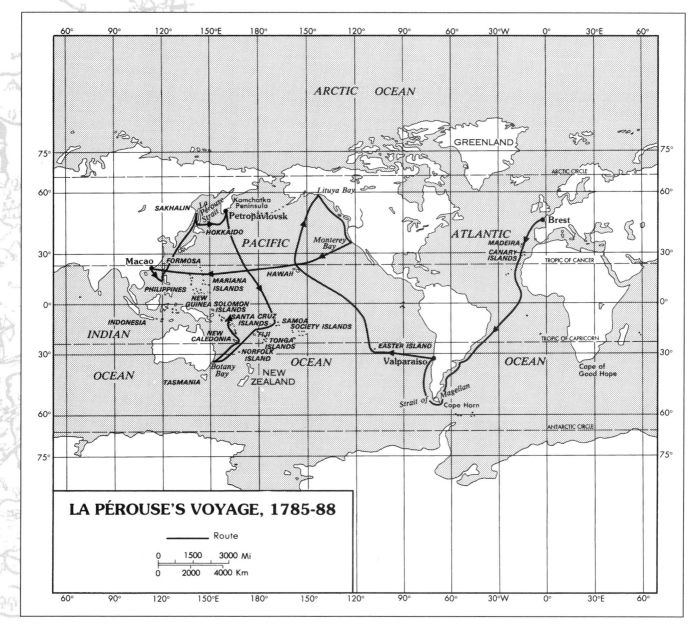

LA PÉROUSE'S VOYAGE, 1785-88

——— Route

0   1500   3000 Mi

0   2000   4000 Km

La Pérouse's voyage took him across two oceans, but it ended mysteriously somewhere in the Santa Cruz Islands.

continuing northeast. On June 23, the explorers sighted Mount St. Elias on the southeast coast of Alaska. They set up camp at what is now called Lituya Bay, where they had to keep watch against thefts by the people native to the area.

Tragedy struck for the first time in July, when three of the expedition's small boats sank in dangerous waters at the narrow mouth of the bay. Twenty-one men lost their lives. At the end of the month, the French left the bay, carrying a cargo of furs acquired through trade. They then sailed south to Monterey Bay, on the California coast, and spent 10 days studying the wildlife and the Spanish settlements in the region.

Encounters in Asia

On September 24, La Pérouse sailed west, discovering Necker Island northwest of Hawaii and landing in the Mariana Islands. On

January 2, 1787, he entered the port of Macao on the Chinese coast. There the *Astrolabe*'s naturalist left the expedition in order to take its logs and maps back to France. After passing through the Philippine Islands, La Pérouse turned his ships toward the northern coast of Asia, which at that time was virtually unknown to western Europeans.

La Pérouse sailed north between Formosa (present-day Taiwan) and the Ryukyu Islands, south of Japan. The inhabitants of Oku-Yeso (now called Sakhalin Island), which lies north of Japan, drew him a map that showed their island, the island of Yeso to the south (now Hokkaido, Japan), and the coast of the Asian mainland. La Pérouse sailed a bit farther north and then turned back south, sailing between Oku-Yeso and Yeso through a waterway now called La Pérouse Strait.

The French reached Petropavlovsk, a city on Russia's Kamchatka Peninsula, on September 6. There La Pérouse received a letter from France, promoting him to squadron commander and ordering him to investigate a British settlement in New South Wales (in what is now Australia). But first he and his men spent four weeks feasting and relaxing with the residents of Petropavlovsk. Before leaving, La Pérouse sent his interpreter, Barthélemy de Lesseps, back to France with more records of the voyage.

Exploring the Southwest Pacific

On the way to Australia, disaster again befell the French explorers. At the Samoan Islands, 1,000 Samoans attacked crewmen who had come ashore to refill the ships' water barrels. Twelve Frenchmen were killed, and 20 were wounded. La Pérouse had no choice but to sail on, stopping at the Fiji Islands and Norfolk Island before receiving a friendly welcome from the British settlers at Botany Bay in Australia. In February 1788, he put his most recent logs and records aboard a British ship headed for Europe. In a letter, La Pérouse outlined his plans for the rest of the voyage. He hoped to explore the islands of Tonga and New Caledonia, the Santa Cruz and Solomon Islands, and the Louisiades near New Guinea. He also planned to explore Van Diemen's Land (now called Tasmania) and the western coast of Australia. On May 10, 1788, La Pérouse sailed from Botany Bay and was never heard from again.

The Search for La Pérouse

In 1791 the French Admiral Antoine de Bruni d'ENTRECASTEAUX was sent to look for La Pérouse, but he abandoned the search in July 1793 and died shortly thereafter. Thirty-three years later, a British merchant captain heard rumors that La Pérouse had reached the Santa Cruz Islands. The French explorer Jules DUMONT D'URVILLE investigated this clue in 1828 and found evidence that La Pérouse's ships had run aground near Vanikoro Island in the Santa Cruz group. La Pérouse's former interpreter, de Lesseps, identified wreckage there as belonging to the *Boussole* and *Astrolabe*. Apparently, some of La Pérouse's men had been killed by the islanders, and the survivors had built a small boat from the wreckage of the ships. They may have ventured back onto the water, but what happened to them from that point remains a mystery.

SUGGESTED READING John Dunmore, *Pacific Explorer: The Life of Jean François de la Pérouse, 1741–1788* (Naval Institute Press, 1985); Frank Horner, *Looking for La Pérouse: d'Entrecasteaux in Australia and the South Pacific, 1792–1793* (Melbourne University Press, 1996); Jean François La Pérouse, *The First French Expedition to California: Lapérouse in 1786,* edited and translated by Charles N. Rudkin (Glen Dawson, 1959); Geoffrey Rawson, *Pandora's Last Voyage* (Longmans, 1963).

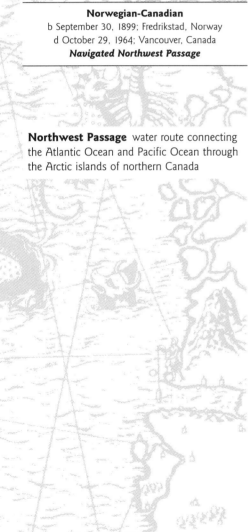

Larsen, Henry Asbjorn

Norwegian-Canadian
b September 30, 1899; Fredrikstad, Norway
d October 29, 1964; Vancouver, Canada
Navigated Northwest Passage

Northwest Passage water route connecting the Atlantic Ocean and Pacific Ocean through the Arctic islands of northern Canada

Henry Larsen, one of the greatest Arctic navigators of the 1900s, led the second sea voyage through the **Northwest Passage.** He was the first to do so traveling from west to east. He was also the first to accomplish this feat without stopping for the winter along the way.

The Canadian Mounties

Larsen was born in a port town at the mouth of Oslo Fjord in Norway, just 10 miles from the hometown of the great polar explorer Roald AMUNDSEN. When Larsen was seven years old, he was thrilled by Amundsen's triumphant return to Norway from his successful navigation of the Northwest Passage. Three years later, Larsen went to sea in search of his own adventures. He spent over 15 years at sea, became a Canadian citizen in 1927, and joined the Royal Canadian Mounted Police (RCMP) the next year. He soon received an assignment to sail on the *St. Roch,* a new RCMP vessel designed especially for the Arctic Ocean. Within a year, he had become the ship's captain.

The Passage There and Back

Larsen had been patrolling the waters of the Canadian Arctic for 10 years when he finally received the assignment he had hoped for. In previous years, his instructions had been to head back to the Pacific Ocean when his winter patrol was over. But in 1940 his orders were to sail to the Atlantic Ocean instead. He left Vancouver, British Columbia, in June and followed nearly the same route that Amundsen had taken, although in the opposite direction. Larsen had hoped to make the trip in about 90 days, but his ship was caught in the ice pack for two winters. He finally reached his destination of Halifax, Nova Scotia, in October 1942. When asked by reporters what the difficult 7,500-mile journey had been like, he replied: "Routine."

Larsen began the return trip to Vancouver on July 22, 1944. With much better ice conditions, the return journey took just 86 days—almost exactly the time he had predicted. This time he took William PARRY's route through Viscount Melville Sound and then followed Prince of Wales Strait to Amundsen Gulf. After his arrival in Vancouver, Larsen continued to serve the RCMP, eventually overseeing police operations throughout the Yukon Territory and the Northwest Territories, an area almost half the size of the United States. He retired in 1961.

SUGGESTED READING John M. Bassett, *Henry Larsen* (Fitzhenry and Whiteside, 1980); F. S. Ferrar, *Arctic Assignment: The Story of the* St. Roch (Macmillan of Canada, 1974); Henry A. Larsen, *The North-West Passage, 1940–1942 and 1944: The Famous Voyages of the Royal Canadian Mounted Police Schooner* St. Roch (City Archives, 1954).

La Salle, René Robert Cavelier de

French
b November 22, 1643; Rouen, France
d March 19, 1687; Texas
Followed Mississippi River to its mouth

Jesuit member of the Society of Jesus, a Roman Catholic order founded by Ignatius of Loyola in 1534

New France French colony that included the St. Lawrence River valley, the Great Lakes region, and until 1713, Acadia (now called Nova Scotia)

René Robert Cavelier de La Salle received an audience with the French king, Louis XIV, to present his plan to build a French empire in North America.

René Robert Cavelier de La Salle had a grand vision of expanding the French Empire in North America. In pursuit of this goal, he canoed down the Mississippi River to its mouth at the Gulf of Mexico. Unfortunately, France was unable to make La Salle's dream a reality, and the explorer met an early death in what is now eastern Texas.

A Born Adventurer

La Salle was educated to become a **Jesuit** priest, but he realized that he was more suited to a life of adventure. In 1666 he settled on the frontier of **New France,** west of Montréal. After working three years as a farmer, he sold his land to become an explorer. His first expedition was to find a river to the west that the natives called the Ohio. From their description, La Salle thought that it might empty into a body of water called the Vermilion Sea that was believed to exist on the continent's west coast. If so, the Ohio River would be a water route to the Pacific Ocean and Asia. La Salle set out in 1669, but little is known about his movements over the next two years. He returned to Montréal with a rich load of furs.

In 1672 La Salle was put in charge of Fort Frontenac, a trading post on Lake Ontario. While there, he learned that the explorers Louis JOLLIET and Father Jacques MARQUETTE had traveled down the Mississippi River as far as what is now called the Arkansas River. They were sure that the Mississippi emptied into the Gulf of Mexico. Since the Ohio flows into the Mississippi, this new information ended La Salle's hope that the Ohio would lead to the Pacific Ocean. But his dreams of exploring the Mississippi River and expanding the French empire were still alive.

Plans Fall Through

In 1677 La Salle traveled to France to present his plans to King Louis XIV. The king approved, but he could not afford to finance these activities—La Salle would have to pay for the expedition himself. La Salle returned to New France in 1678 with an Italian adventurer named Henri de Tonti, who would be his lifelong friend and companion explorer.

Near the end of the year, La Salle, Tonti, and Father Louis HENNEPIN established a fort near Niagara Falls. They built a ship, *Le Griffon,* and

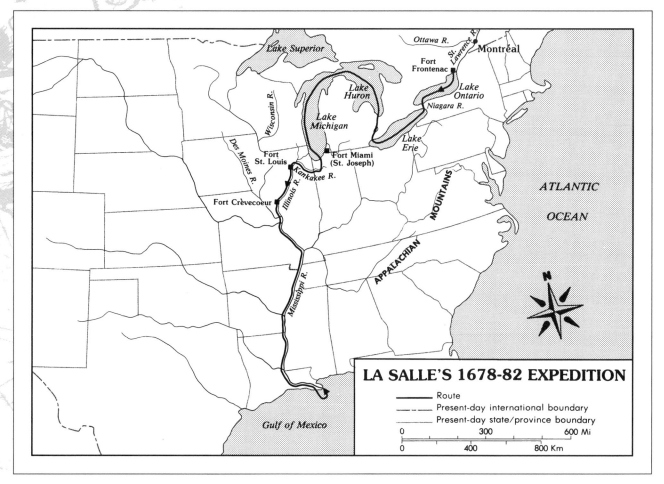

LA SALLE'S 1678-82 EXPEDITION

Route

Present-day international boundary

Present-day state/province boundary

| 0 | 300 | 600 Mi |
| 0 | 400 | 800 Km |

La Salle followed the Mississippi River to its mouth, where the city of New Orleans is located today.

sent an advance party west to gather furs that would be sold to raise money. In August *Le Griffon* met La Salle's men at the southern tip of Lake Michigan to pick up the cargo of furs. The ship headed back to the Niagara River, but it was never heard from again. Unaware of the loss of this source of money, La Salle proceeded with his plans. He built Fort Miami on the southeast shore of Lake Michigan, and by December he was ready to set out for the Mississippi River. After canoeing down the St. Joseph, Kankakee, and Illinois Rivers, he built an outpost near the site of present-day Peoria, Illinois. La Salle named it Fort Crèvecoeur, which means Fort Heartbreak in French.

Disaster on the Illinois River

The expedition quickly suffered several setbacks. First, Father Hennepin and two others left to explore the Illinois River, but they were captured by Sioux Indians and never rejoined La Salle. Meanwhile, the party's supplies were running low, and La Salle decided to return to New France. He reached Montréal after a difficult 1,000-mile journey through melting ice and mud, only to find that *Le Griffon* had been lost. However, he succeeded in raising money in Montréal to continue the expedition.

alliance formal agreement of friendship or common defense

When he returned to the Illinois River, he found Fort Crèvecoeur in ruins, destroyed by Iroquois. Tonti and the other Europeans were nowhere to be found. The coming winter weather forced La Salle to give up his search for Tonti and return to Fort Miami. In the meantime, he formed an **alliance** with tribes who were enemies of the Iroquois.

In June 1681, La Salle was reunited with Tonti and other survivors of the destruction of Fort Crèvecoeur. They had been captured by the Iroquois but had escaped. The friendly Ottawa tribe had helped Tonti and his companions travel to what is now Michigan, where they met La Salle.

The Mighty Mississippi

La Salle resumed his expedition on December 21, 1681. He entered the Mississippi River seven weeks later and reached the Arkansas River on March 13. There the explorers heard Indian war cries and saw a party of Quapaw Indians paddling toward them in canoes. La Salle displayed the peace pipe of his Indian allies, and the delighted Quapaw took the explorers to their village. As the unsuspecting Indians looked on, La Salle claimed the village for France; then he feasted and celebrated with his hosts, whom he considered to be new subjects of the French king. La Salle repeated these actions in all the Indian villages that he visited as he made his way down the Mississippi.

On April 6, the explorers reached the point where the Mississippi splits into several channels as it spills into the Gulf of Mexico. They formed three groups to follow the three main channels and were reunited at the gulf three days later. La Salle claimed the river and its valley for France and named the region Louisiana in honor of King Louis XIV.

To Build an Empire

La Salle had hoped to establish two French colonies, one on the Illinois River and one on the Gulf of Mexico. The first, Fort St. Louis, was built in 1683, but the governor of New France would not allow a settlement at the mouth of the Mississippi. La Salle went to France to seek the king's approval, received it, and set sail for North America in July 1684. From that point on, he was beset by troubles. He quarreled with the ship's captain, the ship was attacked by pirates and wrecked in the Caribbean Sea, and La Salle became ill while in the Caribbean region.

When he finally entered the Gulf of Mexico, La Salle sailed right past the Mississippi River. It is possible that the king had ordered him to find and raid Spanish mines in Texas. In any case, La Salle and his would-be colonists were put ashore just west of what is now Galveston, Texas, about 400 miles west of the Mississippi. After establishing a temporary colony, La Salle tried several times to reach the river by land. On one such journey, he behaved strangely and did not communicate with his men. Dissatisfied and frightened, they murdered him somewhere in the Texas wilderness on March 19, 1687.

SUGGESTED READING Francis Parkman, *La Salle and the Discovery of the Great West* (Little, Brown, 1942); John Upton Terrell, *La Salle: The Life and Times of an Explorer* (Weybright and Talley, 1968).

Las Casas, Bartolomé de

Spanish
b 1474; Seville, Spain
d 1566; San Cristóbal, New Spain (Mexico)
Worked for rights of American Indians

conquistador Spanish or Portuguese explorer and military leader in the Americas

Council of the Indies governing body of Spain's colonial empire from 1524 to 1834

This painting depicts Bartolomé de Las Casas, a champion of the rights of Indians, mourning the cruelty of the Spanish colonists.

Father Bartolomé de Las Casas spent 50 years fighting for the rights of American Indians and eventually became one of the most influential men in the Spanish colonies. Early in his adult life, he was a wealthy slaveholder, but he became a priest, sold his slaves, and devoted the rest of his life to defending American Indians against injustice. He was also a historian and kept records of Pánfilo de NARVÁEZ's conquest of Cuba and Francisco PIZARRO's conquest of Peru.

Slavery in Cuba

Las Casas was born in Seville, Spain, and attended the University of Salamanca. He first saw an American Indian in 1493, one of several brought to Spain by Christopher COLUMBUS. Las Casas moved to the island of Cuba in 1502 and built a large estate. He purchased Indians as slaves to work in his mines. In 1510 Las Casas took holy vows and became a priest, before accompanying the Narváez expedition to explore and conquer the rest of the island. Las Casas left Narváez after witnessing the Spanish massacre of over 2,000 Indians.

A Champion of Human Rights

While preparing a sermon in 1514, Las Casas had what he called a "sudden illumination" that changed the direction of his life. He freed his slaves and vowed to work for "the justice of these Indian peoples, and to condemn the robbery, evil, and injustice committed against them." He saw how Spanish laws failed to protect the Inca during Pizarro's brutal conquest of Cuzco (in what is now Peru) from 1532 to 1533. It is true, however, that his accounts of the Spanish conquests contained some exaggerations of Spanish brutality.

Eleven years later, Las Casas was appointed bishop of the province of Chiapas (in what is now Mexico). In this position, he continued to pressure the king of Spain to protect the rights of American Indians. In 1550 Las Casas participated in a unique debate in Valladolid, Spain. Las Casas argued the case for Indians' rights. Juan Ginés de Sepúlveda represented the **conquistadors** and Spanish colonists. The council hearing the debate made no immediate decisions, but new laws favoring the Indians were passed soon afterward. Las Casas was appointed to the newly formed **Council of the Indies,** which was in charge of enforcing those laws.

Las Casas's forceful efforts led Spain to recognize that Indians were entitled to protection even if they did not convert to Christianity. Las Casas died on the church's estate in San Cristóbal (present-day San Cristóbal de las Casas, Mexico) in 1566.

SUGGESTED READING Bartolomé de Las Casas, *The Devastation of the Indies, A Brief Account*, translated by Hera Briffault (Seabury, 1974).

La Vérendrye, Pierre Gaultier de Varennes de

French-Canadian
b November 17, 1685; Trois-Rivières, Canada
d December 6, 1749; Montréal, Canada
Explored Lake Winnipeg region

New France French colony that included the St. Lawrence River valley, the Great Lakes region, and until 1713, Acadia (now called Nova Scotia)

This statue of Pierre Gaultier de Varennes de La Vérendrye stands at the Parliament Building in Québec, Canada.

Pierre Gaultier de Varennes de La Vérendrye explored central Canada, searching for a waterway to the Pacific Ocean. Along with several members of his family, La Vérendrye discovered and described Lake Winnipeg, Lake Winnipegosis, Lake Manitoba, and the rivers that flow into Hudson Bay from the west and south. He also explored the upper reaches of the Missouri River. However, his motive for exploring was a subject for debate among his fellow Frenchmen. Some said he was driven by curiosity and devotion to France. But others claimed that he only wanted to control the fur trade in central Canada.

Search for the Western Sea

La Vérendrye was born into one of the best-known families in **New France.** His father was governor of Trois-Rivières, a colony on the St. Lawrence River. After serving in the French army in Europe, La Vérendrye returned to New France. Between 1715 and 1727, he managed his family's fur trading business north of Lake Superior. During that time, he heard local Indians tell tales of a large lake from which a river flowed west. The river was said to end in water that moved with waves and tides. La Vérendrye suspected that the river led to what the French called the Western Sea, a mythical inland sea that was believed to lead to the Pacific Ocean.

In 1730 La Vérendrye asked the French king for permission to explore this route. Although the king approved the mission, he refused to support La Vérendrye with money. Instead the explorer was guaranteed a monopoly on the fur trade in the area of Lake Winnipeg. In exchange he was expected to build fortified trading posts to secure the area for France. The king hoped that La Vérendrye could persuade local Indians to trade furs with the French rather than with the English, who had established trading posts at Hudson Bay. Profits from these activities could be used to finance the search for the Western Sea.

La Vérendrye left Montréal on June 8, 1731, with a party that included his nephew and three of his sons. By August they had reached the high ground separating the area that drains east toward Lake Superior from the area that drains west toward Lake Winnipeg. La Vérendrye decided to spend the winter there, and he later claimed that his hired trappers had refused to go farther. His critics, however, suggested that he had stayed to collect furs. In any case, he did send a party west to construct a fort at

Rainy Lake. It was the first of eight forts La Vérendrye built as trading posts to purchase furs from the Indians.

Rumors at the Mandan Villages

By 1733 La Vérendrye had learned that the river flowing north out of Lake Winnipeg (now called the Nelson River) empties into Hudson Bay, not the Western Sea. Because of this disappointment, he lost interest in finding a route to the Pacific Ocean. The French court, however, was becoming more interested in the search and demanded that La Vérendrye fulfill the terms of his agreement. Fortunately, he had picked up some new information. He was told that an Indian tribe that lived on a river called the "River of the West" knew the way to the Western Sea. These Indians were actually the Mandan tribe on the upper Missouri River. Meriwether LEWIS and William CLARK visited the Mandan 70 years later on their journey to the Pacific.

In October 1738, La Vérendrye left Fort La Reine on the Assiniboine River with 20 men. They traveled up the river until rapids and shallow water made it impossible to use canoes. They then headed south by land to look for the Mandan villages. The Frenchmen reached the first village on December 3, and in the excitement of their arrival, the bag of gifts they had brought for the Mandan was stolen. Unable to participate in the ritual of gift giving, the French could not ask for any favors from the Indians.

La Vérendrye decided to return to Fort La Reine in February, but he left behind two men to learn the Mandan language. By September the pair had rejoined him at the fort. They said that a group of western Indians had appeared at the Mandan villages with tales of white men living in brick houses. It is possible that they had seen Spanish missionaries in California. The western Indians offered to take the Frenchmen to see these other white men. La Vérendrye sent his son Pierre to pursue this rumor, but Pierre was unable to find guides and was forced to return to Fort La Reine the next summer.

Unfinished Business

In spring of 1742, Pierre and his younger brother left Fort La Reine with two other men to look for the route west mentioned by the Mandan's visitors. They traveled for over a year, being passed from one tribe to another. They always believed that they were nearing the Western Sea. On January 1, 1743, they saw a mountain range that may have been either the Bighorn Mountains of Wyoming or the Black Hills of South Dakota. Later that winter, they buried a plate of lead engraved with the coat of arms of the French king. The plate was dug up by a schoolgirl 170 years later near Pierre, South Dakota. The mountains and the lead plate are the only clues to the route taken by the explorers, who gave up their search and returned to Fort La Reine on July 2, 1743.

The next year, La Vérendrye returned to Montréal to request financial support for further explorations. However, the governor of New France ordered him to stay in the east and gave control of his trading posts to someone else. La Vérendrye protested this unfair treatment, but he was not granted permission to return to the western lands until a new governor took office six years later. La Vérendrye then traveled to the Saskatchewan River, which he had concluded was the most likely route to the Western Sea. He asked local tribes where the river came from, and they all told him that it flowed out of a distant, mountainous land. Beyond the mountains, they said, was a great lake whose salty water was undrinkable. La Vérendrye felt sure that the Indians were referring to the Pacific Ocean, and he made plans for the long journey to the mountains. However, he died before he could begin, and his sons were not allowed to continue his work.

SUGGESTED READING Hubert G. Smith, *The Explorations of the La Vérendryes in the Northern Plains, 1738-1743* (University of Nebraska Press, 1980).

Legazpi, Miguel López de

Spanish
b 1510; Guipúzcoa province, Spain
d August 20, 1572; Philippine Islands
Established Spanish rule in Philippines

New Spain region of Spanish colonial empire that included the areas now occupied by Mexico, Florida, Texas, New Mexico, Arizona, California, and various Caribbean islands

archipelago large group of islands or a body of water with many islands

Miguel López de Legazpi is remembered as the conqueror of the Philippine Islands. In the late 1500s, he established Spanish rule over those islands in the Pacific Ocean. He also served as the colony's first governor.

Legazpi was born in northern Spain and settled in Mexico, which was then part of the Spanish colony of **New Spain.** In 1564 the Spanish king, Phillip II, asked him to establish a colony in the island group that Ferdinand MAGELLAN had claimed for Spain in 1521. Philip also ordered Legazpi to convert the islanders to Christianity.

On November 21, 1564, Legazpi left Mexico in an expedition headed by his cousin, Andrés de URDANETA. With five ships carrying 6 monks and 400 soldiers and sailors, the Spaniards landed in the islands in February 1565. Spies sent by the prince of the island of Cebu to observe them brought back tales of men who ate rocks and breathed smoke. The sources of these rumors were probably the hard biscuits and tobacco that the Spanish had brought from Mexico. The prince decided to befriend these strange visitors. On April 27, Legazpi and his soldiers entered the town now known as Cebu City and took control. The islanders resisted at first, but they eventually submitted to Spanish authority. Legazpi's main weapons were his own persistence and the monks' missionary work. He used force rarely and only when necessary.

Over the next four years, Legazpi extended Spanish rule to the other islands in the group, which he named the Philippine Islands in honor of his king. In 1570 Legazpi's grandson subdued a Muslim stronghold on the island of Luzon and secured a treaty that gave Spain control over the entire **archipelago.** Legazpi established a capital city at Manila in June 1571 and was named the first governor of the Philippines. He died in the islands in 1572, at the age of 62.

SUGGESTED READING Andrew Sharp, *Adventurous Armada; The Story of Legazpi's Expedition* (Whitcombe and Tombs, 1961).

Leichhardt, Friedrich Wilhelm Ludwig

German
b October 23, 1813; Trebitsch, Prussia
(now Třebíč, Czech Republic)
d after April 3, 1848; Queensland, Australia
Explored northeastern Australia

Despite a poor sense of direction, Friedrich Wilhelm Ludwig Leichhardt led several expeditions into the Australian bush country.

bush land that has not been cleared or settled, usually covered with short trees and other plants

surveyor one who makes precise measurements of a location's geography

scurvy disease caused by a lack of vitamin C and once a major cause of death among sailors; symptoms include internal bleeding, loosened teeth, and extreme fatigue

specimen sample of a plant, animal, or mineral, usually collected for scientific study or display

Friedrich Wilhelm Ludwig Leichhardt was one of the most unlikely explorers in the history of Australia. After deserting from the army of Prussia, he made several expeditions into the interior of his new homeland, Australia. He was proclaimed a hero in both Australia and Europe before disappearing mysteriously into the Australian **bush** country in 1848.

An Appearance in Australia

Leichhardt was born in Prussia (a former German state in northern and central Europe) and was educated as a naturalist at the universities of Berlin and Göttingen. He joined the Prussian army but deserted and made his way to Australia in February 1842. He planned to make a name for himself by exploring the Australian interior, even though he had a poor sense of direction. After being turned down for a job with the **surveyor** general of the New South Wales province, he earned money by lecturing on natural history.

Leichhardt spent most of his first two years in Australia in Sydney, where he was often seen wearing a Southeast Asian hat and carrying a sword—not the more usual gun—because he was afraid of firearms. He also made several plant-collecting trips, one of which was a 480-mile walk up the east coast from Newcastle to Moreton Bay, near Brisbane.

The Australian Bush Country

Leichhardt's first journey of exploration was an overland trek from Sydney to Port Essington, located west of the Gulf of Carpentaria on the continent's northern coast. He and his supporters hoped that Port Essington would be a gateway for trade between southern Asia and Australia. Leichhardt left Sydney on October 1, 1844, with a small group that included an experienced scientist named John Gilbert. They headed north, always staying within 10 miles of water, since each man carried only a small flask. This lack of proper equipment was typical of the hardships the party faced. Leichhardt frequently became lost, and the group's supply of food was soon exhausted.

The men pressed on, however, reaching the Mitchell River, just east of the Gulf of Carpentaria, in June 1845. Along the river, Gilbert was killed in an attack by Australian Aborigines. **Scurvy** soon afflicted the rest of the men, and the difficult journey lasted until December 17, when they arrived at Port Essington. Leichhardt had lost most of his **specimens** during the trip, but he had discovered good grazing lands for livestock, a valuable find at that time. Therefore, he was given a hero's welcome when he returned to Sydney, and the king of Prussia even pardoned him for his desertion.

In 1846 Leichhardt developed a plan to cross the continent from Sydney by traveling north and then west. He covered only 500 miles in six months before returning, defeated, to Sydney. He began a similar attempt in March 1848 and was last seen a month later. Two of his campsites were found, but there was no other trace left of him.

SUGGESTED READING Marcel Aurosseau, compiler and translator, *The Letters of F. W. Ludwig Leichhardt*, 3 volumes, (Cambridge University Press, 1968); Jo Jensen, *Ludwig Leichhardt* (Future Horizons Publishing, 1996).

Leif Erikson. See *Erikson, Leif.*

Le Moyne, Pierre d'Iberville. See *Iberville, Pierre Le Moyne d'.*

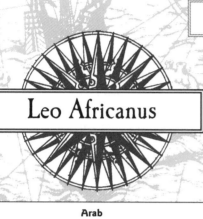

Leo Africanus

Arab
b 1494?; Granada, Spain
d 1554?; Tunis (in present-day Tunisia)
Explored Africa south of Sahara

sultan ruler of a Muslim nation

Leo Africanus was a living link between the two dominant cultures of the medieval Mediterranean world—the Christian countries of Europe and the Islamic empire of North Africa and the Middle East. He was an Islamic Arab, born in Spain, who was converted to Christianity as an adult by Pope Leo X. Living in Rome, he wrote a book that gave the Europeans of his time their first detailed account of the African kingdoms that flourished south of the Sahara desert region.

Travels in Africa

Leo Africanus was born with the name al-Hassan ibn Muhammad al-Wizaz al-Fasi in Granada, Spain. He and his family were Moors, Islamic people originally from Morocco in North Africa. Before al-Fasi's birth, the Moors had controlled parts of Spain for hundreds of years. In 1492, however, Christian rulers and armies conquered the last Islamic kingdom in Spain, forcing most of the Moors to leave within a few years. Al-Fasi and his family were among them. They crossed the Mediterranean Sea to Morocco, where al-Fasi grew up in the city of Fez, a center of Islamic learning. As a young man, he received training in religion and law and began the travels that would make him famous. He appears to have served on diplomatic missions for the **sultan** of Morocco.

In the early 1500s, al-Fasi visited Mali and Bornu, kingdoms south of the Sahara. He encountered the Hausa people, who now live in northern Nigeria and southern Niger. Farther to the west, he reached the Gambia River, which flows into the Atlantic Ocean. He visited several towns along the Niger River and followed part of its course. Al-Fasi also traveled to Arabia, Egypt, and Turkey. In 1518 he was on his way back to Morocco from a visit to Constantinople (present-day Istanbul) when pirates captured the ship on which he was sailing.

From Captive to Convert

Realizing that al-Fasi was no ordinary passenger, the pirates took him to Rome and presented him to Pope Leo X as a gift. Leo X was so greatly impressed by al-Fasi's intelligence and experience that he granted the Moor his freedom. Al-Fasi converted to Christianity and was baptized with the pope's own name. From that time on, the new convert was known as Leo Africanus, meaning Leo the African in Latin. He became well known in Rome, where he taught Arabic,

studied Latin and Italian, and wrote several important books. One of these works discussed the Arabic and Spanish languages, and another recounted the lives of leading Arab philosophers. But Leo is remembered chiefly for his contribution to geography, *The History and Description of Africa*.

Facts and Myths

Leo's book about Africa was enthusiastically received by Europeans, whose interest in the wider world around them was developing rapidly. Scholars and geographers quickly accepted Leo as an authority. Most of what he wrote was accurate, but people sometimes misread his words and created ideas of Africa that had more to do with their own imaginations than with what Leo had written.

Leo devoted many pages to the **caravan** trade across the Sahara. He described the desert town of Taghaza, which was built on huge deposits of salt, an extremely valuable product for trade. Taghaza's houses and **mosque** were made of hard salt, and even its water tasted salty. Because food could not be grown in salty soil, all of the city's food was brought in by caravan. Leo also wrote about the Songhai Empire, a large and powerful state that ruled much of western Africa south of the desert in the early 1500s. Its capital was Gao, a city on the Niger River. Leo wrote about this city's slave markets and wealthy merchants.

Up the river from Gao was Timbuktu, a city that Leo had visited several times. Europeans were especially fascinated by this remote city, which was rumored to be a source of gold. Leo wrote of Timbuktu's "magnificent and well-furnished court" and "princely palace." Somehow European readers expanded on Leo's description until they believed that Timbuktu's houses were roofed with gold. The legend of Timbuktu's fabulous wealth lived on until visits by the French explorer René-Auguste CAILLIÉ in 1828 and the German Heinrich BARTH in 1853 disproved such stories.

Leo did make one great error when he claimed that the Niger River flows westward from Timbuktu, when in fact it flows eastward. This mistake confused geographers for several centuries. The question was finally settled by the Scottish explorer Mungo PARK in 1796. Some scholars then came to believe that Leo had simply copied his book from the works of al-IDRISI, an Arab geographer who had made the same error in the 1100s. But today most historians believe that Leo had witnessed the majority of what he described.

Leo made no maps, and he was less interested in physical geography than in the trade and culture of the places he visited. Although his history of Africa was completed by 1526, it did not reach readers until 1550, when another author included it in a collection of travel accounts. Leo, however, did not live to see the fame and controversy caused by his book. By 1550 he had returned to North Africa and settled in the city of Tunis, where he died a few years later.

SUGGESTED READING Leo Africanus, *The History and Description of Africa*, edited by Robert Brown, 3 volumes (Hakluyt Society, 1896); David Mountfield, *A History of African Exploration* (Domus Books, 1976).

---

caravan large group of people traveling together, often with pack animals, across a desert or other dangerous region

mosque Muslim house of prayer and worship

León, Juan Ponce de. *See Ponce de León, Juan.*

Leonov, Aleksei Arkhipovich

Russian
b May 30, 1934; Listvyanka, Soviet Union
living
First person to walk in space

Soviet Union nation that existed from 1922 to 1991, made up of Russia and 14 other republics in eastern Europe and northern Asia

cosmonaut Russian term for a person who travels into space; literally, "traveler to the universe"

orbit stable, circular route; one trip around; to revolve around

astronaut American term for a person who travels into space; literally, "traveler to the stars"

space suit protective gear that allows a person who wears it to survive in space

capsule small early spacecraft designed to carry a person around the earth

When the Soviet space agency canceled its plans for lunar exploration, Aleksei Leonov lost an opportunity to walk on the moon.

Aleksei Leonov was a pioneer of space exploration during the early years of the "space race" between the United States and the **Soviet Union.** He took part in two historic space missions that set new levels of achievement—one technical and the other political.

To Walk in Space

Leonov was born in the region of eastern Russia known as Siberia, where his father was a coal miner. From an early age, he was fascinated by both painting and flying. As a young man, he attended flight school by day and art school by night. By the age of 23, he was a fighter pilot in the Soviet air force. The following year, he answered the Soviet space agency's first call for **cosmonaut** training. More than 3,000 pilots volunteered. Leonov was among the first 8 selected, along with Yuri GAGARIN, who became the first person in space in 1961.

The cosmonauts underwent a demanding training program. The space agency assigned Leonov to be the first person to leave a spacecraft in **orbit.** Leonov prepared in urgent haste for his mission, for American **astronauts** were trying to accomplish the same feat.

On March 18, 1965, Leonov and another cosmonaut made the Soviet Union's eighth crewed spaceflight, a mission known as Voskhod 2. Wearing a specially designed **space suit,** Leonov left his **capsule,** *Diamond,* floating at the end of a 17-foot connecting cable. Gazing down at the earth, as he later recalled, "I said to myself, it's true, the earth is round." After 12 minutes in space, Leonov reentered the capsule, the first person to have made a space walk. On March 19, the capsule landed safely in deep snow in the Soviet countryside.

A Meeting Above the Earth

Leonov's second spaceflight took place in 1975. He commanded the Soyuz 19 mission on a six-day flight that was the world's first international space mission. On July 17, the Soyuz docked in orbit with the American Apollo 18 capsule.

During the $44\frac{1}{2}$ hours that their spacecraft were joined, the astronauts and cosmonauts received greetings from the leaders of their nations and broadcast their own messages to the world. Leonov impressed Americans with his good humor and his knowledge of English. The space travelers also shared meals, exchanged gifts, and visited each other's spacecraft. Leonov had decorated the Soviet capsule with drawings, including a cartoon of the three American astronauts riding like cowboys on their Apollo spacecraft. After many years of tension between the Soviets and the

Americans, the meeting in space was a powerful symbol of peace and cooperation.

During his final years with the Soviet space agency, Leonov was deputy director of the cosmonaut training program. His artistic career also flourished over the years, and some Soviet stamps featured his artwork. In addition, he wrote several books about space, including a children's book called *I Walk in Space.*

SUGGESTED READING Philip Clark, *The Soviet Manned Space Program: An Illustrated History of the Men, the Missions, and the Spacecraft* (Orion Books, 1988); Gordon R. Hooper, *The Soviet Cosmonaut Team*, 2 volumes (GRH Publications, 1990); James E. Oberg, *Red Star in Orbit* (Random House, 1981).

Lewis, Meriwether

American
b August 18, 1774; Albemarle County, Virginia
d October 11, 1809; near Nashville, Tennessee
***Explored Missouri River and
northwestern United States***

militia armed force made up of citizens who are not professional soldiers but who may be called upon to serve the military

Meriwether Lewis led what may have been the greatest journey of discovery by American explorers.

From 1804 to 1806, Meriwether Lewis and William CLARK led a group of American explorers on a historic journey from the Mississippi River to the Pacific Ocean. Their route took them up the Missouri River, across the Rocky Mountains, and down the Columbia River to the ocean's edge. Despite harsh weather conditions and dangerous terrain, Lewis and Clark gathered a great deal of valuable information about the western frontier of the United States.

A Young Man's Responsibilities
Lewis was born in Virginia, where his family had many well-known neighbors, including Thomas Jefferson. When Lewis was about 10 years old, he and his family moved to a plantation in Georgia, where Lewis became an expert hunter and developed interests in both science and literature. He returned to Virginia at the age of 13 and spent the next five years studying to attend William and Mary College. But after his stepfather's death, Lewis decided to stay home to manage his family's estate.

At the age of 20, Lewis joined the local **militia** to put down the Whiskey Rebellion, an uprising of farmers who were rebelling against a tax the government had placed on liquor. He wrote to his mother that he was "delighted" by military life, and he later enlisted in the regular army. Lewis served under General Anthony Wayne in a campaign against the Indians in the region that is now Ohio, Indiana, Illinois, Wisconsin, and Michigan. During this time, he met Clark, a fellow officer who would later become his partner in exploration.

In 1801 Thomas Jefferson was elected the third president of the United States. He wrote to Lewis, offering him the post of private secretary. After obtaining a leave of absence from the military, Lewis traveled to Washington to take up his new duties. For the next two years, he managed the president's household, attended state dinners with important guests, and acted as the president's spokesperson to the Senate.

Preparing for the Corps of Discovery
Jefferson had been considering the idea of a journey to explore a land route to the Pacific for more than 20 years. In 1792, when Jefferson was secretary of state, he proposed that the American

Philosophical Society of Philadelphia sponsor such a project. When Lewis heard about the expedition, he asked Jefferson for permission to join it, but Jefferson thought that Lewis was too young and inexperienced. The mission was canceled when the man chosen to lead it, the French botanist André Michaux, was discovered to be a secret agent for France.

After assisting Jefferson for two years, however, Lewis had proved that he could handle responsibility. On January 18, 1803, the president sent a message to Congress. He proposed an expedition that would trace the Missouri River to its source and cross the Rocky Mountains (then called the Stony Mountains). He stated that the goal was to find the best water route to the Pacific Ocean for commercial purposes. Lewis prepared an estimate of expenses for the trip, and Congress quickly approved the sum he requested.

Jefferson created the Corps of Discovery to carry out the mission, and he placed Lewis in command. The president believed that Lewis had all the qualities necessary to lead such an expedition. Lewis was courageous, determined, observant, and honest. In addition, he was a skilled hunter and outdoorsman, was familiar with Indian customs, and had the ability to maintain discipline among a group. However, Lewis lacked scientific knowledge, so Jefferson sent him to Philadelphia to study with scientists. Lewis learned **geology,** geography, **zoology,** and mapmaking, and he was given access to the most recent maps of the West. He also wrote to Clark and asked him to be co-commander of the Corps.

geology the scientific study of the earth's natural history

zoology the scientific study of animals

While the primary purpose of the journey was to promote commerce by finding an all-water route to the Pacific Ocean, Jefferson's instructions to Lewis revealed a broader plan. Lewis was ordered to establish precise locations of landmarks in order to prepare an accurate map of the region. He was also to make a careful study of the soil, note any volcanic activity, and keep statistics on the weather. Furthermore, he was instructed to make observations about any Indian tribes he encountered along the way. Jefferson wanted to know as much as possible about the lands and peoples to the west.

Shortly before the expedition was to begin, France sold the Louisiana Territory to the United States. This region covered vast stretches of land from New Orleans in the south to Canada in the north and from the Mississippi River in the east to the Rocky Mountains in the west. Its purchase doubled the size of the United States and made Lewis's journey much more important. The activities of the Corps of Discovery would strengthen the American hold on the area by giving the president and Congress a better understanding of the territory they had just bought.

The Expedition Begins

Leaving Washington, D.C., in the summer of 1803, Lewis rode to Pittsburgh, Pennsylvania, where a 55-foot boat was being built for the trip. When it was finished, Lewis had it loaded with supplies—food, clothing, medicine, tools, guns, ammunition, and goods to trade with any Indians he might meet. He then assembled a crew,

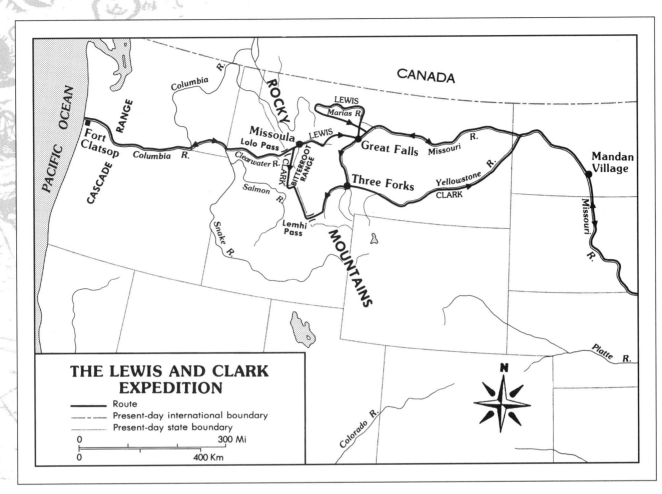

THE LEWIS AND CLARK EXPEDITION

——	Route
– – –	Present-day international boundary
······	Present-day state boundary

0	300 Mi
0	400 Km

Lewis and Clark led the Corps of Discovery through rivers, mountains, and Indian territory to the Pacific Ocean.

voyageur expert French woodsman, boatman, and guide

sailed down the Ohio River, and met Clark at the Clark family estate near Louisville, Kentucky. By late November, the Corps of Discovery was headed up the Mississippi River to St. Louis. Lewis and Clark decided to spend the winter at a site near the mouth of the Wood River, across the Mississippi from St. Louis.

On May 14, 1804, the expedition left St. Louis with three boats and about 40 men. Most of the men were soldiers, but the party also included some French **voyageurs.** The journey up the Missouri River was very slow and difficult at first. The Corps traveled against a strong, unpredictable current and had to contend with hazards such as floating branches and shifting sandbars. The men often had to get out of their boats and haul them along with ropes. The overwhelming heat and the swarms of mosquitoes were a frequent source of irritation. But the explorers were able to avoid hostile encounters with Indians.

Lewis and Clark were fascinated by the variety of plants and wildlife they saw on the journey, much of it previously unknown to white men. By September the expedition reached what is now South Dakota, where vast herds of buffalo, deer, elk, and antelope roamed the prairies. Lewis was especially interested in the small animals he called "barking squirrels." Another member of the party called these creatures prairie dogs, the name by which they have been known ever since. The beauty of the land and the rich soil impressed everyone in the Corps.

Sacajawea Joins the Explorers

In November 1804, the Corps stopped to build winter quarters in what is now North Dakota. The site was located near the villages of the Mandan tribe, visited over 60 years earlier by the French explorer Pierre Gaultier de Varennes de La Vérendrye. During the winter, the men built six canoes for faster travel on the journey westward. They also visited the Mandan villages and tried to learn as much as they could about the lands that lay ahead.

The explorers were visited by a French-Canadian fur trapper named Toussaint Charbonneau. He was married to Sacajawea, a woman from the Shoshone tribe who had been captured by the Minetaree Indians and sold to Charbonneau. Since the Corps planned to travel into Shoshone territory to acquire horses for their journey, having a member of the tribe with them would be helpful. Lewis and Clark invited Charbonneau, Sacajawea, and the couple's newborn son, Jean-Baptiste, to join them when they continued west in the spring.

Indians in the Rocky Mountains

In early April, Lewis and Clark were ready to set out once again. Lewis sent 16 of the men back east to report on the Corps's progress to President Jefferson. They traveled down the Missouri River with supplies, **specimens,** and records of the first part of the expedition. Meanwhile, the remaining members of the Corps headed upriver, looking for a water passage across the Rockies to the Pacific Ocean.

Travel became much more uncomfortable and dangerous as the river's course led the explorers into the foothills of the Rockies. The Corps soon came to a point where the river was joined by another, which flowed from the northwest. A disagreement arose over which branch was part of the Missouri and which was only a **tributary.** Although the other men were sure that the northern branch was the Missouri, Lewis and Clark correctly chose the southern branch, and the party reached the Great Falls (in present-day Montana) in June. Lewis named the northern tributary Maria's River after his cousin (it is now called the Marias River). If the commanders had followed the advice of their men, the explorers would have encountered a maze of mountains and rapids, and their chances of success would have been greatly reduced.

At the Great Falls, however, the journey became even more difficult. The expedition spent an entire month getting around just 10 miles of rapids. By the time they cleared the falls, the explorers were in Shoshone territory, but they did not see any Indians. Near the end of July, the group reached what is now Three Forks, Montana, where three streams join to form the Missouri River. Lewis put Clark in charge of the men on the westernmost tributary, while he himself took a small party by land to find the Shoshone.

On August 12, Lewis followed an Indian trail that led him to the Lemhi Pass through the Rocky Mountains. He recognized that he

specimen sample of a plant, animal, or mineral, usually collected for scientific study or display

tributary stream or river that flows into a larger stream or river

had reached the Continental Divide, the line separating rivers that flow east from those that flow west. He eventually met an elderly woman and a girl who led him to a Shoshone camp. Three days later, Clark, Charbonneau, and Sacajawea joined him there. Reunited with her people, Sacajawea was overwhelmed to discover that her brother, Cameahwait, was chief of the Shoshone tribe.

Rivers to the Pacific Ocean

Lewis and Clark did not stay long with the Shoshone because they were eager to travel west before winter. The Shoshone provided them with a guide and several horses. Lewis led the men down the Salmon River, across the Continental Divide to the Bitterroot Valley, and into the Bitterroot Mountains. After an exhausting month of clearing paths through the wilderness in the snow, the Corps came upon the villages of the Nez Percé tribe. Two chiefs agreed to take the party to the sea and lead the men down the Clearwater River to the Snake River. They finally reached the Columbia River on October 16.

Six days later, the expedition came to the Cascade Mountains, the last major obstacle to be crossed before reaching the Pacific Ocean. The Corps continued on the Columbia River through the Cascades. By November 2, they noticed the ocean's tide rising and falling in the river, and on November 15, they caught their first sight of the Pacific Ocean. Rather than spend the winter on the shore, the Corps built quarters, Fort Clatsop, a short distance inland.

A Violent Return

Lewis had hoped to find ships to take the party back east by sea, but by late March, none had appeared. Since the weather had cleared, he ordered the Corps to return to Missouri by land. Near what is now Missoula, Montana, the party split into two groups. Clark returned to Three Forks and then traveled down the Yellowstone River, while Lewis took an Indian shortcut to the Missouri and Marias Rivers. In late July 1806, the only violent encounter of the trip occurred when Lewis met a group of Blackfoot Indians. He thought that he had convinced them that his expedition was peaceful. The Americans and the Indians even agreed to camp together that night. But in the early morning hours, the Blackfoot tried to steal the party's guns. During the fight that followed, one Blackfoot was shot and another was stabbed.

On August 12, Lewis and Clark were reunited on the Missouri River, near the point where it is joined by the Yellowstone River. They arrived in St. Louis on September 23, 1806. After the expedition, Lewis resigned from the army, and Jefferson appointed him governor of the Louisiana Territory. In October 1809, Lewis headed to Washington to resolve a dispute concerning some money he believed the government owed him. While staying at an inn in Tennessee, Lewis died. Jefferson, who knew Lewis was prone to depression, believed that the explorer had taken his own life. However, Lewis's family and the Tennessee locals believed that he had been murdered, since both his money and his watch were missing. The mystery of his death was never solved.

Despite his early death, Lewis had made an invaluable contribution to knowledge of the West and opened up the area to American settlement and control. Lewis's leadership and skill were major reasons for the success of the expedition. His thoroughness and grasp of detail ensured not only the safety of the party but also the usefulness of the information it gathered. Many of the men who served under him in the Corps of Discovery, including John COLTER and George DROUILLARD, continued his work as explorers in their own right.

SUGGESTED READING John L. Allen, *Lewis and Clark and the Image of the American Northwest* (Dover Publications, 1991); Stephen E. Ambrose, *Undaunted Courage: Meriwether Lewis, Thomas Jefferson, and the Opening of the American West* (Simon and Schuster, 1996); Richard H. Dillon, *Meriwether Lewis: A Biography* (Western Tanager, 1988); Gary E. Moulton, editor, *The Journals of the Lewis and Clark Expedition*, 11 volumes (University of Nebraska Press, 1983–97).

Linschoten, Jan Huyghen van

Dutch
b 1563; Haarlem, the Netherlands
d February 8, 1611; Enkhuizen, the Netherlands
Searched for Northeast Passage

Northeast Passage water route connecting the Atlantic Ocean and Pacific Ocean along the Arctic coastline of Europe and Asia

Jan Huyghen van Linschoten was the first European to propose a shorter route from Europe to China and India by sailing north of Russia. Between 1594 and 1595, he participated in two expeditions to search for this **Northeast Passage.** Although his journeys to the Arctic Ocean were unsuccessful, Linschoten's attempts motivated later explorers to search for alternative routes to Asia.

An Opportunity to Improve Trade
In 1583 Linschoten sailed from Holland (now the Netherlands) to the Portuguese colony of Goa, on the west coast of India. He spent six years there working as a bookkeeper. During this time, he collected much information on trade between Goa and other ports in the area controlled by the Portuguese. He also became convinced that finding a northern route to China and India would enhance trade relations between Europe and Asia.

When he returned to Holland, Linschoten wrote two books about the people and customs of India. He also organized an expedition to find a northern route to Asia. Merchants from his hometown of Enkhuizen financed part of the voyage, while the Dutch government gave one ship, and merchants from Amsterdam offered two more. Willem BARENTS agreed to act as chief pilot for the expedition and to command two of the fleet's four ships.

Blocked by Ice
In June 1594, the fleet set out, according to Linschoten, "to sail into the North seas, to discover the kingdoms of Cathaia [Cathay] and China." When the ships reached the islands of Novaya Zemlya, Barents sailed up the west coast while Linschoten continued east into the Kara Sea. Bad weather and ice forced the ships to return home, but Barents and Linschoten tried again the following year. The Dutch government outfitted seven ships for the voyage into the Kara Sea. However, the ice pack once again stopped the explorers' progress, and they failed to reach their goal. This voyage was Linschoten's last attempt to find a Northeast Passage, but in 1597 Barents made another try that cost him his life. In 1601 Linschoten

published an account of the voyages, which inspired later Dutch and English expeditions.

SUGGESTED READING Charles McKew Parr, *Jan Van Linschoten: The Dutch Marco Polo* (Crowell, 1964).

Litke, Fyodor Petrovich. See *Lütke, Fyodor Petrovich.*

Livingstone, David

Scottish
b March 19, 1813; Blantyre, Scotland
d May 1, 1873; near Lake Bangweulu
(in present-day Zambia)
Explored central and southern Africa

fossil trace left in rocks by a plant or animal that lived long ago

David Livingstone sparked great public interest with his lectures on the wonders of Africa and the evils of the slave trade.

David Livingstone went to Africa as a missionary doctor in 1841, hoping to spread Christian faith and European medicine among the people of central and southern Africa. He was the first European to visit huge areas of the African interior. The people of Europe were captivated by his books, his lectures, and the dramatic search for him led by Henry Morton STANLEY. As a result, Livingstone did more than any other explorer to bring Africa to the attention of Europe.

His successes were possible largely because of his remarkable perseverance and his great abilities as an observer. As he traveled into the unknown regions of central Africa, he recorded all the wonders that he saw. His writings contain endless descriptions of African geography, customs, medical practices, diet, birds, animals, trees, and flowers. Livingstone eventually published three books, which are closely studied by scholars even today.

A Poor, Hard Life in Scotland

Livingstone's childhood was filled with poverty and hard work. He, his parents, and his four brothers and sisters lived in a single small room. To earn money, he began working 14 hours a day in a cotton mill when he was just 10 years old.

With his first wages, the young Livingstone bought a Latin grammar book. He brought it with him to the mill and read it as he worked; then he continued his studies with a teacher every night. On his rare holidays, he collected insects, plants, and **fossils** in the countryside around his hometown, Blantyre. This hobby was an early sign of the intense interest in natural history that would make his explorations in Africa so valuable to scientists.

A Deep Religious Devotion

The Livingstones taught all their children a strong Christian faith and the need to share that faith with others. By the time David turned 20, he had decided to devote his life to the relief of human suffering. That decision influenced his thoughts and deeds for the rest of his days. His first step toward his goal was to become a doctor so that he could serve as a medical missionary in China. He continued to work at the mill part-time while studying Greek, religion, and medicine in Glasgow, Scotland.

In 1838 Livingstone was accepted into the London Missionary Society. He moved to London to complete his medical studies and prepare for his first assignment, but a war in China forced him to change his plans. Around this time, Livingstone met Robert Moffat,

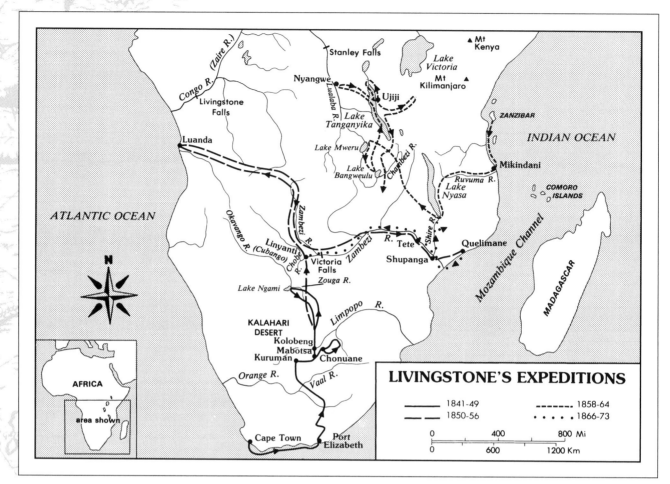

Among Livingstone's geographical discoveries was his proof that the Kalahari and Sahara desert regions are separated by tropical rain forest.

a famous Scottish missionary who worked in southern Africa. Moffat later wrote: "I observed that this young man was interested in my story. . . . By and by he asked me whether I thought he would do for Africa. I said I believed he would, if he would not go to an old station, but would advance to unoccupied ground . . . where no missionary had ever been." Livingstone decided to follow Moffat's advice. On November 18, 1840, after qualifying as a doctor, he was officially named a missionary. He spent one night at home—the last time he would see his father—and three weeks later, he sailed for southern Africa.

Trek into the Wilderness
Livingstone landed at Cape Town (in present-day South Africa) on March 14, 1841. Although explorers had sailed around Africa and roughly mapped it during the 1400s and 1500s, the enormous continent was still mostly a mystery to Europeans of the 1800s. Africa had few natural harbors, and exploration beyond the coastal areas was a difficult task. The climate in the dense forests and wide deserts was often extreme, and insects carried many deadly diseases. Livingstone, however, was unconcerned by these obstacles. He headed west and north in an ox-drawn wagon on a 700-mile, three-month journey to Kuruman, Moffat's **mission.** North of

mission settlement founded by priests in a land where they hoped to convert people to Christianity

Kuruman lay the Kalahari Desert, which no European had crossed. Beyond the desert lay the unexplored interior of central Africa.

At Kuruman, Moffat and his wife had built a comfortable settlement with thatched houses and gardens, but Livingstone wanted to move on. Within two months, he left for the Kalahari Desert. Over the next few years, Livingstone made several trips north searching for sites where he might found new missions. On each trip, he pushed farther into the Kalahari than any European before him. His journals from that period reveal a strong missionary determination, a delight in geographical discovery, and a growing respect for African peoples and their customs.

Attack and Recovery

In 1844 Livingstone set out to build a mission at Mabotsa, about 220 miles northeast of Kuruman. Along the way, he was nearly mauled to death by a lion. In Livingstone's words, the lion "caught my shoulder as he sprang, and we both came to the ground below together. Growling horribly close to my ear, he shook me as a terrier dog does a rat."

Livingstone survived, but the damage was serious. He wrote: "Besides crunching the bone into splinters, he left eleven teeth wounds on the upper part of my arm." Livingstone returned to Kuruman, where the Moffats nursed him back to health, but he never regained full use of his left arm.

In 1845 Livingstone married Robert Moffat's daughter, Mary. Over the next several years, the couple explored the region south of the Kalahari Desert. They built missions at Mabotsa, Chonuane, and Kolobeng (near the border between present-day Botswana and South Africa), and they had three children. Soon, however, Livingstone became restless. He wanted to investigate the other side of the Kalahari Desert, where he had heard that a body of water called Lake Ngami was located. Beyond the lake, he was told, lay the fertile land of the Makololo tribe, who were led by a powerful ruler named Sebituane. The thought of new geographical discoveries—and new missionary settlements—drew Livingstone north.

Rivers, Swamps, and Fame

Leaving his family in Kolobeng, Livingstone traveled north in June 1849 with three big-game hunters and a supporting party of about 40 Africans. The expedition skirted the edge of the desert and then reached the Zouga River, which the local people said flowed out of Lake Ngami. Livingstone wrote: "It was on 1st August 1849 that we first reached the northeast end of Lake Ngami, and for the first time this fine-looking sheet of water was beheld by Europeans."

This accomplishment had an great impact on Livingstone's future explorations. Britain's Royal Geographical Society heard of his discovery and awarded him a gold medal and a cash prize. More important, the society encouraged Livingstone to continue his work in Africa and promoted his achievements to the British public.

Livingstone wanted to continue northward, but the local Africans refused to supply guides or food. He returned to Kolobeng and prepared for another attempt to reach the Makololo tribe. He was

accompanied on this new journey by his wife—who was pregnant with their fourth child—and his three children, aged four, three, and one. Two months and 600 miles later, an outbreak of fever forced them back to Kolobeng. The Livingstones tried yet again in April 1851 and finally reached the land of the Makololo. Sebituane, the Makololo chief, came 400 miles to meet them on the banks of the Chobe River.

Livingstone suddenly decided to look for a route to the west coast of Africa, which was about 1,800 miles away. He left his family camped by the Chobe River and pushed on through the swamps for about 130 miles. He was then "rewarded by the discovery of the Zambezi, in the center of the continent. This was a most important point, for that river was not previously known to exist at all." Meanwhile, Mary gave birth to their fourth child, and David finally decided to send his family back to the safety of England. After a difficult 1,500-mile trek to Cape Town, Mary and the four children boarded a ship for home.

Encounters with the Slave Trade

After his family's departure, Livingstone rejoined the Makololo people. However, he soon became ill with a fever for the first time. Even worse, he discovered evidence of an active slave trade operated in the area by Portuguese. This information strengthened his desire to find a route to the west coast. He hoped that if he could bring Christianity and European commerce to the interior, the slave trade would be discouraged and displaced.

But his task was not easy. The journey could well have been Livingstone's last, as he hinted in a letter to Moffat: "I shall open up a path to the interior, or perish." Nevertheless, in November 1853, Livingstone and 27 Makololo companions left the village of Linyanti and began paddling up the Zambezi River. They traveled through the edges of the central African rain forests. Along the way, Livingstone filled his notebooks with detailed descriptions of central Africa's **geology,** plants, animals, and people.

During the trip, Livingstone fought such illnesses as **malaria** and **dysentery,** and the party's supplies ran low. As the explorers approached the west coast of Africa, local tribes refused to help because Livingstone had nothing to trade. However, Portuguese and Arab slave traders came to the party's rescue. Livingstone and the Makololo reached the Atlantic Ocean at Luanda (in what is now Angola) on May 31, 1854.

Waterfall on the Zambezi River

At Luanda, Livingstone was offered passage to Britain on a British ship, but instead he decided to help his companions return to their homes. After a short rest, he and the Makololo headed east down the Chobe and Zambezi Rivers. Livingstone eventually reached what he said was "the most wonderful sight I had witnessed in Africa"—the majestic, thundering falls of Mosi-oa-tunya. The overwhelmed explorer named it Victoria Falls after the British queen. He said it was "the only English name I have affixed to any part of the country."

geology the scientific study of the earth's natural history

malaria disease that is spread by mosquitoes in tropical areas

dysentery disease that causes severe diarrhea

On May 20, 1856, Livingstone and his party reached the Indian Ocean and the city of Quelimane (now in Mozambique). He decided to return to Britain, since he had not seen his family in four years. He arrived in December to find that he was already a national hero. He published his first book, *Missionary Travels and Researches in South Africa,* and received many honors. But he soon began preparing for his return to Africa.

Thanks to his fame, Livingstone won support from the British government for his plan to explore the Zambezi River further. The government was mostly interested in the region's geography and resources. Livingstone had his own plan—to start an English colony that would help establish Christianity and end the slave trade.

A Troubled Voyage

Livingstone left England on March 12, 1858, for an exploration of the Zambezi River that he estimated would last two years. In fact, six unhappy years would pass before he returned from the expedition that began his long decline into illness and depression. He began the journey with abundant supplies and impressive equipment, including a steamboat with a paddle wheel. Traveling with him were his wife Mary, his brother Charles, 3 other Europeans, and 10 Africans.

The group faced difficulties from the start. The steamboat could not travel well through the shallow waters of the Zambezi, and most of the Europeans fell ill with fever. Livingstone sent word back to England that he needed a more suitable vessel. Meanwhile, he set up a base to store supplies at the town of Shupanga. He then decided to explore the Shire River, one of the **tributaries** of the Zambezi.

In July 1859, Livingstone sailed up the Shire and then crossed a region called the Shire highlands, which he thought was an ideal site for a European settlement. After traveling for a few more weeks, Livingstone discovered Lake Nyasa (also known as Lake Malawi). But his excitement faded when he learned that the southern end of the lake was a crossroads for several slave trading routes. By this time, Livingstone was also suffering from severe bleeding **hemorrhoids,** the medical problem that eventually contributed to his death. After traveling 1,400 miles, Livingstone arrived in Tete (in what is now Mozambique) in November 1860. Early the next year, a new boat arrived from England, but it too was unfit for the Zambezi River.

Anger and Sorrow

Meanwhile, Livingstone's opposition to the slave trade had grown stronger, and in July he began freeing all the slaves he came across. Before long, he had freed more than 100 and set up a village for them, complete with a school. He then returned to Lake Nyasa for more exploration, collecting valuable information on the lake's geography and the region's slave trade.

On April 27, 1862, Livingstone's wife, Mary, died at Shupanga. After burying her there, the saddened missionary wrote, "I feel willing to die." The following January, he and the rest of the party

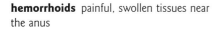

tributary stream or river that flows into a larger stream or river

hemorrhoids painful, swollen tissues near the anus

boarded their newest steamboat, *Lady Nyasa*, as well as a smaller boat, *Pioneer*, and returned to the Shire region. Livingstone was horrified to find that slave traders had rampaged through the area since his previous visit. Entire villages had been burned to the ground, and the river and the ground were strewn with the bodies of dead Africans.

After this shocking experience, Livingstone received more bad news: the expedition had been called back to England. He tried to find a buyer for the *Lady Nyasa*, but the only people who were interested were Portuguese slave traders. Instead of selling his ship to his enemies, Livingstone and a small crew sailed the vessel from Zanzibar (an island off the east coast of what is now Tanzania) and made a risky crossing of the Indian Ocean. Livingstone left the ship for sale in Bombay, India, before returning to Britain on July 23, 1864.

A Brief Visit

With the help of his brother Charles, Livingstone wrote his second book, *Narrative of an Expedition to the Zambezi and its Tributaries*. The work sold 5,000 copies on the first day after it was published. On a lecture tour, Livingstone spoke out fiercely against the Portuguese slave traders in Africa. He also spent time with his five-year-old daughter, whom he had never before seen. But once again it did not take long for him to plan his next trip to Africa.

Livingstone's final expedition was supported by the Royal Geographic Society and private donors. His two personal goals were, as usual, to carry on his missionary work and to end the slave trade. But he also had a new, highly ambitious mission—to find the sources of the Zambezi, Congo, and Nile Rivers. He left Britain in August 1865, stopped in Bombay to complete the sale of the *Lady Nyasa*, and arrived at Mikindani on Africa's east coast the following March. Livingstone was healthy and glad to be back on the continent, but the feeling did not last long.

Theft and Desertions in the Interior

Traveling with a group of 57 men, Livingstone set out for Lake Nyasa and the unknown country beyond. Before long, familiar difficulties arose. Most of the pack animals died, the expedition ran out of food, and Livingstone had trouble controlling the men. The party frequently saw evidence of the slave trade, which discouraged everyone in the group.

Livingstone reached Lake Nyasa on August 8, 1866, and the Shire region a month later. There all but 11 of his companions deserted him, taking most of his supplies as they fled. Livingstone continued trekking northwest but soon faced another problem. An escaped slave whom he had hired ran off with the medicine chest. This loss was serious, because Livingstone had begun to suffer severe attacks of a fever that caused **rheumatism.**

Despite these hardships, Livingstone reached the Chambezi River in January 1867. Livingstone thought that the Chambezi might be the source of the Nile River, and he spent the rest of his life trying to confirm this. On April 1, he caught sight of Lake Tanganyika and

rheumatism physical condition that causes pain in the joints or muscles, making movement uncomfortable

promptly collapsed to the ground. Almost a month passed before he could travel again.

Livingstone pressed on into the continent's interior. By early November, he had discovered Lake Mweru, but his spirits were low. He wrote in his journal: "I am so tired of exploration without a word from home or anywhere for two years, that I must go to Ujiji on Lake Tanganyika for letters before doing anything else." The rainy season began, however, and travel was almost impossible. Livingstone wandered around the area for a few months and then made another important geographical find—Lake Bangweulu, a large, marshy lake southeast of Lake Mweru. By now he was desperately ill with pneumonia. He was saved by Arab merchants, who gave him medicine and carried him to Ujiji in March 1869.

Despair and Hope

Later in 1869, Livingstone set out again to find the source of the Nile River. This journey was by far his most difficult. He was constantly sick and hungry, was almost killed in an ambush, and never did solve the puzzle of the Nile. On March 29, 1871, he reached the town of Nyangwe (in what is now the Democratic Republic of Congo), the northernmost point of all of his African travels. When he returned to Ujiji in October, his sickness and sense of failure crushed him. "I felt as if dying on my feet," he wrote. To make matters worse, the Africans with whom he had left his belongings had sold them while he was gone and spent the money they had made.

A new friend then came to the rescue. On November 10, 1871, Henry Morton STANLEY, a reporter from New York City, arrived in Ujiji. He had come to find the famous explorer, who everyone feared was lost or dead. Stanley's greeting, "Dr. Livingstone, I presume," became the most famous remark in the history of exploration. This visitor brought much-needed food, medicine, and companionship. After Livingstone recovered, he and Stanley searched together for the Nile's **headwaters** near the northern part of Lake Tanganyika. Stanley begged Livingstone to leave Africa with him, but the doctor stubbornly refused. When Stanley left, he was the last non-African whom Livingstone would ever see.

The Last Days of Dr. Livingstone

The Scottish missionary tried one more time to find the source of the Nile. Within a month, he was seriously ill again. By early 1873, he was approaching Lake Bangweulu in the middle of the drenching rainy season. His **chronometers** and **sextant** were damaged, and for the first time during his travels, he became lost. Livingstone's illness and bleeding worsened, and he contracted dysentery again. The expedition paused in a small village near the lake, and on the morning of May 1, his companions found Livingstone dead in his hut.

Livingstone's heart and other organs were buried under a tree in the village. His body was then carried by his fellow travelers 900 miles to the coast, where it was placed on a ship for Britain. Livingstone was buried in London in April 1874.

headwaters source of a river

chronometer clock designed to keep precise time in the rough conditions of sea travel

sextant optical instrument used by navigators since the 1750s to determine distance north or south of the equator

In his own mind, Livingstone had failed in many ways. He did not settle the question of the Nile's source, end the slave trade, or establish permanent missions in Africa. But soon after his death, the slave trade lessened while Christian missions flourished, thanks in large part to his pioneering efforts to promote those causes. Moreover, his contributions to the geographical knowledge of central and southern Africa were unequaled by any other explorer.

SUGGESTED READING Tim Jeal, *Livingstone* (G. P. Putnam, 1973); David Livingstone, *Missionary Travels and Researches in South Africa* (Ayer, 1972); Oliver Ransford, *David Livingstone: The Dark Continent* (St. Martin's, 1978); I. Schapera, *Livingstone's African Journals, 1853-1856* (Chatto and Windus, 1963).

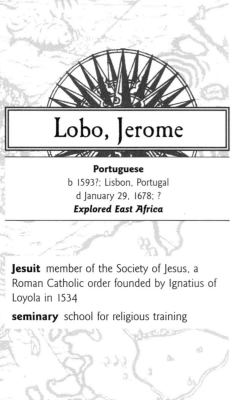

Lobo, Jerome

Portuguese
b 1593?; Lisbon, Portugal
d January 29, 1678; ?
Explored East Africa

Jesuit member of the Society of Jesus, a Roman Catholic order founded by Ignatius of Loyola in 1534

seminary school for religious training

tributary stream or river that flows into a larger stream or river

Father Jerome Lobo was one of the first Europeans to visit Lake Tana, the source of the Blue Nile River. A **Jesuit** priest, Lobo explored the Juba River and Malindi (now Kenya) in 1624 before beginning missionary work in Abyssinia (now Ethiopia). He later wrote two books about his experiences in Africa. Though the Scottish explorer James BRUCE later questioned the accuracy of Lobo's reports, the priest's claims were ultimately proven true.

Travels to India and Africa

Lobo entered the **seminary** at the age of 16 and became a priest 11 years later. After teaching at a Portuguese college, he was sent in 1622 to Goa, a Portuguese colony on the west coast of India. There he was to complete his religious studies and prepare for missionary work in Abyssinia. The same year, Father Pero Páez, the Jesuits' missionary leader in Abyssinia, died. Father Lobo was chosen to accompany the new Jesuit leader to the country. The ruler of Abyssinia had already become a Roman Catholic, so Lobo did not expect resistance from the local people.

Lobo left India in 1624. He was unable to reach Abyssinia at first, so he traveled south to the Juba River and Malindi. The following year, he arrived in Abyssinia and began his missionary work. He also took time to explore the region. He traveled to Lake Tana as Father Páez had done 10 years before. This visit made Lobo the second European known to have seen the source of the Blue Nile, the smaller of the Nile River's two **tributaries.** He also went southeast to the falls of Lake Tana, known as Tisisat Falls.

Telling and Defending Lobo's Story

Lobo spent seven years as a missionary in Abyssinia. But after the death of the country's Catholic emperor, Lobo and the other Jesuits were eventually forced to leave. In 1634 Lobo sailed back to Goa and then on to Madrid and Rome. He reported to the religious leaders of Spain and to the Pope on the situation in Abyssinia. Lobo unsuccessfully tried to convince them to ask the new government to allow the Jesuits to return. Unable to go back to Africa, Lobo returned to Goa, where he stayed almost 20 years before going home to Portugal. He spent most of the rest of his life writing about his experiences in Africa. He described his travels to Lake Tana poetically in a journal later published as *A Voyage to Abyssinia.* This work led to claims that Lobo had lied about his travels.

More than 150 years after Lobo explored Abyssinia, Scotsman James Bruce became the next European to visit Tisisat Falls. Highly competitive and fiercely anti-Catholic, Bruce declared that Lobo could not have possibly reached the falls because Lobo's description of the area was inaccurate. Bruce said that some of the experiences Lobo had described—such as sitting on a ledge and seeing the rushing waters—were impossible. Later explorers determined that the falls were very different from one season to the next, proving that Lobo had reached them, just as he had claimed.

SUGGESTED READING James J. Walsh, *These Splendid Priests* (Sears, 1926).

Long, Stephen Harriman

American
b December 30, 1784; Hopkinton, New Hampshire
d September 4, 1864; Alton, Illinois
Explored American West

Stephen Harriman Long's claim that the Southwest was a "Great American Desert" discouraged Americans from settling there for over 30 years.

scurvy disease caused by a lack of vitamin C and once a major cause of death among sailors; symptoms include internal bleeding, loosened teeth, and extreme fatigue

Stephen Harriman Long made three explorations of the North American interior as a member of the United States Army Corps of Topographical Engineers. His most important journey took place in 1820, when he led a party along the Platte River to the Rocky Mountains and then south to the Arkansas and Canadian Rivers. Long's report of the expedition confirmed the opinion of explorer Zebulon PIKE, who had traveled the area 10 years before. Both men thought that the Southwest was a "Great American Desert," where humans could not live. Long's views kept Americans from settling there for over 30 years.

Pioneering Scientist

After graduating from Dartmouth College, Long joined the army. He taught mathematics for two years at the U.S. Military Academy at West Point, New York, before transferring to the Corps of Topographical Engineers. On his first expedition, in 1817, Long traveled up the Mississippi River to the Falls of St. Anthony at what is now Minneapolis, Minnesota. The United States government wanted to build military forts in the area to help fight hostile Indians and protect American fur traders from British interference. Long's job was to find appropriate sites for these forts. As a result of his work, the government built Fort Snelling where the Mississippi and Minnesota Rivers meet. Long was also involved in the construction of Fort Smith on the Arkansas River.

In 1819 the U.S. government proposed to establish a military outpost near the meeting of the Missouri and Yellowstone Rivers. The fort would help the United States protect its northwestern frontier and extend its fur trade. The proposal led to the Yellowstone Expedition. In the spring of 1819, a party of 1,000 men led by General Henry Atkinson headed up the Missouri in five steamboats. Long sailed on a sixth steamboat that carried scientific explorers and artists. It was the first time steamboats had been used on the Missouri and the first time scientific explorers took part in an expedition to the West. But using steamboats turned out to be a mistake—the ships couldn't sail up the river and were forced to stop at Council Bluffs (in present-day Iowa). With men dying of **scurvy,** and with costs rising, Congress canceled the expedition.

The Second Journey

Long, however, was ordered to continue west. He was instructed to travel along the Platte River through the Great Plains to the Arkansas and Red Rivers in the Southwest. The Red River was considered important because it was assumed to be the boundary between the United States and Spanish territory. On June 6, 1820, Long and his party left Council Bluffs and headed west along the Platte. As they crossed the plains, they saw giant herds of buffalo and met Pawnee Indians. On June 30, the expedition sighted the Rocky Mountains and named the highest peak they could see Longs Peak. In mid-July the party came out of the mountains just south of the site of present-day Denver. A few days later, some members of the party scaled Pikes Peak and became the first recorded climbers of that mountain.

The expedition then followed the Arkansas River as far as the Royal Gorge but failed to reach the river's source. Long decided to divide his party into two groups. The first would descend the Arkansas, traveling east as far as the border of what is now Oklahoma. Long led the second group, which headed south until they reached a river he thought was the Red. They followed the river downstream, heading east.

Long's journey was a difficult one. At times he and his party were forced to eat their own horses, and most of the Indians they met were hostile. When he reached the end of the river, Long was shocked to discover that it flowed into the Arkansas. He realized that he had not been on the Red River, which flows into the Mississippi. He had been traveling on the Canadian River, which is just north of the Red. To make matters worse, Long found out that three deserters from the other group had taken most of the expedition's journals and scientific notebooks.

Last Trip West

Despite the failure of his second expedition, Long was given another chance. In 1823 he was sent to explore the area between the Mississippi and Missouri Rivers. The party followed the Mississippi and then traveled up the Minnesota to its **headwaters.** There the men marked the international boundary between the United States and Canada. When Long arrived in Philadelphia on October 26, 1823, he received a warm welcome, his first upon returning from the West.

Long never explored again, but he continued his career of government service. With the Corps of Topographical Engineers, he earned a reputation as a **surveyor** of routes for new railroads. Eventually, he became an expert in the new field of railroad engineering.

Long's Major Contribution

Long had many disappointments on his second expedition, such as failing to find the Red River and losing his notebooks and journals. Still, after that trip, he managed to produce the most significant report and map of the West since the journey of Meriwether LEWIS and William CLARK. Long supervised the compiling of the report,

headwaters source of a river

surveyor one who makes precise measurements of a location's geography

geologist scientist who studies the earth's natural history

species type of plant or animal

which was actually written by Edwin James, the chief **geologist** of the trip. It contained complete descriptions of plants and animals of the plains, and it even included a number of animal **species,** such as the coyote, that were discovered and named on the trip. In an additional 17-page section, Long made the first attempt to record the sign language used by many tribes on the plains. The writer James Fenimore Cooper used details of the report in one of his novels, *The Prairie.*

Although the report was useful, it also created a negative image of the plains. Long wrote that the land was not fit for farming and that it lacked enough water and timber to support settlers. Historians later criticized Long for creating a myth of the "Great American Desert." But Long had based his opinion on what he had seen, including the harsh winters and hostile Indians. In a sense, Long was right. Americans of the 1820s probably did not yet have the resources to settle that land.

SUGGESTED READING John Moring, *Men with Sand: Great Explorers of the North American West* (Falcon Publishing, 1998); Roger L. Nichols, *Stephen Long and American Frontier Exploration* (University of Oklahoma Press, 1995).

Lopes de Sequeira, Diogo

Portuguese
b ?; ?
d 1520?; ?
Led first European fleet to explore Malay Archipelago

archipelago large group of islands or a body of water with many islands

Today the Portuguese explorer Diogo Lopes de Sequeira is not as well known as his countryman and fellow explorer Ferdinand MAGELLAN. But Lopes de Sequeira was the first European navigator to sail the Pacific seas described centuries before by Marco POLO. He was also the commander on Magellan's first voyage to the islands of Southeast Asia. In the early 1500s, Lopes de Sequeira led a Portuguese fleet to explore the Malay **Archipelago,** near the islands now called the Philippines.

Little is known about Lopes de Sequeira's early life or exactly when he traveled from Portugal to the Pacific Ocean. Historians know that Magellan volunteered for service in India in 1504 and sailed under Lopes de Sequeira's command. They also know that Magellan reached the coast of India in 1509. Upon their arrival, the Europeans met resistance from the people of Goa and Cochin, two cities located on the southwestern coast of India.

That same year, Lopes de Sequeira's fleet left the Indian port of Calicut, rounded Ceylon (now Sri Lanka), and crossed the Bay of Bengal. The expedition finally landed somewhere on the northern part of Sumatra, in what is now Indonesia. Lopes de Sequeira signed a treaty with the local chief and sailed on to the Moluccas (also in Indonesia), which he reached in September.

The Portuguese captain and his crew were surprised by what they saw. The port city was crowded with ships and traders from Arabia, Persia (now Iran), Bengal (India), Burma (now Myanmar), Java (Indonesia), China, and the Philippines. Lopes de Sequeira soon established friendly relations with the foreign traders, and he purchased spices to bring back to Portugal. The local leader, however, was not as hospitable. He plotted to kill Lopes de Sequeira and his men. Luckily for Lopes de Sequeira, a kind trader warned him of the plot, and he sailed to safety. Some of his crew, however, had already been taken prisoner.

During his travels, Lopes de Sequeira sailed as far east as Ternate, in the Moluccas. His fleet arrived back in Portugal in 1512, marking the end of his career as an explorer.

SUGGESTED READING Ronald Bishop Smith, *Diogo Lopes de Sequeira* (Silvas, 1975).

López de Legazpi, Miguel. See *Legazpi, Miguel López de.*

Lucid, Shannon Wells

American
b January 14, 1943; Shanghai, China
living
Set endurance record for women in space

NASA National Aeronautics and Space Administration, the U.S. space agency

astronaut American term for a person who travels into space; literally, "traveler to the stars"

After Shannon Lucid's 188-day stay aboard the *Mir* space station in 1996, she had spent more time in space than any other American astronaut.

As a child, Shannon Wells Lucid dreamed of exploring space. As a young woman, she was frustrated by the fact that **NASA's** first **astronauts** were all men. But after she became an astronaut herself, she spent more time in **orbit** around the earth than any other American and any other woman.

Women in Space

Lucid was born Shannon Wells in China, where her parents were missionaries. In 1949 the Wells family left China and settled in Bethany, Oklahoma. Shannon read a great deal about the history of the American frontier and later recalled: "I was very interested in being a pioneer." Space, she thought, was a frontier she could explore. However, all of the astronauts in the early years of America's space program were men. She remembers feeling angry because there was "absolutely no reason not to have any females." In 1963 the **Soviet Union's** Valentina TERESHKOVA became the first woman in space. Twenty years passed before the American Sally RIDE became the second.

Meanwhile, Wells earned degrees in chemistry and biochemistry at the University of Oklahoma. Although she was a skilled and qualified pilot, she could not get a job as a commercial pilot because she was a woman, so she worked as a chemist instead. She married Michael Lucid and started a family.

In 1978 NASA was ready to train its first women astronauts, and Lucid was one of the six women chosen that year. In 1985 she made her first spaceflight, aboard the **space shuttle** *Discovery.* By 1993 Lucid had been part of three more shuttle missions, in which she carried out scientific experiments. She had logged a total of nearly 840 hours in space, more than any other American woman.

Setting a New Record

On March 22, 1996, Lucid rode the shuttle *Atlantis* into space for her fifth mission. The shuttle carried her to the Russian **space station** *Mir.* She spent 188 days aboard *Mir,* during which time the station orbited the earth more than 3,000 times and traveled 75 million miles. Her time aboard the cramped station was often uncomfortable. She compared it to "living in a camper in the back of your pickup with your kids . . . when it's raining and no one

orbit stable, circular route; one trip around; to revolve around

Soviet Union nation that existed from 1922 to 1991, made up of Russia and 14 other republics in eastern Europe and northern Asia

space shuttle reusable spacecraft designed to transport people and cargo between the earth and space

space station spacecraft that circles the earth for months or years with a human crew

cosmonaut Russian term for a person who travels into space; literally, "traveler to the universe"

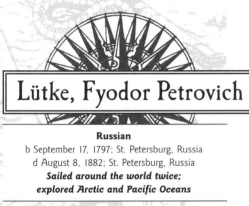

Lütke, Fyodor Petrovich

Russian
b September 17, 1797; St. Petersburg, Russia
d August 8, 1882; St. Petersburg, Russia
*Sailed around the world twice;
explored Arctic and Pacific Oceans*

circumnavigate to travel around

circumnavigation journey around the world

aide-de-camp assistant to a high-ranking military officer

czar title of Russian monarchs from the 1200s to 1917

specimen sample of a plant, animal, or mineral, usually collected for scientific study or display

can get out." But she worked well with the two Russian **cosmonauts** aboard *Mir* and enjoyed e-mail and video communication with her family, which by then included three children.

Lucid conducted dozens of scientific experiments aboard *Mir,* studying, for example, the way crystals grow in the weightlessness of space. Other studies began when she returned to earth in October 1996. The lack of gravity in space causes bones and muscles to weaken, but to the amazement of scientists, Lucid was able to stand and walk out of the shuttle. She had spent hundreds of hours exercising aboard *Mir* to keep fit. Lucid had been in space longer than anyone so far except one Russian cosmonaut, and she gave America's space scientists an opportunity to study the effects—and the future—of life in space.

SUGGESTED READING Carmen Bredeson, *Shannon Lucid: Space Ambassador* (Millbrook Press, 1998).

From 1826 to 1829, Fyodor Petrovich Lütke **circumnavigated** the globe as captain of the *Senyavin.* By completing this voyage, he led one of the most valuable Pacific explorations of the 1800s.

An Experienced Sailor

Lütke attended the Russian school for naval cadets and became a career naval officer. In 1817 he made his first **circumnavigation** as part of the *Kamchatka* expedition to determine the position of several islands in the Bering Sea. From 1821 to 1824, Lütke took the *Apollo* into Arctic waters, mapping the Murmansk Coast of Russia's Barents Sea. He also charted the western and southern coasts of the island of Novaya Zemlya.

In 1825 Lütke became an **aide-de-camp** of **Czar** Nicholas I. The following year, the Russian ruler put Lütke in command of a major expedition to the Pacific Ocean. Lütke's ship, the *Senyavin,* sailed from Kronstadt (now Kronshlot), on the Gulf of Finland, on September 1 with a crew that included a team of scientists. They reached the Canary Islands, off western Africa, in November and then crossed the Atlantic Ocean to South America. Lütke rounded Cape Horn and stopped for a three-week rest ashore in Valparaíso, Chile.

From Chile he sailed north to Sitka, Alaska, in April 1827 and then headed west to the Aleutian Islands in late August. After sailing north into the Bering Sea, he mapped St. Matthew Island and then charted part of the coast of Asia.

Scientific Advances

In December, Lütke headed south to the Carolines, where the expedition's naturalists found the only known **specimen** of a bird they called the Caroline rail. Lütke reached Guam on February 26, 1828; then, in April, he visited the Bonin Islands near Japan. There a naturalist discovered another rare bird, the Bonin finch. Lütke visited the Carolines again and then the Philippines before returning home by way of Africa. He reached Kronstadt on September 16, 1829.

species type of plant or animal

During the three-year voyage, his scientists had discovered more than 300 **species** of birds, 700 insects, and 150 shellfish. They collected more than 4,000 plants and the largest number of algae species to date. Lütke later became an admiral and served in several government posts. He helped found the Russian Geographical Society in 1845 and was a member of several other scientific societies. Lütke wrote about his last expedition in a book called *Voyage Around the World.*

SUGGESTED READING A. I. Alekseev, *Fedor Petrovich Litke,* edited by Katherine L. Arndt, translated by Serge LeComte (University of Alaska Press, 1996).

Mackenzie, Alexander

Scottish
b 1764?; Stornoway, Scotland
d 1820; near Pitlochry, Scotland
*Explored western Canada;
reached Pacific Ocean by land route*

Northwest Passage water route connecting the Atlantic Ocean and Pacific Ocean through the Arctic islands of northern Canada

voyageur expert French woodsman, boatman, and guide

The world did not learn of Alexander Mackenzie's daring explorations until his journals were published in 1801, eight years after his last expedition.

Sir Alexander Mackenzie made two daring expeditions into the northernmost reaches of Canada's Alberta province. In 1789 he followed the river that now bears his name to the Arctic Ocean. Four years later, he crossed the Rocky Mountains to become the first person to reach the Pacific Ocean by an overland route.

Search for the Northwest Passage

After moving to Canada, Mackenzie became involved in the fur trade in Montréal. He eagerly accepted the job of running a trading post at Lake Athabasca, in what are now the Canadian provinces of Alberta and Saskatchewan. Mackenzie replaced the American explorer Peter POND as director of the post.

Many years earlier, Captain James COOK had described a river that flowed into the Alaskan bay now known as Cook Inlet. Pond believed that the river flowing out of the Great Slave Lake, located northwest of Lake Athabasca, was the same river Cook had described. Mackenzie supported Pond's theory and wanted to test it. He hoped to discover the **Northwest Passage** that so many explorers had sought unsuccessfully. Mackenzie spent the winter of 1788 preparing for his journey.

Mackenzie left Fort Chipewyan, on Lake Athabasca, on June 3, 1789. His party included four Canadian **voyageurs,** two of their wives, a German, and a Chipewyan Indian called English Chief and his family. Traveling up the Peace River to the Slave River and then northwest, they reached Great Slave Lake on June 9 and found it still covered with ice. For two weeks, they picked their way north through the breaks in ice. When they came to the north shore of the lake, they spent another six days searching for what is now called the Mackenzie River.

Once on the river, Mackenzie was pleased to discover that it ran west, and in some places southwest, for 300 miles. Because of this new information, he believed that the river might eventually reach the Pacific Ocean. On July 2, the morning fog lifted to reveal the snow-capped Rocky Mountains in the distance. Although Mackenzie saw the mountains as another sign of his party's westward progress, he found out that the river did not flow through the mountains as he had expected. Instead it soon turned north.

latitude distance north or south of the equator

longitude distance east or west of an imaginary line on the earth's surface; in 1884 most nations agreed to draw the line through Greenwich, England

portage transport of boats and supplies overland between waterways

Arctic Explorations

Disappointed, Mackenzie and his party continued along the river. They eventually met Slave and Dog-Rib Indians, who warned them of monsters and other dangers down the river. According to Mackenzie, the Indians predicted "that it would require several winters to get to the sea," and that old age would come upon them before they returned. Despite the warning, the expedition continued by canoe. On July 10, they entered the river's mouth on the Arctic Ocean. Mackenzie took a **latitude** reading at this point and was surprised and discouraged to learn how far north he was. Two days later, the party reached open water at a point now called Mackenzie Bay in the present-day Beaufort Sea. For five days, the men cautiously paddled their bark canoes between the shore and the ice field, exploring the bay.

Mackenzie then hurried to return home before winter set in. The party reached Fort Chipewyan on September 12, two days after the first snowstorm. In 102 days, Mackenzie had traveled almost 3,000 miles, mapped one of the world's great rivers, and almost entirely put to rest the idea of a Northwest Passage to the Pacific Ocean. But he was still determined to reach the Pacific.

West to the Pacific

Mackenzie realized that if his explorations were to have any scientific value, he needed to know more about mapping and finding exact geographic positions. In 1791 he went to England to study astronomy, navigation, and geography, and he bought the latest instruments for determining **longitude** and latitude. By the fall of 1792, he was back at Lake Athabasca, making final preparations for his next journey.

Before winter came, Mackenzie quickly built a crude fort 200 miles up the Peace River. This location would give him a head start in the spring. On May 9, 1793, Mackenzie set out with 10 people and 3,000 pounds of supplies. The group rowed a large, extremely lightweight canoe that Mackenzie had designed. In addition to Mackenzie's second-in-command, Alexander Mackay, the party included six French-Canadian voyageurs and two Indian interpreters and hunters. By May 17, the men had spotted the Rocky Mountains.

The next part of the journey was a dangerous one, as they entered the Peace River canyon. The canyon was a rough 22-mile run of falls and rapids, much of it between rocky cliffs. For six days, they towed the canoe up the river. They then **portaged** the craft 9 miles up a steep mountain and across wooded hills before finally reaching a calmer stretch of the river.

After a week of easy paddling, they came to a fork in the river. Mackenzie thought one branch, the Finlay River, was more likely to lead to the Pacific Ocean. But he chose the other branch, now known as the Parsnip River, because a Beaver Indian he had previously met had recommended that route. For the next month, the party was surrounded by mountains and traveled up rapid, shallow rivers. Heat, gnats, and mosquitoes added to their troubles. They next crossed the Continental Divide, the line separating the

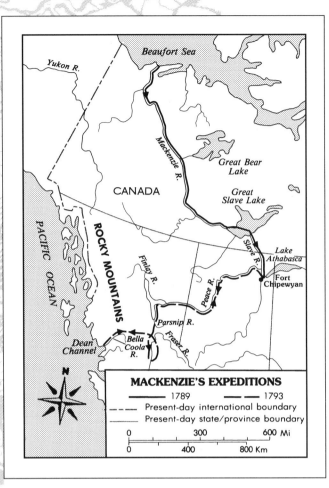

MACKENZIE'S EXPEDITIONS

——— 1789   - - - 1793
- - - Present-day international boundary
——— Present-day state/province boundary

| 0 | 300 | 600 Mi |
| 0 | 400 | 800 Km |

The Mackenzie River was originally named the Disappointment River by the explorer because he thought that his 1789 trip was a failure.

rivers that flow east from those that flow west. When they reached what is now the Fraser River, local Indians told them that the river canyon was nearly impassable and that the route to the sea was a long one.

A Wise Change of Plans

Mackenzie now decided that the only practical route to the Pacific was overland rather than by river. His men, though tired, agreed to backtrack up the Fraser to reach the overland route. On July 4, the party left their extra supplies at the junction of the Fraser and Blackwater Rivers and began hiking with heavy packs.

For 15 days, they marched toward the sea, surrounded by new sights. They saw gigantic trees and met Indian tribes who lived on salmon rather than on land animals. They marveled at the Indians' large houses, which were covered with carvings and paintings, and their huge seagoing canoes made from cedar logs.

On July 17, the party arrived at a village on what is now called the Bella Coola River. After receiving a warm reception from the Indians there, the explorers called the place Friendly Village. Mackenzie then continued toward the Pacific coast and arrived at the mouth of the Bella Coola. The river emptied into a narrow bay of the sea now called Dean Channel (in present-day British Columbia).

The Indians Mackenzie met on the coast were hostile, but he had a job to do before he could leave. He needed to find a spot where he could stay long enough to take daytime and nighttime readings so as to determine his exact latitude and longitude. After being followed by anxious Indians for two days, Mackenzie selected a rock ledge on the Dean Channel. Later he used a mixture of purple dye and melted grease to write on the rock: "Alexander Mackenzie, from Canada, by land, the twenty-second day of July, one thousand seven hundred and ninety-three." That rock was later made into a monument, with the same words chiseled into its surface. At last he was ready to head home. While the trip west had taken 10 hard weeks, the return trip took only 4. By August 24, he was back at the fort on the Peace River, and his exploring days were over.

Alexander Mackenzie was a man of courage and imagination. His determination and leadership skills helped him complete two of the most difficult explorations ever undertaken in North America. His accomplishments are honored with a river, a mountain range, and a bay that bear his name.

SUGGESTED READING Barry M. Gough, *First Across the Continent: Sir Alexander Mackenzie* (University of Oklahoma Press, 1997); Alexander Mackenzie, *The Journals and Letters of Sir Alexander Mackenzie*, edited by W. Kaye Lamb (Macmillan of Canada, 1970) and *Voyages from Montreal on the River St. Lawrence Through the Continent of North America to the Frozen and Pacific Oceans in the Years 1789 and 1793* (Tuttle, 1971); James K. Smith, *Alexander Mackenzie, Explorer, the Hero Who Failed* (McGraw-Hill Ryerson, 1973).

MacMillan, Donald Baxter

American
b November 10, 1874; Provincetown, Massachusetts
d November 10, 1970; Provincetown, Massachusetts
Explored Arctic Ocean by sled and plane

anthropologist scientist who studies human societies

Inuit people of the Canadian Arctic, sometimes known as the Eskimo

glacier large, slowly moving mass of ice

schooner fast, easy-to-maneuver sailing ship with two or more masts and triangular sails

Donald Baxter MacMillan pioneered the exploration of the Arctic Ocean with modern equipment, such as airplanes and snowmobiles.

Donald Baxter MacMillan began his Arctic explorations as an assistant on Robert PEARY's final expedition to the North Pole in 1908. Afterward, MacMillan made 30 more trips to the Arctic Ocean and spent several of these journeys filling in gaps on Peary's map of the region. From 1913 to 1917, he tried to find Peary's mythical Crocker Island, said to lie northwest of Canada's Ellesmere Island. But Peary's sighting had been an illusion.

Scientist and Student of Culture

MacMillan was an **anthropologist** by training, but he had a wide academic background. He taught Latin and physical education at a private school and served as principal of a high school in Maine. He also ran a summer camp, where he taught Peary's son outdoor skills.

Unlike Peary, MacMillan pursued serious scientific projects in the Arctic Ocean. He studied many topics, including the lifestyle of the **Inuit** and the movement of **glaciers.** He also proved that trees had once grown in the polar regions. On the Sverdrup Islands, he found a coal deposit formed by trees that had rotted and sunk into the earth millions of years before. After his journey with Peary, MacMillan spent three years in the Labrador region of Newfoundland, Canada, doing research on the culture of the area. As was true of the Arctic explorer Vilhjalmur STEFANSSON, his interest in people was closely connected to his passion for exploring the lands they inhabited.

Breaking New Ground in Exploration

In 1920 MacMillan visited Canada's Hudson Bay area to report on possible sites for trading posts. The next year, he sailed north for the first time in the *Bowdoin*, a **schooner** specifically designed to navigate in Arctic waters. He used it regularly on later trips to the region. In 1925 MacMillan helped introduce a new era in Arctic exploration. While Roald AMUNDSEN was preparing for an Arctic flight, MacMillan helped organize an expedition that successfully flew across Ellesmere Island. This trip was the first of Richard BYRD's and Floyd BENNETT's flights in Arctic conditions.

MacMillan's career in the Arctic continued for many years. He eventually earned the rank of rear admiral in the U.S. Naval Reserve and worked on various military and civilian projects. His expeditions introduced the use of aircraft, snowmobiles, and shortwave radios in Arctic exploration. MacMillan took his last trip in 1957 at the age of 82.

Magellan, Ferdinand

Portuguese
b 1480?; Portugal
d April 27, 1521; Mactan Island, Philippines
Led first expedition to sail around the world

circumnavigation journey around the world

Ferdinand Magellan's pride and determination made him a great explorer, but they also led to his dismissal from the royal court of Portugal, his homeland.

junk Chinese ship with sails made of fiber mats

SUGGESTED READING Everett S. Allen, *Arctic Odyssey; the Life of Rear Admiral Donald B. MacMillan* (Dodd, Mead, 1962); Donald B. MacMillan, *Four Years in the White North* (Hale, Cushman, and Flint, 1933).

Ferdinand Magellan achieved what Christopher Columbus had attempted about 30 years earlier—he reached Asia by sailing west from Europe. Though he did not live to see its conclusion, Magellan led the first expedition to sail completely around the world. This **circumnavigation** stands out in history as one of the greatest feats of exploration. A fearless navigator, Magellan found a strait through South America into what was then called the South Sea. He renamed that sea the Pacific Ocean and became the first European to cross it.

Magellan overcame many hardships during his historic voyage into the unknown. Stern and self-disciplined, he led with a firm but fair hand. He asked his crew to make great sacrifices, yet he demanded even more from himself. However, the strength that made Magellan a great captain also led to his death when he stubbornly fought a battle with inhabitants of the Philippine Islands.

First Voyage and First Battle

Ferdinand Magellan was born in Portugal around 1480. His father was a trusted officer of John II, king of Portugal. Magellan began his schooling at age 7. At 12 he went to the king's court to study mathematics, geography, mapmaking, and navigation. Three years later, Magellan entered the service of Portugal's new king, Manuel I, who was known as "Manuel the Fortunate." The king allowed Magellan to go to sea with a fleet that would fight to advance Portugal's trading interests in the Indian Ocean.

On March 25, 1505, Magellan sailed for India under the command of Francisco de Almeida. The fleet of 22 ships, with nearly 2,000 men, was the largest ever to leave Portugal. The expedition reached Cannanore, a city on the southern part of India's west coast, known as the Malabar Coast. There Magellan was wounded in battle. It was the first of several serious wounds he would receive during his life.

Pirates and Prisoners

After building a fort at Cannanore, the Portuguese sailed for the east coast of Africa. For the next 18 months, they destroyed Arab settlements and replaced them with Portuguese trading posts protected by soldiers. Magellan returned to India in 1507, and two years later, he was wounded again at the Battle of Dui, in which 19 Portuguese ships defeated 200 Arab vessels in the Indian Ocean.

After recovering from his injury, Magellan joined Diogo Lopes de Sequeira on a mission to Malacca, on the Malay Peninsula in Southeast Asia. When they arrived in September 1509, Magellan and his cousin, Francisco Serrano, heard of a plot against the Portuguese by a local ruler, but no one in command believed the tale. When an attack came as Magellan had warned, the Portuguese lost 60 men.

Shortly afterward, the Portuguese were attacked again, this time by a pirate **junk,** and Serrano was taken captive. Magellan sneaked

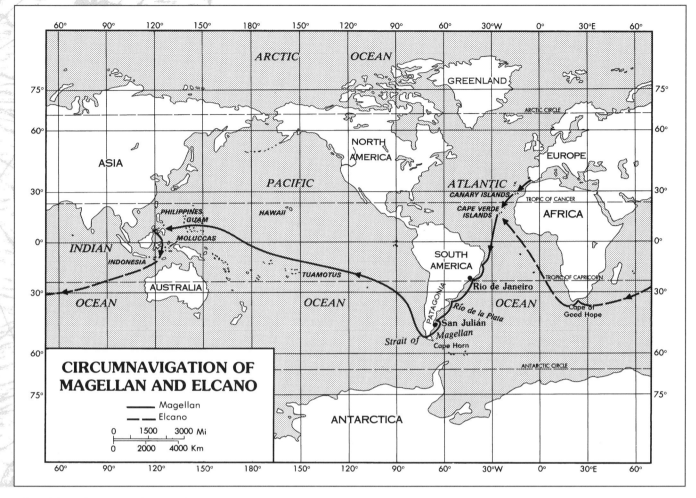

CIRCUMNAVIGATION OF MAGELLAN AND ELCANO

—— Magellan
— — Elcano

| 0 | 1500 | 3000 Mi |
| 0 | 2000 | 4000 Km |

Magellan did not live to see the completion of the first sea voyage around the world.

aboard the junk, freed his cousin, and captured the pirates' ship and treasure. However, his tour of duty in southern Asia continued to be difficult. He was wounded yet again in a battle at Calicut, India, and was later shipwrecked in the Arabian Sea. His heroic efforts in that crisis were highly praised by Portuguese writers of the time.

Promoted for Valor

In October 1510, Magellan's bravery was recognized by the new Portuguese governor in India, Afonso de ALBUQUERQUE. The governor promoted Magellan to captain and gave him command of a **caravel.** The next month, Albuquerque carried out a vicious attack on the Indian port of Goa. Some historians believe that Magellan did not like the slaughter and looting that accompanied the Portuguese efforts in India. It may have been at this time that his interests turned more toward exploration.

The next summer, Magellan accompanied Albuquerque on a successful mission to capture Malacca. There Magellan acquired as a slave a 13-year-old Malay boy who became known as Black Henry or Malacca Henry. Henry served Magellan until the captain's death 10 years later.

In December 1511, Albuquerque sent ships from Malacca to find the Spice Islands, also called the Moluccas. Magellan's cousin Serrano

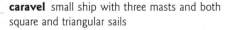

caravel small ship with three masts and both square and triangular sails

When Ferdinand Magellan sailed from Spain in 1519, he flew a white flag with a shield that showed the castles of Castile and the lions of León.

Treaty of Tordesillas agreement between Spain and Portugal dividing the rights to discovered lands along a north-south line

courtier attendant at a royal court

took part in this voyage and eventually settled in the Moluccas, sending out letters with tales of the islands' endless riches. Some scholars believe that Magellan may have gone on this mission as well, while others suggest that he spent the time patrolling the coast off Malacca. In any case, he did make at least one such side trip, sailing as far as Luzon and Mindanao, islands in the Phillipines.

Rejection at Court

Magellan went back to Portugal in 1512. He had by then begun to fall out of favor with both Albuquerque and King Manuel, and he soon left the royal court. In August 1513, he volunteered for military duty in Azamor, Morocco, where he received another wound. The injury left him lame in one leg for the rest of his life. After the fighting, Magellan was placed in charge of the prisoners and property that the Portuguese had captured. He was then accused of selling a herd of captured cattle back to the enemy. King Manuel was unsympathetic to Magellan's case, and though the charges were later dropped, Magellan never forgot the poor treatment he had received.

Three years later, Magellan asked King Manuel I for a larger salary and a chance to lead an expedition to Asia. The king denied both requests, so Magellan asked if he could leave Manuel's service. The king dismissed him with an insult. Furious, Magellan left the court and traveled to Pôrto, a port city in northern Portugal. There he met a renowned navigator, John of Lisbon, and an old friend from the fighting in India, Duarte BARBOSA. John of Lisbon told Magellan that there was a water passage through the Americas. Meanwhile, Barbosa said that he had relatives in Spain who wanted to finance an expedition to the Spice Islands. The Barbosas were willing to put Magellan in command. His opportunity had come at last.

Pledging a New Allegiance

Magellan left for Spain on October 12, 1517. He soon met with King Charles I of Spain, who immediately approved the planned voyage to the Spice Islands. Spain could benefit by finding new lands for trade and colonization, and the Moluccas were thought to be a valuable source of spices, timber, and other goods. Magellan hoped to prove that the Moluccas were in the part of the world that Spain could claim according to the **Treaty of Tordesillas.** He planned to sail west, avoiding Africa's Cape of Good Hope, which was controlled by the Portuguese.

Magellan began his voyage with five ships and a crew of about 250 men. Many of these men were **courtiers** and their servants, not experienced sailors. Many of the lower-ranking crewmen were Spanish, but most of the officers and pilots were Portuguese, probably handpicked by Magellan. This division created tension on board, as did Magellan's decision to keep his route and destination a secret from the crew.

Magellan commanded a vessel called the *Trinidad.* The other four were named *San Antonio, Concepción, Victoria,* and *Santiago.* All five were small or medium-sized merchant ships. Their supplies included 213,800 pounds of biscuits; 72,000 pounds of salted beef; and 57,000 pounds of salted pork, as well as cheese, beans, rice, and other foods. The ships also carried cannons; supplies for making repairs; and a cargo of bells, knives, mirrors, and other items to be traded in the Spice Islands.

Trouble Comes Quickly

The expedition sailed from Sanlúcar de Barrameda on September 20, 1519. Trouble began almost immediately. When the ships turned to the west—away from the coast of Africa—the Spaniard Juan de Cartagena, captain of the *San Antonio,* led a **mutiny** against Magellan. Unwilling to cross the Atlantic Ocean, the rebels tried to anger Magellan and provoke him into taking some action that would justify killing him. But Magellan stood his ground, and most of the sailors sided with him. He removed Cartagena from command and made him a prisoner.

Even so, the mood aboard the ships remained tense as the fleet encountered terrible storms and then drifted listlessly in the **doldrums.** Finally, on December 8, the coast of Brazil was sighted. The ships anchored five days later at a place Magellan called Porto de Santa Lucia (the site of present-day Rio de Janeiro). There the crew gathered more food and made repairs to the ships. Two weeks later, the fleet proceeded south along the South American coast.

On January 11, 1520, Magellan reached a bay that appeared to be a passage west. He sent Juan Serrano, a relative of his cousin Francisco Serrano, to investigate in the *Santiago.* The passage turned out to be a wide river, now called the Río de la Plata. South of the river mouth lay waters that no European had explored before.

Giant Visitors

After nearly two months of sailing south, Magellan decided to spend the winter on land, near the site of present-day San Julián, Argentina. The five ships anchored on March 31, and there the men were the first Europeans to see strange birds that could not fly and had flippers for feet—penguins.

On Easter another of Magellan's Spanish captains, Gaspar de Quesada, led a revolt. He freed Cartagena and promised to turn the ships back toward Spain. However, most of the sailors again sided with Magellan, and with their help, he ended the mutiny. Quesada was executed, and Cartagena was stranded on shore along with a French priest who had taken part in the rebellion.

Shortly after this incident, the explorers were visited by a very tall man who lived in the area. Magellan named him Juan the Giant, and several more large visitors soon arrived. Magellan called them Patagonians, from the Spanish word *pata,* which means paw, because the skins they wore on their feet looked like paws. The crew captured two of the Patagonians to take back to Europe, but they died during the voyage.

In May Magellan sent Serrano south to scout the coast. The *Santiago* ran aground near the mouth of what is now the Santa Cruz River, and the crew had to walk 60 miles back to camp. The winter of the southern hemisphere was then approaching, so the explorers spent five more months at their camp, cleaning and repairing the ships. During this time, it became clear that the Portuguese merchants who had supplied the ships' food had cheated Magellan.

mutiny rebellion by a ship's crew against the officers

doldrums areas of calm or light winds in ocean regions near the equator

They had provided only half the food he had paid for, in hopes of sabotaging his mission. Magellan estimated that there was enough food left for only three months.

The Strait of Magellan

In mid-October, Magellan sailed south again. On October 21, after a storm cleared, he saw that the coastline turned west. He sent the *San Antonio* to investigate and ordered its captain to return in three days. Magellan never saw the ship again, for the captain sailed it back to Spain. With his three remaining ships, Magellan then entered the strait that now bears his name.

The passage was difficult. The ships plowed through large waves and threaded their way around whirlpools while avoiding the rocky cliffs on each side. The land to the south was lit with fires, and Magellan named it Tierra del Fuego, which means Land of Fire. On November 27, 1520, after spending 37 days in the strait, Magellan and his ships reached the open sea at the other end. At that time, Magellan said, "We are about to stand into an ocean where no ship has sailed before. May the ocean always be as calm and benevolent as it is today." He named it Pacific, meaning peaceful.

Hunger on the Ocean

Magellan pointed the ships northwest and began the journey across the Pacific Ocean. The food supply soon ran low, and the men put rags on hooks and fished from the sides of the ships. By Christmas the expedition had reached the **latitude** of the Spice Islands, but there was no land in sight. The penguin and seal meat that the men had brought on board in Patagonia rotted in the tropical heat, and maggots consumed what little remained. The crew members were forced to eat sawdust and leather. They mixed the small supply of freshwater with salty seawater with so that it would last longer. Gradually, men began to sicken and die of **scurvy.** Driven by hunger, they caught rats in the ships' holds and sold them to one another.

Magellan had expected the journey to the Moluccas to last four weeks, but it dragged on, seemingly without end. In anger he threw his maps into the sea, saying, "With the pardon of the **cartographers,** the Moluccas are not to be found at their appointed place." The next day, an island was sighted, probably in what are now called the Tuamotu Islands. Magellan named the island San Pablo because it was the feast day of St. Paul. The captain and his crew spent a week at that uninhabited spot, collecting rainwater in the sails to refill the ships' water barrels. When they sailed again, they sighted another island. They could see no people, and sharks seemed to be the only fish in those waters. They sailed on and crossed the equator on February 13.

Welcome and Celebration

On March 4, the men on the *Trinidad,* Magellan's ship, ate the very last of their food. Two days later, land was sighted again, and the explorers went ashore on the island of Guam after four months on the open sea. They called the island group (now the Marianas), the

latitude distance north or south of the equator

scurvy disease caused by a lack of vitamin C and once a major cause of death among sailors; symptoms include internal bleeding, loosened teeth, and extreme fatigue

cartographer mapmaker

Ladrones which is Spanish for thieves, because the islanders, though friendly, stole everything they could from the ships.

Magellan took his time in the Ladrones, obtaining coconuts, yams, and rice on shore to feed his sick and hungry crew. When all aboard had regained their strength, the fleet sailed southwest. On March 16, Magellan sighted an island chain that he called the **Archipelago** de San Lazaro (now known as the Philippine Islands) and dropped anchor off shore. Two days later, nine islanders arrived with food to trade. Magellan noticed that although the visitors appeared to be poor and wore little clothing, they had gold bracelets and earrings.

On March 28, Magellan left for another of the islands. When he anchored, men in a large canoe rowed out to greet the Europeans. Magellan's servant Henry called out to the men and was answered in his own language, Malay. Magellan then knew that he had reached Southeast Asia, where he had already been in his earlier travels. Three days later, he and his crew celebrated their success and the Easter holiday on shore. They were joined by the island's **raja,** Colambu.

A Christian Mission

After trading in the Philippines, Magellan's crew was eager to sail for the Spice Islands, but the captain wanted to stay longer. He hoped to find a familiar landmark to verify that he had indeed **circumnavigated** the world, reaching lands that he and other Europeans had already visited. He also hoped to find gold. In addition, King Charles had promised him that if he found a group of six or more islands, he could claim two for himself.

Magellan had one more objective in mind. Like most of the explorers who sailed for Spain, Magellan was deeply religious, and he hoped to win converts to Christianity. Colambu, the local leader, seemed open to the idea, and he thought that his relative, the raja of the nearby island of Cebu, would accept this new religion too. In early April, Colambu took Magellan to Cebu, where the Europeans obtained supplies, built a stone chapel on shore, and celebrated mass again. Colambu and his relative then asked to be baptized— perhaps because Magellan had told them that the Christian god would help them conquer their enemies.

Magellan also told the local chiefs that they must obey the Christian king, Charles. When one chief refused, Magellan attacked and burned his village and then erected a cross at the site. Cilapulapo, chief of an island called Mactan, also refused to swear allegiance to Charles. Against the advice of Serrano and the raja of Cebu, Magellan decided to punish Cilapulapo. At midnight on April 26, 1521, the determined captain sailed for Mactan with 60 of his crew and 1,000 men of Cebu.

A Violent Death

Magellan landed on Mactan with 48 of his men. Defenders appeared on both sides of Magellan's force, armed with stones, arrows, and spears, and a battle raged all morning. The Europeans were better armed, with crossbows and muskets, and wore armored helmets. But the Mactan warriors grew bolder as the fighting went on. Just as

archipelago large group of islands or a body of water with many islands

raja chief in India or the Pacific Islands

circumnavigate to travel around

Magellan ordered a retreat, a poisoned arrow pierced his leg. Another wound followed, this time in his sword arm. When a Mactan warrior again struck Magellan's already wounded leg, the captain fell forward and died.

"And so they slew our mirror, our light, our comfort and our true and only guide." These words were written by Antonio PIGAFETTA, an Italian nobleman who had joined the expedition as an observer and kept a journal of the trip. He also noted that if it had not been for Magellan, "not one of us in the boats would have been saved, for while he was fighting, the rest retired."

With Magellan's death, command of the expedition fell to Juan Serrano and Duarte Barbosa. Both men were killed just a few days later at a banquet held by the raja of Cebu. João Lopes Carvalho was then elected leader. He burned one of the remaining three ships, the *Concepción,* and took the *Victoria* and *Trinidad* on a spree of piracy. But he was unable to find the Moluccas, and leadership passed to Juan Sebastián de ELCANO. He captained the *Victoria* to the Moluccas and then back to Spain, carrying 18 Europeans and 3 Pacific Islanders. They arrived in Spain on September 8, 1522. The *Trinidad,* meanwhile, had been captured by the Portuguese and wrecked. Over the next few years, only four or five of its crew straggled into Spain.

Magellan's Accomplishment

Pigafetta was one of the men who returned on the *Victoria.* Since Magellan's logs of the expedition had been lost with the *Trinidad,* Pigafetta's journal is the only written record that exists of the three-year voyage and the man he called "so noble a captain." Magellan, he wrote,

> was more constant than any one else in adversity. He endured hunger better than all the others, and better than any man in the world did he understand sea charts and navigation. . . . The best proof of his genius is that he circumnavigated the world, none having preceded him.

SUGGESTED READING F. H. H. Guillemard, *The Life of Ferdinand Magellan* (AMS Press, 1971); William Jay Jacobs, *Magellan: Voyager with a Dream* (F. Watts, 1994); Antonio Pigafetta, *Magellan's Voyage,* translated by R. A. Skelton (Yale University Press, 1969); Edouard Roditi, *Magellan of the Pacific* (McGraw-Hill, 1972).

Malaspina, Alejandro

Italian
b November 2, 1754; Mulazzo, Italy
d April 9, 1810; Pontremoli, Italy
Sailed around the world; explored Pacific Ocean and North and South America

circumnavigate to travel around

From 1789 to 1794, Alejandro Malaspina led one of the most important scientific voyages ever sponsored by Spain. His expedition was the first to the Pacific Ocean backed by the Spanish since Pedro Fernandez de QUIRÓS sailed those waters in 1605.

Reward for a Brave Sailor

Born to a noble Italian family, Malaspina moved to Cadiz, Spain, at the age of 20. He entered the Spanish navy and proved his bravery in several military campaigns. As a result, he was rewarded with a promotion to commander of the ship *Astrea,* in which he **circumnavigated** the world. Malaspina was later chosen to lead a voyage to survey South America. On this expedition, he was instructed to prepare sea charts to make navigation easier. He was also ordered to report on the political and economic situation in the vast Spanish Empire.

Alejandro Malaspina made a scientific and political study of Spain's colonial empire, but his conclusions were unpopular, and he was jailed.

surveyor one who makes precise measurements of a location's geography

specimen sample of a plant, animal, or mineral, usually collected for scientific study or display

Northwest Passage water route connecting the Atlantic Ocean and Pacific Ocean through the Arctic islands of northern Canada

glacier large, slowly moving mass of ice

circumnavigation journey around the world

Malaspina left Spain on July 30, 1789, aboard the *Descubierta.* He headed for Brazil, where **surveyors** mapped the coastline in great detail. The expedition continued south, exploring and mapping the coasts of Argentina and Patagonia. After stopping at the Malvina (now Falkland) Islands and Tierra del Fuego, the ship rounded Cape Horn and proceeded up the western coast of South America. On both coasts, biologists collected many **specimens** and made drawings of even more. When the expedition reached Guayaquil, one biologist left the party to travel inland to Bolivia, where he studied that country's plant life. Malaspina continued to sail north, visiting the Galápagos Islands, Panama, and Mexico. He collected political and economic information from the Spanish colonies along the way.

In 1791 Malaspina sailed as far north as southeastern Alaska, possibly in search of the **Northwest Passage.** Near what is now Juneau, he discovered a **glacier** that bears his name. The Malaspina Glacier is a river of ice that covers about 1,500 square miles and is over 1,000 feet thick. The following year, Malaspina sailed across the Pacific Ocean to the Philippines. He spent 1793 in the southwest Pacific, visiting New South Wales (in present-day Australia), New Zealand, and Tonga. He returned to Spain in 1794, but it is not clear whether he sailed back by way of South America's Cape Horn or continued west around Africa's Cape of Good Hope. If he did sail by way of Africa, he completed his second **circumnavigation.**

Triumph and Disgrace

Malaspina arrived in Spain on September 21, 1794, and was soon promoted to brigadier for his accomplishments. His glory, however, did not last long. His trip had convinced him that Spain should free its colonies in America. These ideas offended the Spanish authorities, and Malaspina was imprisoned and stripped of his titles. He spent six years in jail and was released only on the condition that he leave Spain. He settled in his native Italy, where he died in 1810.

As a result of his conflict with the Spanish, much of Malaspina's work was lost, and the rest was forgotten for 30 years. The findings from his voyage were kept secret until 1885. Despite Malaspina's opposition to Spain's colonial rule, his trip actually helped strengthen the country's empire in the Pacific Ocean.

SUGGESTED READING Donald C. Cutter, *Malaspina and Galiano: Spanish Voyages to the Northwest Coast, 1791 and 1792* (University of Washington Press, 1991).

Marchand, Jean-Baptiste

French
b November 22, 1863; Thoissey, France
d January 13, 1934; Paris, France
Explored Niger River, Sudan, and Ivory Coast

Jean-Baptiste Marchand was a professional military officer who explored the Niger River, the Sudan, and the Ivory Coast. He is best known for his role in France's attempt to prevent the larger and more powerful British forces from controlling Africa's White Nile River. In 1898 he led what was known as the Marchand Mission across Africa in a bold attempt to block British expansion in the Sudan. This expedition resulted in what became known as the Fashoda Incident, which almost led to war between France and England.

Jean-Baptiste Marchand led French troops across central Africa to face a larger British force at Fashoda in the Sudan.

chevalier member of the French knighthood

watershed ridge of high ground forming the boundary between regions where the water of each region flows into a different river system

Early Service in Africa

Marchand joined the French army as a youth and served for four years before being trained as an officer. He was named a sublieutenant in 1887 and saw active duty in West Africa two years later. During this time, he fought against two of the area's local tribes. He was wounded several times and was made a **chevalier** of the Legion of Honor. The next year, he began a series of journeys to investigate the sources of the Niger River. Marchand explored the western Sudan in 1892, and from 1893 to 1895, he traveled through the inland region of the Ivory Coast. In 1896 Marchand was in Gabon, in the French Congo, when he received orders for a mission to the Sudan.

Britain and France Clash in Africa

The dispute between Britain and France arose because each side wanted to connect its widely separated colonial territories in Africa. Britain wanted to link Uganda to Egypt by building a railway from the Cape of Good Hope, at the southern tip of Africa, to Cairo. France, on the other hand, hoped to extend its control over central Africa and the Sudan. The French wanted to break Britain's colonial hold over the Sudan by seizing the Nile River. In this way, they hoped to establish France's claim to ownership of the region.

After several months of preparation, Marchand and his men set out from Brazzaville (in what is now the Democratic Republic of Congo) in January 1897. They undertook a difficult journey east across central Africa, arriving in the Sudanese town of Fashoda (now Kodok) on the White Nile on July 10, 1898. Marchand's troops, however, did not occupy the town for long. A British force, commanded by H. H. Kitchener, had been sent from Egypt at the same time as Marchand left Brazzaville. Marchand arrived first, but the British force sent to oppose him was much larger. The incident came close to erupting into full-scale combat. While neither Marchand nor Kitchener wanted war, neither wanted to give up his claim to the fort. They finally agreed that Egyptian, British, and French flags should all fly over the fort.

The Situation is Resolved

Although the French public was outraged by the British action, the country needed Britain's support against Germany. Therefore, the French foreign minister ordered Marchand to withdraw from Fashoda on November 4. The Fashoda Incident was the closest France and Britain ever came to waging war over territories in Africa. In March 1899, the British and French agreed that the **watershed** of the Nile and Congo Rivers should mark the dividing line between the two countries' possessions in Africa. France would control land west of the watershed; land east of the watershed would belong to Britain.

Marchand's campaign was unsuccessful, but he was still hailed as a hero upon his return to France. Because of his courage, both in crossing the African continent and in facing British troops,

Marchand was promoted to commander of the Legion of Honor. He later served as a general in World War I and died in Paris in 1934.

SUGGESTED READING Charles Anthony Langdon Richards and James Place, editors, *East African Explorers* (Oxford University Press, 1959).

Marcos de Niza

French
b ?; Nice, France
d 1558; Mexico
Explored southwestern United States

New Spain region of Spanish colonial empire that included the areas now occupied by Mexico, Florida, Texas, New Mexico, Arizona, California, and various Caribbean islands

Father Marcos de Niza served as chaplain to Pedro de Alvarado during his conquest of Guatemala and his expedition to Quito, in what is now Ecuador. However, Marcos is most famous for his exploration of the region north of the frontier of **New Spain.** From his journey to the region that is now Arizona and New Mexico, he brought back tales of the seven enchanted cities of Cíbola. His stories inspired a later expedition led by Francisco Vásquez de Coronado to find and conquer the cities.

Marcos's Explorations in America

Scholars know that Marcos de Niza was born in Nice, France, because his name in Spanish means "Marcus of Nice." No one knows when he first arrived in New Spain, but from 1523 to 1526, he served as chaplain on Alvarado's march through what are now the countries of Guatemala and El Salvador. He then accompanied Alvarado on his expedition to Quito in 1533. Marcos later did missionary work among the Indians in Arizona, gaining valuable knowledge of the region.

As a result of his experiences in Arizona, Marcos was chosen to lead an expedition north of New Spain. He was ordered to explore the lands beyond the Spanish territory's frontier and to verify reports by the explorer Álvar Núñez Cabeza de Vaca. Marcos was also instructed to assure the Indians that Spain's intentions were peaceful—even though they were not. Marcos set out from the town of Culiacán in New Galicia (the modern Mexican states of Sinaloa and Nayarit) on March 7, 1539. He was accompanied by a slave named Estéban, who had also journeyed with Cabeza de Vaca.

There has been much dispute over where Marcos traveled and exactly what he saw. His route can be traced by modern scholars because places in his journal correspond to descriptions from other reliable sources. However, the journal is also full of exaggerations and wild stories of camels, elephants, and unicorn-like animals.

The Seven Cities of Cíbola

Marcos arrived in Arizona, where local Indians told him of a great country to the north, which they called Cíbola, where there were seven rich cities. Marcos believed that these might be the seven enchanted cities mentioned in a legend he had heard. According to the story, the cities were founded by seven Portuguese bishops who had fled Iberia (the peninsula occupied by Spain and Portugal) when it was invaded by Arabs in the 700s. The Indians told Marcos that the people of these cities wore cotton clothes, had pots and jars made of gold, and even used little blades made of gold to wipe the sweat off their bodies.

Since the Spanish had already found great wealth in the Aztec Empire of Mexico and the Inca Empire of Peru, Marcos believed the tales of Cíbola. To search for these cities, he headed northeast through empty stretches of southeastern Arizona into what is now New Mexico. He became known as Sayota (meaning "man from heaven") to the local Indians, who came from miles away to receive his blessing. Some of them gave him gifts of turquoise and finely worked leather, which supported his belief in the existence of a rich empire nearby. The Indians also told him stories of cities with buildings four and five stories high.

Estéban went ahead to scout for the cities. Marcos told him to send back white crosses when he discovered anything significant. The size of each cross he sent would indicate the importance of his discovery. After several trips, Estéban sent back a cross as tall as a man, with the news that Cíbola was close. Marcos hurried ahead, even after he learned that the Zuñi tribe had killed Estéban.

The Legend Explodes

In May 1539, Marcos was convinced that he had found Cíbola. After climbing a hill, he looked down on a scene that he described in his journal. "[T]he houses are . . . all of stone, with their stories and flat roofs. As far as I could see from a height where I had placed myself to observe, the settlement is larger than the city of Mexico." He was probably looking at the Hawikuh **pueblo,** one of six Zuñi Indian communities united in a confederacy. Remembering Estéban's fate, Marcos was afraid to enter the city, so he returned to Mexico City to tell his tale of Cíbola.

As a result of Marcos's story, Coronado led a major expedition to Cíbola the next year. With Marcos as his guide, the Spaniard set out to conquer the cities of Cíbola. However, when he arrived at the pueblo, Coronado found only "a collection of huts." Marcos was sent back to Mexico City in disgrace and was called the "Lying Monk" for his tall tales. He spent the last 15 years of his life as an invalid and died in New Spain in 1558. Even though he did not discover the fabled cities of Cíbola, Marcos did explore much of what has become Arizona and New Mexico. In addition, his tales provided the motivation for Coronado's remarkable journeys in North America.

SUGGESTED READING Adolph F. Bandelier, *The Discovery of New Mexico by the Franciscan Monk Friar Marcos de Niza in 1539*, edited and translated by Madeleine Turrell Rodack (University of Arizona Press, 1981); Cleve Hallenbeck, *The Journey of Fray Marcos de Niza* (Greenwood, 1949).

pueblo Indian village or dwelling in the American Southwest, often built of sun-dried bricks

Marquette, Jacques

French
b June 10, 1637; Laon, France
d May 18, 1675; territory of Illinois Indians
Explored Mississippi River

Jesuit member of the Society of Jesus, a Roman Catholic order founded by Ignatius of Loyola in 1534

Jacques Marquette was a **Jesuit** priest who is best known for accompanying Louis JOLLIET on his voyage of discovery down the Mississippi River. Marquette's journal is the only surviving record of their historic journey.

To the Wilds of Canada

Marquette had always felt the urge to explore faraway places. This desire was still strong even after he spent 11 years studying for the priesthood. In 1665 he asked his superior to allow him "to set out for foreign nations of which I have been thinking from my earliest boyhood." His wish was granted and on September 20, 1666, he arrived in Québec.

A letter Marquette gave to Indians on the Mississippi was found 220 years later among the papers of an Englishman named Robert Harley.

mission settlement founded by priests in a land where they hoped to convert people to Christianity

portage transport of boats and supplies overland between waterways

Marquette spent his first year in Québec studying Indian languages and eventually became fluent in six. The following year, he worked among the Ottawa Indians at a **mission** located near Sault Ste. Marie. Marquette then founded a new mission at Chequamegon Bay near the western end of Lake Superior, where he first met members of the Illinois tribe. He later set up the mission of St. Ignace on the Straits of Mackinac, between Lake Michigan and Lake Huron. Here he met Louis Jolliet.

Jolliet had come to the settlement on December 8, 1672, during the first stage of his exploration of the Mississippi River. His orders were to find out whether the river flowed west to the Pacific Ocean or south to the Gulf of Mexico. At the suggestion of the Jesuits, Marquette joined Jolliet's expedition as chaplain and as a Christian ambassador to the Indians.

The men spent the winter gathering information from the local Indians about the route they were to travel. Some of this information was not very comforting—or reliable. The Green Bay tribe, for example, tried to discourage the explorers with tales of savage Indians who "never show mercy to strangers, smashing their heads without any cause." The tribe also warned of terrible heat and "horrible monsters, which devoured men and canoes together." Marquette thanked them for their advice but told them that he had to make this journey, "because the salvation of souls was at stake and for this I would be willing to give my life."

Exploring the Mississippi

Marquette, Jolliet, and five other men left the mission in May 1673, paddling birch-bark canoes to the west shore of Lake Michigan and entering the Fox River. After a short **portage** to the Wisconsin River, they entered the Mississippi River on June 17. Marquette's journal records many new forms of wildlife. He mentioned "monstrous fish [probably catfish], one of which struck our canoe so violently that I thought it was a great tree which was going to break our canoe into pieces." He also described what was probably a lynx, seen swimming in the water. The party shot a bison so huge, "it took three men to move it, and they had difficulty."

The first Indians they met were the friendly Illinois tribe. A tribal elder greeted them with his hands lifted toward the sun, saying, "How beautiful the sun is, O Frenchmen, when you come to visit us." The Illinois gave the two men a peace pipe to use when they first encountered new tribes. Marquette was impressed with their generosity, and he promised to return to live with them and teach them.

As their journey continued, the explorers quickly realized that the river flowed south, not west. One day in June, they heard the roar of rapids and soon saw "floating islands of debris" pouring into the Mississippi from another river—the Missouri. Realizing that this river was probably the route west, Marquette wrote, "One day I hope to discover the California Sea by following its course." But they continued down the Mississippi to a point just north of what is now called the Arkansas River. In four months, they had paddled over 2,500 miles. At this point, they met Indians who said that they

This picture illustrates the arrival of Jacques Marquette and Louis Jolliet at the upper Mississippi River.

For a map of Marquette's route, see the profile of Louis JOLLIET in this volume.

were only about 10 days from the sea. However, the Indians also said that it was dangerous to go on because of warlike tribes who possessed guns. The explorers decided not to risk capture by Indians or the Spanish, who were probably the source of the guns. On July 17, 1673, the expedition headed back north.

The trip back up the Mississippi was extremely difficult because the explorers had to paddle against the river's strong current. At the mouth of the Ohio River, the party met a group of Indians who said that they traded with other Europeans. The tribesmen suggested that the explorers leave the Mississippi and take an easier route up the Illinois River. The party took the Indians' advice and returned by way of the Illinois and Chicago Rivers. Upon his return, Marquette went to Green Bay to recover from the difficult voyage. Jolliet explored further before joining him there in the winter.

Marquette's Final Days

In October 1674, Marquette set out to keep an earlier promise to return to a Kaskaskia village on the Illinois River. However, ill health caused him to delay his trip until the spring. When he finally arrived at the village, he preached to a circle of 500 chiefs with 1,500 braves standing behind them. But Marquette knew that he could dysentery disease that causes severe diarrhea

not stay at the village because he was dying of **dysentery,** so he left to return to St. Ignace. However, he was too weak to finish the trip, and he died at the mouth of the river that now bears his name.

Since Jolliet's papers were lost in a canoe accident, Marquette's journal is the only record of their trip. But some historians claim that the journal was actually written by Marquette's superior, Father Dablon, using Jolliet's recollections and Marquette's notes. The question remains unsolved. Whoever wrote it, the journal shows that Marquette was both a dedicated missionary and a courageous adventurer.

SUGGESTED READING Zachary Kent, *Jacques Marquette and Louis Jolliet* (Childrens Press, 1994).

Martínez, Estéban José

Spanish
b December 9, 1742; Seville, Spain
d October 28, 1798; Loreto, Baja California, Mexico
Explored northwest coast of North America

New Spain region of Spanish colonial empire that included the areas now occupied by Mexico, Florida, Texas, New Mexico, Arizona, California, and various Caribbean islands

In 1788 Estéban José Martínez commanded an expedition to the northwest coast of North America to investigate Russian activity in the Aleutian Islands. While he was there, he learned that Russia was planning to establish a settlement at Nootka Sound. Martínez's trip led to the Spanish settlement of Nootka in 1789, but his behavior would ultimately prove harmful to Spanish interests in the area.

Competition in the Northwest

Martínez entered the Spanish naval academy at age 13 and went to sea at 16. He was eventually assigned to the Spanish naval command at San Blas, **New Spain.** In 1774 he was second-in-command to Juan Josef Pérez HERNÁNDEZ on the first Spanish expedition to the northwest coast of North America. That voyage was made in response to rumors of Russian expansion into the area.

From 1776 to 1788, Martínez sailed supply ships between San Blas and new Spanish settlements in California. In 1788 Spain once again became alarmed by reports that Russia was trying to expand its control over the Aleutian Islands. Martínez was ordered to sail north to investigate the new rumors of Russian settlements in the region. He was also to take possession of new lands for Spain wherever he could do so conveniently.

Leaving San Blas with two ships on March 8, Martínez arrived at Prince William Sound (in present-day Alaska) by mid-May. He then began to act strangely, quarreling violently with his crew. Some of his men later said that he had been drunk. After several days, he proceeded to Unalaska Island in the eastern Aleutians, off the west coast of Alaska. He arrived on July 21 and was warmly welcomed by the one Russian at the outpost.

The Russian told Martínez that Russia planned to settle Nootka Sound, an island off what is now Vancouver Island, the next year. The Russians hoped to limit British fur-trading activity in the area. Martínez then performed a brief ceremony claiming possession of the island for Spain, even though the Russians were there before him.

A Hollow Victory for Spain

Returning to San Blas, Martínez reported what he had learned and volunteered to lead an expedition to settle Nootka immediately. His offer was accepted, and Spain took control of the island. However, his poor treatment of British ships and citizens in Nootka caused Britain to protest to Spain. As a result, the two nations signed the Nootka Convention in 1790. This agreement opened to all nations any territory not settled by Spain as of that year.

Martínez's violent temper and aggressive treatment of others caused him great trouble. Many complaints were filed against him, both by men under his command and by foreigners who had to deal with him. Although he wanted to serve his country, his actions eventually hurt Spain. Thus Martínez, who had worked so hard to establish Spanish supremacy in North America, ended up weakening Spain's hold over the Pacific Northwest.

SUGGESTED READING Richard Whitehead, editor, *The Voyage of the Frigate* Princesa *to Southern California in 1782, as Recorded in the Logs of Juan Pantoja y Arriaga and Estéban José Martínez,* translated by Geraldine V. Sahyun (A. H. Clark Company, 1982).

Martínez de Irala, Domingo. See *Irala, Domingo Martínez de.*

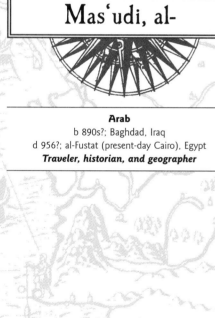

Mas'udi, al-

Arab
b 890s?; Baghdad, Iraq
d 956?; al-Fustat (present-day Cairo), Egypt
Traveler, historian, and geographer

Al-Mas'udi was one of the many great scholars of the medieval Islamic world. He traveled widely and was the first Arab to write about some of the lands that lay beyond the borders of Islam. Like modern geographers, al-Mas'udi explored the relationship of geography and history to human culture.

A Son of Islam

Abu al-Hasan Ali ibn al-Husayn al-Mas'udi was born around A.D. 895 in Baghdad (in modern-day Iraq). At that time, Baghdad was a flourishing city that was a center of learning, commerce, and politics. Nothing is known about al-Mas'udi's background except that his family claimed to be descended from Mas'ud, a companion of the prophet Muhammad who had founded Islam in the 600s.

Al-Mas'udi became a traveler and a writer of historical and geographical texts. His books contain a record of his travels, although the sequence and dates are not always clear. Another source of uncertainty is that al-Mas'udi, like many ancient and medieval travel writers, did not limit his writings to places and events he saw or experienced firsthand. He also wrote about myths, tales, legends, and his discussions with learned men and other travelers. As a result, it is difficult to know which of the places he described he actually visited. It is clear, however, that he began traveling at an early age.

Temples and Traders

Al-Mas'udi spent at least part of 915 in Persia (present-day Iran). He visited several ancient sites, including Persepolis, one of Persia's ancient capitals. Persia had become an Islamic land, but al-Mas'udi—unlike some Islamic travelers—was especially interested in non-Islamic peoples and religions. He made a point of visiting the temples of Zoroastrianism, Persia's ancient religion.

After leaving Persia, al-Mas'udi went to India. He wrote about China, India, and the lands that are now Sri Lanka and Indonesia, but modern scholars are unsure whether he journeyed to those places himself or simply relayed what others had told him. On his way back to Baghdad, al-Mas'udi stopped in southern Arabia and noted the region's trade with eastern Africa. It is likely that he then sailed to Zanzibar, an island off the African coast where Arabian traders had established thriving ports and markets.

Religions of the Middle East

After a few years at home, al-Mas'udi was on the road again, traveling through Iraq, Syria, and Arabia. He also went to the city of Jerusalem, where he visited Christian churches and met with learned Christians and Jews. He wrote about several of the region's ancient religious **sects** that had remained apart from Judaism, Christianity, and Islam. Modern historians of religion value al-Mas'udi's accounts of these peoples and their beliefs.

By the late 920s, al-Mas'udi seems to have been back in Baghdad. He soon resumed traveling, however, and made at least one more long journey. He went north through Persia to the Caspian and Aral Seas that lie between southern Russia and central Asia. Al-Mas'udi left the first known written description of the Aral Sea. He also correctly claimed that the Caspian Sea was a closed body of water and not, as some people of the time believed, connected to the Black Sea.

Around 941 al-Mas'udi returned to the Arabian Peninsula. He visited the holy cities of Mecca and Medina; then he went to Egypt, where he witnessed a festival held by the country's Christian minority. In the years that followed, al-Mas'udi apparently divided his time between Syria and Egypt and set to work on his books.

Al-Mas'udi's Works

Al-Mas'udi wrote several books, some of which are now lost. He dealt with a broad range of topics, including science, language, religion, and philosophy, but his works on history and geography interested readers the most. His major work was a 30-volume history of the world called *Reports of the Age,* of which only the first volume still exists. Much of the material contained in that volume also appears in another of his works, *Meadows of Gold and Mines of Precious Stones.* In this book, al-Mas'udi recounted how philosophers in ancient Greece, India, and the Middle East had explained the origin and shape of the earth. The book also contains an Arabic version of writings by the Greek geographer PTOLEMY. Al-Mas'udi summed up many of these ideas in his last book, *The Book of Warning and Supervision.*

Like many other medieval geographers, al-Mas'udi was particularly interested in the goods produced by various regions and the routes by which people traded these goods over long distances. Among these products were costly luxury items such as ivory, emeralds, and incense.

Al-Mas'udi also gave much attention to what is now called human geography, the study of the relationships between people and their physical environment. He was one of the first geographers to consider how environmental factors such as climate, water, and

sect small religious group or subdivision of a larger religion

vegetation influence the people who live in a region. To illustrate the effect of geography on human history, he described what had happened when the course of Iraq's Euphrates River changed. The port city that had previously been at the river mouth was economically ruined, while the city at the river mouth's new location prospered.

Al-Mas'udi eventually settled in al-Fustat, a town in Egypt that later became the city of Cairo. He died there in about 956. Although some of his information was unreliable, and some of his ideas were mistaken, he made pioneering efforts in the study of geography, religion, and economics. His books have remained important sources of historical knowledge to this day.

SUGGESTED READING Ahmad M. H. Shboul, *Al-Mas'udi and His World: A Muslim Humanist and His Interest in Non-Muslims* (Ithaca Press, 1979).

Maury, Matthew Fontaine

American
b January 14, 1806; Spotsylvania County, Virginia
d February 1, 1873; Lexington, Virginia
*Collected, compiled, and published
scientific data concerning world's oceans*

oceanography the scientific study of the ocean and underwater life

meteorology the scientific study of weather and weather forecasting

In the mid-1800s, Matthew Fontaine Maury compiled data that are still used today to prepare ocean charts.

Matthew Fontaine Maury was one of the most important pioneers in the field of **oceanography.** In the mid-1800s, he prepared the first truly accurate charts of the world's oceans. He also wrote the first modern oceanographic textbook, led the effort to establish **meteorology** as a universal science, and recommended the first set of traffic rules for the sea.

The Accident that Changed Everything

Maury joined the U.S. Navy in 1825 at the age of 19. By 1830 he had sailed around the world, and six years later, he was promoted to lieutenant. In 1839 he was involved in a stagecoach accident that left him lame and ended his active sea duty. But within three years, he was put in charge of the navy's Depot of Charts and Instruments. This unit later became the U.S. Naval Observatory and Hydrographic Office.

In his new position, Maury developed special logbooks in which sea captains could record data on ocean currents, depths, tides, winds, and temperatures. Maury used this information to prepare an intensive study of the world's oceans, which he published in 1847. The wind and current charts that he created resulted in the establishment of new and more efficient sea routes. The average sailing time from New York to San Francisco by way of Cape Horn, for example, dropped from 180 days to 153 days.

Charting the World's Oceans

Maury later helped to organize a conference of the world's coastal nations in 1853. This conference eventually led to the creation of an international organization for the study of the oceans. At this conference, Maury gathered oceanic data from the majority of the sea captains from the nations that attended. He used this information to prepare accurate charts of the Atlantic, Pacific, and Indian Oceans. With these charts, Maury directed the collection of deep-sea measurements that produced the first profile of the floor of the Atlantic Ocean. This information established that it was possible to lay a telegraph cable along the ocean floor, connecting Europe with America.

In 1855 Maury published *Physical Geography of the Sea,* regarded as the first textbook of modern oceanography. In the same year, he also published *Sailing Directions.* This book described new sea routes that were shorter and safer than those in use at the time. Maury was also the first person to recommend that eastbound and westbound ships travel in separate shipping lanes to avoid collisions.

Maury's achievements and his name are still a part of almost every sailor's life. All ocean charts issued by the U.S. Oceanographic Office today bear the words: "Founded upon the researches made in the early part of the nineteenth century by Matthew Fontaine Maury, while serving as a lieutenant in the U.S. Navy."

SUGGESTED READING Charles Lee Lewis, *Matthew Fontaine Maury, the Pathfinder of the Seas* (U.S. Naval Institute, 1927); Matthew Fontaine Maury, *Physical Geography of the Sea* (Harper and Brothers, 1855); Francis Leigh Williams, *Matthew Fontaine Maury: Scientist of the Sea* (Rutgers University Press, 1963).

Mawson, Douglas

Australian
b May 5, 1882; Bradford, England
d October 14, 1958; Adelaide, Australia
Explored Antarctica

---

geology the scientific study of the earth's natural history

sledge heavy sled, often mounted on runners, that is pulled over snow or ice

Douglas Mawson organized and led the Australian Antarctic Expedition of 1911 to 1914.

Sir Douglas Mawson was a professor of **geology** who carried out the most thorough scientific examination of Antarctica in the 1900s. Unlike most polar explorers, who were interested in fame or adventure, he always knew that his main mission in Antarctica was scientific. Nevertheless, he pleased the public with daring exploits and narrow escapes as exciting as those of any other polar explorer.

The Explorer-Scientist

Mawson's family moved from England to Sydney, Australia, when he was only four years old. Mawson attended the University of Sydney, specializing in chemistry, mining, and geology. In 1903 he joined the first geological survey of New Hebrides (present-day Vanuatu). Two years later, he was appointed as a lecturer at the University of Adelaide, where he received an advanced degree.

At Adelaide, Mawson began working with the geologist T. W. Edgeworth David, who was later named scientific director of the Antarctic expedition led by Sir Ernest SHACKLETON. On David's recommendation, Mawson was appointed physicist for the expedition. While traveling in Antarctica, Mawson, David, and Dr. Alistair Forbes MacKay climbed Mount Erebus, an active volcano on James Ross Island. They also journeyed by **sledge** to the South Magnetic Pole and back, a round trip of over 1,300 miles. On this expedition, they were the first to see and study the geological structure of Victoria Land.

Surveying Antarctica

Mawson was later asked to join the polar expedition of Robert Falcon SCOTT. He turned down the offer, however, in order to organize the first careful scientific survey of Antarctica. To accomplish this task, three land bases were linked with a ship by radio so that the surveyors could cover the maximum possible amount of territory. The expedition left Australia aboard the *Aurora* on December 2, 1911. The first party landed on Macquarie Island, some 600 miles off the coast. Mawson traveled on to the Antarctic mainland with a second party to explore the flat, windswept George V Coast. Winter camp was set up there, and his crew split up into five groups that spread out to examine and map the area. They roamed as far west as Adélie Coast, which had been explored by Jules DUMONT D'URVILLE more than 70 years before. The third landing party sailed west for uncharted shores.

Disaster on the Ice

glacier large, slowly moving mass of ice

Mawson's party headed east toward Oates Land, traveling across **glaciers** and deep cracks in the ice. Along the way, one of the men lost control of his dogs and fell into a seemingly bottomless split in the ice. Most of the party's food was on his sledge, so the remaining members of the party were forced to return to base. As their dogs starved to death, the men were forced to eat them, but this source of food was quickly consumed. Mawson's colleague Dr. Xavier Mertz died on the way to the base, but Mawson persevered. Hauling his own sledge, Mawson finally reached base 31 days later, only to find that he had just missed the *Aurora*. Shortly before his arrival, the ship had left to resupply the third base 1,200 miles to the west.

Mawson, suffering from exposure to the cold, spent another winter with a group left behind by the *Aurora*. When he recovered, he continued his work. In all, the expedition explored nearly 2,000 miles of coast and 4,000 miles of the interior by the time it returned to Australia.

After World War I, the British asked Mawson to return to Antarctica for the purpose of claiming rights to lands there. From 1929 to 1931, he covered much new territory in a seaplane, which he flew from the *Discovery,* the ship formerly used by Robert Scott. Mawson's work formed the basis of claims to Mac Robertson Land and Princess Elizabeth Island, in what is now Australian Antarctic Territory. Britain surrendered its claims to these lands to Australia in 1936. Mawson spent the rest of his life editing scientific data collected on his expeditions.

SUGGESTED READING Paquita Mawson, *Mawson of the Antarctic: The Life of Sir Douglas Mawson, F.R.S., O.B.E.* (Longmans, 1964).

McClintock, Francis Leopold

Anglo-Irish
b July 8, 1819; Dundalk, Ireland
d November 17, 1907; London, England
Explored Canadian Arctic

sledge heavy sled, often mounted on runners, that is pulled over snow or ice

Francis Leopold McClintock was one of the most unusual of all Arctic explorers. The sole purpose of his 11-year career was to locate the lost Arctic expedition party of Sir John FRANKLIN. In the 10 years after Franklin's disappearance, many men were involved in this search, but McClintock was the leading figure among them. During his quest, McClintock also charted hundreds of miles of Arctic territory. At first McClintock hoped to save the lost explorer. Later he hoped simply to find Franklin's body. Finally, in 1859, he located the remains of the fated expedition.

Sledding Across the Arctic Ocean

McClintock entered the navy at age 12, but his first Arctic experience came years later, in 1848. At that time, he joined the crew of the *Enterprise* under James Clark ROSS, Britain's first commanding officer in the Arctic. Ross pioneered the use of **sledges** hauled by men

Admiralty governing body of Britain's Royal Navy until 1964

Inuit people of the Canadian Arctic, sometimes known as the Eskimo

In 1853 Francis McClintock set a record for distance traveled by sledge, covering more than 1,200 miles.

to travel across the Arctic ice, but McClintock perfected the technique and is often considered its originator. McClintock also became an expert in the use of dogsleds. But he found it hard to locate well-trained dogs on short notice, so he rarely used this more effective form of Arctic transportation.

Under orders from the British **Admiralty,** McClintock began his first expedition to look for Franklin in early 1849. McClintock and Ross traveled by sledge along the coast of Somerset Island (in the present-day Northwest Territories of Canada). Two years later, McClintock journeyed from Cornwallis Island to Melville Island. His third ice voyage occurred in 1853, when he journeyed from Melville Island to Prince Patrick Island—which he discovered—and beyond. In the end, McClintock made four sledge journeys in his career, covering more than 3,000 miles. He later became general coordinator of sledging operations in the Canadian Arctic. In this position, he was responsible for charting enormous lengths of coastline.

Continuing the Search for Franklin

McClintock returned from his journey to Prince Patrick Island in 1854. Although the British navy had by then given up the search for the lost Franklin expedition, Franklin's widow had not. She insisted that no one had yet searched in the most likely place—off the coast of King William Land (now King William Island). Her suspicion was confirmed by Scottish explorer John RAE. He had heard from the **Inuit** that a party of white men had been seen in that area. McClintock was the obvious choice to command the mission. Since Lady Franklin was covering most of the expenses for the journey, McClintock agreed to take on the job without pay.

In the summer of 1857, McClintock prepared the *Fox* for navigation in the polar region and traveled to Greenland to obtain sled dogs and Inuit drivers. On the way to Lancaster Sound, the *Fox* became caught in sheets of floating ice and was trapped until the following April. After drifting almost 1,200 miles, the ship narrowly missed destruction when it finally was released from the ice.

Sailing through Barrow Strait and Peel Sound, McClintock settled in at the entrance to Bellot Strait for the winter of 1858. He spent the time setting up supply depots that three search expeditions would use as their bases of operation. The method of using depots was later copied by other Arctic explorers. He also met local Inuit at the site who possessed a number of European artifacts that had obviously been taken from a shipwreck.

Locating the Lost Expedition

In the spring, three parties set out, each with one man-hauled sledge and one sled pulled by dogs. McClintock took the southernmost route and led a party to the mouth of the Great Fish River (now the Back River). The most promising route—around the north and west coast of King William Land—was given to William Hobson. As a result, it was Hobson who located the only surviving written record of Franklin's expedition. He found it in a pile of stones on Victory Point. Hobson then saw a sledge loaded with a mountain of heavy, unnecessary items and two skeletons. McClintock himself had found a skeleton on the south shore of King William Land. A few days later, he came across the sledge first discovered by Hobson.

McClintock's expedition had finally solved the mystery of Franklin's fate, ending his widow's long years of dread. McClintock had also completed the survey of Arctic coastal land begun by John Rae. He was knighted and honored as a hero upon his return to London in September 1859. He returned to the Arctic in 1860 to conduct ocean measurements for the first North Atlantic telegraph line. He was promoted to admiral in 1884 and died in London in 1907 at the age of 88.

SUGGESTED READING Clements Markham, *The Life of Admiral Sir Leopold McClintock* (John Murray, 1909); F. L. McClintock, *The Voyage of the "Fox" in the Arctic Seas: A Narrative of the Fate of Sir John Franklin and His Companions* (reprint, M. G. Hurtig, 1972).

McClure, Robert John Le Mesurier

Anglo-Irish
b January 28, 1807; Wexford, Ireland
d October 17, 1873; London, England
Explored Alaskan and Canadian Arctic

Northwest Passage water route connecting the Atlantic Ocean and Pacific Ocean through the Arctic islands of northern Canada

mate assistant to the commander of a ship

While on a rescue mission in the Arctic Ocean, Robert McClure discovered the Northwest Passage, a route explorers had been seeking for almost 400 years.

Vice Admiral Sir Robert John Le Mesurier McClure was one of several commanders sent by the British navy in 1850 to search for the missing Arctic expedition party led by Sir John FRANKLIN. During this rescue mission, McClure became, according to many historians, the first European to navigate the **Northwest Passage.**

Searching for Franklin

As a youth, McClure had the finest education offered in England. He attended Eton College and then Sandhurst, Great Britain's military academy. An unpredictable, sometimes brutal person, McClure joined the navy after his schooling. He was eventually chosen as **mate** for Captain George BACK's expedition to Hudson Bay from 1836 to 1837. McClure later held a series of minor posts on ships from Canada to the Caribbean islands. In 1848 he returned to the Arctic Ocean aboard the *Investigator* as part of Sir James Clark ROSS's unsuccessful mission to rescue the Franklin party.

In January 1850, McClure left Plymouth, England, on another attempt to find Franklin's lost expedition. This time McClure was commander of the *Investigator*. He rounded South America's Cape Horn and sailed north for the Bering Strait. That fall he reached the Prince of Wales Strait between Banks and Victoria Islands before being pushed back by ice from Melville Sound. With this accomplishment, he discovered the Northwest Passage, a route for which explorers had been searching since the late 1400s.

Trapped in the Ice

The next summer, McClure tried to sail up the west coast of Banks Island, but his ship became trapped in the ice. He and his crew spent the next two winters there. Finally, in the spring of 1853, McClure decided that the weakest members of the crew should attempt an overland escape. He felt that they could not survive another winter on the ship. On April 6, just before the group was to set out, a rescue party from Sir Edward Belcher's *Resolute* found McClure's starving men. McClure and his men abandoned the *Investigator* and traveled

sledge heavy sled, often mounted on runners, that is pulled over snow or ice

archipelago large group of islands or a body of water with many islands

by **sledge** to Melville Sound, where the *Resolute* had dropped anchor. After spending winter aboard the *Resolute,* McClure and his crew returned to a hero's welcome in England on September 28, 1854. The British Parliament also awarded McClure a large cash prize for discovering the Northwest Passage.

Although his discovery was a great one, McClure did not actually sail the entire passage, since he abandoned his ship on the north coast of Banks Island. Nevertheless, his party's sledging expeditions traced the shores of the westernmost island in the Arctic **archipelago,** showing that the passage linked east and west in a continuous waterway. His party had also managed to survive 21 months in the Arctic wilderness with no human contact, an amazing feat of endurance. McClure was knighted for his accomplishments and continued to serve in the British navy until his retirement in 1861.

SUGGESTED READING Robert Le Mesurier M'Clure, *The Discovery of the North-West Passage* (M.G. Hurtig, 1969); Sherard Osborn, *The Discovery of the Northwest Passage by Robert Le Mesurier M'Clure,* edited by William C. Wonders (M.G. Hurtig, 1969).

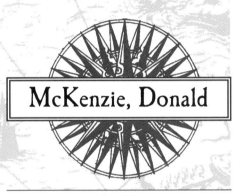

McKenzie, Donald

Scottish
b June 16, 1783; near Inverness, Scotland
d January 20, 1851; Mayville, New York
Explored Snake River region of American West

Donald McKenzie, like so many explorers of the American West, was a fur trader. As an employee of Montréal's North West Company, he made three important explorations of the Snake River region between 1818 and 1821.

New Approach to the Fur Trade

McKenzie had been in the fur trade for 10 years when he joined John Jacob Astor's Pacific Fur Company in 1811. That year he took part in a long and nearly disastrous journey west from St. Louis to the mouth of the Columbia River, under the command of Wilson Price HUNT. McKenzie was the only member of the expedition who recognized the potential of the Snake River as fur trapping country. When Astor sold his business to the North West Company, McKenzie again pushed his ideas about fur trading in the Snake River region. By 1816 the North West Company had put him in charge of reviving the fur trade east of the Columbia River.

McKenzie's first act was to abandon the old method of setting up trading posts and waiting for Indians to bring in pelts. He realized that the Indians of that region were not used to trapping beaver and would rather spend their time on other activities. McKenzie decided to bring Canadian and American trappers out to the region and support them with supplies from the trading post. He was the first to use this technique, which became standard practice in the Rocky Mountain fur trade.

River Explorations

McKenzie built Fort Nez Perce near the junction of the Columbia and Snake Rivers and began his explorations. He headed up the Snake River before turning southeast to the area between the Snake and Green Rivers. The region had plenty of beaver—and hostile Indians as well. On his next expedition, he traveled up the Snake River to see if it could be used as a route to supply his men in the field. On this trip, he became the first non-Indian to cross Hells Canyon (now on the border between Oregon and Idaho). In 1819 he sent out trappers who eventually made it as far south as Bear Lake (in present-day Utah).

Before leaving the area in 1821, McKenzie made one more trek into the Snake River country. Since he disliked keeping a journal, little is known of this trip. Nevertheless, McKenzie was a fearless explorer and a bold trader who made lasting contributions to the exploration of the Snake River region.

SUGGESTED READING John Upton Terrell, *Furs by Astor* (William Morrow, 1963).

M'Clintock, Francis. See *McClintock, Francis.*

Mendaña de Nehra, Alvaro de

Spanish
b 1541; ?
d 1595; Santa Cruz Islands
Discovered Solomon, Marquesas, and Santa Cruz Islands

viceroy governor of a Spanish colony in the Americas

cosmographer scientist who studies the structure of the universe

Alvaro de Mendaña de Nehra made two ambitious voyages across the Pacific Ocean, searching for lands that were said to be rich in silver and gold. Although he never found those fabled lands, he became the first European to discover islands in the present-day Solomon, Marquesas, and Santa Cruz groups. He would also be the last European to see the Solomons for 200 years.

The Legend of Tupac Yupanqui

Mendaña was 26 years old when his uncle, the **viceroy** of Peru, chose him to lead an expedition to the Pacific Ocean. The viceroy had learned from the historian and **cosmographer** Pedro Sarmiento de Gamboa about the Inca legend of Tupac Yupanqui. According to the legend, Tupac Yupanqui crossed the sea and found islands rich with silver and gold off the coast of a large continent. The Spanish believed that this landmass was *Terra Australis Incognita,* the unknown southern continent that geographers thought dominated the Pacific. Mendaña wanted to sail westward to find the islands and the great continent. He planned to start a Spanish colony there and convert any nonbelievers to Catholicism.

Mendaña sailed from Callao, Peru, on November 19, 1567. His two ships carried 150 men, including soldiers, Franciscan monks, and slaves. Although their journey would take them 7,000 miles, they brought only enough provisions for a trip one-third that length. Heading west and southwest, Mendaña sailed between the island groups now known as the Tuamotus and Marquesas, missing both of them. After turning northwest, he finally spotted land on January 15, 1568, somewhere in the Ellice Islands (now Tuvalu), north of Fiji. The Spaniards tried to land to obtain fresh water, but dangerous currents and hostile islanders in canoes drove them off.

Land at Last

After nearly running aground on reefs, Mendaña finally found a place to land in February. He named the site Santa Isabel after the saint whose festival fell on the day the expedition had left Peru. The ships had been at sea for 80 days. At first Mendaña believed that he had discovered a continent, but further exploration showed that Santa Isabel was an island—one of the group now called the Solomons.

The Spaniards' first meeting with the local Melanesian islanders was friendly. The explorers gave the people beads and bells, and the local chief promised the Spaniards food. When the food did not arrive after a few days, Mendaña sent men in search of supplies. The Spaniards had been advised to trade rather than use force, but they met resistance from inland villagers, and a battle broke out. This incident would be typical of their encounters with the islanders they met over the next six months. Relations with the local people ranged from peaceful to very hostile.

Soon after their landing at Santa Isabel, the Spaniards built a **brigantine** that could safely navigate the island's reefs. They used it to explore not only Santa Isabel but also the islands now called Guadalcanal, Malaita, and San Cristóbal. In August, Mendaña asked his crew to vote on their next course of action. Mendaña himself wanted to look for the great continent, and a few of his men wanted to stay in the Solomons and look for gold. Most of the crew, however, wanted to go back to Peru because food was in such short supply. Therefore, on August 15, 1568, the ships began the return trip across the Pacific Ocean.

Two Disappointments and a Third Chance

In October the expedition came within sight of Wake Island, but a hurricane struck soon after, and the ships were separated. With its crew exhausted and suffering from **scurvy,** Mendaña's ship reached Baja California, Mexico, in December. The second vessel arrived some months later. After repairing the ships, the expedition sailed southward, reaching Peru in July 1569.

Despite the failure of the first mission, Mendaña spent several years in Spain trying to convince the court to sponsor a second expedition. The authorities finally agreed, and in 1576 Mendaña set sail from Spain. But when he reached Panama, he was imprisoned by enemies of his uncle, ending his second journey. Years later he received one more chance, largely as a result of the activities of the English **privateer** Sir Francis Drake. The Spanish were so concerned about Drake's advances in the Pacific that they approved Mendaña's idea to establish a colony in that region. Mendaña set out in June 1595 with four ships carrying nearly 400 people—soldiers, sailors, women, and children.

Failure at Ndeni

In late July, the expedition reached the islands that Mendaña called the Marquesas. A battle erupted when the islanders there tried to take the Spanish ships. The soldiers killed 200 islanders, and the Spaniards moved on to find another spot for the colony. In September they reached the Santa Cruz Islands, which Mendaña also named, and anchored at Ndeni.

The members of the expedition had been arguing with each other since their departure from Peru, and their continued disagreements prevented them from organizing a permanent settlement. Fever also

brigantine two-masted sailing ship with both square and triangular sails

scurvy disease caused by a lack of vitamin C and once a major cause of death among sailors; symptoms include internal bleeding, loosened teeth, and extreme fatigue

privateer privately owned ship hired by a government to attack enemy ships

broke out among the Spaniards and eventually claimed Mendaña's life. He died without seeing the Solomon Islands again. No other European would see the Solomons until they were rediscovered by Philip CARTERET in 1767. They were not identified as Mendaña's islands until 1792.

The Spanish settlement on Ndeni ended in failure. All the would-be colonists, including Mendaña's widow, ultimately sailed on under the command of Pedro Fernandez de QUIRÓS. The party eventually reached the islands that are now the Philippines.

SUGGESTED READING Lord of Hackney Amherst and Basil Thompson, *The Voyage of Mendaña to the Solomon Islands in 1568* (Hakluyt Society, 1901); Colin Jack-Hinton, *A Search for the Islands of Solomon, 1567-1838* (Cambridge University Press, 1907).

Messerschmidt, Daniel Gottlieb

German
b September 16, 1685; Danzig, Prussia
(now Gdansk, Poland)
d 1735; St. Petersburg, Russia
Explored Siberia

geology the scientific study of the earth's natural history

czar title of Russian monarchs from the 1200s to 1917

Daniel Gottlieb Messerschmidt began the scientific exploration of Siberia in the 1700s. Siberia, now part of Russia, is an immense region of Asia that stretches from the Ural Mountains to the Pacific Ocean. The first European explorers of this region were fortune-seeking Russian adventurers such as Timofeyevich YERMAK and Yerofei Pavlovich KHABAROV. In contrast, Messerschmidt crossed the Urals to study—rather than plunder—the lands beyond. He compiled a wealth of scientific information about Siberia and is now recognized as a pioneer in the exploration of that region. However, the last years of his life were spent in poverty, depression, and isolation, and his work has remained almost entirely unknown.

Chosen for a Mission

As a young man, Messerschmidt studied medicine, mathematics, and **geology.** He was practicing medicine in his hometown of Danzig (present-day Gdansk) in 1716 when the city received a royal visitor—Peter the Great, the **czar** of Russia. Peter was deeply interested in modernizing his country and making it the equal of other European nations. Therefore, he traveled throughout western Europe, inviting some of the finest artists, scholars, and scientists he met to come to Russia. In Danzig, Peter asked Messerschmidt to make a scientific survey of Siberia. The young doctor accepted, and he arrived in the capital city of St. Petersburg, Russia, in 1717.

The following year, Messerschmidt and the Russian government signed a contract. Messerschmidt would receive a yearly salary in return for leading a wide-ranging expedition into central Siberia. Geography, natural resources, wildlife, plants, peoples, languages, customs, diseases, and medicines—Messerschmidt's mission was to study these subjects and more, over an area larger than all of the European part of Russia.

The Scientist in Siberia

Leaving St. Petersburg in the summer of 1720, Messerschmidt headed east. He passed through Moscow and then crossed the Ural Mountains into a land known to few Europeans. A handful of

Russian towns, forts, and settlements dotted western Siberia. But in the hundreds of miles of pine forests, rivers, and marshes beyond, dozens of different Siberian tribes still practiced their traditional ways of life.

In the Russian city of Tobolsk, in western Siberia, Messerschmidt befriended an officer in the Swedish army, a German named Philip Tabbert. During a war between Russia and Sweden, the Russians had taken Tabbert prisoner and sent him to Siberia. A friendship grew between Messerschmidt and Tabbert, and local Russian authorities assigned Tabbert to help Messerschmidt in his enormous task. The pair worked together for over a year, until a peace agreement between Russia and Sweden restored Tabbert's freedom. Messerschmidt's diary records, "I parted from the pious, honest, industrious, loyal Tabbert, my only friend and support, with many tears. . . ."

Messerschmidt continued his work in Siberia until 1727. His travels carried him as far as the eastern realm of Manchuria, a part of China. He entered the Arctic regions to the north, and in the south, he explored the area near Lake Baikal and Mongolia. Among his many finds was the complete skeleton of a prehistoric woolly mammoth, which he sent back to St. Petersburg. In the Arctic, he was the first to describe permafrost, soil that remains permanently frozen to depths of hundreds of feet. He also collected old manuscripts that showed the links among the languages of various Siberian peoples.

Return to the West

When Messerschmidt returned to St. Petersburg, he brought wagons full of rocks, plants, animals, bones, ancient manuscripts, and thousands of pages of his own maps and notes—the fruits of seven years of hard work. Government officials were pleased by his reports of copper, iron, and silver deposits in various regions of Siberia.

But Messerschmidt's fellow scientists did not give him the enthusiastic reception he might have expected. Apparently, Messerschmidt returned from his long journey utterly exhausted, and perhaps even mentally disturbed. He arranged his notes into a detailed report in 10 volumes, but no one seemed especially interested. In 1728 Messerschmidt gave all of his work to the Academy of Sciences in St. Petersburg. His notes are still there, but they have never been published or translated from the Latin in which he wrote.

Messerschmidt then fell wildly in love with a Russian woman, whom he believed he had seen in a dream while in Siberia. They married and tried to move to Danzig, but they lost all of their possessions in a shipwreck and were forced to return to St. Petersburg. Depressed and unable to find work, Messerschmidt lived with his wife in poverty. But he was not entirely forgotten. A naturalist named Georg Steller sought his advice in preparing for an expedition to Siberia led by Vitus BERING. After Messerschmidt died, Steller not only kept some of his records but also married his widow.

Nachtigal, Gustav

German
b February 23, 1834; Eichstedt, Prussia (now Germany)
d April 19, 1885; Gulf of Guinea
Explored North Africa

plague contagious disease that quickly kills large numbers of people

The German explorers Gustav Nachtigal and Heinrich BARTH made great contributions to the exploration of Africa.

SUGGESTED READING Yuri Semyonov, *Siberia: Its Conquest and Development* (International Publishers Representatives, 1963); Leonhard Stejneger, *Georg Wilhelm Steller: The Pioneer of Alaskan Natural History* (Harvard University Press, 1936).

Gustav Nachtigal spent 22 years in North Africa leading expeditions, fighting a **plague,** and undertaking a dangerous diplomatic mission for Prussia's King William I. One of the greatest German geographers, he laid a solid foundation for German exploration and colonization of Africa.

Curing and Being Cured in Africa

Nachtigal, the son of a minister, never planned to go to Africa. He enjoyed his post as a military surgeon in Cologne. But when he was 28 years old, Nachtigal fell ill with a lung ailment, and he knew that the best place to recover was in the dry climate of North Africa.

After recovering from his illness in 1862, Nachtigal joined an expedition with the Tunisian army and became familiar with the terrain. On this journey, Nachtigal spent a year in the desert treating wounded soldiers and finding a new sense of purpose. He became fascinated with Africa and with exploration, reading widely on both subjects and learning the Arabic language.

The time he spent with the army gave Nachtigal a taste for adventure. Although he was unwilling to resume his normal medical work

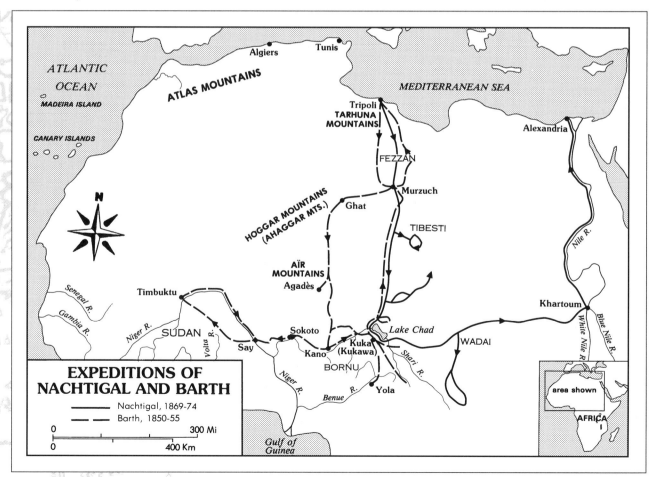

EXPEDITIONS OF NACHTIGAL AND BARTH

——— Nachtigal, 1869–74
– – – Barth, 1850–55

0   300 Mi
0   400 Km

in Tunis, he did lend his services during a deadly **typhus** epidemic in 1868, working without pay. Later that year, he received an offer that promised him both the travel and excitement he was seeking.

A German explorer, Friedrich Gerhard RoHLFS, had been chosen by German officials for a diplomatic mission to the Sudan. Rohlfs, however, did not want the assignment, and he recruited Nachtigal to take his place. Nachtigal readily agreed to serve as an ambassador for King William I of Prussia and visit **Sultan** Omar of Bornu (in present-day Nigeria).

Nachtigal the Diplomat

Nachtigal set out from the North African coast for Bornu, located some 2,000 miles to the south. He traveled east over the Tarhuna Mountains and then crossed the central Sahara. After reaching Murzuch (in present-day Libya), he decided to make a side trip to Tibesti, near the border of the present-day countries of Chad and Libya. The area, inhabited by the hostile Tibbu tribe, had never been visited by Europeans. Traveling through heat that reached over 100° Fahrenheit, Nachtigal arrived at the region's main village to find the tribesmen near starvation. Although he gave them almost all of his supplies, the Tibbu jailed him. Nachtigal eventually managed to escape and make his way to Bornu for his meeting with the sultan.

The German ambassador brought the sultan gifts, including life-size statues of the royal family, a large throne, and an arsenal of weapons. His mission was a great success, and the sultan allowed Nachtigal to use Kuka, his capital, as a base for further explorations. During the next three years, he made a number of memorable journeys. Nachtigal's final expedition in 1874 took him to Khartoum, where he received a hero's welcome.

Nachtigal took very detailed notes on all of his journeys, which helped the Germans better understand Africa and its people. The German authorities successfully used the information to colonize Togo and Cameroon. Nachtigal later was named consul general in Tunis and also served as a negotiator for several treaties. He died at sea off the Ivory Coast in 1885, at the age of 51.

SUGGESTED READING Gustav Nachtigal, *Sahara and Sudan*, translated by Allan G. B. Fisher and Humphrey J. Fisher (Humanities Press International, 1974–1987).

Nachtigal's detailed writings included reports on Africa's natural history and weather and the social and political conditions of the local tribes.

typhus disease that causes high fever, dizziness, and rashes; often transmitted by body lice

sultan ruler of a Muslim nation

Nansen, Fridtjof

Norwegian
b October 10, 1861; Froen, near Oslo, Norway
d May 13, 1930; Lysaker, near Oslo, Norway
Explored Greenland and Arctic Ocean

zoology the scientific study of animals

Fridtjof Nansen was a scientist, writer, and artist who later won the Nobel Peace Prize. In the rough-and-tumble field of Arctic exploration, he was a man of unusual grace and intelligence. He was the first to cross both the Greenland ice cap and the Arctic Ocean. Both expeditions involved simple and astonishing methods of travel, and both involved great risk. The experts on Arctic exploration at the time thought that Nansen's plans were dangerous and even insane, but no lives were lost.

An Idea Takes Hold

Nansen's parents taught him to love nature, and in 1880 he entered the University of Oslo to study **zoology** so that he could spend much

This photograph of Fridtjof Nansen was taken by fellow explorer Frederick Jackson on the day that they met on Franz Josef Land.

sledge heavy sled, often mounted on runners, that is pulled over snow or ice

of his time outdoors. In 1883 he read that Baron Nils Adolf Erik NORDENSKIÖLD had led an expedition to the ice sheets of Greenland. Two men who had gone with the baron had reported that the skiing was excellent. Nansen had an idea that he said "struck me with all the speed of lightning"—he would ski right across Greenland. He had been to Greenland recently on a field trip and could hardly wait to go back.

It took four years to plan the expedition, all while he was doing important work in zoology and histology, the study of body tissues. The experts doubted that he could cross Greenland with the small group he planned to take, but he was able to get the support he needed. Baron Nordenskiöld, who had retired from exploring by then, gave Nansen his snow boots and cautioned him to "look after your feet."

Across Greenland

Nansen was an excellent skier and a careful planner. He even invented a stove, called the Nansen cooker, just for this trip. But he was still taking a great gamble. If the land was not smooth enough for skiing all the way across Greenland, Nansen and his party would be trapped without supplies for the winter. Nansen knew, however, that he would have the wind at his back. He believed in leaving himself no way out so that he could not choose to give up. "I have always," he later explained, "regarded the much-praised line of retreat as a trap for people who want to reach their goal."

In early August 1888, the group had a rough landing on the east coast of Greenland, but Nansen, Otto SVERDRUP, and the others were all well-trained skiers. In a little more than a month, they reached their highest point, roughly 9,000 feet above sea level. Just 10 days later, they reached the west coast, and on October 3, the group arrived in the coast town of Godthaab in boats they had built. Because the landing at the start had not gone well, they had made up the lost time by turning the skis and **sledges** into sailing rafts. Nansen wrote that the rafts had "square Viking-like sails showing dark against the white snowfield."

Return to the Arctic

Nansen was a hero when he returned to Norway, but experts outside Norway still expressed doubt when he announced his next daring plan. An American general said that it was a crazy idea that would lead to disaster. Like the first plan, this one came to Nansen suddenly while he was reading. Two scientists had written about the wreckage of George Washington DE LONG's ship, *Jeannette.* They thought that the wreckage could have drifted from north of Siberia to the southwest coast of Greenland on the pack ice near the North Pole. They even suggested that an explorer could attach his ship to the ice and be carried by the drift. Nansen decided to try it and had the right kind of ship built. De Long's ship had been crushed when the ice it was locked in had expanded. Nansen's ship had a round and shallow hull so that the growing ice would slip right under it.

The *Fram* was the first vessel designed especially for the Arctic Ocean. Shaped almost like a bathtub, it was built like a rock. The oak rails in front were three feet thick and were covered with sheets of iron. It took two years to build.

At last, nine years after the idea had come to him, Nansen and 12 others left the northern tip of Norway on June 26, 1893. They sailed for Russia's New Siberian Islands, where the *Jeannette* had been wrecked. By September they were fighting through ice in waters that Nordenskiöld himself had had to give up on 15 years before.

On September 20, the *Fram* ran into the solid ice pack. The ship was tied to the ice, and in a few days, the ice had frozen around it. Soon the *Fram* was squeezed to the top of the ice, and by December a three-year drift had begun.

The ship became a floating science lab, and Nansen quickly made some important discoveries. He found that the Arctic Ocean was much warmer and deeper than people thought. He also added to the proof that there was no land continent over the North Pole.

Trying for the Pole

The crew kept a busy scientific schedule, and they got along well by living and working as equals. But by the second winter, Nansen was restless. It became clear that the *Fram* would miss the North Pole by hundreds of miles, so Nansen left Sverdrup in command of the ship. He and a companion set out on the ice, heading north with dogsleds.

Nansen's expeditions set records not only for northern progress but also for daring and originality.

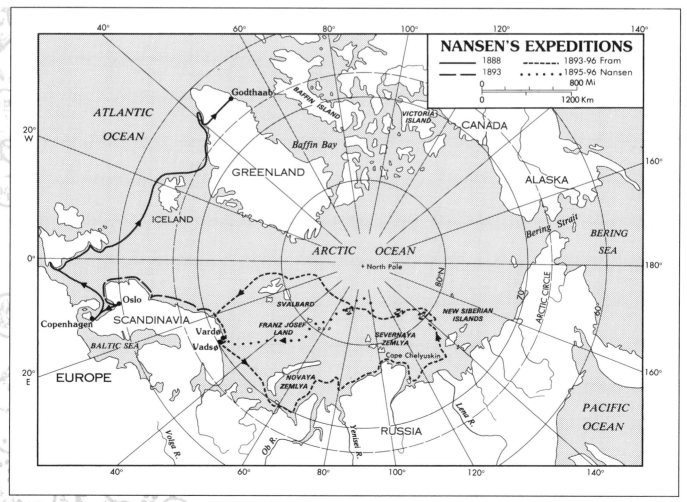

NANSEN'S EXPEDITIONS

—— 1888	------ 1893-96 Fram
– – 1893	••••• 1895-96 Nansen

0   800 Mi
0   1200 Km

latitude distance north or south of the equator

League of Nations worldwide diplomatic organization founded after World War I

They left the ship on March 14, 1895, and set a record by getting as far as 86°14′ north **latitude** on April 18. They headed back and had to spend a miserable winter in a walrus-hide hut on Franz Josef Land. They continued their journey in May 1896. With incredible luck and completely by chance, they ran into another explorer, Frederick Jackson. Jackson had planned to look for land north of Franz Josef Land, but Nansen convinced him that there was no land to be found. Therefore, Nansen argued, Jackson might as well rescue these two filthy and exhausted Norwegians.

Nansen returned to Norway on August 13, 1896, and the *Fram* returned a few days later. Sverdrup and the crew had reached a record high latitude for a ship—85°55′ north. That record was not broken until the U.S. atomic submarine *Nautilus* went under the pole in 1958. The return of both Nansen and his ship created a huge sensation in Norway, but these adventures of his youth seemed normal to Nansen. He had a full life of important work and responsibilities ahead.

A Distinguished Life

Nansen continued his work as a scientist and traveled around the world. His fame and abilities made him an important public figure. In 1906 he became Norway's first minister in London, and he also played a key diplomatic role during World War I. After the war, he started his greatest adventure yet as a leading figure in the new **League of Nations.** He took on the enormous job of finding homes for the millions of refugees from the world war and from the Russian Revolution. In 1921 he headed an international effort to stop a famine in Russia, and later he did the same for Greece and Armenia. In 1922 he received the Nobel Peace Prize.

After his death in 1930, the League of Nations created the Nansen International Office for Refugees to continue his work. Nansen had spent much time in the Arctic, working shoulder to shoulder with people whom he treated as his equals. He had drifted through the beautiful Arctic night, which he described as a "dreamland, painted in the imagination's most delicate tints. . . ." It was time he had spent preparing for the even harder task of bringing peace.

SUGGESTED READING Liv Nansen Hoyer, *Nansen: A Family Portrait*, translated by Maurice Michael (Longmans, Green, 1957); Fridtjof Nansen, *Farthest North*, 2 volumes (Harper and Brothers, 1898); Edward Shackleton, *Nansen the Explorer* (H. F. and G. Witherby, 1959); J. Edward Whitehouse, *Nansen: A Book of Homage* (Hodder and Stoughton, 1930).

Narváez, Pánfilo de

Spanish
b 1470?; Valladolid, Spain
d 1528; Gulf of Mexico
Explored Florida and Cuba

conquistador Spanish or Portuguese explorer and military leader in the Americas

Pánfilo de Narváez was a ruthless leader who made serious mistakes during two expeditions to Mexico and Florida. He had originally won fame for his role in the conquest of Cuba, but his first error led to a devastating defeat at the hands of the **conquistador** Hernán CORTÉS in Mexico. The second mistake cost Narváez and many of his men their lives in the Gulf of Mexico.

Military Exploits in Mexico and the Caribbean

Narváez was born in Valladolid, Spain. At the age of 28, he moved to Hispaniola (the island now occupied by Haiti and the Dominican Republic) to seek his fortune as a soldier. In 1509 he accompanied

During his campaign to conquer Cuba, Narváez reportedly killed more than 2,000 of the local tribesmen.

New Spain region of Spanish colonial empire that included the areas now occupied by Mexico, Florida, Texas, New Mexico, Arizona, California, and various Caribbean islands

Juan de Esquirel in his conquest of Jamaica. Two years later, Narváez led a mission to survey and conquer Cuba. During this seven-year expedition, he gained a reputation for both bravery and cruelty. Bartolomé de LAS CASAS, the expedition's priest, reported that the campaign against Cuba's people was a bloody slaughter.

In 1520 Narváez was sent to **New Spain** by the governor of Cuba, Diego Velásquez. Cortés, who had conquered New Spain, had disobeyed the governor's orders and was going to be replaced by Narváez. On April 23, 1520, Narváez arrived in Vera Cruz. He began negotiations with aides to Cortés while also secretly meeting with representatives of the captured Aztec emperor, Montezuma II. During the negotiations, the clever Cortés managed to sneak his men into Narváez's camp and carry out a surprise attack. Although outnumbered five to one, Cortés's forces defeated Narváez and imprisoned him for two years.

Expedition to Florida

Once he was released, Narváez went to Spain to seek permission to conquer new lands. In 1527 he was authorized to explore and conquer the area from the River of Palms in northeastern Mexico (the present-day Rio Grande) to Florida. Despite his problems in New Spain, Narváez was confident in his ability. He sailed from Spain on June 27, 1527, with 600 men in five ships. However, by the time he landed on the west coast of Florida the following April, he had lost much of his force. One ship and several men had been lost in a hurricane, and 140 men had refused to continue beyond Hispaniola.

Narváez next made an error that would prove fatal for him and for many of his men. Against the advice of Álvar Núñez CABEZA DE VACA, the treasurer and high sheriff of the expedition, Narváez divided his force. He marched inland with 300 men while the rest sailed up the coast of Florida. The two groups planned to reunite somewhere farther north. But the crew aboard the ships searched for the land party for a year before giving up and heading for Vera Cruz.

Meanwhile, Narváez and his party made slow progress toward the interior of Florida, marching through swamps filled with poisonous snakes and alligators. Some captured Indians then told Narváez of a place called Apalachen where there was supposedly much gold. For two weeks, the men marched northwest to look for Apalachen. They crossed what is now the Suwannee River and finally reached their destination near the site of present-day Tallahassee. But they did not find gold—just 40 huts and golden fields of corn. With supplies running low, Narváez was forced to head for the coast of the Gulf of Mexico.

Narváez Pays for His Mistakes

Narváez and his men reached the coast at a place called Aute, near modern Apalachee Bay. Recent evidence suggests that the site is

barge flat-bottomed boat without sails

now occupied by the St. Marks Wildlife Refuge. Here they realized that they had missed the ships. With little food left, they were forced to kill and eat their horses. For this reason, Narváez named the place Bahía de Caballos, which means Bay of Horses.

The party knew that they could not survive on the mainland, so they built **barges** to try to sail to Pánuco, on the northeastern coast of what is now Mexico. They used iron from their riding equipment and crossbows to make nails for the barges. Then the men covered the frames of the barges with the skins from their horses and used their own shirts for sails. All the while, they were harassed by the local Indians. Several men died of disease and hunger during the 16 days it took to complete the barges. Finally, on September 22, 1528, Narváez and his men were ready to sail.

The five barges, with about 200 men aboard, were overloaded, and no one knew how to navigate. They stayed close to the coastline and landed occasionally to search for food. When they reached the mouth of the Mississippi River, the strong river current and violent winds carried them out to sea. Eventually, the vessels drifted apart, and only two of them reached Galveston Island, Texas. Cabeza de Vaca was one of the survivors, but Narváez was never seen again. It is believed that Narváez drowned near the mouth of the Mississippi.

SUGGESTED READING Cyclone Covey, translator, *Cabeza de Vaca's Adventures in the Unknown Interior of America* (University of New Mexico Press, 1983).

Nearchus

Greek
b 360 B.C.?; ?
d 312 B.C.; ?
Opened up sea route from India to Arabian peninsula

galley ship with oars and sails, used in ancient and medieval times

Nearchus, one of the greatest geographers of ancient times, made a historic journey from the Indus River (in present-day Pakistan) to the Euphrates River (in present-day Iraq). His record of this trip gave the Mediterranean world its first knowledge of the sea route to India.

Crocodiles in the River

Nearchus's journey was commissioned by ALEXANDER THE GREAT, who ruled Greece and conquered much of the ancient world between 336 B.C. and 323 B.C. As Alexander's armies marched across Asia, they came to the Indus River and were surprised to find crocodiles in it. Knowing that the Nile River also contained crocodiles, they thought that the Indus might be the source of the Nile and that India and Africa might be linked. To explore this possibility, Alexander had Nearchus build a fleet of **galleys** and cargo ships. However, Nearchus soon sent back reports that the Indus flowed into a "Great Sea." While this report convinced Alexander that the Indus and the Nile were not connected, he was still interested in the possibility of a direct water route from India to the Mediterranean Sea.

Completing the Mission

After eight years of marching and fighting, Alexander's men finally refused to continue east into an unknown land where elephants were said to live. Alexander, however, was determined to explore the coast between the Indus and Euphrates Rivers. On his return to Greece in 325 B.C., Alexander joined Nearchus and his fleet on the

tributary stream or river that flows into a larger stream or river

Hydaspes (now the Jhelum) River, a **tributary** of the Indus. They proceeded downriver to the Indian Ocean, where Alexander continued his journey overland, and Nearchus and his fleet of 150 ships took a sea route to the Persian Gulf.

Nearchus kept a precise record of how far the fleet traveled each day, where it anchored, the features of the coastline, and the location of natural harbors. Later explorers confirmed the observations Nearchus made in his logbook. Alexander then ordered Nearchus to continue his exploration of the water route between India and the Mediterranean Sea by sailing around the Arabian peninsula. This journey was a remarkable achievement for the time. More than 400 years after Nearchus lived, the Greek historian Arrian included a summary of Nearchus's account of his travels in a book entitled *Indica*.

SUGGESTED READING Aubrey de Selincourt, *The Campaigns of Alexander* (Penguin Books, 1976).

Nehra, Alvaro de Mendaña de. See *Mendaña de Nehra, Alvaro de.*

Nicollet de Belleborne, Jean

French
b 1598?; Cherbourg, France
d October 27, 1642; Sillery, Canada
Explored Lake Michigan and Green Bay

New France French colony that included the St. Lawrence River valley, the Great Lakes region, and until 1713, Acadia (now called Nova Scotia)

Jean Nicollet de Belleborne spent many years as a representative of **New France,** living among the Indians of the Great Lakes. In 1634, on a mission for Samuel de CHAMPLAIN, he became the first European to see Lake Michigan and Green Bay.

Life Among the Indians

Nicollet arrived in New France in 1618, at about the age of 20. He was one of several young men sent by Champlain to live among the Indians and learn their languages and customs. For two years, he lived with the Algonquin on Allumette Island, on the Ottawa River. During that time, he learned both their language and that of the Huron Indians. After returning to Québec, he was sent to live among the Nipissing between the Ottawa River and Lake Huron. The Nipissing were an important link between the French and the tribes further west and on Hudson Bay. Nicollet's task was to win their loyalty so that they would trade furs with the French instead of with the English.

When the English captured Québec in 1629, Nicollet went west to persuade the Huron not to trade with them. Four years later, Québec was back under French control, and Nicollet requested a job as a clerk at Trois-Rivières, a town whose name means Three Rivers, on the St. Lawrence River. Champlain agreed to give him the post but asked him to undertake one last mission.

Search for the China Sea

Nicollet had two goals on this expedition. He was to establish relations with the Winnebago tribe on Lake Michigan and prevent them from trading with the Dutch. He was also to search for the fabled China Sea, which the Indians had told him was west of Green Bay.

This illustration depicts Jean Nicollet de Belleborne at Lake Itasca, the source of the Mississippi River.

Jesuit member of the Society of Jesus, a Roman Catholic order founded by Ignatius of Loyola in 1534

Nicollet was given a robe of fine cloth, covered with flowers and birds of many colors, so that he could greet the Chinese leaders he might meet in proper style.

When he arrived at Green Bay, Nicollet put on his robe, which made him appear godlike to the Winnebago. After signing a peace treaty with them, he began to search for the China Sea, but he was unable to locate such a waterway. He returned to Québec in 1635 and took up his duties as a clerk at Trois-Rivières.

Seven years later, Nicollet drowned while sailing on rough waters between Québec and Trois-Rivières. The memoirs of the **Jesuit** priests who knew him say that Nicollet was a man of the highest character. They described him as "equally and singularly loved" by the French and the Indians.

SUGGESTED READING Morris Bishop, *Champlain* (Macdonald, 1949).

Niza, Marcos de. *See Marcos de Niza.*

Nobile, Umberto

Italian
b January 21, 1885; Lauro (near Naples), Italy
d July 29, 1978; Rome, Italy
Explored Arctic Ocean by air

General Umberto Nobile was a brilliant engineer who specialized in the design of **dirigibles.** In 1926 he became the first person to pilot an aircraft across the Arctic Ocean. He was joined on his historic flight by the great Norwegian polar explorer Roald AMUNDSEN.

Rivalry Between Explorers
Nobile became the director of the aircraft factory in Rome in 1919, when he was just 34 years old. Three years later, Italy's new

dirigible large aircraft filled with a lighter-than-air gas that keeps it aloft; similar to a blimp but with a rigid frame

archipelago large group of islands or a body of water with many islands

sledge heavy sled, often mounted on runners, that is pulled over snow or ice

In this photograph, taken in 1926, Umberto Nobile walks inside the gasbag of his dirigible, the *Norge.*

government created a military corps of aeronautical engineers, and Nobile was made a lieutenant colonel. In 1925 he received a telegraph from Roald Amundsen and his American sponsor, Lincoln ELLSWORTH. The pair wanted to buy the dirigible *N-1,* which Nobile had designed.

Amundsen and Ellsworth planned to fly across the Arctic Ocean, and they wanted Nobile to be their pilot. Negotiations between the parties were difficult because Amundsen wanted to play a more active role in the flight. It was his idea, and he had done a great deal of work planning the expedition. However, he eventually settled for being merely a passenger on what turned out to be his last Arctic journey. Amundsen renamed the aircraft the *Norge* to honor his home country, Norway.

The *Norge* left the Norwegian **archipelago** of Svalbard on May 11, 1926, and arrived at the North Pole the next day. Despite ice on the aircraft and dangerous fog, the party landed in Alaska on May 14. The men had been in the air for 70 hours straight and had covered 3,400 miles. It was an outstanding accomplishment for everyone involved, but Amundsen became upset when Nobile received most of the attention and praise. Amundsen also saw that the successful expedition brought glory to the Italian government and to its dictator, Benito Mussolini. The Norwegian explorer worried that he had unknowingly played a part in promoting Mussolini's undemocratic cause.

Nobile Plans His Own Expedition

Nobile, however, had no interest in politics, and he was humiliated by Amundsen's attempt to take credit for the trip. He decided to lead his own Arctic expedition. He planned three separate flights, including a landing at the North Pole. Mussolini approved Nobile's plan over the objection of Air Marshal Italo Balbo, commander of Italy's air forces. Nobile's countrymen agreed with Mussolini's decision. Even Pope Pius XI, head of the Roman Catholic Church, became excited about the prospect of the flights. He personally gave Nobile an oak cross to plant at the pole. But this time there was little glory for the Italians.

Nobile approached the veteran Arctic explorers Fridtjof NANSEN and Otto SVERDRUP for advice on supplies. He loaded his dirigible *Italia* with **sledges,** canvas boats, and other articles for Arctic travel. Nobile took off from Svalbard on May 11, 1928, but he had to return because of bad weather. Four days later, the *Italia* headed for Siberia, successfully covering 2,500 miles on the journey. Nobile had high hopes for his flight to the pole.

Disaster at the Pole

Nobile departed on May 23 and reached the pole easily, but poor weather conditions prevented him from landing. On the flight back to Svalbard, the wind grew stronger, and ice built up on the dirigible. The propellers threw sharp pieces of ice into the soft sides of the craft. Fog

Nobile's dirigible *Italia*, photographed here over Stolp, Prussia (now Słupsk, Poland), reached the North Pole in 1928 but crashed during its return trip.

Soviet Union nation that existed from 1922 to 1991, made up of Russia and 14 other republics in eastern Europe and northern Asia

made accurate navigation impossible, and ice jammed the *Italia*'s steering gear. The gear was finally freed of ice, but the aircraft soon began to sink steadily, about 180 miles northeast of Svalbard.

The craft crashed on the ice, and its cabin was torn off, leaving the 10 men who had been inside it stranded. The rest of the ship bounced back into the air with six crew members still hanging from it—they were never seen again. Of those men who landed on the ice, one mechanic had been killed in the crash, and Nobile and a technician were injured. Fortunately, a tent, a radio, and about a month's worth of food were found in the wreckage. These supplies enabled all but one of the survivors to endure the long wait for rescuers. Swedish scientist Finn Malmgren set out across the ice to seek help, but he died in the attempt.

News of the crash led to a huge international rescue effort. Despite his differences with Nobile, Amundsen immediately joined the hunt for the survivors. He died, however, when his plane became lost over the Barents Sea. Several other searchers also lost their lives. Nobile was finally rescued by the Swedish Air Force on June 24, and a Soviet ship picked up the other survivors on July 12.

Air Marshal Balbo used the crash to discredit Nobile, who was stripped of his rank and all of his honors. In 1932 Nobile left Italy to build dirigibles in the **Soviet Union.** After World War II, he returned to Rome, where he later died at the age of 93.

SUGGESTED READING Umberto Nobile, *My Polar Flight* (Muller, 1961).

Nordenskiöld, Nils Adolf Erik

Swedish-Finnish
b November 18, 1832; Helsinki, Finland
d August 12, 1901; Stockholm, Sweden
*Explored Canadian and Norwegian Arctic;
navigated Northeast Passage*

Northeast Passage water route connecting the Atlantic Ocean and Pacific Ocean along the Arctic coastline of Europe and Asia

geologist scientist who studies the earth's natural history

latitude distance north or south of the equator

botanist scientist who studies plants

After his successful Arctic travels, Nordenskiöld became a distinguished historian of exploration.

Nils Adolf Erik Nordenskiöld was one of the greatest Arctic explorers of the late 1800s. Unlike other explorers of that era, Nordenskiöld was interested in promoting commerce, rather than in simply charting remote stretches of ice or competing with others to reach the poles. Nordenskiöld's most important accomplishment was proving the existence of a **Northeast Passage.** By navigating the passage in 1878, he showed merchants that they could connect by sea with the great rivers of northern Asia and Europe. The route became an important link in the world's trade network.

From Scholar to Explorer

As a child, Nordenskiöld explored mineral deposits all over Finland with his father, who was a geologist. After he graduated from the University of Helsinki in 1853, Nils and his father conducted experiments on metals from Russia's Ural Mountains. Back home in Finland, Nordenskiöld used his extensive research to write a handbook on mineral deposits. His work won him positions with both the government and the university.

Although these jobs gave him the time and money to continue his studies, Nordenskiöld soon abandoned his academic career. During that time, the Russian authorities ruling in Finland were nervous about Finns who were loyal to Scandinavia. Nordenskiöld, whose family was Swedish, expressed his anti-Russian views and was fired from both of his posts in 1855. After several conflicts with the authorities, he eventually moved to Sweden.

Early Explorations in the Arctic

In 1858 Nordenskiöld accompanied the Swedish **geologist** Otto Torell on a scientific expedition to Spitsbergen (now part of Svalbard), in Norway. The expedition was successful, and the two teamed up again in 1861. They set up bases in Spitsbergen, where they hoped to measure the curvature of the earth. Torell had wanted to try to reach the North Pole by dogsled, but they arrived too late in the season make the attempt.

Three years later, Nordenskiöld led another expedition to Spitsbergen to continue work on measuring the earth's curvature. By this time, he was completely dedicated to Arctic exploration, and in 1868 he returned to the region again. This trip was financed by the Swedish government and the wealthy businessman Oscar Dickson, who became one of his main supporters. Nordenskiöld was determined to sail closer to the North Pole than anyone had before him, and this journey was also a success. Aboard the *Sofia*, Nordenskiöld reached the highest **latitude** yet achieved in the Northern Hemisphere.

When he returned to Sweden, Nordenskiöld got involved in politics, and he was elected to Parliament in 1869. But the next year, he was off again to Greenland, becoming the first to explore any significant distance into the country's interior. Traveling with a **botanist** and two

Inuit people of the Canadian Arctic, sometimes known as the Eskimo

sledge heavy sled, often mounted on runners, that is pulled over snow or ice

Inuit, Nordenskiöld made many important discoveries about the nature of the region.

In 1872 Nordenskiöld planned to make an attempt to reach the North Pole by **sledge.** However, ice prevented his supply ships from returning south, and he found himself with twice the number of people to feed and care for over the winter. Nordenskiöld's well-planned trip suddenly became a dangerous adventure. In addition, a storm scattered the party's reindeer, ending any hope of reaching the pole. Remarkably, only two members of the expedition died. Nordenskiöld even led some members of his crew on a 150-mile journey on foot to survey northeastern Spitsbergen.

The Northeast Passage

After this trip, Nordenskiöld decided to give up his quest for the North Pole and concentrate on opening the Northeast Passage. This passage had been a dream of northern European explorers in the 1500s and 1600s, when Spain and Portugal dominated the southern sea routes to Asia. Earlier explorers, such as Hugh Willoughby and Willem BARENTS, had lost their lives trying to discover a Northeast Passage. Even so, their sacrifices had led to positive discoveries, such as the rich whaling and fishing grounds off Spitsbergen and trade in the White Sea.

By Nordenskiöld's day, however, Spain and Portugal no longer controlled the southern sea routes. Furthermore, cargo could now be carried efficiently across North America by rail. The recently opened Suez Canal made trade easier than ever, and there were also plans for a canal to be built across Central America. No one thought that there was a need for a Northeast Passage, and most critics felt that such a route would always be dangerous and impractical.

Nordenskiöld did not share their opinions. He studied fishing journals and historical accounts of the area. This research, along with his own travels, convinced him that sailing the passage was possible. Nordenskiöld was convinced that the main Siberian rivers—the Ob, the Yenisei, and the Lena—warmed the sea north of Siberia. He assumed that the waters were warm enough during the summer to open a narrow but reliable passage. Previous explorers had made the mistake of sailing too far from the coast to find an open polar sea. Nordenskiöld decided instead to stay close to the mainland. His careful preparations and vast knowledge would make this historic voyage almost routine—not the dangerous venture such a journey had been hundreds of years before.

Conquering the Northeast Passage

Nordenskiöld's first step was to take the steamship *Pröven* north of Siberia, to the mouth of the Yenisei River in the Kara Sea. Soon after he reached the mouth, a Russian fisherman took Nordenskiöld and five companions in a small boat on a slow 1,000-mile trip up-river to the city of Yeniseisk, in central Russia. This trip proved the possibility of reaching the Siberian rivers by sea. Despite Nordenskiöld's anti-Russian views, the Russian government went out of its way to welcome him because he had opened the Siberian coast to European trade. A wealthy Russian merchant named Alexander

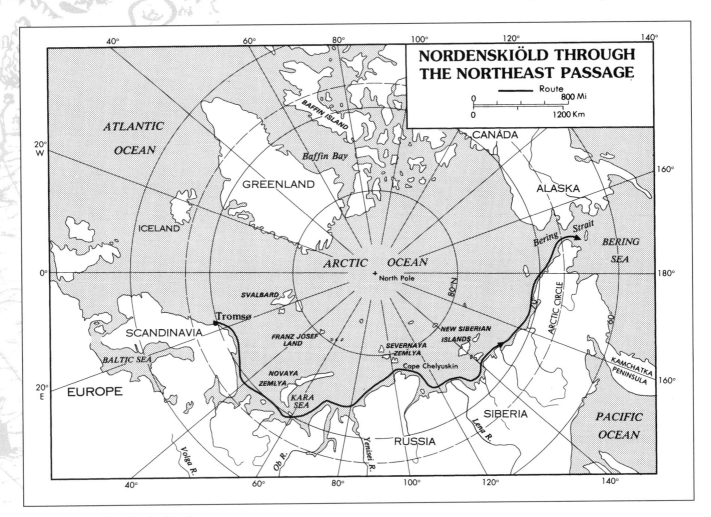

During his voyage through the Northeast Passage, Nordenskiöld was stopped by ice only once, when he tried to reach the New Siberian Islands.

Sibiryakov became one of Nordenskiöld's loyal financial backers. The merchant was so impressed with Nordenskiöld's accomplishment that he immediately sent a ship from Yeniseisk to the Russian city of St. Petersburg, by way of Sweden.

Nordenskiöld returned to Sweden in November 1875, and after two years of preparation, he was ready for his final expedition to the passage. Both the Swedish government and his supporter Oscar Dickson backed the journey. Sibiryakov provided three ships to carry coal and supplies for Nordenskiöld's ship, the *Vega*.

On July 31, 1878, the four ships met in the strait leading to the Kara Sea to begin their journey. It proved to be uneventful, with Nordenskiöld following the coast as he had planned. When he reached the Bering Strait, he stopped for the winter. On July 20, 1879, the *Vega* was freed from the ice, and it sailed easily through the strait and into the Pacific Ocean. Nordenskiöld was hailed as a hero on his return trip to Sweden. He arrived home in Stockholm on April 24, 1880, a date now known as Vega Day in Sweden. He was later made a baron for his accomplishment.

In 1883 Nordenskiöld made one more trip to Greenland, traveling 140 miles inland with two companions. On this Arctic expedition, he demonstrated that ice probably covered the continent. It was this trip that inspired the young Fridtjof NANSEN to ski across Greenland four years later. Nordenskiöld retired shortly afterward, though he continued his scholarly research and advised other explorers. He also remained active in the fight for Finnish independence from Russia until his death in 1901.

SUGGESTED READING L. P. Kirwan, *A History of Polar Exploration* (W. W. Norton, 1960); George Kish, *North-east Passage: Adolf Erik Nordenskiöld, His Life and Times* (Nico Israel, 1973); L.H. Neatby, *Discovery in Russian and Siberian Waters* (Ohio University Press, 1973).

Novaes, Bartolomeu de.   See *Dias, Bartolomeu.*

Nuñez de Balboa, Vasco.   See *Balboa, Vasco Nuñez de.*

Odoric of Pordenone

Italian
b 1286?; Villanova (near Pordenone), Italy
d January 14, 1331; Udine, Italy
Traveled in Middle East, Asia, and Indonesia

junk Chinese ship with sails made of fiber mats

khan title of an Asian ruler

In about 1316, Odoric of Pordenone became a Franciscan monk and went to Asia as a missionary. By the time he returned to Italy, 14 years later, he had baptized more than 20,000 people. He had also written vivid descriptions of Asian life that influenced European thought for several hundred years. Odoric's stories combined facts with a creative flair for exaggeration. His accounts were probably the basis for the English work *The Voyage and Travels of Sir John Mandeville, Knight,* written in the 1300s.

On the Way to Asia

Odoric's journey to Asia first took him to Franciscan communities in Asia Minor (the peninsula now occupied by Turkey) and Persia (now Iran). After a brief stay in Hormuz, at the eastern end of the Persian Gulf, Odoric sailed for India. He landed near Bombay in about 1322 and went on to visit many parts of India. From India, Odoric traveled to Southeast Asia on a **junk.** This voyage took him through Sumatra, Java, and Borneo. He arrived in China only 10 years after Marco POLO had left the region.

Travels Through China and Tibet

Odoric's journals include colorful descriptions of his three-year stay in Beijing, China. He also wrote about his visit to the court of the Great **Khan** and his many travels throughout Asia. Odoric described the Chinese city of Hangzhou as the "greatest city in the world. It is one hundred miles in circumference, and in this vast area there is not a single spot that is not inhabited." Odoric was the first European to comment upon the long fingernails of Chinese noblemen and the ritual binding of girls' feet to keep the feet from growing. He also noted the methods of Chinese fishermen, who used large, diving birds to catch fish.

When Odoric decided to return to Italy, he set out by land and traveled through the uncharted regions of central Asia. He was probably the first European to visit Lhasa, the capital and holy city of Tibet. Odoric wrote that the people of Tibet lived in tents made of black felt. He called Lhasa "very beautiful: it is built of white stone and its streets are well paved." When Odoric reached Italy, another monk wrote down the story of his travels in simple Latin. Odoric died several months later, in 1331.

SUGGESTED READING James Joseph Walsh, compiler, *These Splendid Priests* (Books for Libraries Press, 1968).

Canadian
b 1794; Québec City, Canada
d September 27, 1854; Oregon City, Oregon
Explored American West

For most of his life, Peter Skene Ogden worked in the fur trade on the North American continent. From 1824 to 1830, he led six expeditions in the American West. In the course of these travels, Ogden thoroughly explored the Snake River area. He also became the first non-Indian to see the present-day Humboldt River in what is now Nevada, and he traveled as far south as the Gulf of California.

A Ruthless Trader

Ogden became a fur trader with the North West Company at the age of 15 or 16. Over the next 12 years, he gained a reputation as a ruthless trader who would do anything to get what he wanted. He used violence and threats to compete with the traders of his company's rival, Hudson's Bay Company. When Hudson's Bay took over the North West Company in 1821, Ogden lost his job. But he convinced the Hudson's Bay Company that his rough style could be of value. By 1823 he was working for Hudson's Bay in what is now eastern Washington State, and he was asked to lead a trapping expedition to the Snake River in the spring of 1824.

At that time, there was no firm boundary between the United States and Canada in the northwestern region known as the Oregon Territory. Although this area was open to both British and American trappers, the British knew that someday the Americans would want to take over the region. Ogden's fur company, which was British, wanted to take as many beaver pelts as possible before the Americans restricted their access to the furs. The British hoped to empty every stream in the Oregon Territory of beaver, leaving nothing for the Americans. Ogden's job was to trap every beaver in sight.

The Unknown River

During the trapping season of 1824 to 1825, Ogden thoroughly explored the Snake and Bear River country. But Ogden's most important expedition came three years later, when he discovered the Humboldt River in what is now Nevada. He followed the river from its source to the Humboldt Sinks, a series of marshy lakes where the river ends. Ogden called it the Unknown River. Years later, John Charles FRÉMONT named the river after the German explorer Alexander von HUMBOLDT, who never even saw it. The river soon became an important stage of the trail that led American settlers to the West. Ogden had unintentionally helped his company's rivals gain a stronger foothold in the region.

Peter Skene Ogden was the first non-Indian to travel the length of the American West from north to south.

California Travels

In August 1828, Jedediah SMITH and two of his men arrived at Fort Vancouver after narrowly escaping an Indian attack in which the rest of their party had been killed. Ogden arrived at the fort and heard Smith discussing two of his expeditions across the Mojave Desert and into California. This report gave Ogden the idea for his last and most interesting exploration of the West. He headed south, possibly traveling as far as the Gulf of California. Unfortunately, his written accounts of this expedition were lost in a whirlpool on the Columbia River shortly before the end of the journey. Nine of Ogden's men drowned in the deadly currents.

Historians have pieced together a record of the journey from Ogden's letters and later reports. It is believed that Ogden and his skilled party of 30 men traveled south from the Columbia River to the Humboldt Sinks. There they turned southeast and traveled through what Ogden called the Great Sandy Desert of the Great Salt Lake. They were probably in the Great Basin of what became modern Nevada. On this difficult trip, Ogden and his men were forced to eat the flesh of horses that died on the trail. They even drank the horses' blood to quench their thirst.

Eventually, they came to the southwest branch of the Colorado River, near the site of present-day Needles, California. This spot was probably where Smith had been attacked by a band of Mojave Indians while traveling to the Mojave Desert in the summer of 1827. Unlike Smith, Ogden and his men were ready when an attack came. They quickly fought the Indians off with guns and handmade spears and then headed down the Colorado River. When they reached the Gulf of California, they had traveled the entire length of the American West from north to south.

Drinking Mud and Other Adventures

Peter Ogden spent another 24 years in the fur trade, but none of his later travels matched his explorations of the American West. Ogden was a tough character who liked to overcome challenges. On one western expedition, liquid mud was the only drink available to him and his men. Ogden wrote: "This is certainly a most horrid life. . . . Man in this Country is deprived of every comfort that can tend to make existence desirable." Ogden survived many hardships and added greatly to what was known about the North American West.

SUGGESTED READING Archie Binns, *Peter Skene Ogden: Fur Trader* (Binfords and Mort, 1967).

Ojeda, Alonso de

Spanish
b 1468?; Cuenca, Spain
d 1515?; Hispaniola
(now Haiti and the Dominican Republic)
Explored coasts of Venezuela and Colombia

conquistador Spanish or Portuguese explorer and military leader in the Americas

Alonso de Ojeda was a ruthless and violent **conquistador** who looted the lands he explored and treated the Indians who lived there with great cruelty. He commanded a ship on Christopher COLUMBUS's second voyage across the Atlantic Ocean, from 1493 to 1495. On this expedition, Ojeda explored Hispaniola (the island now occupied by Haiti and the Dominican Republic) in search of gold. Later he led several of his own expeditions to South America and founded San Sebastián on the gulf of Urabá, in what is now Colombia. San Sebastián was the first Spanish settlement on South American soil, though it was later abandoned.

The Pearls of Little Venice

Ojeda was born into a noble Spanish family, sometime between 1466 and 1470, in the town of Cuenca. As a youth, he had a quick temper and was always getting into fights. He later gained fame as a soldier in the Christian campaign to recapture Spain from the Moors, the

Alonso de Ojeda earned early fame for leading Spanish soldiers in the interior of Hispaniola, as illustrated in this drawing.

cartographer mapmaker

Arabic people who had ruled much of the peninsula for over 700 years. Ojeda then joined Columbus on his second voyage to the Americas and proved his ability as an explorer. Ojeda fought Indians, thick undergrowth, and heat to reach the inner regions of Hispaniola.

When Ojeda returned from this voyage, the Spanish king commissioned him to search for more riches in the Americas. The expedition departed from Cadiz on May 16, 1499. On board were the **cartographer** Juan de LA COSA, and the king's financial representative, Amerigo VESPUCCI. After passing the Cape Verde Islands off the coast of western Africa, the ships split up. Vespucci explored to the southeast of South America, and Ojeda sailed along the northwest coast of the continent. Ojeda passed the mouths of two large rivers—most likely the Essequibo, now in modern British Guiana, and the Orinoco in Venezuela. He then reached the Gulf of Paria.

Ojeda made his first landfall on the island now known as Trinidad. There he met people whom he described as "Caribs or cannibals of gentle disposition." Sailing west, he rounded what is now called the Paraguaná Peninsula, which juts into the Caribbean Sea, and entered the waters now known as the Gulf of Venezuela. Heading south, Ojeda found what is now Lake Maracaibo. The people there fished for pearls and lived in houses built on stilts in the shallow part of the lake. When Ojeda saw these dwellings, he named the land Venezuela (Little Venice). After traveling along the northern coast of South America, Ojeda sailed to Hispaniola to rejoin Vespucci. The expedition returned to Spain with enough pearls and Indian slaves to make the voyage a financial success.

adelantado Spanish leader of a military expedition to America during the 1500s who also served as governor and judge

Conqueror and Convict

Ojeda was awarded the title of **adelantado** of Coquibacoa (the area around Lake Maracaibo). In 1501 he was given permission to cut brazilwood on Hispaniola and nearby islands and to continue to develop the pearl trade. His next expedition reached the Peninsula of Paria, Venezuela, in March 1502. He worked his way along the coast, trading with the Indians for pearls. The area became known as the Pearl Coast.

Whenever supplies ran low, Ojeda attacked Indian villages. He would enslave or kill the entire population and take everything he could find. When supply ships finally came from Jamaica, Ojeda was accused of not paying the required portion of his profits to the Spanish king. Ojeda was taken to Hispaniola, where he was convicted, but he managed to return to Spain and clear himself of the charges.

In 1508 Ojeda undertook a major expedition to found a settlement in South America. When he landed at the site of what is now Cartagena, Colombia, his finances were dwindling. Ojeda decided to attack a Carib Indian village to capture slaves, whom he could sell. His lieutenant warned him against this violent act, but Ojeda ignored him and slaughtered or enslaved all the Indians of the village. Neighboring Carib then took revenge by attacking the Spaniards with poisoned darts that caused a slow, painful death. Ojeda was the only one able to escape. He was small enough to hide behind his shield, which took some 300 arrow hits.

The Abandoned Settlement

In 1510 Ojeda established a settlement called San Sebastián, on the Gulf of Urabá. Indian attacks and food shortages forced him to leave and seek help for his colony. After being shipwrecked on the shore of Cuba, he reached Hispaniola. There he found out that his colonists had abandoned the settlement. Their desertion ruined Ojeda's finances. According to some accounts, Ojeda entered a community of Franciscan monks in Hispaniola and died there in poverty in about 1515.

Alonso de Ojeda is known both for his extreme cruelty toward Indians and for his successful explorations. His expeditions opened up parts of Venezuela and Colombia for further Spanish exploration and colonization. Today Ciudad Ojeda stands along the shore of Lake Maracaibo, near the site where Ojeda first came across the pearl fishers almost 500 years ago.

SUGGESTED READING C. Edwards Lester, *The Life and Voyages of Americus Vespucius* (H. Mansfield, 1867).

Oñate, Juan de

Spanish
b 1549?; Mexico
d 1624; Spain
Explored and colonized American Southwest

Juan de Oñate was one of the richest men in **New Spain** when he volunteered to pay for and lead an expedition to New Mexico. Oñate wanted to explore and colonize the region, but he was also eager to search for a legendary land of incredible wealth called Quivira. Francisco Vásquez de CORONADO had sought the same land almost 60 years earlier. But neither Oñate nor Cornonado ever discovered Quivira. They found only a vast wilderness and modest Indian villages.

New Spain region of Spanish colonial empire that included the areas now occupied by Mexico, Florida, Texas, New Mexico, Arizona, California, and various Caribbean islands

pueblo Indian village or dwelling in the American Southwest, often built of sun-dried bricks

Council of the Indies governing body of Spain's colonial empire from 1524 to 1834

A Slow Journey

Oñate's wealthy father was a former governor of New Galicia (now the Mexican states of Nayarit and Sinaloa). Oñate also became a powerful man in New Spain. He gained even more influence when he married the great-granddaughter of the Aztec king Montezuma II. Oñate always combined a strong sense of duty with great ambition and pride. He was determined to lead an expedition to New Mexico, and he waited a long time for approval from the king of Spain and his representative in New Spain.

In the summer of 1597, Oñate left New Spain with 400 men (130 brought their wives and children). The party also included several monks of the Franciscan order, as well as Indians who were assigned to carry supplies. Oñate brought articles to trade with the local Indians and four bells for a church.

The expedition moved slowly, trying to find their way in the wilderness. At first they were delayed by heavy rains. Then they endured five days of desert travel and terrible thirst. Eventually, Oñate found the Rio Grande and followed it north. He entered New Mexico on April 30, 1598, and claimed the land for Spain. Continuing up the Rio Grande, the party marched through a mountain pass that Oñate named El Paso del Norte (near present-day El Paso, Texas). They crossed to the east bank of the river and headed north across a vast plain. Oñate encountered many friendly Indian **pueblos** along the way, and seven Indian chieftains pledged obedience to the king of Spain.

On August 11, 1598, the expedition came to the site where the Rio Chama and the Rio Grande meet. Oñate chose this site for his capital, calling it San Juan de los Caballeros. It was the first European settlement west of the Mississippi River. By early October, Oñate had left the area with a small party to explore the wilderness to the west. Another group attempted to join him but was massacred during an uprising at the pueblo of Acoma. When Oñate heard this news, he returned to the capital at once. He received the priests' permission to wage war on the Acoma Indians. Oñate defeated the Acoma, but he found it hard to keep peace with the other Indian pueblos after the conflict.

Battles in Court

In his continuing search for Quivira, Oñate explored the region that became Kansas, the mouth of the Colorado River, and the Gulf of California. After several years of searching, many of the colonists were frustrated. By 1607 secret reports that criticized Oñate had reached the king's officials in New Spain. To make matters worse, no vast riches had been found. Two years later, Oñate was ordered to return to New Spain. He was removed from his position and put on trial for various crimes, including cruelty against the Acoma and issuing false reports about conditions in New Mexico. Oñate was found guilty and was banished from New Mexico in 1614. Oñate then took his case to the **Council of the Indies.**

Over the next seven years, Oñate spent his entire fortune pleading the case. In 1622 the Council recommended that he be forgiven, but the king delayed his decision. At age 75, Oñate went to Spain to

adelantado Spanish leader of a military expedition to America during the 1500s who also served as governor and judge

Orellana, Francisco de

Spanish
b 1511?; Trujillo, Spain
d 1546; Amazon, Brazil
Explored Amazon River; crossed South America

conquistador Spanish or Portuguese explorer and military leader in the Americas

El Dorado mythical ruler, city, or area of South America believed to possess much gold

appeal personally to the king. In 1624 the king pardoned him, restored his title of **adelantado,** and gave him a government position. Oñate died in Spain the same year. He had lost his money, but he had won back his honor.

Oñate's explorations opened up New Mexico for future settlement. He established the first permanent colony there and found a more direct northern route to New Mexico from New Spain. Today visitors to New Mexico can still see Oñate's name carved on the face of the huge sandstone rock called El Morro.

SUGGESTED READING Robert McGeagh, *Juan de Oñate's Colony in the Wilderness: An Early History of the American Southwest* (Sunstone Press, 1990).

In the early 1530s, Francisco de Orellana fought beside **conquistador** Francisco PIZARRO to conquer the Inca in the land that is now Peru. In 1541 Orellana joined Gonzalo Pizarro on the first recorded expedition eastward across the Andes Mountains in search of **El Dorado** and cinnamon forests. On this journey, Orellana unintentionally became the first European to cross South America by way of the Marañón River (now known as the Amazon). But this Amazon adventure caused Gonzalo Pizarro to accuse Orellana of abandoning his mission and betraying his country.

The Power of the Pizarros

Orellana was born in Trujillo, Spain, in about 1511. He was related to Francisco Pizarro. When he was about 16, Orellana traveled to Spain's distant American colonies to seek fame, fortune, and adventure. Although the exact location of his landing is not known, it was probably in what is now Panama, since the Pizarro family had some power there. In 1531 Francisco Pizarro set out to conquer Peru, and young Orellana went with him. Orellana won honors for his service in the campaign against the Inca. During one battle, he lost an eye.

Once Peru was under Pizarro's control, Orellana settled in Portoviejo, now a port in present-day Ecuador. He went to war again to help fight off Indian attacks at Cuzco and Lima. He also fought on Pizarro's side against another conquistador, Diego de ALMAGRO, who was battling Pizarro for control of Cuzco. To keep other conquistadors from challenging his authority, Pizarro ordered them to explore and conquer new lands. Orellana was appointed to explore the province of Culata, which he conquered. In 1537 he rebuilt a destroyed Spanish settlement on the site of what is now Guayaquil, Ecuador.

Difficult Times

Four years later, Orellana joined Gonzalo Pizarro, Francisco's half brother, on an expedition east of the Andes. They hoped to find the legendary land of cinnamon, which was almost as valuable as gold at that time. They were also seeking the fabled El Dorado. According to legend, the king of El Dorado covered himself in gold dust

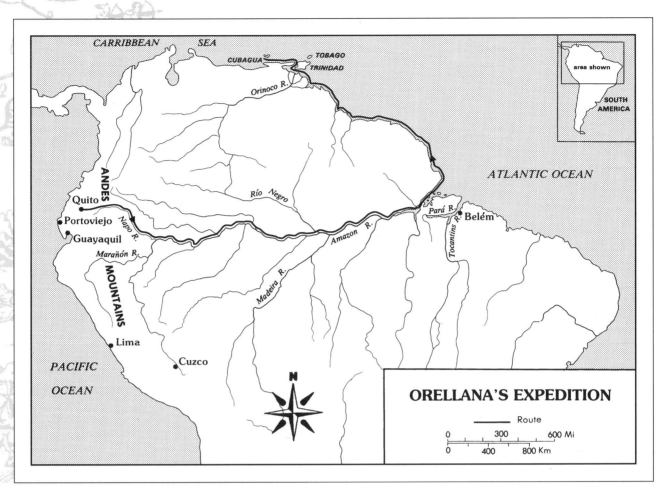

ORELLANA'S EXPEDITION

Francisco de Orellana was the first European to succeed in navigating the entire length of the Amazon River.

every day. He then washed it off in a lake while his aides showered him with emeralds and golden objects. Motivated by a thirst for riches, the conquistadors were ready to face any hardship in order to find this lake filled with gold.

Orellana and his small party missed the expedition's original departure from Quito (now in Ecuador). They survived near starvation and Indian attacks before they finally joined Pizarro and the main group. A monk named Gaspar de Carvajal, who kept a journal of the expedition, wrote that Orellana had only a sword and shield left when he finally reunited with Pizarro and his men. By the end of December 1541, the Spaniards had set up camp on the Coca River. They had found no great wealth, and all their Indian slaves had been killed by disease. Exhausted and nearly starved, the Spaniards lived on "grass, nuts, and poisonous worms." At this point, Orellana headed downstream to search for food. He took 57 men in a small boat and 10 canoes.

Amazon Adventure

Orellana's party sailed down the Coca into the Napo River. They traveled 700 miles through a remote region where there was absolutely nothing to eat. Their supplies ran out, and Orellana and his men were forced to eat their leather belts and shoes, cooked with herbs. When they arrived at an Indian village in January 1542, the

tributary stream or river that flows into a larger stream or river

Spaniards were able to trade for food. At this point, Orellana decided to continue downstream to the Atlantic Ocean. This decision caused controversy for years to come. He was accused of cruelly abandoning Pizarro. Some historians, however, think that Orellana and his men believed that it would be impossible to return upstream against the swift current. Documents from the journey do not provide clear answers.

Orellana persuaded the Indians to help him build another boat, and he set out again on April 24. About a month later, Orellana reached a major branch of the Amazon River, which he named the Rio Negro, meaning Black River. He and his party continued the length of the Amazon and fought through the great tidal surges at the river's mouth. They reached the Atlantic Ocean on August 26, 1542. Orellana's expedition then made a slow, difficult voyage along the South American coast. They had no compass or other tools for navigation, and they used blankets for sails.

According to Carvajal's account, this epic journey covered over 3,000 miles—down the Amazon River and its **tributaries,** through unknown territory. Its primary goal was survival rather than exploration. The party spent most of its time trying to get food, either from nature or from Indians. The group also had to face extreme heat, swarms of biting insects, man-eating piranha fish, and giant water rodents.

The Amazon Women

During his travels, Orellana heard stories of a tribe of tall, white women warriors, to whom many Indian villages paid tribute. The women allowed no men in their villages except once a year for mating purposes. They sent male children to be raised in their fathers' villages. Carvajal recorded the legend of these women, and he also reported that 10 to 12 of them had been sighted during a battle with an Indian tribe. He described them as being "very robust" and "doing as much fighting as ten men."

Orellana called these women Amazons because they reminded him of the Amazons of Greek legend. The Greek Amazons were said to be a tribe of women warriors who lived north of the Black Sea. When Orellana crossed the Amazon River, it was known as the Marañón. However, as a direct result of Orellana's stories, it has been called the Amazon ever since his journey.

In May 1543, Orellana returned to Valladolid, Spain. The next year, King Charles I of Spain made Orellana governor-general of the lands he had discovered (named New Andalucia), granting him permission to explore and colonize the region. However, it took more than a year for Orellana to organize his trip. Then, with four ships, he and his young wife left Spain on May 11, 1545. By the time he arrived on the Brazilian coast seven months later, he had already lost a ship and many men. His expedition continued to suffer from shipwrecks and desertions. Weak and frustrated, Orellana died during an attempt to travel up the Amazon in 1546.

SUGGESTED READING Gaspar de Carvajal, *The Discovery of the Amazon: According to the Account of Friar Gaspar de Carvajal, and Other Documents,* edited by H. C. Heaton (American Geographical Society, 1934).

Palliser, John

Irish
b January 29, 1817; Comragh, Ireland
d August 18, 1887; Comragh, Ireland
Explored western Canada

geology the scientific study of the earth's natural history

John Palliser was a wealthy man who loved to hunt and live off the land. He made good use of his outdoor skills when he volunteered to survey a large section of southwestern Canada for the British government. His expedition eventually helped the British settle the region.

New Land for Starving People

In 1856 Palliser proposed an expedition to what was then called the British West (now southwestern Canada) to see if the area was suitable for colonization. Seven years earlier, hundreds of thousands of Irish had begun moving to North America to flee starvation caused by a terrible famine. Palliser's plan addressed an urgent need, and the British government agreed to fund his expedition. He would survey the land from Lake Superior to the Red River and then continue west to the Rocky Mountains and beyond.

Palliser's party was to report on soil conditions, geography, and possible trade routes. Dr. James Hector was responsible for **geology** and the health of the group. Other scientists were hired to take magnetic readings, collect plant specimens, and record astronomical data. The area targeted for study lay just north of the border between Canada and the United States. Palliser was also encouraged to find a pass through the Rocky Mountains for a railway.

With supplies and guides from the Hudson's Bay Company, Palliser and his companions spent the summer of 1857 traveling from Sault Ste. Marie (in present-day Ontario) to Red River Settlement (now Winnipeg, Manitoba). From there they journeyed along Canada's border with the United States into Saskatchewan and headed northwest. Palliser then turned back and traveled overland to Montréal and New York to ask British officials for more time and money. He also took this time to repair the expedition's damaged scientific instruments.

In the spring and summer of 1858, the party split up to find new ways to pass through the Rockies. Palliser had returned, and he explored North Kananaskis Pass and North Kootenay Pass. Then he joined the rest of the party at Fort Edmonton, Alberta, for the winter. Dr. Hector explored Kicking Horse Pass, which later became the route used by the Canadian Pacific Railway.

Laying the Foundation

The next year, the expedition spent more time in the southern plains and foothills east of the Rockies. Palliser once again took the North Kootenay Pass through the Rockies and pressed on to the Columbia River at Fort Colvile. He was joined there by Hector, who came through the Howse Pass. Together they traveled on land and downstream to Portland; then they went by steamboat to Victoria on Vancouver Island. Since the overland journey had been difficult, Palliser wrongly concluded that it would cost too much to build a railway through the Canadian Rockies.

Despite his mistaken assumption, Palliser had laid the groundwork for future settlement in the area. He had made accurate charts and had found fertile land beyond the most barren sections of prairie. Palliser continued to hunt and to travel, but he spent his final years managing his property in Ireland and serving as a justice of the peace.

SUGGESTED READING Irene M. Spry, *The Palliser Expedition: The Dramatic Story of Western Canadian Exploration, 1857–1860* (Fifth House Publishers, 1995).

Park, Mungo

Scottish
b September 10, 1771; Fowlshiels, Scotland
d January 1806?; near Bussa, Nigeria
Explored Niger River

species type of plant or animal

caravan large group of people traveling together, often with pack animals, across a desert or other dangerous region

In 1805 Park discovered that the Niger River turns sharply southward below Timbuktu, disproving his theory that the Niger flowed into the Congo.

While exploring the northern reaches of Africa's Niger River in the late 1700s, Dr. Mungo Park settled an age-old question as to the direction of the Niger's flow. Despite a grueling 11-month journey—during which he was robbed, imprisoned, and almost died of fever and starvation—he managed to return safely to England. There he published a best-selling account of his adventures and earned international fame for his achievements.

An Easy Target

Park, the son of a farmer, was educated as a surgeon at Edinburgh University. In 1792 he became a medical officer on a merchant ship heading to Sumatra (in present-day Indonesia). While stationed there, Park studied the island's plant and animal life and discovered eight new **species** of fish. He later described his discoveries in a scientific publication. His work impressed English scientist Joseph BANKS of the Africa Association, a group that promoted exploration of the interior of Africa. Banks needed a capable traveler to explore the Niger River, and he chose Park for the assignment.

Park arrived on the west coast of Africa in July 1795. He had traveled only 200 miles inland when he fell ill, delaying the expedition by several months. While recovering in the village of Pisania on the banks of the Gambia River, Park studied the local language and customs. He then headed north to the Senegal River.

Park had hoped to travel into the interior with a **caravan,** but the local tribes were suspicious and refused to go with him. He left on his trip with only two servants, and this small party was an easy target for robbers. On Christmas Day, thieves took all of Park's money and belongings in the kingdom of Kajaaga in Senegal. For several days, Park traveled through forests, swamps, and mountain terrain. He was then captured by Arab soldiers from the kingdom of Ludamar.

The Scotsman was imprisoned for several months by the Arabs, who had never seen a white man before. Park grew more and more afraid that he would be murdered, but in early July, he managed to escape. Even though he had lost all of his supplies, he decided to continue east toward the Niger rather than return to the west coast.

Although Park nearly died of thirst on the first day of his journey, he was saved when a thunderstorm struck. He sucked the rainfall out of his clothes. Luck came to his rescue again when he came across a group of refugees. Park traveled with them to Ségou (in present-day Mali). In late July, they came to a market town on the banks of the Niger River. Park had reached his destination.

Changing Direction

Park saw the river for the first time at daybreak. He later wrote that the wide river was "glittering to the morning sun" and "flowing slowly to the eastward." Park ran to the river and drank the water. He then said a prayer of thanks for having achieved his goal.

The explorer stayed in Ségou for several days, hoping to meet with King Mansong, who ruled the territory. Although the sight of the white stranger disturbed the local people, this time their fear worked to Park's advantage. Royal officials paid the penniless explorer a large sum of money to leave the area. Park's mission was officially completed, but now he had the funds to continue exploring the Niger. He traveled downstream for six days and reached the town of Silla. But he decided not to travel any farther. He realized that heavy tropical rains would have slowed his progress, and there were hostile tribes nearby.

Park began his return trip in August. He encountered many of the same problems as he had experienced on the first part of his journey. Many of the local tribes eyed him with suspicion. He was robbed again of nearly all his belongings except his hat—and the journal notes he had hidden inside it. When Park fell ill with a fever, he was nursed back to health by local people in a small village on the Niger. They were kind because they were amazed by his ability to write.

In April 1796, Park joined a westward caravan and reached Pisania two months later. A small group of European settlers nearby did not recognize the thin, tired explorer. They had thought that he was dead. Park proved who he was, and the settlers congratulated him. He was the first explorer to return from the previously unknown inner regions of the continent.

Home to Glory

Park enjoyed even greater glory in London. He returned there at Christmas and published *Travels in the Interior Districts of Africa.* The book made him an instant celebrity. Europeans loved his writing, which blended adventure, humor, and emotion. After sales of his book had earned him a large sum of money, Park married in 1799 and set up a medical practice in Scotland. But he wanted to lead another expedition—this time to follow the Niger along its course. After repeated requests to the government, his plan was finally approved.

Park believed that the mystery of the Niger was still not solved, and he was right. His discovery that the Niger flowed eastward had created more questions than it had answered. Park had disproved the idea that the Niger was a **tributary** of the Nile. He believed that the Niger linked with the Congo River (also known as the Zaire River) to the east. Park hoped to prove this theory as he sailed up the Gambia River in April 1805.

The Luck Runs Out

Park started out with an expedition of 40 men. They sailed as far as Kaiaf and then traveled by land to the Niger River. Since they were traveling during the rainy season, **malaria** and **dysentery** attacked

tributary stream or river that flows into a larger stream or river

malaria disease that is spread by mosquitoes in tropical areas

dysentery disease that causes severe diarrhea

the crew. Only 11 men remained when the party reached Bamako (in what is now Mali). Park sighted the Niger in August. By the time he reached Sansanding, to the north of Ségou, he set sail down the river with only a guide and 3 servants.

The story of what happened to Park next was pieced together long after he disappeared, using information gathered from the local tribes. He seems to have followed the river past Timbuktu, where it curves sharply southward, and traveled more than half of its remaining length. Then the rapids at Bussa (in present-day Nigeria) blocked his passage.

Park had probably angered many of the communities along the river by refusing to pay their tolls. To avenge their losses, a local tribe attacked his party at Bussa. One of Park's former servants reported that Park fell into the rapids and drowned while trying to get away from his attackers.

SUGGESTED READING Kenneth Lupton, *Mungo Park: The African Traveler* (Oxford University Press, 1979); Mungo Park, *The Travels of Mungo Park* (E. P. Dutton, 1907).

Parry, William Edward

English
b December 19, 1790; Bath, England
d July 8, 1855; Ems, Germany
Explored Canadian Arctic and Norwegian Arctic

archipelago large group of islands or a body of water with many islands

frigate small, agile warship with three masts and square sails

Northwest Passage water route connecting the Atlantic Ocean and Pacific Ocean through the Arctic islands of northern Canada

Rear Admiral Sir William Edward Parry was a highly successful Arctic explorer, combining careful planning and observation with good humor and good luck. He charted a major part of the **archipelago** that lies between the west coast of Greenland and the Beaufort Sea. Parry's expeditions broke the barrier that had separated Europe from much of the Arctic region. This barrier had not been crossed since the voyages of William BAFFIN in the early 1600s.

Off to a Good Start

Parry began his career as a sailor early in life, joining the navy in 1803, at the age of 13. He immediately went to sea with the fleet that blockaded the French coast of the English Channel. He also served in the North Sea and the Baltic Sea, quickly working his way up the ranks. From 1810 to 1813, he received training in the Arctic region as a lieutenant aboard the **frigate** *Alexandria.* Parry's crew was sent to protect the whaling fleet off Spitsbergen (now part of Svalbard, Norway).

During these years, Parry became a skilled navigator. He wrote a training manual, *Nautical Astronomy by Night,* which was published in 1816. Parry's book impressed the second secretary of the navy, John BARROW. In 1818 Barrow put Parry in command of the *Alexander.* Parry's new assignment was to join John Ross's *Isabella* on an expedition to the Arctic Ocean.

This mission was headed for the waters west of Greenland, where William Baffin had explored more than 200 years earlier. But Ross's goal was not simply to rediscover Baffin Bay. He wanted to search the inlets on the bay's western shore in order to find a **Northwest Passage.** Baffin had also searched for such a route around North America to the Pacific Ocean. But John Barrow was convinced that the modern British navy could succeed where earlier explorers had failed.

brig small, fast sailing ship with two masts and square sails

Breaking the Barrier

Barrow was disappointed when Ross did not find a passage through Baffin Bay. Parry pointed out that Ross could have seen a mirage that looked like a mountain. Such a mirage might have tricked Ross into thinking that Lancaster Sound was a dead end. Barrow agreed with Parry's theory and decided to send another expedition to Baffin Bay the following year. Parry was put in charge of two ships, the 375-ton vessel *Hecla* and the less seaworthy **brig** *Griper.* The boats were loaded with enough supplies to last three years.

Parry left England on May 11, 1819, and soon demonstrated that he was right about Ross's mistake. Parry boldly charted a course straight through the sheets of floating ice in Davis Strait. He then sailed through Lancaster Sound and continued west. When he turned south into Prince Regent Inlet, ice blocked further progress. However, he decided to sail west again and was able to thread his way through the broken sheets of ice until he reached what is now Melville Island. At this point, Parry had passed beyond all of the major landmasses that stood in the way of a Northwest Passage. He had finally charted a link between the Atlantic and Arctic Oceans. But Parry also saw that the sea so far north is never clear of ice and could never become an open water passage. This discovery was important in itself.

Warm Spirits in the Cold

On September 22, Parry decided to stop forcing his way through the ice in Melville Sound. His crew sawed a long channel through the ice pack to Melville Island, where they set up winter quarters. Parry came up with a creative way to cope with the long, intensely cold winter. He did away with strict naval discipline and turned the *Hecla* into a kind of winter resort, with music, theater, and opera. He even composed a comic opera, which he titled *Northwest Passage.* Parry also established a newspaper, a school, and an exercise area.

This expedition marked the first time that Europeans had wintered in the islands north of North America, and only one man died, from a disease that was not related to the Arctic conditions. It helped that all of Parry's officers were young. Parry had also chosen good-natured sailors who would get along. He offered "good wages, good feeling, and good treatment." Parry's concern for the well-being of his crew certainly played a part in his success.

In late spring, a party explored Melville Island to its north coast. When the ice cleared in midsummer, Parry tried to push farther west. The effort failed, so he gave up at Cape Dundas and led a smooth voyage back to Peterhead, Scotland. When he arrived in October 1820, Parry was greeted with a hero's welcome. He was promoted to commander and received a large financial award from the British Parliament.

In addition to exploring the Arctic, William Parry was put in charge of worldwide mapping operations for the British fleet.

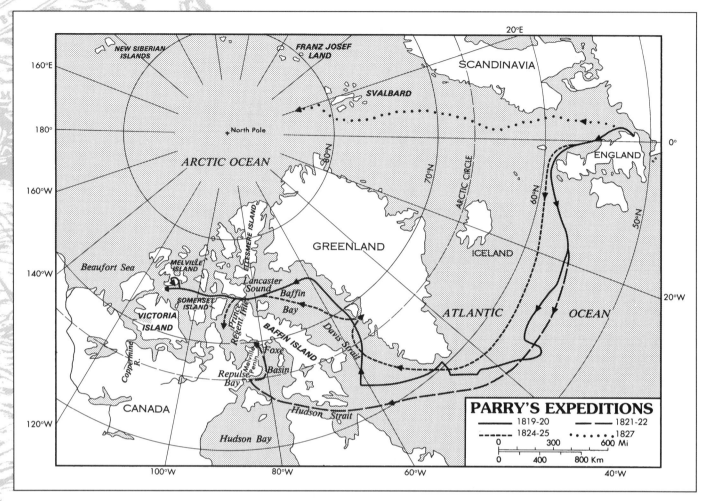

PARRY'S EXPEDITIONS
— 1819-20   — — 1821-22
- - - 1824-25   •••••• 1827

Parry's lengthy expeditions marked the start of the modern era of Arctic exploration.

Another Try for the Passage

Parry believed that a Northwest Passage might still be possible if it were tried farther south along the coast of the North American mainland. He suggested an attempt to reach the waters of Prince Regent Inlet from the south by way of Hudson Bay. He had previously explored these waters from the north.

The waters north of Hudson Bay, in Foxe Basin, had been iced over during every attempt to navigate them since the 1600s. Although Barrow and Parry were aware of these unsuccessful attempts, they believed that favorable ice conditions made their plan worth a try. Much of Britain's push into the polar region was due to a fear of Russia's efforts in the area. If the Russian navy found a Northwest Passage from Alaska to the Atlantic Ocean, it could claim control over the route. Still, Parry thought that this expedition would "probably end in disappointment."

In May 1821, Parry set off with the *Fury* and the *Hecla.* He skillfully navigated the ice fields of Frozen Strait and arrived at Repulse Bay on August 22, well before winter. Parry confirmed an earlier report that the bay had no outlet. He then headed north up the coast of Melville Peninsula in search of an open waterway. When winter came, Parry once again set up his seasonal quarters off what is now Winter Island. The Europeans were visited by the local **Inuit,** who

Inuit people of the Canadian Arctic, sometimes known as the Eskimo

set up a village of igloos near the ships. Parry took careful notes that described their customs and songs. An Inuit woman named Iligliuk shared her knowledge of local geography with Parry. She drew a sketch of Melville Peninsula and the strait to its north. The strait leads from Foxe Basin in the east to the waters at the bottom of Prince Regent Inlet in the west.

In the summer of 1822, Parry followed Iligliuk's map up the coast of the peninsula to the strait. He named it Fury and Hecla Strait after his ships. Parry waited there for the ice to melt—for the rest of the summer and for most of the following summer too. In the meantime, Parry and his crew explored the strait and much of the Melville Peninsula by foot and by boat. Parry also began to learn the Inuit methods of Arctic travel. Although Parry's attempts at dogsledding were unsuccessful, one of the young crew members, John Ross's nephew James Clark Ross, eventually became famous for his dogsledding abilities.

The End of the Fury

Parry returned to England in October 1823. He found that his failure to find a passage had not discouraged the navy. His superiors were determined to continue Arctic exploration. The British public was also excited by Parry's voyage. John FRANKLIN's return from a daring journey across northern Canada had added to the Arctic fever. In 1824 Parry was again sent to Arctic waters with the *Fury* and the *Hecla*. This time he was to explore the southern parts of Prince Regent Inlet. Unfortunately, the results were again very disappointing.

Parry's course through Davis Strait and Lancaster Sound was much more challenging this time. It took two summers to sail into Prince Regent Inlet, which he had so easily entered in 1819. As the ships headed down the inlet's west coast, they were squeezed ashore by the ice pack, causing serious damage to the *Fury*. The ships were forced ashore again a month later. Parry had no choice but to leave the *Fury* and move the entire crew onto the *Hecla* for the trip back to England. Parry left his extra supplies on Somerset Island, and these provisions later saved the lives of John Ross's expedition of 1829 to 1833.

Despite a worsening case of **rheumatism,** Parry made one more Arctic voyage. In the spring and summer of 1827, he became the first in a long line of brave explorers who tried to reach the North Pole. Parry's method was to pull heavy **boat-sledges** over the polar ice cap north of Spitsbergen. However, with this inefficient method, he could cover no more than seven miles a day. To make matters worse, his progress north was often reversed when the ice pack drifted in the opposite direction. Nevertheless, in July 1827, he reached a northern **latitude** that was not surpassed for almost 50 years.

When Parry returned to England, he was knighted and honored with a degree from Oxford University. He then held a series of prominent civilian jobs until his death in 1855.

SUGGESTED READING Pierre Berton, *The Arctic Grail* (Viking, 1988); Brendan Lehane, *The Northwest Passage* (Time-Life Books, 1981); Jeannette Mirsky, *To the Arctic* (University of Chicago Press, 1970); Ann Parry, *Parry of the Arctic* (Chatto and Windus, 1963).

rheumatism physical condition that causes pain in the joints or muscles, making movement uncomfortable

boat-sledge boat mounted on sled runners to allow travel on both ice and water

latitude distance north or south of the equator

Pasha, Emin. See *Schnitzer, Eduard.*

Pavie, Auguste-Jean-Marie

French
b 1847; Dinan, France
d 1925; Thourie, France
Explored and colonized Laos

alliance formal agreement of friendship or common defense

protectorate weak state that yields political control to a stronger state in exchange for military protection

pirogue canoe usually made from a hollow tree trunk

In the late 1800s, Auguste-Jean-Marie Pavie knew as much as any European about the region then called Indochina (now comprising the modern nations of Vietnam, Cambodia, and Laos). Pavie traveled tirelessly for years in the service of France, learning about Indochina and its peoples. Using his knowledge and his skill as a diplomat, he shrewdly involved himself in local political conflicts—and almost singlehandedly expanded the French colonial empire in Southeast Asia.

An Interest in Empire

Europeans of the early 1800s had little knowledge of the geography of Southeast Asia. However, their interest in this region and its resources was growing. The sea route between the Indian and Pacific Oceans runs around Southeast Asia, so control of the area's waters was very important. Europeans also hoped that Indochina might offer an overland trade route northward into China. Britain, which ruled nearby India and Burma (now known as Myanmar), sent out several expeditions to explore that possibility.

France, anxious not to be left behind in the scramble for Asian colonies, turned its attention to Cochin, as southern Vietnam was then called. By the 1860s, the French were established in Cochin's capital city, Saigon (present-day Ho Chi Minh City). The colonial authorities worked to widen French influence among the surrounding kingdoms and tribes through **alliances,** treaties, and trade. French explorers such as Francis GARNIER investigated the region's rivers and rain forests.

The French Colonial Service

In the 1860s, many thousands of French colonists lived and worked in the coastal regions of what is now Vietnam. To protect its coastal colony, France tried to win control over the many small kingdoms and tribes in the area that is now Laos and Cambodia. That area had long been caught between the stronger kingdoms of Vietnam and Siam (present-day Thailand). To protect themselves, the Lao peoples had often agreed to become **protectorates** of one or both of their stronger neighbors. The French wanted the Lao to become protectorates of France rather than of any Asian nation. To support and enforce these alliances and to protect its colonies, France sent troops to Indochina. Auguste Pavie arrived as a marine, sometime in the 1860s.

By 1868 Pavie was employed as a telegraph operator by the Cochin's colonial government, which then sent him to a post in coastal Cambodia. Over the next few years, he studied Cambodia's Khmer language and culture and made several journeys inland. Pavie's interest in exploration earned him a special assignment in 1880. He oversaw the construction of the first telegraph line from Phnom Penh, Cambodia, to Bangkok, Siam.

As a supervisor, Pavie traveled widely, climbing into a **pirogue** at a moment's notice. Along the region's many rivers and over its dangerous mountain trails, he carried out a series of surveys to map parts of Cambodia and Laos that were unknown to Europeans. He believed that his careful explorations would help the French to secure control of Indochina.

Exploration and Politics

In 1886 the French colonial government appointed Pavie as its first representative in Luang Prabang, a city in northern Laos, where the political situation was tense. The Ho, bands of armed raiders from China, had been terrorizing Lao villages for years. An elderly Lao king named Oun Kham invited Siam to send an army of Thai soldiers into Laos to protect the Lao from the Ho. The Thai army arrived, but it was clear that Siam also wanted political control of Laos—a prize that Pavie intended to win for France.

When Pavie reached Luang Prabang in early 1887, Thai officials greeted him politely, although they prevented him from meeting with Oun Kham. A few months later, matters grew worse. In their effort to control the region, Thai troops captured four brothers of a local chieftain as hostages. The Thai then abandoned Luang Prabang. In anger, the chieftain gathered a Ho army, which burned and looted the undefended city. The raiders killed many people, but Pavie was able to escape with Oun Kham, the Lao king.

Oun Kham, seeing that the Thai had proven unreliable and that Pavie had saved his life, decided that France would make a better protector than Siam. In 1893 Pavie helped to negotiate a treaty under which Siam gave up its claims to Lao territory east and north of the Mekong River. Laos became a French protectorate, part of French Indochina. Pavie then worked to build ties between the Lao and the French by visiting and befriending the area's many princes and tribal chieftains. He persuaded them to pledge their loyalty to France.

While crisscrossing the region, Pavie continued the geographic efforts that had helped him to achieve his political aims. Drawing on his years of experience as a geographer and **surveyor,** he helped to establish the borders of Laos, Thailand, Vietnam, Burma, and China. He also drew the first accurate maps of Laos. When Pavie retired from colonial service in 1895, he had traveled about 18,000 miles in 15 years. He described his activities in 10 volumes, which he published in Paris between 1898 and 1919.

SUGGESTED READING Arthur J. Dommen, *Conflict in Laos,* 2nd edition (Praeger Publishers, 1971); James McCarthy, *Surveying and Exploring in Siam* (John Murray, 1900).

surveyor one who makes precise measurements of a location's geography

Payer, Julius von

Austrian
b September 1, 1842; Teplitz-Schönau, Austria
(now Teplice, Czech Republic)
d August 30, 1915; Bled, Slovenia
Explored Russian Arctic;
discovered Franz Josef Land

Julius von Payer was a lieutenant in the army of the Austro-Hungarian Empire. In 1871 he set out on a military expedition to the Arctic Ocean north of Europe and Russia. Two years later, he discovered the northernmost **archipelago** of the region and named it Franz Josef Land. After making several **sledge** trips around the islands, Payer mistakenly concluded that there was a large continent surrounding the North Pole.

Unanswered Questions

Despite many attempts to explore the Arctic Ocean north of Europe and Russia, the geography of that region beyond the coast was still

archipelago large group of islands or a body of water with many islands

sledge heavy sled, often mounted on runners, that is pulled over snow or ice

unknown in the late 1800s. Payer hoped to determine whether there was a continent or a sea north of the Russian islands of Novaya Zemlya. If there was a sea, he would find out whether open waters lay north of the ring of ice that had blocked the way of explorers for centuries. To answer these questions, Payer and his naval companion, Lieutenant Karl Weyprecht, sailed north from Tromsø, Norway, in June 1871. They hoped to follow the Gulf Stream, a warm ocean current. But they soon discovered that there was no passage through the solid ice that stretched from Spitsbergen (an island north of Norway) east to Novaya Zemlya.

Fooled by the Fog

Payer returned to the region the next year in the *Tegethoff,* a steamship equipped for ice travel. He reached Novaya Zemlya on August 3. A few weeks later, the ship became stuck in the ice. Payer and his crew remained on board the *Tegethoff* as it slowly drifted northwest with the ice. They hoped to make new discoveries the following summer. In August 1873, the expedition sighted an archipelago and named the islands Franz Josef Land in honor of Austria-Hungary's emperor.

After another winter on the ship, Payer made several sledge trips across Franz Josef Land in the spring of 1874, taking time to climb the peaks he found. He came to the inaccurate conclusion that the group of small islands was actually two large landmasses. Looking north through the Arctic fog, he mistakenly believed that he could see another large landmass. This theory was later disproved by the Norwegian explorer Fridtjof NANSEN on his 1893 voyage to the Russian Arctic.

Payer and his crew finally abandoned their icebound ship on May 20, 1874, and began the difficult trek home. They took three small boats south over the ice and then into open sea, where a Russian fishing boat picked them up. After this expedition, Payer retired from exploring, took up painting, and gained recognition with his depictions of the Arctic region.

SUGGESTED READING Julius Payer, *New Lands Within the Arctic Circle: Narrative of the Discoveries of the Austrian Ship "Tegetthoff," in the Years 1872–1874* (D. Appleton and Company, 1877).